PLACE
AND REPLACE

ESSAYS ON WESTERN CANADA
PLACE AND REPLACE

EDITED BY ADELE PERRY, ESYLLT W. JONES, AND LEAH MORTON

UMP
University of Manitoba Press

University of Manitoba Press
Winnipeg, Manitoba
Canada R3T 2M5
uofmpress.ca

17 16 15 14 13   1 2 3 4 5

Printed in Canada
Text printed on chlorine-free, 100% post-consumer recycled paper

Cover and Interior Design: Jessica Koroscil
Cover image: "New Year's Family Dinner" (2009) by Alex Janvier,
watercolor on paper, 30" x 22.5"

Library and Archives Canada Cataloguing in Publication

Place and replace : essays on Western Canada / Adele Perry, Esyllt W.
Jones, Leah Morton, editors.

Based on papers presented at a joint meeting of Western Canada Studies
and the St. John's College Prairies Conference held at St. John's College,
University of Manitoba, Winnipeg, Man., from Sept. 16–18, 2010.

Includes bibliographical references.
ISBN 978-0-88755-740-8 (pbk.)
ISBN 978-0-88755-431-5 (PDF e-book)
ISBN 978-0-88755-433-9 (epub e-book)

1. Canada, Western—History. 2. Canada, Western—Social conditions.
3. Canada, Western—Politics and government. I. Perry, Adele II. Jones,
Esyllt Wynne, 1964– III. Morton, Leah

FC3237.P63 2013   971.2   C2012-902594-1

The University of Manitoba Press gratefully acknowledges the financial
support for its publication program provided by the Government of Canada
through the Canada Book Fund, the Canada Council for the Arts, the Manitoba
Department of Culture, Heritage, Tourism, the Manitoba Arts Council,
and the Manitoba Book Publishing Tax Credit.

CONTENTS

PLACE, POLITICS, AND STUDYING WESTERN CANADA: AN INTRODUCTION[1]

ADELE PERRY, LEAH MORTON, AND ESYLLT W. JONES

For forty years scholars have discussed how to best define the related terrains of "western Canada," "the Prairies" and, less often, the "prairie West." Is it best understood as a unit of geography—defined by land, space, and the human experience of environment? If so, where does this geographical unit end and begin? What borders does western Canada cross or stop at, and what areas are situated at its core, assigned to its margins, or located outside of it? Is western Canada more or less the Prairies, or does it include the territories lying west of the Rocky Mountains, north of the treeline, or in what is now northern Ontario? Should western Canada be seen as part of a continuous history that encompasses the American West? Is western Canada given shape by a common past or at least one common enough to hang a workable and meaningful historical narrative on? If we accept that the past provides western Canada with its meaning, we may not agree on what parts of that history take precedence over others. Is western Canada best approached as a unit of culture, a space that is imagined or challenged in conversation, in books, or on screens? If western Canada is a space brought into being by literary and artistic imaginations, is this sufficient reason to retain it as an analytic category?

To some extent, these discussions about how to define western Canada are one part of a wider Canadian dialogue about the power and purchase of region as an analytic category and identity. But the conversations about how we might best understand western Canada are also particular to the circumstances of these specific places. This book is made up of sixteen essays that discuss western Canada in the nineteenth and twentieth centuries. These essays are informed by this ongo-ing debate about how to best define and understand western Canada, but they are not preoccupied by it. Sometimes the essays question the very terms of the discus-sion. More often, contributors to *Place and Replace* proceed as if these questions are either unanswerable or not terribly important. Rather than debate, discuss, and dissect regional frameworks, the essays here analyze the histories, cultures, and politics that unevenly constitute western Canada.

This book began with a conference held at the University of Manitoba in the fall of 2010. "Place and Replace: A Joint Meeting of the St. John's College Prairies Conference and Western Canadian Studies" represented a merging of two schol-arly meetings, each possessing its own specific history and different but related mandate. In its first incarnation, Western Canadian Studies began in 1969 and met annually and then biannually, mainly at the University of Calgary but in later years, in a range of locations. These conferences were inflected with the politics of regional identity and grievance. The first Western Canadian Studies conferences were interdisciplinary, and reached beyond the conventional academy to engage a wider community, but reflected the disciplinary interests of historians. Different meetings deployed different definitions of western Canada, and the volumes of essays that were produced out of them did too.[2] This conference stopped meeting in 1990, and after an almost twenty-year hiatus, Western Canadian Studies was revived and redefined in 2008 by a group of historians.[3] A meeting at the Univer-sity of Alberta and, in time, a fine collection of essays edited by Sarah Carter, Peter Fortna, and Alvin Finkel were the concrete results.[4]

The St. John's College Prairies Conference began after the first incarnation of Western Canadian Studies ceased to meet. The first St. John's College Prairies Conference was held in 1990, and it has met every three years since then, always at St. John's College at the University of Manitoba in Winnipeg. These meetings built on the College's ongoing commitment to Canadian Studies and the confer-ences hosted in 1989, 1990, and 2004.[5] The St. John's College Prairies Conferences both sustained the work of Western Canadian Studies and shifted its interests. If the first iteration of Western Canadian Studies had a wide scope but a practical focus on history and historical scholarship, the St. John's College Prairies Confer-ences were interdisciplinary but tended to emphasize literature and the study of it. The two volumes of essays produced out of these conferences were both edited by historians, but the conferences themselves built on the remarkable literary com-munity associated with Winnipeg in general and St. John's College in particular, including Robert Kroetsch, David Arnason, and Dennis Cooley. The St. John's College Prairies Conference reflected its particular geographic location in Win-nipeg and focused on modern-day Saskatchewan and Manitoba and, to a lesser extent, Alberta.[6]

As a conference, "Place and Replace" attempted to synthesize these two conferences and their respective emphases on history and literature, and their slightly—but importantly—varying definitions of region. As a book, *Place and Replace: Essays on Western Canada* follows a long and well-established tradition of rigorously multidisciplinary examination of this particular Canadian region. It features articles written by historians, by scholars trained in the interdisciplinary practice of Native or Indigenous Studies, by literary and film scholars, by political scientists, and by scholars of city planning. The essays' authors are at a wide variety of career-stages, ranging from graduate students completing their dissertations to well-established scholars. The theme of "place and replace" calls attention to the layered and changeable histories and politics of location in western Canada. By invoking "place," we continue a longstanding tradition of situating questions of place at the centre of analyses of western Canada's cultures, pasts, and politics. By modifying this focus with the word "replace" we make clear that place is not stable, universal, or static. Places and people's relationship to them are variable, and they are frequently uncomfortable and conflicted. Place is not simply a secure location, but a shifting terrain that has excluded and disempowered as well as included and nourished. The sixteen essays here confirm the topical importance to western Canada of Indigenous peoples, dispossession, and colonialism; migration, race, and ethnicity; gender and women's experiences; the role of the natural or built environment; and the impact of politics and the state. But read carefully, these essays also make clear that the ties that connect these themes are not always where we expect to find them. Rather than organize the essays along chronological, disciplinary, or strictly topical lines, the collection is structured around four kinds of literal and metaphoric places: farms; trails, trains, and airplanes; books, films, and journals; and parks, towns, and polls. To connect the essays around these locations emphasizes the connections between topics, issues, and subjects that are sometimes presumed to be discrete and builds on the capacity of interdisciplinary scholarship about western Canada to work around and beyond the usual divisions between disciplines and departments.

FARMS

In *Farms*, three authors prompt us to rethink how we have understood the place of agriculture in western Canada. Agriculture has long played a pivotal role in the remaking of North American space along European lines.[7] The connection between agriculture and empire took on new political weight in the last years of the nineteenth and the first years of the twentieth century, when western Canada was transformed from an Indigenous and hybrid colonial space to a settler society organized around commercial agriculture, predicated, as Sarah Carter elsewhere explains, on "complementary assumptions of British superiority and white male dominance."[8] But the meanings of farms and farming were not fixed and eternal. For much of the twentieth century, agriculture and farming have served as powerful bases for alternative and radical politics in western Canada.[9] As Alison Calder argues forcefully in her essay in this volume, the farm figured as the location of "traumatic experience of white, largely male settlers" and has played a telling role in western Canadian literature and scholarship.

The essays in this section unsettle our assumptions of what farms meant and mean to western Canada. The authors map very different experiences of farms as locations of family and intimacy, as well as of labour and agricultural production. Carter, a historian, builds on her earlier work on prairie Indian reserve farming to address property rights for First Nations farmers in Manitoba and the Northwest. She reminds us that prairie Indigenous people practised agriculture long before Europeans arrived.[10] She demonstrates, too, just how far state officials were willing to go to keep First Nations people from having the basic property rights upon which participation in the commercial agricultural economy of the reconstituted western Canada was premised. Bret Nickels works in the interdisciplinary context of Native Studies. His essay on the Manitoba Indian Agriculture Program deals with a very different time period than does Carter. But for all the difference between the late nineteenth century and the late twentieth century, Carter and Nickels tell strikingly similar stories of underfunding, confusion, and lost opportunities; ones that offer valuable insights into the history of Indigenous peoples and the state in Canada.

Both Carter's and Nickels' essays confirm the centrality of Indigenous histories to the current study of western Canada. Questions of Indigenous peoples, dispossession, and colonization played a key role when scholarly discussions were first developing in the 1930s. For all their differences, George F. Stanley's interest in seeing western Canada as part of a wider empire and Harold Innis' emphasis on economy in general and the fur trade in particular both made room for Indigenous peoples as historical actors.[11] Indigenous histories and issues played a smaller role in western Canadian studies at the height of their popularity in the 1960s and early 1970s. As Calder's trenchant critique of laments for "prairie literature" in this collection suggests, this search for prairie culture was rooted in settler histories and idioms that did and do not easily accommodate Indigenous pasts or presents. Recent scholarship, however, has re-placed Indigenous peoples, colonization, and resistance at the core of the analysis, having benefitted from the upsurge in scholarship on Indigenous history in Canada that marked the last decades of the twentieth century. More work was published on Canadian Aboriginal history in the 1990s than in the five preceding decades.[12] This shift has continued in the twenty-first century, and is reflected in the prominent place of Indigenous histories and cultures in the essays by Carter, Nickels, and, later in the volume, by Emma LaRocque, Calder, and Elspeth Tulloch.

Gender and women's history also complicate the histories we attach to farms in western Canada. Pernille Jakobsen's essay offers a sensitive and careful reading of a 1973 Supreme Court Case in which an Alberta farm-wife unsuccessfully fought to have the court acknowledge her claims to the ranch she had maintained with her husband. Jakobsen reminds us of the continuities between first- and second-wave feminism, and highlights their common concern with women's lack of property rights within agricultural economies. Historians are more familiar with work explaining the impact of first-wave feminism on late nineteenth- and early twentieth century western Canadian society, but Jakobsen suggests that the revived and reoriented women's movement of the late twentieth century made its own decisive impact. The second wave of modern feminism, like the first, changed western Canada's landscape.

Jakobsen reminds us of the need to examine western Canada as gendered space. Women's history gained new popularity and a modicum of institutional support in the 1970s, at roughly the same time that the study of western Canada gained some sustained academic legitimacy. The history of western Canadian first-wave feminists such as Nellie McClung and Margret Benedictsson was central to early forays into Canadian women's history published in the 1970s and 1980s.[13] Works such as Sylvia Van Kirk's *"Many Tender Ties": Women in Fur-Trade Society 1670–1870* and Jennifer S.H. Brown's *Strangers in Blood: Fur Trade Company Families in Indian Country* pressed the connection between Indigenous history, family history, and women's history.[14] The genre of Canadian gender history that flourished in the 1990s and 2000s was arguably less concerned with the particulars of this regional experience. As western Canadian women's and gender history faded somewhat from the limelight, it continued to be explored in a handful of monographs and several collections of essays.[15] Contributors to *Place and Replace* such as Jakobsen, Lisa Chilton, and Heather Stanley continue to build upon this body of work.

TRAILS, TRAINS, AND AIRPLANES

The essays in *Farms* collectively reconfigure the meaning attached to agriculture in western Canadian studies. Those in *Trails, Trains, and Airplanes* prompt us to think in different ways about migration—movement to, within, and from western Canada—and the attendant politics of race, ethnicity, and nation. Long before Europeans arrived, Indigenous peoples were mobile. They had well-developed trade networks that stretched across much of North America, and contact among groups that spoke different languages, ate different foods, and reckoned the world in different terms. With the arrival of the fur trade came men tied to and labouring on behalf of European capital. Many of them would marry into the Indigenous societies they traded with. Most of these men were Scots, French Canadian, and Orcadians, but others were drawn from a maritime world with global ties and sources of labour. At Fort William in 1816, one trader found men from "England, Ireland, Scotland, France, Germany, Italy, Denmark, Sweden, Holland, Switzerland, United States of America, the Gold Coast of Africa, the sandwich Islands, Bengal, Canada, with various tribes of Indians, and a mixed progeny of Creoles, or half-breeds."[16]

In the late nineteenth and early twentieth century, western Canada was remade, in no small part though the process of global migration. Waves of settlers from the United Kingdom, elsewhere in Canada, the United States, and continental Europe arrived in what was Indigenous and fur-trade space, buttressing the small pockets of European settlement at Red River and Victoria and, in time, radically transforming the region. The first two essays in this section address the mechanics by which the diverse Indigenous and settler spaces between the Great Lakes and the Rockies were remade as Canadian in the closing years of the nineteenth century and the first years of the twentieth century. Amanda Nettlebeck and Robert Foster, both historians based in Australia, examine an iconic North-West Mounted Police and the work it did in asserting British authority, and continues to do in mainstream Canadian popular memory and culture.[17] Like Carter and Nettlebeck and Foster, Lisa Chilton analyzes an episode in the remaking of western Canada as a British settler society. Chilton's essay examines the massive and state-orchestrated migration of British people to the Prairies in the early twentieth century, the anxieties it provoked, and the considerable efforts made to control it. Chilton's essay is very much about labour, and by situating the question of work and the work immigrants might do at the core of her analysis, Chilton also reminds us of the critical role that questions of labour and class have played in western Canadian historiography and suggests some of the ways they might continue to do so.[18]

The essays in this section remind us that the politics of migration, and the experiences and identities it brings in its wake, are not straightforward. Not all migrants were the ones sought by official state programmes premised on related ideals of nation and empire-building. Alison Marshall is trained as a scholar of East Asian religions, and here she discusses Chinese Canadians and the train in the early twentieth century Prairies. Along with Marshall's recent monograph, this essay serves as a salutary reminder that Chinese-Canadian history did not take shape on the West Coast or in major cities alone, and that historians' conventional focus on European migration to the Prairies does not tell the whole story of this region.[19] Royden Loewen uses the train as a vehicle for rethinking western Canadian history and the place of migration in it. Loewen builds on his voluminous work on transnational Mennonite history to examine German-speaking Mennonites leaving western Canada for South America in the 1920s, '30s, and '40s.[20] Loewen's analysis provides attention to the process of return migration that historians have called recent attention to, and makes clear the value of oral history as an archive and methodology.

The essays in *Trails, Trains, and Airplanes* illustrate that immigration has changed, and is still changing, western Canada. As Loewen and Gerry Friesen have demonstrated elsewhere, the patterns of migration that were so critical to shaping twentieth century western Canada began to shift significantly in the 1970s. Increasingly, immigrants to western Canada, and more especially western Canadian cities, would come from the Global South—Latin America, Asia, the Middle East, and Africa.[21] Joyce Chadya's essay here deals with how current-day migrants from Zimbabwe recreate the rituals of death, mourning, and memory within the city of Winnipeg. Chadya is a historian whose primary research area is southern Africa, and here she examines some of the ways that a diaspora community deals with the most intimate of rituals—those around death—in present-day western Canada. The essays in this section offer a substantial corrective to work that acknowledges and laments the erasure of western Canada's multicultural and multiracial past from scholarly study but does not substantially address it.[22]

BOOKS, FILMS, AND JOURNALS

The third section, *Books, Films, and Journals*, deals with images of western Canada in literature, medical writing, and film. Alison Calder is a literary critic and a poet, and in her essay she analyses the racial and gendered meanings of "prairie literature" and asks what is at stake in it. Calder's is a powerful challenge to western Canadian studies as it has been practised for much of the last four decades, and a call for a different kind of critical practice, one that challenges rather than reinforces the gendered violence of settler colonialism. It is appropriate that Calder's essay is placed alongside Emma LaRocque's. LaRocque is also poet and scholar, and here she reckons with Métis literature and its interpretation of prairie place. LaRocque's highlighting of Métis literature is part of a wider recuperation and recognition of Indigenous writing in western Canada.[23] Métis invocation of place, LaRocque argues, fundamentally challenges popular images of Métis as placeless or out of place. The gaps between this Indigenous literature and the mainstream and even canonical works studied by Calder make it clear that western Canadian place, and the politics of it, are structured and given meaning by social difference.

Other essays in this section deal with the images of western Canada that circulate through films, medical literature, and novels and short stories. Lindy Ledohowski, a literary scholar, examines images of Ukrainian-Canadian women in

English-language literature. She argues that images of the iconic "baba" are more complicated than scholars have often assumed, and suggests that our ideas of both women and Ukrainian-Canadian understanding of space and home in the Prairies are due for revision. Elspeth Tulloch is also a literary critic, but here she turns to the medium of film. Picking up on themes identified by LaRocque and Calder, Tulloch examines how National Film Board films have dealt with the presence of francophones—most notably franco-Manitoban author Gabrielle Roy and Métis leader Louis Riel—in western Canada. Here, we see how filmmakers struggled to acknowledge the French-language histories of the region, and how this compli-cated twentieth century Canada's dominant national discourses. Heather Stanley, a historian, addresses the charged topic of marital sexuality as it was represented in mid-twentieth century medical literature. Along with Jakobsen, Ledohowski and Stanley both engage with feminist historical and literary practice to produce new readings of western Canada and the history of women and sexuality within it.

PARKS, TOWNS, AND POLLS

The final section brings together three essays that analyze three kinds of ex-plicitly political places in twentieth century western Canada: parks, polls, and towns. Historian Sterling Evans' essay draws on the rich scholarship on the en-vironmental history of the American West to piece together a careful study of the making of Alberta's Dinosaur National Park in the mid-twentieth century. Evans' essay shows us in very concrete ways how places are produced through human activity and history. Beverly Sandalack, an expert in city planning, ad-dresses the particular form of the "prairie town" in a richly illustrated and evoca-tive essay. Studies of western Canada have tended to emphasize urban or rural space, and not been much concerned with the small towns that complicate the presumed schism between them. Sandalack acknowledges and explores the small town as a central feature of the settler landscape. Throughout much of the twentieth century, western Canada's physical environment was often assigned a critical and sometimes even overarching place in scholarly discussions, lo-cated at the core of identity, lived history, and cultural expression. While both Evans and Sandalack put the emphasis on the western Canadian environment, their stress is on how people have shaped it rather than having been shaped by it. The last place dealt with in this section is the poll. Scholars have long been concerned with mapping out western Canada's particular political history, ask-ing what marks it as distinct from the rest of Canada. In his essay, political sci-entist Jared Wesley builds on his 2010 monograph to analyze regional patterns of electoral politics.[24] By examining recent information about voting patterns in the provinces of Manitoba, Saskatchewan, and Alberta, he concludes that there are enormous differences among the three provinces. Wesley's argument here prompts us to return to a comment made by historian Ramsay Cook some thirty years ago. Given the difficulty of defining region, "why not call a region what it really is—a province."[25]

Cumulatively, these essays give us new ways to think about western Canada from the late nineteenth century to the present day. The essays show us how canonical aspects of western Canadian studies like the farm can be refigured by putting women and Indigenous people at the centre of our analysis. By exploring the work of Indigenous authors and recent social policies around Indigenous people and agriculture, contributors to this volume remind us that Indigenous histories are modern ones that stretch well beyond the early years of contact and settlement to profoundly shape the western Canada of today. The studies of migration make clear that migration was a part of colonization policy. They also remind us that these policies never succeeded in wholly shaping practice. As Loewen's essay demonstrates, people left western Canada, as well as arrived there. In the early twentieth century, Chinese Canadians who were formally banned from entry to Canada came nonetheless and made meaningful lives. People from around the world continue to do so, in numbers and from places that challenge our older assumptions of western Canada's ethnic and racial constitution.

These essays focus on questions of place within a specific regional frame in ways that make clear western Canada's location in a wider world. In the past decade, scholars of western Canada have been interested in investigating the possibilities of transnational and comparative work that stretches across the borders that separated the Canadian from the American West and North America from the Pacific and Atlantic worlds.[26] Nettlebeck and Foster and Chilton all imagine their subjects in wider, imperial terms. Evans stresses Alberta's location within a continental North American history and in doing so helps correct for a scholarship that, as Betsy Jameson and Jeremy Mouat point out, has failed to adequately account for the cross-border histories of the Canadian prairies and the American plains.[27] The essays by Chadya, Loewen, Marshall, Ledohowski, and Chilton are each aware that studying migration necessitates a transnational lens. In a variety of ways, the essays in *Place and Replace* fulfill American historian Patricia Limerick's exhortation to go west and end up global[28] or, perhaps, go global and end up western.

The essays that make up *Place and Replace* push us to think in new ways, but they also confirm some of the themes that scholars of western Canada have returned to repeatedly over the last three decades. They recognize the centrality of Indigenous peoples, colonization, and resistance; migration, race, ethnicity, and nation; literary and other representations; politics, both formal and informal; and the built and natural environment and interactions between them. While some new scholarly vocabularies have a clear imprint here, others do not. Gender and, to a lesser extent, sexuality is an important theme in these essays, but none take up Valerie Korniek's urge to better acknowledge the queer histories of western Canada.[29] The geographic boundaries employed here are also largely familiar. Scholars have long debated which territories, exactly, are included in western Canada. There is not a lot to add to this discussion, but it is worth noting that the essays in this collection reiterate a definition of western Canada essentially analogous with "present-day southern Manitoba, Saskatchewan, and Alberta" as it is generally constituted. It was not the editors' formal intention to counter Finkel, Carter, and Fortna's decision to "not limit the West to Prairie Canada, but rather to recognize multiple Wests and include British Columbia, northern Ontario, Northern Canada, and the borderlands with the United States."[30] Yet in practice *Place and Replace* returns to a working definition of region that equates western Canada with "the Prairies." It is worth thinking about why this might be so and the costs and benefits it might have for our analyses.

Along with previous volumes arising from Western Canadian Studies and St. John's College Prairies Conferences, *Place and Replace* is best read as a collection of recent interdisciplinary research into western Canada. These have played an invaluable role in promoting and making available to a keen readership new scholarship on western Canada. *Prairie Forum* has been a stable vehicle for interdisciplinary scholarship on the prairies since 1976, and each of the western provinces has a historical journal focusing on its particular history.[31] But there are no journals devoted to western Canada, and in this context the publication of *Place and Replace* and anthologies like it serves a critical scholarly purpose. It demonstrates some recent ways that scholars have examined western Canada's multiple pasts and presents around the rubric of "place and replace," reminds us of the possibility and productivity of interdisciplinary discussion, and suggests new opportunities and directions for emerging scholarship.

NOTES

1   We would like to thank Barry Ferguson, Alison Calder, Dennis Cooley, Donald Smith, and Gerry Friesen for their comments on and assistance with this introduction. Adele Perry also acknowledges the support of the Canada Research Chairs programme.

2   See *Prairie Perspectives: Papers of the Western Canadian Studies Conference*, ed. David Gagan (Toronto: Holt, Rinehart and Winston, 1970); *The Twenties in Western Canada*, ed. Susan Mann (Ottawa: National Museum of Man, 1972); *Prairie Perspectives 2: Selected Papers of the Western Canadian Studies Conference*, eds. Anthony W. Rasporich and Henry C. Klassen (Toronto: Holt, Rinehart and Winston, 1973); *Western Perspectives 1*, ed. David J. Bercuson (Toronto: Hold, Rinehart, and Winston, 1974); *Western Canada Past and Present*, ed. A.W. Rasporich (Calgary: McClelland and Stewart

West, 1975); *The Settlement of the West*, ed. Howard Palmer (Calgary: University of Calgary Press, 1977); *The Canadian West: Social Change and Economic Development*, ed. Henry Klassen (Calgary: University of Calgary Press, 1977); Ian A.L. Getty and Donald B. Smith, *One Century Later: Western Canadian Reserve Indians Since Treaty 7* (Vancouver: UBC Press, 1978); *Eastern and Western Perspectives: Papers From the 1978 Joint Atlantic Canadian Western Canadian Studies Conference*, eds. David Bercuson and Phillip Buckner (Toronto: University of Toronto Press, 1981); *The Dirty Thirties in Prairie Canada*, eds. Doug Francis and Herman Ganzevoort (Vancouver: Tantalus Research, 1980); *The New Provinces, 1905–1980, Alberta and Saskatchewan*, eds. Howard Palmer and Donald Smith (Vancouver: Tantalus Research, 1980). Thanks to Donald Smith and Lindsay Moir for tracking these down.

3   http://www.arts.ualberta.ca/~wcsc/, accessed 4 December 2011.

4   Sarah Carter, Alvin Finkel, and Peter Fortna, "Introduction," in *The West and Beyond: New Perspectives on an Imagined Region*, eds. Carter, Finkel, and Fortna (Edmonton: Athabasca University Press, 2010).

5   The 2004 meeting on Indigenous history produced *Intersecting Worlds: Rural and Urban Aboriginal Issues*, eds. Denise Fuchs and Mary Jane McCallum (Winnipeg: St John's College Press, 2004).

6   Two published volumes have come out of these conferences: *Toward Defining the Prairies: Region, Culture, and History*, ed. Robert Wardhaugh (Winnipeg: University of Manitoba Press, 2001); *The Prairies Lost and Found*, ed. Len Kuffert (Winnipeg: St. John's College Press, 2007). A related project is *History, Literature, and the Writing of the Canadian Prairies*, eds. Alison Calder and Robert Wardhaugh (Winnipeg: University of Manitoba Press, 2005).

7   See Ramsay Cook, *1492 and All That: Making a Garden out of Wilderness* (Toronto: Robarts Centre for Canadian Studies, 1992).

8   Sarah Carter, *The Importance of Being Monogamous: Marriage and Nation Building in Western Canada* (Edmonton: Athabasca University Press, 2008), 292. Also see Doug Owram, *The Promise of Eden: The Canadian Expansionist Movement and the Idea of the West, 1856–1900*, 2nd ed. (Toronto: University of Toronto Press, 1992).

9   See, for instance, Jeffrey M. Taylor, *Fashioning Farmers: Ideology, Agricultural Knowledge and the Manitoba Farm Movement, 1890–1925* (Regina: Canadian Plains Research Center, 1994).

10   See Catherine Flynn and E. Leight Syms, "Manitoba's First Farmers," *Manitoba History*, 31 (Spring 1996): 4–11.

11   See, for instance, George Stanley, *The Birth of Western Canada: A History of the Riel Rebellions* (Toronto: University of Toronto Press, 1992 [1936]); Harold Innis, *The Fur Trade in Canada: An Introduction to Canadian Economic History*, revised ed. (Toronto: University of Toronto Press, 1984 [1930]). This point is made in the wider Canadian context in Marlene Shore, "Introduction," *The Contested Past: Reading Canada's History—Selections from the* Canadian Historical Review (Toronto: University of Toronto Press, 2002).

12   See Keith Thor Carlson, Melinda Marie Jetté, and Kenichi Matsui, "An Annotated Bibliography of Major Writings in Aboriginal History, 1990–99," *Canadian Historical Review*, 82, 1 (2001): 132.

13   See, for instance, Veronica Strong-Boag, "Canadian Feminism in the 1920s: The Case of Nellie McClung," *Journal of Canadian Studies* 12, 4 (Summer 1977): 58–68; Mary Kinnear, "The Icelandic Connection: Freyja and the Manitoba Woman Suffrage Movement," *Canadian Woman Studies/les cahiers de la femme* 7, 4 (1986): 25–28.

14   Sylvia Van Kirk, *"Many Tender Ties": Women and Fur Trade Society, 1670–1870* (Winnipeg: Watson and Dwyer, 1980); Jennifer S.H. Brown, *Strangers in Blood: Fur*

Trade Company Families in Indian Country (Vancouver: UBC Press, 1980). Two recent volumes explore the legacies of these books and their authors: *Gathering Places: Fur Trade and Aboriginal Histories*, eds. Carolyn Podruchny and Laura Peers (Vancouver: UBC Press, 2010); *Finding a Way to the Heart: Feminist Writings on Aboriginal and Women's History in Canada*, eds. Robin Jarvis Brownlie and Valerie Korinek (Winnipeg: University of Manitoba Press, 2012).

15   The monographs include Sarah Carter, *Capturing Women: The Manipulation of Cultural Imagery on the Prairie West* (Montreal: McGill-Queens, 1997); Myra Rutherdale, *Women and the White Man's God: Gender and Race in the Canadian Mission Field* (Vancouver: UBC Press, 2003); Mary Kinnear, *A Female Economy: Women's Work in a Prairie Province, 1870–1970* (Montreal: McGill-Queen's, 1998). Important collections are *Contact Zones: Aboriginal and Settler Women in Canada's Past*, eds. Myra Rutherdale and Katie Pickles (Vancouver: UBC Press, 2005); *Unsettled Pasts: Reconceiving the West Through Women's History*, eds. Sarah Carter, Lesley Erickson, Pat Roome, and Char Smith (Calgary: University of Calgary Press, 2005); *Telling Tales: Essays in Western Women's History*, eds. Catherine A. Cavanaugh and Randi R. Warne (Vancouver: UBC Press, 2000).

16   Ross Cox, *The Columbia River, or Scenes and adventures during a residence of six years on the western side of the Rocky Mountains among various tribes of Indians hitherto unknown; together with 'A Journey across the American Continent'*, ed. Edgar I. Steward and Jane R Stewart (Norman, OK: University of Oklahoma Press, 1957 [1831]), 333.

17   See, for instance, The Mounted Police and Prairie Society, 1873–1919, ed. William M. Baker (Regina: Canadian Plains Research Center, 1998); Michael Dawson, *The Mountie from Dime Novel to Disney* (Toronto: Between the Lines, 1998).

18   On this, see David Bright, "The West Wants In: Regionalism, Class, and *Labour/Le Travail*, 1976-2002," *Labour/Le Travail*, 50 (Fall 2002): 159–162.

19   Alison Marshall, *The Way of the Bachelor: Early Chinese Settlement in Manitoba* (Vancouver: UBC Press, 2011). Also see "Manitoba Chinese Stories," found at http://www.youtube.com/watch?v=7WwNJGkHfwQ, accessed 7 April 2012.

20   See, for instance, Royden Loewen, *Diaspora in the Countryside: Two Mennonite Communities in Mid-20th Century North America* (Urbana: University of Illinois Press and Toronto: University of Toronto Press, 2006); Royden Loewen, *Hidden Worlds: Revisiting the Mennonite Migrants of the 1870s* (Winnipeg: University of Manitoba Press, 2001).

21   See Royden Loewen and Gerald Friesen, *Immigrants in Prairie Cities: Ethnic Diversity in Twentieth century Canada* (Toronto: University of Toronto Press, 2010), Chapters 5 and 7.

22   See "Introduction" in *The Prairie West as Promised Land*, eds. R. Douglas Francis and Chris Kitzen (Calgary: University of Calgary Press, 2007).

23   See *Manitowapow: Aboriginal Writings from the Land of Water*, eds. Niigaanwewidam James Sinclair and Warren Cariou (Winnipeg: Portage and Main Press, 2011).

24   Jared J. Wesley, *Code Politics: Campaigns and Cultures in the Canadian Prairies* (Vancouver: UBC Press, 2010).

25   Ramsay Cook, "Regionalism Unmasked," *Acadiensis*, 8, 1 (1983): 140. Also see Gerald Friesen, "Defining the Prairies: Or Why the Prairies Don't Exist," in *Toward Defining the Prairies*.

26   See, for instance, Sterling Evans, *The Borderlands of the American West: Essays on Regional History of the Forty-Ninth Parallel* (Lincoln: University of Nebraska, 2006); *One Step Over the Line: Toward a History of Women in the North American Wests*, eds. Elizabeth Jameson and Sheila McManus (Edmonton: Athabasca University Press,

2008); *One West, Two Myths: A Comparative Reader,* eds. Carol Highman and Robert Thacker (Calgary: University of Calgary Press, 2004).

27   See Betsy Jameson and Jeremy Moat, "Telling Differences: The Forty-Ninth Parallel and the Historiographies of the West and the Nation," *Pacific Historical Review,* 75, 2 (May 2006): 217.

28   Patricia Nelson Limerick, "Going West and Ending Up Global," *The Western Historical Quarterly* 32, 1 (Spring 2001): 5–24.

29   See Valerie Korinek, "A Queer-Eye View of the Prairies: Reorienting Western Canadian Histories," in *The West and Beyond.* The University of Manitoba's Lesbian, Gay, Bisexual, and Two-Spirited Oral History and Archives initiative is also noteworthy here. See http://umanitoba.ca/faculties/arts/departments/humanities/umih_lgbtt_initiative. html, accessed 16 December 2011.

30   Alvin Finkel, Sarah Carter, and Peter Fortna, "Introduction," in *The West and Beyond,* xvi.

31   See http://www.cprc.ca/prairieforum, accessed 4 December 2011. Provincial journals include *BC Historical Quarterly, Alberta History, Saskatchewan History,* and *Manitoba History.*

ERASING AND REPLACING
PROPERTY AND HOMESTEAD RIGHTS OF FIRST NATIONS FARMERS OF MANITOBA AND THE NORTHWEST, 1870s – 1910s[1]

SARAH CARTER

An article in *The Canadian Indian* in 1891 tidily summed up a prevailing view of Aboriginal people and agriculture in North America: "Prior to the advent of the Europeans, the North American Indians were not an agricultural people; the cultivation of the soil was considered among them as a degrading occupation for the men of the tribes, who left it to the old women and the children."[2] The view that First Nations people were not agricultural—and even if there was some farming it was left to women and was thus half-hearted, sporadic, sloppy, and negligible—prevailed despite clear evidence to the contrary. Well before the treaties of the 1870s there was plenty of evidence to the contrary in the region that became Manitoba. In some cases there were agricultural settlements with communally cultivated land, and in others, individual farms.[3] Agriculture long predated the arrival of Europeans in Manitoba, and later drew on and absorbed techniques and crops brought by fur traders, missionaries, and early settlers.

At the time of the treaties of the 1870s the presence of First Nations farming should have been welcomed by the new Canadian regime, as the encouragement of agriculture was presented as a government priority. Pre-treaty farming activity in Manitoba was used as a rationale for not providing the same level of assistance in the establishment of reserve agriculture as was offered to First Nations further west. Yet the agriculture of First Nations people also posed vexing problems. If they were farmers, they had property, and were land owners in actual occupation.

But it was vital to the enterprise of establishing colonial rule in western Canada to cast First Nations as the antithesis of agriculturalists—as hunters, incapable and ignorant of farming, and thus having no concept of true land ownership. It was important to draw clear distinctions between the "settlers" who were the farmers and homesteaders (and who would have virtually unrestricted access to farm land) and the "Indians" who would need very little, would be restricted to reserves and have almost no opportunity to expand their holdings. The presence of First Nations farmers needed to be suppressed—erased, even—and confined to reserves. Deliberate and strenuous efforts were needed to accomplish these goals. Torturous twists and turns were required to ensure that no one defined as "Indian" actually owned land off or on reserves, even in cases where land was occupied and farmed before the treaties. As Patrick Wolfe has noted, the object of settler-colonization was the land, and settlers wanted Indigenous people to vanish from the land. The dominant feature of settler-colonization was replacement.[4] The presence of First Nations farmers, particularly off reserves, posed vexing questions and they had to vanish from the post-1870 landscape.

Any window of opportunity to retain or acquire individual parcels of land was boarded up and nailed shut, yet First Nations farmers and would-be homesteaders tried to open these windows. They asked pointed questions about their rights to individually own and sell land on and off their reserves, and about whether they had the right to the homestead grant of 160 acres available to male (and some female) newcomers. Did the assignments of land under the treaties include individual plots of land they already possessed? Could an Indian who resided on and farmed land in advance of the treaties claim that land as his homestead? Could an "enfranchised Indian" homestead? Could an Indian from eastern Canada move west and file on a homestead on the prairies? Answers were almost always "no," and if "yes," each case had to be carefully scrutinized. The priority of the Canadian government was the settlement of new immigrants on the land, and they had many advantages and opportunities to expand their property beyond the initial grant of land. By contrast, First Nations had virtually no opportunity to expand their land base after reserves were surveyed; the treaties provided a mechanism to diminish but not to increase reserve land. This article focuses on present-day Manitoba, as it is part of a co-authored study of First Nations agriculture in that province, but sources from other locations are also included to shed light on the larger region of western Canada.

In *How the Indians Lost Their Land: Law and Power on the Frontier*, legal historian Stuart Banner found that in the eighteenth century and earlier Europeans generally viewed Native Americans as the proprietors of their land with rights to that land. This perception was altered in the nineteenth century when they were uniformly perceived as wandering hunters who did not actually own any land.[5]

The survey and rapid sale of the land during the era of intensive settlement was expedited by this new perception of all Aboriginal people as rambling hunters who might occupy but not own the land, and as being uninterested in agriculture. In western Canada this change of emphasis developed in a more condensed period of time; the two views overlapped for a while because of the presence of First Nations agriculture. Members of the 1857 H.Y. Hind Red River Exploring Expedition found Aboriginal agriculture in many localities in present-day Manitoba. At this point—when there was debate in the Canadas about whether "Rupert's Land" would be a valuable addition to the proposed confederation of British colonies—it was useful to describe and even to praise the nature and extent of Aboriginal agriculture rather than to erase this evidence. Assigned to assess the fertility of the soil and potential for agricultural settlement, members of the expedition acquired a great deal of information on soil quality, crops, the growing season, and frost from Aboriginal farmers.

Members of the 1857 Hind expedition found many generations-old Aboriginal agricultural sites located at strategic provisioning sites along well-worn fur trade routes.[6] At Garden Island, northwest of the Red River settlement, there were "considerable fields of corn." The Aboriginal farmers reported to a member of the 1857 expedition surveyor Simon W. Dawson that "they had cultivated the land from time immemorial," and that they had not once "known an instance where their crops had been injured by frost." At Fairford, crops of potatoes, onions, and turnips were grown; it was a stopping place for the brigades, and had long raised produce to support the fur trade. At Islington Mission or the White Dog or Chien Blanc, "all kinds of farm and garden crops" succeeded well. At Fort Alexander, crops of wheat and potatoes "of great size and excellent quality" were observed in early September 1857. Crops of Indian corn were reported as successful in many parts of the southeastern rim of Lake Winnipeg. The most substantial agricultural "Indian settlement" was St. Peter's on the banks of the Red River north of the Forks (present-day Winnipeg).

While the presence of Aboriginal agriculture was useful to the 1857 expedition, it was less so just a few years later once it was determined that "Rupert's Land" was to be absorbed by the new Dominion of Canada. The erasure of the presence of Aboriginal agriculture was now more important; farmers had to be recognized as having property rights, and if they were truly farmers they might need more than a little land. Hunters and fishers might have some occupancy rights, but were not regarded as actually owning the land; it was helpful to cast all First Nations as hunters without fixed abode, as it was then easier to claim that the land was in fact not theirs. Architects of the new region of the Dominion assumed that the land was Canada's after the 1869–70 transfer from the Hudson's Bay Company, even though First Nations remained "the real sovereigns and owners of land in most of Rupert's Land in 1870."[7] Canada, however, proceeded as if it were sovereign; key decisions about how the land was to be parcelled out were made well before the first treaty of 1871. It had already been decided, for example, that the majority of the territory would be Crown land, that a vast amount of land would go to the Hudson's Bay Company and to the Canadian Pacific Railway, and that 1.4 million acres would go to the Métis. A small circle in Ottawa decided on the survey system and land policy well in advance of treaties, and there was almost no debate in Parliament about these measures; great haste in moving forward with the survey was stressed by parliamentarians. It was the survey, and the maps to be produced that documented that survey, that would declare the land as belonging to Canada. In May 1869 Sir George Cartier stated that "It was important that not a month or day should be lost, after the territory became ours, in organizing a Government and having the lands surveyed, and their character made known throughout this country and Europe."[8] As soon as the Queen's Proclamation was issued declaring the transfer of Rupert's Land to Canada, no time should be lost in "laying out townships" for settlement, Cartier declared. The presence of First Nations farmers proved inconvenient to all of these plans and the haste required for these measures.

Representations of First Nations people as incapable, disinterested, and unwilling farmers—and instead as hunters, fishers, and gatherers—took root in the late nineteenth century. The Plains people were cast as "thoughtlessly, carelessly living on the surface. Like the butterfly flitting from plant to plant, so these men roamed and camped and dreamed, not of mines and means which were above and beneath them on every hand."[9] It was useful to insist that First Nations had a weak and very different concept of land ownership and property—to declare that they had fuzzy and imperfect ideas about communal property that did not imply legal ownership. Their "tribal communism" was condemned as "hurtful to individuality, and without this no race of man can progress." "This is communal; the individual has not yet come in. It is our work to bring in the individual."[10] Department of Indian Affairs officials insisted their "wards" had no concept of private property, and claimed their goal was to introduce individual ownership, as this was critical to the abolishment of what was described as the "tribal" or "communistic" system.[11]

When treaty relations began in 1871, the presence of First Nations farmers should have been welcomed, as Canadian federal authorities claimed that the encouragement of agriculture was a goal of their administration and of the Great Mother, Queen Victoria, herself. Lieutenant-Governor Adams Archibald told the First Nations assembled at the negotiation of Treaty One at Lower Fort Garry that the Great Mother "would like them to adopt the habits of the whites, to till land and raise food, and store it up against a time of want. She thinks this would be the best thing for her red children to do, that it would make them safer from famine and distress, and make their homes more comfortable."[12] Yet Archibald also noted that there were First Nations farmers who were long established in Manitoba. Referring to St. Peter's he said:

> I drove yesterday through the village below this Fort. There I saw many well-built houses, and many well-tilled fields with wheat and barley and potatoes growing, and giving promise of plenty for the winter to come. The people who till these fields and live in these houses are men of your own race, and they show that you can live and prosper and provide like the white man. What I saw in my drive is enough to prove that even if there was not a buffalo or a fur-bearing animal in the country, you could live and be surrounded with comfort by what you can raise from the soil.[13]

At one level the knowledge of and proficiency in agriculture of Manitoba's First Nations was welcomed by federal authorities. Their agriculture was used as a rationale for providing little to no instruction and assistance compared to the First Nations further west, where a program of home farms and farm instructors began in 1879. Indian Commissioner J.A.N. Provencher wrote in 1875 that because the Manitoba First Nations were "sufficiently familiar with the elements of industry and agriculture," and because the Manitoba reserves were near to settlements "the government is exonerated from the obligation, which it has to fulfill elsewhere, of establishing model farms, erecting mills etc...."[14] Settlements surveyed as reserves such as St. Peter's were also useful, as they could illustrate the immediate successes of the agricultural objectives of the federal government.

At the treaties, Manitoba First Nations negotiators conveyed knowledge of the land requirements for successful agriculture, and were concerned that they have an adequate land base, particularly for future generations. Commissioner Provencher wrote in 1875 that, "the Indians, as may be expected, claim the exclusive right of property to lands: they deny to the Government the right to possess without their consent; and, as a natural conclusion, reserve to themselves the right of stating their terms, and of selecting their Reserves."[15] They initially asked for very large reserves; according to Commissioner Wemyss Simpson, "the quantity of land demanded for each band amounted to about three townships per Indian, and included the greater part of the settled portions of the Province."[16] They expressed concerns—not only about the present generation, but their future needs; as one Manitoba chief stated at the Treaty One talks, "I understand thoroughly that every 20 people get a mile square; but if an Indian family of five settles down, he may have more children. Where is their land?"[17] The response of the Canadian and Crown representatives at the Treaty One talks was that reserves could expand to meet growing needs. Adams Archibald stated "whenever his children get more numerous than they are now, they will be provided for further West. Whenever the reserves are found too small the Government will sell the land, and give the Indians land elsewhere."[18] This never happened; in fact, First Nations reserves were diminished, no mechanisms were provided to expand reserve land, and they were unable to acquire homestead land outside of reserves as individuals.

An adequate land base for successful agriculture was less likely for Manitoba First Nations than for newcomers, or for other Indian reserve farmers to the west as well as to the east. The Manitoba treaties (One, Two and Five) provided much less land to First Nations (160 acres per family of five or less in proportion to family size) than to newcomers (160 acres to individual males regardless of marital status and family size and to women who qualified as sole heads of families.) The Manitoba treaties also provided considerably less land than those negotiated with First Nations to the west and east.[19] In Treaty Three, of the North-West Angle Treaty, reserves were not to "exceed in all one square mile [640 acres] for each family of five, or in that proportion for larger or smaller families."[20] Treaty Four, which included a small portion of central western Manitoba, also provided one square mile or 640 acres per family of five. The Dakota of Manitoba, who were not regarded as "British" Indians, were provided with even less land. They were excluded from the treaties, and were granted reserves as "a matter of grace and not of right."[21] Two reserves were allotted in 1874, at Oak River and Bird Tail Creek, and a third at Oak Lake in 1876; these were surveyed on the basis of 80 acres for each family of five.

The First Nations of Manitoba proved complicated to deal with and to dismiss as non-agriculturalists and thus non-land owners. There were a number of settlements with cultivation well before the treaties, and several of these were surveyed as reserves. St. Peter's, the largest and most prosperous of the Aboriginal agricultural settlements, was surveyed as reserve one.[22] This raised a great number of vexing issues, not to be entirely "resolved" in the case of St. Peter's until the complete surrender and closure of the reserve in 1907–1908. One of the rationales for the surrender was the complicated and competing claims over land on the reserve. Before treaties there were also First Nations settlements, or individual farms outside of the land surveyed as reserves. This situation posed thorny questions, as did the issue of whether an individual defined as an "Indian" had the right to sell a parcel of land owned before the treaties. Altogether there were murky distinctions between the "Indians" who were not supposed to be interested in farming and owning land, and the "settlers" who would be the farmers and land owners of the new day.

In early 1875, St. Peter's First Nations settlers insisted to federal authorities that it was agreed in treaty talks that the land that was individually owned at the time of the treaty "should be considered their own property," and that the reserve was to comprise enough land to give each family 160 acres "exclusive of any land [they] held as settlers at the time of signing."[23] The St. Peter's Aboriginal land owners were in some cases selling their land, within the reserves, to "outsiders"—either Métis or whites. Authorities were alarmed that "property that changed hands since the Treaty is very large, and I have reason to believe that it is always increasing." Provencher wrote in a December 1875 memo that "many Indians have acquired properties within the actual limits of the Reserve, before the Treaties. They had cleared and improved them and thought they had the power to dispose of them in virtue of a right of absolute property. Many of these lands were sold to whites, or to Halfbreeds, and it is this matter which now makes conflicting claims, which should be settled as soon as possible by a Treaty, or by special legislation, or by an order in Council."[24]

Commissioner Molyneux St. John addressed these questions in an 1875 memorandum "in reference to understanding with Indians as to the proprietary rights of Indians in property held by them prior to the negotiation of the Stone Fort or No. 1 Treaty."[25] St. John remembered that he was asked by St. Peter's First Nations settlers during the treaty talks whether the land set aside for each family was "meant to include the land already occupied by them." He told them at the time of the treaty that "the allotment now provided for was irrespective of and in addition to their holdings." While St. John did not recall anything being said about their right to sell the properties they had in advance of the treaties, "the impression on my mind was that the small farms already in possession of the Indians should be theirs absolutely." Commissioner Wemyss Simpson had the same opinion, and believed that St. Peter's settlers therefore had the right to sell their property as they had freely before the treaty and before the survey of the reserve.[26] Meanwhile, the First Nations settlers of Fort Alexander, who also had occupied land well before the same land was surveyed as their reserve, were told a different story:

> All the lands occupied by them inside of the Reserve at the time of the
> Treaty was returning to and would be kept by the Government for the
> use of the occupiers who could dispose of it in favour of some member
> of the same band with the approval of the Indian commissioner, but of
> nobody else. They have accepted this interpretation of the Treaty, but
> it is not the same thing at St. Peters, where they say that Mr. Simpson
> assured them that all the land held by them was private property and
> that it could be disposed of as they pleased.[27]

By late 1875, it was decided that the Fort Alexander approach would apply to all First Nations farmers/settlers whose individual property became part of a reserve—they could sell their land, but only to another treaty band member and reserve resident. According to a report prepared by Provencher in December 1875, "all property held by Indians within the limits of the Reserve may remain in the hands of the possessor who would have full power with right to dispose of it in favour of another member of the same Band, but not in favour of persons who were strangers to his tribe."[28] All transfers of property could be made only with the consent of the government.

The 1876 Indian Act further complicated the situation of prior ownership of what became reserve land in Manitoba. After treaties and according to the Indian Act, the legal title to all reserve land was "in the Crown" and was set aside for the use or benefit of a particular band. Plots of land owned and improved before treaties that then became part of a reserve were *not* truly owned by the individual, although they had the right to occupy the land through a location ticket. Section 10 of the Indian Act declared that "any Indian or non-treaty Indian in the Province of British Columbia, the Province of Manitoba, in the North West Territories, or in the Territory of Keewatin, who has, or shall have, previously to the selection of a reserve, possession of and made permanent improvements on a plot of land which has been or shall be included in or surrounded by a reserve, shall have the same privileges, neither more nor less, in respect of such plot, as an Indian enjoys under a location title."[29] Through a "location ticket," an individual could occupy the land and it could be passed down to heirs; it was "transferable," but only "to an Indian of the same band," and all only with the consent of government authorities.[30] Further ensuring that no outsider could purchase, use, or live on land on a reserve, the Indian Act further stipulated that "no person, or Indian other than an Indian of the band, shall settle, reside or hunt upon, occupy or use any land." Transgressors could be evicted, removed, and punished if they returned.[31]

Then there was the murky question of land owned individually pre-treaty that was beyond the boundaries of reserves. In the same 1875 memorandum mentioned above, St. John addressed this issue and wrote that at the time of the treaties—and ever since these occupants had been told—their land "would be protected by the Government."[32] Under the Manitoba Act of 1870, it was enacted that "all persons in peaceable possession of tracts of land at the time of the transfer to Canada in those parts of the Province in which the Indian Title has not been extinguished, shall have the right of pre-emption of the same, as such terms and conditions as may be determined by the Governor in Council."[33] Among other directives that dealt with this issue was an 1871 order-in-council that read "parties found upon the lands at the time of survey, having settled upon and improved the same in good faith as settlers under the land regulations, will be protected in the enjoyment of thereof, whether the same be pre-emption or homestead right provided they respectively enter for such right with the Land Office and otherwise carry out the provisions of the said legislation... within three months after the survey shall have been made."[34]

In 1875 St. John believed that this clause applied to those categorized as Indians, although in his view Indian land owners were not to have very much land. He described their dwellings as "huts," suggesting impermanence of the residences that were surrounded by small patches of cultivated land. St. John emphasized that the occupants had been told "they must be content with such small portions of land round their several huts as the government might think proper to give them." (It might have been drawn to St. John's attention that most immigrant homesteaders lived in shacks or huts and cultivated only small patches of land for the first several years, yet they remained entitled to the full 160 acres if they satisfied the qualifications when applying for land patents.)

The 1875 policy on land occupied and farmed by Indians before the treaties that remained outside of reserves was that "they would be allowed to hold that property as ordinary settlers by giving proper notice to the officer in the Land Office and that they could sell to whom they pleased with the consent of the agent... but in that case they would have to go and live afterwards in the reserve where they would take their share from the lands not yet divided."[35] They were not to be allowed the option of homesteading the land, as was possible for non–First Nations settlers who occupied land before the transfer. When Indians sold their land, they had no option but to go to live on their reserves. This policy too made its way into Provencher's December 1875 report: "in regard to those who at the same time possess properties outside of the Reserve, they should have permission to dispose of them in favour of Whites, but only for the purpose of going to reside on the Reserve assigned to the Band of which they are members."[36]

The rights of treaty people to the individual parcels of land they owned prior to the treaties should have been bolstered by the Indian Act. Section 70 (a) stipulated that "he shall not be disturbed in the occupation of any plot on which he has or may have permanent improvements prior to his becoming a party to any treaty with the Crown."[37] But they were permitted to occupy this land—not to have legal title to the land—although the Government could compensate them for any improvements. In 1877 it was decided that First Nations individuals who had been in "undisturbed occupancy of certain lands in Manitoba not subsequently included in any reserve" were not "persons" (according to 38 Victoria, Chapter 52) and were not therefore entitled to a patent, or outright ownership, of land they occupied before the treaties. Through an 1875 amendment to "An Act Respecting the Appropriation of Certain Dominion Lands in Manitoba" it was enacted that "persons satisfactorily establishing undisturbed occupancy of any lands within the Province prior to, and being by themselves or their servants, tenants or agents, or those through whom they claim in actual peaceable possession thereof, on the

15th day of July, 1870, shall be entitled to receive Letters Patent therefore, granting the same absolutely to them respectively in fee simple."[38]

Were Indians "persons" under this legislation? The minister of the interior, David Laird, consulted with the deputy minister of justice who, in June 1877, "was of the opinion that an Indian does not come within the word 'persons' in the Act referred to. By 'Indian' I mean one of Indian blood reputed to belong to a particular band and who has not been enfranchised under the provisions of the law." The position adopted by the Department of the Interior officials as recommended by Surveyor General J.S. Dennis was that "an Indian does not come within the class of 'persons' referred to in the Act…and cannot therefore claim a Patent for land of which he was in occupation at the time of the transfer of the territory."[39]

If a First Nations owner sold an individual plot of land, the transfer was not valid or binding. Settlers who had purchased land from Indians were given two options—they could buy the land from the federal government at $1.00 per acre, or they could homestead the land, gaining title after three years if they cultivated the land and lived on the claim for a portion of each year. The question was tested in 1876–7 when M.T. Hunter, of St. Andrew's parish, bought land from an Indian outside of a reserve, "upon which he [the Indian – not named] has resided during the last 25 years and has permanent improvements."[40] Hunter had taken legal advice before he purchased the land and had been told that "an Indian has the undoubted right to dispose of any real estate lying outside of a Reserve." However, Hunter was informed in 1877 that the transaction was not valid, and that he had to purchase the land from the government or homestead the land. Chief Surveyor J.S. Dennis wrote a memorandum stating that an assignment of land from an Indian was not valid, "although such assignment may have been made previous to" the 1876 Indian Act.[41] This was because, according to Dennis, Indians were not "persons." An 1880 amendment to the Indian Act clearly distinguished an "Indian" from a "person": "The term 'person' means an individual other than an Indian, unless the context clearly requires another construction."[42] Anyone defined as "Indian," therefore, could not gain a patent to land they had owned and cultivated before the treaties.

The Proclamation of 1763 was another rationale for not recognizing the individual ownership of land by Indians prior to treaties and consequently denying them the right to sell that land. According to the Proclamation, the foundation of the approach that Canada took to treaties, all sales and leases could only be made through the Crown, no private person could presume to make purchases from Indians. Land was to be purchased "only for Us, in our Name, at some public Meeting or Assembly of the Said Indians."[43] Laird referred to "an old proclamation" during debate about the Indian Act in the House of Commons in 1876, when the issue of land owned and sold by Indians of Manitoba emerged.[44] Manitoba MPs supported the rights of Indian owners to buy and sell, in order to make the sales to non-Aboriginal settlers legal. Likely referring to St. Peter's, Andrew Bannatyne said that "some Indians in Manitoba had sold land to settlers in good faith," and Donald A. Smith said he "thought it was only fair that something should be done to legalize these sales."[45] Laird's reply as summarized in the House of Commons debates was: "this would be opening up a wide field. If they admitted the right of giving titles to the Indians, they would probably find the whole North-West in the hands of other persons. He found in an old proclamation of the British Government that purchases of lands from Indians were strictly forbidden. It was understood that Indians could not dispose of land except by treaty to the Crown. If an Indian occupied a piece of land outside a reserve, although he was allowed to enjoy the results of his improvements he had no right to sell the property."[46]

Donald Smith advanced the argument that through the Selkirk Treaty of 1811, rights to the land (below Sugar Point to the Peguis or St. Peter's people) were established, and that "this land had been given to these Indians by Lord Selkirk for services rendered." There was no further debate; when Hector Langevin said that "he thought it would be a great hardship to deprive some Indians of their acquired rights" and that "some Indians had bought lands from others," Laird simply responded that "such a purchase was illegal."[47]

Did an individual Indian have the right to buy or otherwise acquire land outside of reserves and sell it after the treaties? This right was tested in 1909 when, in the Manitoba King's Bench case Sanderson v. Heap, it was decided that an Indian did have the right to sell outright his individual property; it was also clearly stated that an Indian had the right to acquire real and personal property outside of a reserve.[48] A treaty Indian and member of the St. Peter's band had sold land to a resident of the town of Selkirk, and he later wanted the sale made void, arguing that under the Indian Act he was not entitled to make the sale. The judge decided that the Indian Act did not restrict his right to sell, that "nothing forbids him to acquire real and personal property outside of a reserve or special reserve or to dispose of it, *inter vivos* at all events, as freely as persons who are not Indians." Justice Thomas Mathers wrote that "unlike the Indians of the United States who are aliens, the Indians of Canada are British subjects and entitled to all the rights and privileges of subjects." He quoted an earlier judgement in Upper Canada by Justice Robinson, who stated that the government had "never attempted to interfere with the disposition which any individual Indian has desired to make of land that had been granted to him in free and common soccage by the Crown."[49]

First Nations people could not be legally prevented from buying and then selling land off reserve after this 1909 decision. In our study we hope to be able to trace the extent to which this happened. The price of land would have been a barrier, but there are indications of land purchases. In 1910, Winnipeg journalist

Lillian Beynon Thomas wrote about a visit to St. Peter's and Selkirk: "An Indian stood against the rail near us and an over-inquisitive white man on the other side of him said: 'You live on the reserve?' in that idiotic fashion Anglo-Saxons have of thinking that bad English is easier of comprehension than good for an alien. 'No' was the quiet answer in which could be detected dignity and pride. 'I do not take treaty. My father and mother stopped taking treaty money and have their own land.'"[50]

While free to purchase land, no one defined as "Indian" could apply to homestead the 160 acres of land available to (mostly male) newcomers. This prohibition lasted until 1951, when there was virtually no homestead land left, except in north-central Alberta. The issue of whether Aboriginal people could claim land on the "public" domain in western Canada first emerged in 1862 in British Columbia, when an Aboriginal man sought to buy land at a public sale.[51] The official conducting the sale wrote for guidance to the Governor of British Columbia, who replied that there could be no objections, but soon after Aboriginal people were deliberately forbidden the right of pre-emption—the method of acquiring provincial Crown land in BC similar to the homesteading in the prairie provinces—in BC where most of the land, except along the "railway belt," was administered by the province. The provincial legislation read that "such right of pre-emption shall not be held to extend to any of the Aborigines of this Continent, except to such as shall have obtained the Governor's special permission in writing to that effect."[52] Most First Nations farmers in BC had to be content with twenty acres per family of reserve land.[53]

Section 70 of the 1876 Indian Act specifically prohibited those defined as "Indian" from the right to homestead. The Act stipulated that "no Indian or nontreaty Indian, resident in the province of Manitoba, the North-West Territories or the territory of Keewatin, shall be held capable of having acquired or of acquiring a homestead or pre-emption right."[54] This contrasted with the many ways newcomers could acquire land. Architects of the Dominion Land policy clearly recognized that 160 acres would not be enough to sustain a farming family and there were liberal provisions to expand holdings. First, there was the free homestead of 160 acres, obtained for a filing fee of $10.00 (although the land was not owned outright until after first five and later three years of occupancy and cultivation). A homesteader could make a second homestead entry and through the right of pre-emption could also acquire an additional neighbouring 160 acres. Families could expand their holdings as sons (not daughters) could file homesteads on adjoining lands. Well-to-do settlers could also purchase the odd-numbered public lands, CPR land, school lands, and HBC land. First Nations farmers were also excluded from a host of other initiatives intended to foster settlement on what had become the "public domain," which included policies that made woodlots available to homesteaders, and the regulations governing the issue of permits to cut hay and the leasing of lands for grazing purposes.

The goal of the homesteading scheme was to quickly populate the land, replacing First Nations with newcomers. As economist Douglas Allen has written, the land policies of both the U.S. and Canada were "efforts to 'hire' settlers" due to the "Indian's simultaneous claim on public lands and the cost imposed by this dispute over property rights."[55] Homesteading helped to establish Canadian claims in their western territories and was a "least-cost strategy," a "substitute for direct military force [that] acts to mitigate the costs of violence." Allen argues that "when the sovereignty of a region is threatened, settlement is promoted to help establish property rights and mitigate the enforcement costs by violence."[56] A preponderance of fit and preferably youthful white males suited this purpose best and they were given many incentives, including the initial grant of land, and the relatively easy opportunities to acquire more land.

It was not natural and inevitable that all those defined as Indian in western Canada would be deliberately and legally denied the right to homestead. In his 1869 book *Red River Country, Hudson's Bay and North-West Territories Considered in Relation to Canada*, Alexander Russell advocated a system of homesteads for Indians, urging the Dominion to provide "that any Indian of any such tribe might, at any time forever thereafter and anywhere, obtain a free grant of two hundred acres of land, on his choosing to become a settler, as an inalienable homestead."[57] Russell was not alone—during debates about the Indian Act in 1876, the matter was raised by Gavin Fleming, Liberal Member of Parliament for Brant North. He "thought it strange that Indians should be prohibited from obtaining land in the North-West when the most ignorant and illiterate immigrant could enjoy that pre-emption right."[58] Fleming also "did not see why an Indian had not as good a right to emigrate to Manitoba and get a homestead as a white man."[59] Manitoba Member of Parliament John Christian Schultz agreed, saying "it seemed to be held by the Government that because they gave the Indians an annuity of $5 per head the latter were to be deprived of every right and privilege which a white man holds dear." Schultz "did not see why the Indians of the North-West, when they became as intelligent as those in Brant, should not have the right to get homesteads for themselves."[60]

Other advocates of homesteads-for-Indians emerged from time to time. Robert Steinhauer was an Anishinabe Methodist missionary who was enfranchised in 1896. He was also an advocate for homestead rights for First Nations; in 1903 the *Toronto Globe* quoted him as saying that if Indian boys and girls were "given the same chance as other children who are brought into Canada, and given the opportunity of studying at the public schools, and afterwards allowed to homestead land, they would stand shoulder to shoulder with any class of people in the country."[61] From the late nineteenth century there were also many calls for policies that would allot reserve land to individuals. The editor of *The Canada School Journal and Weekly Review*, for example, wrote on September 24, 1885 that in order to be spared "periodical Indian wars" a policy of "separate homesteads" was needed. Through a "method of settling them as individuals... wild and troublesome Indians [in the U.S.] have been peaceably induced to give up savagery, to practically give up its tribal relations, and to take to civilized ways." There were many Canadian admirers of the 1887 Dawes Act in the U.S. that divided up and allotted reserve land individually. A somewhat similar plan was implemented in western Canada by Indian Affairs beginning in 1889 on agricultural reserves with the subdivision survey into small plots and the introduction of a "peasant" farming policy.[62]

Laird's reply to questions about homestead rights in the debates about the Indian Act in 1876, however, was that "the Indians must either be treated as minors or as white men. If they should be found intelligent enough to exercise the rights of white men they could become enfranchised."[63] According to Laird, enfranchisement, to be discussed below, was the way to acquire land individually. Once enfranchised, it might be possible to homestead, although this was not obvious and the issue was debated. A reason for the clause prohibiting homesteading was detailed in an 1899 "Memorandum on the Legal Status of British North American Indians" that contained "information relating to the disabilities and restrictions" imposed upon them. Indians were denied the right to homestead because "the public lands in the Province, Territories and District mentioned are vested in the Crown for the benefit of the government of the Dominion. The surrender of the so-called Indian title over these lands having accrued to the benefit of the Dominion, the Dominion has been party to the reservation of large tracts of land for the benefits of the Indians, which, speaking generally, far exceed in extent the areas to which they would have been entitled individually, under the Homestead and Pre-emption Clauses of the Dominion Lands Act."[64]

Indians had "large tracts of land" reserved for their benefit. Reserves provided land for Indians, scrip provided land for the Métis, and homesteads were for those "not enrolled as Indians," as John A. Macdonald explained in the House of Commons in 1885.[65] Indians could not homestead or take Métis scrip; the same section of the Indian Act that dealt with homestead rights stated that Indians did not have "the right to share in the distribution of any lands allotted to half breeds."[66] There was, however, a brief opportunity in 1886 and 1887 when treaty Indians who met the necessary ancestry qualifications could withdraw from treaty and receive Métis scrip.

In Department of Indian Affairs correspondence the question of whether Indians could homestead was discussed and debated many times and from many angles; extensively debated was the question of whether an enfranchised Indian could homestead. First legislated under the Gradual Civilization Act (1857), this was the process through which an individual lost Indian and wardship status and (supposedly) gained the full rights of citizenship. It was a complicated and protracted process with many hoops to jump through. According to the 1876 Indian Act, consent of the band had to be approved before an applicant ("any Indian man, or unmarried woman of the full age of twenty-one years") could begin the process. The applicant was then assigned a "suitable allotment," the precise amount being unspecified. In allotting the land, the quantity was to be in proportion to the size of the family "compared with the total quantity of land in the reserve, and the whole number of the band." The power to decide how much land was to be allotted was left with the band. If the Indian agent and superintendent general of Indian Affairs decided the allotment was "equitable" then a "competent person" was asked to "report whether the applicant is an Indian who, from the degree of civilization to which he or she has attained, and the character for integrity, morality and sobriety which he or she bears, appears to be qualified to become a proprietor of land in fee simple."[67] If a favourable report was received, a location ticket was issued. There was then a probationary period of three years, or longer in the event of unsatisfactory conduct, after which the superintendent general could grant title to the land in fee simple. Later amendments made the process even more challenging. After 1884 the applicant had to furnish a certificate:

> to be made under oath before a judge of any court or justice of the peace, clergyman or minister of the religious denomination to which the applicant belongs or by two Justices of the Peace, to the effect that, to the best of the knowledge and belief of the deponent or deponents, the applicant for enfranchisement is and had been for at least five years previous, a person of good moral character, temperate in his or her habits, and of sufficient intelligence to be qualified to hold land in fee simple and otherwise to exercise all the rights and privileges of an enfranchised person.[68]

The band council then had thirty days to provide affidavits before a judge or magistrate containing their reasons for or against endorsing the applicant, and then the superintendent general had another thirty days to decide whether a location ticket ought to be granted. Even once all of these criteria were met, and the fee simple title granted, the land was still not his or hers; it could not be sold, leased, or otherwise alienated without the sanction of the Governor-in-Council.[69]

The process of acquiring a small plot of reserve land to call one's own was long and tortuous, and in 1886 even this process was denied to most of the western Canadian First Nations. From that date, the enfranchisement clauses were no longer to apply "to any band of Indians in the Province of British Columbia, the Province of Manitoba, the North-West Territories, or the District of Keewatin" except "by proclamation of the Governor-in-Council from time to time."[70]

Reviewing all of this in 1895, a clerk in the Department of the Interior recommended that an enfranchised Indian should be allowed to homestead. The enfranchisement process was "a sufficient guarantee, I think, that he will be as well able as the average homesteader to carry out the homestead conditions." But he did not want to open the floodgates, and thought they were better off on reserves. He further recommended that "to guard against the danger of enfranchised Indians leaving their lands in the Reserves, which lands are in all probability better suited to their requirements than any land open to homestead entry...each case should be dealt with on its own merits after consultation with the Deputy Superintendent-General of Indian Affairs or the Indian Commissioner."[71]

Based on this advice, the 1895 opinion of Indian Affairs was that upon enfranchisement a male could homestead, as the "disqualification arising from this section [of the Indian Act] will cease to apply to an Indian."[72] That year a circular letter was sent to all agents of Dominion Lands in Manitoba and the North-West Territories announcing that "in future an enfranchised Indian, who disposes of the land allotted to him on the Reserve, is to be furnished with a certificate to that effect. The production of this certificate will therefore enable you to decide whether the applicant is entitled to the privilege of making an entry."[73] Thus the ultimate decision was left in the hands of individual land agents when presented with such a certificate, but this stipulation was quickly amended a few weeks later when it was decided that a certificate indicating enfranchisement, "or other evidence of that fact as might be satisfactory to this Department," was all that was required in order to make homestead entry. It was made clear that "under no other circumstances, however, should any Indian be permitted to settle upon lands" under the administration of the Department of the Interior.[74] This policy of allotting land on their own reserves was also applied in the case of First Nation soldier settlers after World War I, further preventing any "Indian" from acquiring any land on the public domain.[75]

With all of these hoops while enduring years of waiting, it is not surprising that there were very few applicants for enfranchisement. In 1892, Indian agent A.M. Muckle of the Manitoba Clandeboye agency described the problems and challenges the applicant faced, with very little reward at the end of it all.[76] St. Peter's reserve resident Alfred Sinclair, "an intelligent young man twenty one years of age," wanted to leave the band and homestead land outside the reserve. Sinclair had applied to become enfranchised, and this was the first case brought before agent Muckle, who wondered if it was worthwhile for the young man to even apply. All of the clergymen, or magistrates or other acceptable officials, were newcomers, and had not known the young man personally for the last five years (as the Indian Act stipulated), and therefore could not provide Sinclair with a certificate under oath as required. There were other roadblocks. Muckle wrote that the chiefs and councillors:

> will do their utmost to put a stop to any one getting enfranchised, for a person would have to be almost more than human, who could pass through such an ordeal, as having the eyes of Clergymen, or magistrates, the Band of Indians to which he belongs and the Indian Department on him for the space of eight years, or more, without fault being found by some of them in some way, which would invalidate his claim to be enfranchised, and received a patent for say thirty two acres of land, which land strange to say would not be his, as he could not sell it. All the treaty man would gain, after being out as it were on a ticket of leave for eight or fifteen years (if he could pass muster) would be that he was an intelligent voter and had a patent for thirty two acres of land which he could not sell.[77]

Muckle warned that there were other young men of the agency who "had attended school, who have worked in the lumber woods, or steam boats & railways etc, [who were] beginning in a quiet way not to like to be Indians" and who, like Sinclair, wanted to homestead and ultimately own land off the reserve.[78]

Hurdles on the road to enfranchisement were many. The applicant could not complete the process if his or her band refused to allot land; not surprisingly, band councils refused to diminish reserve land by parcelling it out to individuals. This was the case with Augustine Steinhauer (brother of Robert, mentioned above) from Saddle Lake, who in 1915 applied for enfranchisement.[79] Augustine met all of the qualifications set out in the Indian Act, but his band would not allot him any land, so his application for enfranchisement was turned down. The Department of Indian Affairs informed him that the Saddle Lake agent had looked into the matter, finding that the band "absolutely refused to locate you for land," and that "as enfranchisement can only be carried out by location of land in the first place by the Band it is regretted that no further action can be taken towards your enfranchisement."[80] Augustine Steinhauer wrote to the provincial attorney general of Alberta to find out if there was any court of justice he could bring his case before. It is unknown what, if any, reply he received.

There were First Nations settlers who applied for permission to homestead land that they had settled on before the treaties. John Tanner, a member of the Manitoba Gambler First Nation, worked for the North West Mounted Police at Fort Walsh delivering mail across the border, and lived in the Cypress Hills with his family. In 1885 Tanner asked to claim the land as his homestead, stating that when he selected the land in the early 1880s he was told by officials of the police that he would be allowed to hold the land as a homestead.[81] Tanner made considerable improvements and raised horses and cattle in this district, which grew to have a prosperous ranching economy. He was informed that he could not claim the land as a homestead unless he was willing to "give up his annuity as an Indian, or to become enfranchised," which he refused to do.[82] Tanner then asked if his wife Françoise Laronde, who was Métis, could be allowed a homestead entry, but this too was not possible, as a woman was eligible only if she was "a sole head of a family"—that is, if she was without a husband. There was some debate about this among Department of the Interior authorities as it was thought "possible that in a legal sense the wife who is a Half Breed is the sole head of that family, her husband being disqualified from making an entry."[83] Winnipeg Commissioner of Dominion Lands W.H. Smithe also thought that a decision in favour of Tanner "might have a favourable effect in emulating other Indians in the effort to become independent." Another land official wrote that "I shall be very glad if in so deserving a case a favourable decision can be given as I think it might have a very favourable effect in emulating other Indians in the effort to become independent. Both the Lieut. Governor and McDonald—the interpreter—speak in the highest possible terms of Tanner's industry and good character."[84] (Tanner had an interview with Lieutenant Governor Alexander Morris in 1874 about causes of unrest among First Nations, and Morris was impressed with this "remarkable" man.)[85] But neither Tanner nor his wife was permitted to homestead their land. The Department of Indian Affairs proposed to purchase Tanner's land and improvements for $500.00.

Tanner had no option but to abandon his homestead, settling on the Gambler band reserve at Silver Creek Manitoba. In 1900 he was reported to be "the wealthiest Indian within this agency. He has nearly fifty acres of as good wheat and oats as I have seen this season, a good farmhouse, stable, implement-shed and milk-house, besides a new binder, seed-drill, mower wagon and other necessary farm implements. He has over fifty head of good cattle, and about ten horses. His personal property, including buildings and land improvements, is worth at least $3,000."[86]

There were others with Tanner's experience in the prairie provinces. In 1905 a Saulteaux man, a non-treaty Indian, in the Battleford district, requested permission to homestead the land where he lived and had made improvements.[87] He was informed he was not entitled, and had to vacate the land immediately. Non-status Indians lost ownership of their homesteads when they took Treaty Adhesion. In the case of Peter Murdock, however, his land became part of the Fisher River reserve. Murdock had a 160-acre homestead adjacent to the Fisher River reserve that he and his family had occupied since 1903. In 1908 he took Treaty Adhesion and joined the band and the following year the Chief and Council requested that his land be added to the reserve along with another larger tract of land. Inspector of Indian Agencies John Semmens consulted with Murdock and advised him that while Indians were not permitted to acquire homesteads, the Indian Act guaranteed that "he shall not be disturbed in the occupation of any plot on which he had permanent improvements, prior to his becoming a party to any Treaty with the Crown."[88] Murdock's land included a one-and-a-half storey house ("shingle roof, 5 windows with a kitchen lean-to 10' x 14' with two windows"), a small stable and garden. It was valuable to the band because of its hay land and creek.[89] Murdock and his family remained on his land with the consent of the Chief and Council when his land became part of the reserve in 1911.[90]

Land offices and Indian Agents received many requests for permission to homestead. In 1906 two Dakota men, Leo Shields and his son J.Y. Good Shields, applied for homesteads in the Fort Qu'Appelle land office, claiming that "they are not Indians under the Indian Act, as they have never taken treaty." They were informed, however, that "although these persons are Sioux Indians, they are also non-treaty Indians, and as such can not, under Section 126 of the Indian Act, homestead Dominion lands."[91] There were many such inquiries. In 1910 at the Qu'Appelle agency in southern Saskatchewan, Indian agent M. Millar found that when one of the newspapers (mistakenly) reported that an act had been passed granting Indians the same privileges as white men, the people of his agency were soon asking what procedures they should follow to obtain homesteads.[92]

In 1902 a serious challenge to the policy of not permitting Indians to homestead was quickly quashed.[93] Samuel Plain, a resident of the Caradoc reserve in Ontario, planned to move west to homestead, as non-Aboriginal Ontarians were free to do. As mentioned earlier, the Indian Act (section 126 in 1902) stipulated that "no Indian or non-treaty Indian, *resident* in the province of Manitoba, the North-West Territories or the territory of Keewatin, shall be held capable of having acquired a homestead." Plain was a resident of Ontario, so he believed he qualified. A favourable reply could well have led to many First Nations settlers from Ontario, Quebec, the Maritimes provinces and British Columbia taking up homesteads on the prairies. Rain's was but one inquiry—there were frequent such inquiries from Ontario First Nations about whether there were any regulations that stood "in the way of them acquiring land in the Northwest on the same terms as other persons by the performance of homestead duties." Inspector of Indian Agencies in Ottawa J.A. Macrae supported their right to homestead, stating that "the men who would move west would make excellent settlers and cease to be Indians in the ordinary sense, as so many now engaged in business in white communities have done."[94] One had bought half a section of land (presumably in Ontario) and expected to have 150 acres of wheat seeded. An initial opinion of the Department of the Interior was that "it does not appear that the provisions [of the

Indian Act related to homestead rights] apply to an Indian moving to Manitoba or to the North-West Territories from Ontario or any of the other Provinces of Canada…nor does there appear to be any reason why such an Indian should not become a British subject so that letters patent may be issued to him under the provisions of the Dominion Lands Act for a homestead."[95]

The point, however, still needed to be referred to the deputy minister of justice, and he overturned this decision. The prospect of First Nations homesteaders arriving from Ontario and other provinces to populate the prairies was clearly found to be undesirable. It was the opinion of the Justice Department in September of 1902 that "an Indian or non-Treaty Indian who is not a resident of Manitoba or the North-West Territories but who may remove to Manitoba or the Territories is not eligible to obtain a homestead." The tortured reasoning was explained:

> in my opinion such a person cannot legally acquire a homestead. Section 126 of the Indian Act provides that no Indian or non-treaty Indian resident in the Province of Manitoba, the North-West Territories, or the District of Keewatin shall be held capable of having acquired or of acquiring a homestead. Residence upon the homestead for which he has obtained an entry being one of the conditions which the settler must comply with in order to earn his patent, an Indian or non-treaty Indian to whom a homestead has been granted, and who in fulfilment of that condition takes up his residence upon the land selected by him, by that act becomes, if he were not so before, resident in the Province or Territory in which that land is situated, and so subject to the provisions of the section referred to, and incapable of having acquired a homestead right.[96]

Samuel Plain was denied the right to homestead in the West, unlike thousands of other Ontarians. He died on the Caradoc reserve in November, 1904.[97]

By 1914 requests were frequent enough that a Department of the Interior "ruling" was filed on the question of whether Indians could homestead.[98] This was in answer to a letter by John Lecaine, a Lakota of Wood Mountain, Saskatchewan (whose father was a North West Mounted Policeman), as to whether his two half-brothers, "Indians," were eligible for homestead rights. It was decided that they could homestead only if they "do not belong to any particular band of Indians, and if they are not children of any male person of Indian blood who belong to such a Band; or if they are not in treaty and receipt of annuity moneys; or if they do not belong to any irregular band of Indians, or do not follow the Indian mode of life, they may be granted homestead entries." Just what constituted the "Indian mode of life" was not specified. John Lecaine and a number of other Lakota men did secure homesteads, however, in the Wood Mountain district, although this was through unusual and special circumstances involving the establishment of their reserve.[99]

Inquiries about homestead rights also came from those who had been "discharged" from treaty, rather than having gone through the process of enfranchisement. The 1904 request of George Rain, a Nakoda from the Sharphead band, whose reserve was "closed" in 1890, was debated at Indian Affairs offices in Winnipeg and Ottawa, and at the Department of Justice in Ottawa.[100] Rain had been discharged from treaty, and officially had no reserve to call home. Assistant Indian Commissioner J.A.J. McKenna, after consulting with Commissioner David Laird, wrote that being discharged from treaty meant that the person "ceased to be an Indian within the meaning of the [Indian] Act and had therefore all the privileges of ordinary citizenship."[101] The commissioner's position, according to McKenna, was that "the word 'Indian' as used in Sec. 126 has not a racial but a restricted legal significance." McKenna added that

> Now the moment a man is discharged he ceases to belong to a particular band, and can no longer be reputed to belong to any particular band. A non-Treaty Indian is defined to be 'any person of Indian blood who is reputed to belong to an irregular band but who follows the Indian mode of life.' Geo. Rain does not belong to any irregular band, nor is he reputed to belong to any such band. From the report of our Agent it certainly appears that he is not leading what is regarded as the Indian mode of life. He lives as an individual, not as a member of a tribe. When he hunts and fishes he hunts and fishes as a white man. He works at the saw-mill and does freighting. He is settled on land outside of a Reserve, has broken ground and put up fencing. He owns horses and cattle, and other property.

Yet all of this detailed information was not enough to convince the Department of Indian Affairs that Rain could apply to homestead. Department of Justice officials were consulted, and eight months later replied that to have withdrawn from treaty, Rain would have to be a "halfbreed," and "it is not stated that the person in question is a halfbreed."[102] (A "halfbreed" could withdraw or be discharged from a treaty under section 13 of the Indian Act, chapter 22, section 1.) It is not clear whether Rain was ever granted the right to homestead.

This paper has traced the complex twists and turns federal bureaucrats resorted to in order to ensure that First Nations had almost no individual property rights, either on or off reserves. Strategies were many, including declaring that Indians were not "persons," and drawing on the "old proclamation" dug up by Minister of the Interior David Laird in debates about the Indian Act in 1876. Inquiries about homestead rights were dismissed and discouraged.

Enfranchisement was presented as the route to a plot of land in fee simple, but this was a difficult and protracted process that rarely succeeded. Together these schemes and tactics combined to ensure that First Nations people had no land to call their own, and no ability to expand their land base, either as individuals or collectively. The *ad hoc* nature of the reactions to the issues and requests as they arose indicate that there was no master plan plotted and spelled out behind closed doors in the offices of the bureaucracy, but the consistency of the responses over decades suggest that the overall objective was to erase First Nations from the landscape outside of reserves, confine them to those reserves, and replace them with an army of homesteaders. This had very real implications for their agricultural economy. With all the windows of opportunity boarded up, First Nations farmers had no option but to pursue agriculture within the confines of their reserves, and the confines of the Indian Act.

NOTES

1   Thanks to the Social Sciences and Humanities Research Council of Canada for supporting this project through a standard research grant for: "Growing Pains: The Dynamics of First Nations Agriculture in Manitoba." Thanks to my co-investigator Winona Wheeler for the insight and sources she provided for this paper.

2   *The Canadian Indian* 1, 5 (February 1891): 129. For more on this prevailing attitude see Sarah Carter, *Lost Harvests: Prairie Indian Reserve Farmers and Government Policy* (Montreal and Kingston: McGill-Queen's University Press, 1990), Chapter One.

3   We hope that our study can provide precise details on acreages under cultivation by First Nations before treaties, and the extent of individual private property /farms, but we have not yet located the necessary sources. We do not want to exaggerate the extent of private holdings, as this was not the form of land tenure of the majority of First Nations of Manitoba and the west, but this paper clearly establishes their existence.

4   Patrick Wolfe, *Settler Colonialism and the Transformation of Anthropology: The Politics and Poetics of an Ethnographic Event* (London: Cassell, 1999); Patrick Wolfe, "Settler Colonialism and the Elimination of the Native," *Journal of Genocide Research* 8, 4 (2006): 387-409.

5   Stuart Banner, *How the Indians Lost Their Land: Law and Power on the Frontier* (Cambridge: The Belknap Press of Harvard University Press, 2005).

6   H.Y. Hind, *Narrative of the Canadian Red River Exploring Expedition of 1857 and of the Assiniboine and Saskatchewan Exploring Expeditions of 1858* (Rpt.: New York: Greenwood Press, 1969), 45, 111. See also C. Flynn and E. Leigh Syms, "Manitoba's First Farmers," *Manitoba History* 31 (Spring 1996) and D.W. Moodie and Barry Kaye, "The Northern Limit of Indian Agriculture in North America," *Geographical Review* 59, 4 (October 1969).

7   Kent McNeil, "Sovereignty and the Aboriginal Nations of Rupert's Land," *Manitoba History* 37 (Spring/Summer 1999): 7.

8   Canada. *House of Commons Debates.* 28 May, 1869: 485.

9   John McDougall, *On Western Trails in the Early Seventies: Frontier Pioneer Life in the Canadian Northwest* (Toronto: William Briggs, 1911), 18.

10 Quoted in Sarah Carter, "The Missionaries' Indian: The Publications of John McDougall, John Maclean and Egerton Ryerson Young," *Prairie Forum* 9, 1 (1984): 33.

11 Carter, *Lost Harvests*, 196.

12 Alexander Morris, *The Treaties of Canada with the Indians of Manitoba and the North-West Territories Including the Negotiations on Which They Were Based* (1880 rpt.: Saskatoon: Fifth House Publishers, 1991), 28.

13 Ibid., 29.

14 Canada. *Sessional Papers* 9, 9 (1875): 32-3.

15 Ibid, 34.

16 Morris, 39.

17 Quoted in Frank Tough, *As their Natural Resources Fail: Native Peoples and the Economic History of Northern Manitoba, 1870–1930* (Vancouver: UBC Press, 1996), 95.

18 Ibid.

19 Morris, 315.

20 Ibid., 322.

21 Ibid., 279.

22 Sarah Carter, "Site Review: St. Peter's and the Interpretation of the Agriculture of Manitoba's Aboriginal People," in *Manitoba History* 18 (Autumn, 1989): 46-52.

23 The following correspondence is in Library and Archives Canada (LAC), Record Group 10 (RG 10), v. 3614, file 4311. It is not always clear who the author is of each of the documents: W. Simpson, Molyneux St. John, or J.A.N. Provencher.

24 Extract from report of Provencher, 31 December, 1873, in Ibid.

25 Memorandum in reference to understanding with Indians under Treaties Nos. 1 & 2 as to the proprietary right of Indians in property held by them prior to the negotiation of the Stone Fort or No. 1 Treaty. By Molyneux St. John. No precise date; 1875. In Ibid.

26 Wemyss Simpson to E.A. Meredith, 15 February, 1875. In Ibid.

27 Memo "Right of Indians." St. John in Ibid.

28 Extract from report of Provencher, 31 December 1873, in Ibid.

29 *Indian Acts and Amendments 1868–1975: An Indexed Collection*, ed. Sharon Venne (Saskatoon: University of Saskatchewan Native Law Centre 1981), 27. (The Indian Act, 1876. S.C. 1876, co. 18 (39 Vict.)

30 Ibid.

31 Ibid., 28-9.

32 LAC RG10 v. 3614 f.4322. Memo "Right of Indians," St. John.

33 Manitoba Act 1870 available at http://www.solon.org/Constitutions/Canada/English/ma_1870.html

34 Order-in-Council 1871-1036 April 26, 1871 Lands in Manitoba–[Secretary] of State submits regulations respecting persons who settled on lands before survey, setting forth conditions upon which they may hold the same. RG 2, Privy Council Office, Series A-1a, vol. 288.

35 LAC, RG 10, v. 3614 f. 4311 Memo "Right of Indians," St. John.

36 Extract from report of the Provencher, 31 December, 1875. In Ibid.

37   Venne, 43.

38   "An Act to amend 'An Act respecting the approproiation of certain Lands in Manitoba.' 1875 vol. 1 (Canada - 38 Victoria, 3rd Parliament, 2nd Session) Chapter 52, p. 292.

39   LAC, RG 15, file 7052.

40   Letter, M.T. Hunter to Surveyor General of Dominion Lands, Ottawa, 6 December, 1876. LAC RG 10, v. 236, file 7052.

41   Surveyor General J. Dennis to Minister of the Interior, 6 June, 1877. In Ibid.

42   Venne, 57. (The Indian Act 1880 S.C. 1880 c. 28 43 Vict.).

43   See the text of the Royal Proclamation of 1763 at http://www.bloorstreet.com/200block/rp1763.htm

44   Canada, *House of Commons Debates,* 3nd Session, 3rd Parliament, 1876, 872.

45   Ibid.

46   Ibid.

47   Ibid.

48   Sanderson v. Heap, 1909, 11, *Western Law Reports*, 238. Manitoba King's Bench, Mathers, J., June 1909, http://library2.usask.ca/native/cnlc/vol103/631.html.l

49   Ibid.

50   Dame Durden (Lillian Beynon Thomas), "Seeing Lake Winnipeg," *Farmers' Advocate and Home Journal* 10 (August 1910): 1190.

51   Wendy Moss and Elaine Gardner-O'Toole, "Aboriginal People: History of Discriminatory Laws," Government of Canada: Law and Government Division, Nov. 1987, revised Nov. 1991. Available at http://dsp-psd.pwgsc.gc.ca/Collection-R/LoPBdP/BP/bp175-e.htm

52   Quoted in Ibid.

53   This issue of the rights of First Nations to pre-empt or homestead land in British Columbia is murky; however, see a 1903 document in LAC, RG 15, Series D II 1, vol. 750, f. 478,863 in which it is stated that there "are no grounds for refusing an Indian in BC entry for land under the control of the Dept."

54   Venne, 43. This is in the section "Disabilities and Penalties" (The Indian Act 1876 S.C. 1876, c. 18(39 Vict.) ·

55   Douglas W. Allen, "Homesteading and Property Rights: Or, 'How the West Was Really Won,'" *Journal of Law and Economics* 34 (April 1991): 2.

56   Ibid., 3.

57   Alexander Jamieson Russell, *Red River Country, Hudson's Bay and North-West Territories Considered in Relation to Canada* (Ottawa: G.E. Desbarats, 1869), 154.

58   Canada, *House of Commons Debates,* 3nd Session, 3rd Parliament, 1876, 870.

59   Ibid., 933.

60   Ibid., 933.

61   Quoted in Donald B. Smith, "The Steinhauer Brothers: Education and Self-Reliance," *Alberta History* 50, no. 2 (Spring 2002) n.p. Online version available at http://images.ourontario.ca/Cobourg/53460/data

62   Carter, *Lost Harvests*, 193–236.

63   Ibid.

64   *Canada: Memorandum on the Legal Status of British North American Indians.* Presented to both Houses of Parliament by Command of Her Majesty, Dec., 1900 (London: Darling and Son, 1900), 16.

65 Canada, *House of Commons Debates,* 3nd Session, 5th Parliament, 8 May 1885, 1567.

66 Venne, 43.

67 Ibid., 47–50.

68 Ibid., 98 (An Act further to amend "The Indian Act, 1880" S.C. 1884 c. 27 47. Vict.).

69 Ibid., 146.

70 Ibid., 144.

71 LAC, RG 15, D-II-1, vol. 718, file 378753, V.O. Cote to A.M. Burgess, 10 June 1895 "Re: Mr. Hayter Reed's letter respecting the right of an enfranchised Indian to take up a homestead."

72 LAC, RG 15, Series D II 1, v. 750, f. 478, 863, Letter, Lynwoode Pereira to John McKenzie, 31 Aug., 1898.

73 Ibid.

74 Ibid.

75 Sarah Carter, "'An Infamous Proposal': Prairie Indian Reserve Land and Soldier Settlement after World War I," *Manitoba History,* 37 (Spring/Summer 1999): 9–21.

76 LAC, RG 10, v. 3871, f. 89486, Letter, A.M. Muckle to E. McColl, 6 April, 1892.

77 Ibid.

78 Ibid.

79 Provincial Archives of Alberta, Accession number GR 1966.0166/261a. A. Steinhauer to attorney general of Alberta, 1 Dec., 1915.,

80 Quoted in Ibid.

81 LAC, RG10, v. 3739, file 28571, Hayter Reed to superintendent general of Indian Affairs, 15 April 1886.

82 Saskatchewan Archives Board (SAB), homestead file for SE 20 – 11 – 26 – W3. Letter, R.A. Ruttan to A.M. Burgess, 8 August, 1885.

83 W. H. Smithe to A.M. Burgess, 20 August, 1885 in Ibid.

84 Ruttan to Burgess, 8 August, 1885 in Ibid.

85 LAC, RG 10, v. 3610, file 3528, Memorandum of an interview with Kissoway, or John Tanner, 6 June, 1874.

86 Canada. *Sessional Papers* 14, 11, 5th session of Parliament, 1900: 128.

87 LAC, RG 15, Department of the Interior, D – II – 1, vol. 718, file 378753, P.G. Keyes to the agent of Dominion Lands, Battleford, 11 July, 1905.

88 Indian Act R.S., c.43, s. 164(a).

89 LAC, RG 10, v. 7778, file 27136-2. J.D. McLean to John Semmens, Inspector of Indian Agencies, 19 January 1909; J.D. McLean to F. Pedley, Deputy Superintendent of Indian Affairs, 13 January 1909.

90 Ibid,. John Semmens to J.D. McLean, 6 February 1909; Ibid., P.C. Order in Council # 2215, 2 October 1911.

91 LAC, RG 15, series D II 1 v. 990, T 14568, f. 1,237, 946, Letter, _____ unclear secretary, Department of Indian Affairs to secretary, Department of the Interior, 16 August, 1906.

92 LAC, RG 10, v. 1392 H. Nichol to J. McLean, 27 Jan. 1910.

93 LAC, RG 10, v. 3077, file 262, 666.

94 LAC, RG 10, v. 3011, f. 262, 666, J.A. Macrae, to acting deputy minister of the interior, 18 August, 1902.

95 D. Y. Keyes, to J.A. Macrae, 30 August, 1902 in Ibid.

96   D.Y. Keyes to J.A. Macrae, 23 Sept., 1902 in Ibid.

97   See http://familytreemaker.genealogy.com/users/j/o/h/Kimberly-A-John/WEBSITE-0001/ UHP-0344.html.

98   LAC, RG 15, series D2, file 1680 Dominion Lands, 1. L. Pereira to John Lecaine, 27 Nov., 1914.

99   See John Lecaine's homestead files SAB, no. 1890785: NE 27 – T4- R4- W 3, and no. 1954960: T4-R4-W3.

100 Little background information is available on George Rain, but an interview from 1973 with Lazarus Roan, of Small Boy's Camp, Alberta mentions the Rain family and George Rain's efforts to get their reserve back. See http://ourspace.uregina.ca/ bitstream/10294/2182/1/IH-204.pdf, transcript of Eric Stamp's interview with Lazarus Roan, tape number IH – 204, Transcript disc 38. I have assumed this is the same George Rain.

101 LAC, RG 13, Department of Justice, vol. 134, file 1046 –04. J.A.J. McKenna to the secretary, Department of Indian Affairs, 4 Nov., 1904.

102 Ibid., Acting deputy minister of justice to secretary, Department of Indian Affairs, 26 July, 1905.

MURDOCH V. MURDOCH
FEMINISM, PROPERTY, AND THE PRAIRIE FARM IN THE 1970s

PERNILLE JAKOBSEN

On 2 October 1973, the Supreme Court of Canada (SCC) denied Irene Murdoch's claim to any share of the Alberta ranch on which she had laboured alongside her husband of over twenty-five years, leaving her "without even so much as a spoon."[1] Newspapers across Canada reported on the *Murdoch v. Murdoch* case, detailing that a respectable rancher's wife had been turned out of her own home with only the clothes on her back and $200 per month in alimony because her labour amounted to "just about what the ordinary rancher's wife does."[2] Women's organizations across Canada quickly took up Murdoch's story, and turned it into a national feminist *cause célèbre*, using Murdoch's experience to lobby for changes to provincial matrimonial property laws.[3] Certainly, Irene Murdoch's personal plight resonated with men and women across Canada, and *Murdoch* is remembered as *the* pivotal case that "caused" changes to be made in provincial matrimonial property laws by 1980. Yet a national focus obscures the local context of the *Murdoch* case by failing to adequately explain why it was a rural wife's legal maltreatment that came to speak for both urban and rural wives, and blurs the hands-on, grass-roots efforts of the Albertans involved in assisting Irene Murdoch personally and in promoting her cause politically.

Examining the *Murdoch* case *in situ*—in the place in which it occurred—indicates that Murdoch's partnership claim resonated deeply with the Unifarm Women of Alberta (Unifarm Women) and the Calgary Local Council of Women (CLCW), as both of these conservative middle-class women's groups had attempted to achieve "partnership" for married Albertan women since the dower campaign of the early twentieth century. Their *Murdoch*-based initiatives suggest considerable continuity and evolution in their partnership quest, and evidence of rural-urban collaboration. This is important because Murdoch's claim was based on her status as a rural farm wife, and at the time her case was heard, it was neither inevitable that her case would cause a national uproar nor that her story would be applied to both urban and rural wives. Each of these groups clearly articulated their interactions with the *Murdoch* case, and used it to strengthen existing resolutions about the need for wives to attain marital partnership. Unifarm Women advocated for property law reform to maintain and strengthen the institution of marriage and to recognize rural wives' labour contributions. The CLCW played a key role in extending Murdoch's story beyond local parameters. This, combined with CLCW member Patricia Krasinski's personal relationship with Irene Murdoch, provide meaningful glimpses of the woman whose legal maltreatment inspired national outrage.

The details of the *Murdoch* case illustrate the law's continued reluctance to extend partnership to wives in the face of 1970s feminist activism for equality in marriage and improved property rights. Irene Nash married James Alexander (Alex) Murdoch in 1943. Throughout her marriage Irene Murdoch's indoor and outdoor labour was tied to the distinct nature of the rural farm economy which required farm wives to labour on farm land without recognition or remuneration. This stood in stark contrast to the experience of urban wives, whose employment interests were not directly tied to issues of land ownership. In 1952, Irene Murdoch received some money from her mother which was invested in one of the many land transactions Alex Murdoch entered into in his name alone. By 1968, the Murdochs owned a three-quarter section of land near Nanton, Alberta which Alex Murdoch wanted to sell. Irene Murdoch wished to stay in Nanton and refused to sign away her dower rights in the matrimonial home. In response, Alex Murdoch beat his wife to the point where she suffered a fractured jaw, permanent paralysis to her lip and jaw, a speech impediment, $2000 in medical expenses, and the use of a neck collar for two years.[4] Upon returning to her home from the hospital she found the locks had been changed and all of her personal possessions given away. This violent incident brought the couple's rocky marriage to an end, and precipitated Irene Murdoch's legal action.

Irene Murdoch hired Calgary lawyer Ernest Shymka to present her application for child custody, judicial separation, and an equitable partnership interest in the Murdochs' ranch to the Alberta Court of Queen's Bench. In 1971, Judge Macdonald of the Alberta Court of Queen's Bench dismissed Murdoch's partnership claim, but granted her a decree of judicial separation, and monthly alimony in the amount of $200.[5] Alex Murdoch retained custody of their teenage son. Irene Murdoch continued her application for a partnership interest at the appellate level where it was promptly dismissed, largely because she was receiving alimony. At the SCC, Shymka framed Murdoch's claim as a percentage-based interest in trust law rather than as an explicit partnership interest. The majority decided against Murdoch on the basis that they could find no evidence of a resulting trust. Only Judge Laskin, in his dissent, was prepared to suggest that Irene Murdoch's "extraordinary" labour might substantiate a different form of constructive trust than was currently known to the law.[6] The SCC's decision outraged women and men across Canada, nowhere more so than in Alberta, where Unifarm Women and the CLCW discovered in Irene Murdoch the perfect exemplar of a respectable hard-working ranch wife whose labour commanded personal attention and a partnership claim.

Irene Murdoch succeeded generations of Alberta farm and ranch wives who experienced complicated, and sometimes bitter, relationships with the land. On one hand, the physical labour required from early twentieth century wives in building western farms and ranches alongside their husbands "earned" these women a measure of equality. This idea has encouraged some scholars to suggest that the frontier was liberating, in that it "equalized" men and women, and helps to explain the organizing drive of first-wave western-Canadian women in attaining suffrage.[7] On the other hand, farm and ranch wives have endured discriminatory legal treatment, as Canadian laws regarding marriage, land ownership, and inheritance have historically privileged men.[8] Canada's common law entailed a civil death for women upon marriage as the married couple became one person under coverture—that person being the man. As *femmes covert*, wives could not freely enter into contracts, and became their husbands' dependants for many legal purposes.[9] The marriage contract created an exchange of services whereby wives were bound to provide their services, including sex and labour, in exchange for the care and protection of their husbands.[10] Prevailing inheritance customs typically awarded farmland to male children, often favouring the claims of sons over their widowed mothers. Thus, in the event of a marital break-up or husband's death, many farm and ranch wives experienced tremendous difficulty in asserting any claim to the land on which they had laboured and relied upon as their means of subsistence.[11]

This complicated relationship with the land helps to explain why western women's organizations embarked upon a vociferous campaign for partnership rights in the early twentieth century. The campaign to secure property rights for women began in 1909; however, it lagged until 1916, when rural women, through Unifarm Women's predecessor organization, the United Farm Women of Alberta, joined forces with the CLCW.[12] According to Cavanaugh, the "UFWA was instrumental in introducing the concept of matrimonial property, or the equal division of family assets between wife and husband, into the dower debate."[13] Women such as Louise Crummy McKinney, Henrietta Muir Edwards, Emily Murphy, Nellie

McClung, and Irene Parlby, president of the UFWA in 1916, recognized women's doubly disadvantaged status as farm and ranch wives. They wished to own property as equals with their husbands, yet they also understood that they required special protections because of women's social role as wives and mothers, and because the law discriminated on the basis of sex alone.[14]

Recognizing that they were not equal to their husbands, western women undertook a series of campaigns to change the law in order to protect their interests. In 1917, Alberta became the second prairie province to pass a Dower Act.[15] Unlike the earlier system of common-law dower, which granted widows a life estate in their husbands' property upon his death and which was abolished in western Canadian provinces by the Real Property Act of 1886, Alberta's 1917 Act incorporated features of American homestead law. The "homestead" was defined as the residence or dwelling part of the ranch or farm operation in which the wife resided, and granted a married woman the right to live out her life (a "life estate") in the homestead.[16] Significantly, section three of the new Act required the wife's consenting signature before the property could be sold to a third party.[17] In 1968, Irene Murdoch's refusal to relinquish her dower rights would lead to a vicious fight with her husband Alex, but in 1917, some women's organizations praised the Dower Act for protecting women's special interests. Many rural women, however, quickly recognized that it provided them with little more than the ability to live out their lives in a house devoid of furnishings, equipment, livestock, or even seed with which to sustain themselves.

By the mid-1920s the UFWA perceived dower as a stumbling block to women's rights and focused on establishing a very controversial "community of property" regime.[18] This "community of property" interest was based on their recognition that farm and ranch wives provided valuable labour. Arguing that they contributed one-half of the labour required to operate and maintain farms and ranches, rural wives believed they were entitled to a one-half share with their husbands. In 1925, UFWA president Irene Parlby attempted to get "An Act Establishing Community of Property as Between Husband and Wife" to the legislature.[19] While the UFWA and the UFA supported this idea, the provincial government was not ready to embrace the idea of wives as "partners" with their husbands, and the bill was defeated.[20]

Ideas about partnership slowly gained increased acceptance between the 1920s and 1970s, partly because human rights issues came to transcend international boundaries. Local Alberta women increasingly exchanged ideas and held meetings across international borders. During the interwar period, Unifarm Women participated in a variety of educational "peace" initiatives designed to shape youth, "as children can be made to believe as firmly in the possibility of peace as those of a generation ago believed in the necessity of war."[21] To this end, they encouraged Albertan children to participate in "Goodwill Day" by sending messages of goodwill and peace via overseas radio lines. The UFWA strongly encouraged its members to educate themselves about international women's peace initiatives including literature, types of resolutions being adopted, and writing to newspapers commenting on peace articles.[22]

In the aftermath of World War II and Canada's participation in the United Nations' Declaration of Human Rights, Canadian women came to realize that they lacked many of the rights and freedoms enshrined in the Declaration.[23] In this context, the CLCW's relationship with the International Council of Women helped orientate the CLCW to international trends and concerns. At their 1951 meeting, for example, the International Council of Women discussed "equal rights for both spouses in the management and sharing of property held in community and of family property."[24] Likewise, Betty Pedersen, as Unifarm Women's representative, gained exposure to the ideas and opinions of women from fifty-six other countries when she attended an Associated Country Women of the World (ACWW) meeting in Oslo, Norway in 1970.[25] Pedersen, herself married to a Danish immigrant, noted that Scandinavians held very equitable views regarding marital and rural property issues.

Unifarm Women and the CLCW advocated numerous resolutions, especially in the context of labour, inheritance, and tax law reform, which grappled with "equality" and presented wives as partners with their husbands. Ruth Gorman, lawyer and chairman of the CLCW's Laws and Resolutions Committee between 1940 and 1964, supported resolutions aimed at "equal pay for equal work."[26] Unifarm Women fought for greater recognition of their labour contributions. According to Betty Pedersen, they fought many years for the right to receive wages for work they did on their own farms. Pedersen pointed out the ludicrous situation in which neighbouring male farmers had to "exchange wives" in order to pay them wages for driving tractors because they could not legally pay their own wives for this type of labour.[27] Rural wives could become employees on other men's ranches, but could not be legally treated as partners in their own agricultural enterprises, further emphasizing the fragility of rural women's place in the farm economy. In seeking to address this injustice, Unifarm Women drafted a submission to the federal government on the Royal Commission on the Status of Women, arguing that the:

> Canada Pension Plan discriminates against women because only those women who work outside the home in paid employment may claim benefits...due to the fact that it is becoming increasingly difficult to obtain competent, reliable farm labour, many rural women accept a double work load.... These women cannot claim remuneration for work performed in fields and farm yard, nor, if the husband is willing

to pay for such services, can he deduct such wages from his income tax as a legitimate farm expense. This is rank discrimination against rural families, and we, as rural women, ask that this situation be legally rectified and the employment of one spouse by another should be regarded as payable, pensionable and deductable employment.[28]

In seeking redress through the Canada Pension Plan, Unifarm Women drew upon their experience in campaigning for tax reform to achieve a partnership interest in the farm. Through their predecessor organization, the Farm Women's Union of Alberta (FWUA), they had helped to secure legislation to amend the Intestate Succession Act.[29] Prior to this amendment, one-third to one-half of the estate went to the children and was inaccessible to the widow to carry on with the farming operation. After the amendment, widows were awarded $20,000 and the residue was divided between the widow and children.[30]

The issue of divorce gained increasing importance in the partnership debate as both Unifarm Women and the CLCW lobbied for "fairness" in divorce. In 1951, the CLCW's stance on divorce reflected their conservatism, as evidenced by their statement that "no divorce [shall be granted] without its motives having been submitted to the judgment of an independent authority."[31] By 1958 the CLCW advocated extending the grounds for divorce to include incurable insanity, long desertion, and extreme cruelty. In 1960, Beth Underhill, President of the National Council of Women, urged the CLCW to make itself knowledgeable about divorce law. Underhill cautioned, however, that "the fact that you are making yourself aware of divorce legislation in Canada, and the criticism thereto, in no way means that the Council of Women will ever take a stand on this matter, however, it is our responsibility to be informed upon such important legislation."[32] Unifarm Women also stayed abreast of international divorce trends. Through their predecessor, the FWUA, Unifarm Women established a committee on divorce laws that compared Canadian law with changes that had occurred in other countries.[33] They also wished to reform divorce laws, and lobbied for the inclusion of "marriage breakdown" as a cause for divorce during the 1950s and 1960s.[34]

Unifarm Women's idea of partnership was linked to the preservation of marriage. The 1968 Divorce Act included many of the reforms that Unifarm Women had advocated, including extending the grounds of divorce to include the concept of permanent marriage breakdown. Nevertheless, it retained some of the old "fault-based" grounds for divorce, most commonly adultery, cruelty, and desertion. Husbands and wives could apply for divorce on the same grounds, whereas in the past wives could apply for divorce only on the grounds of adultery.[35] With the introduction of the 1968 Act, the divorce rate rose alarmingly in the early 1970s; by 1974, Canada's divorce rate was 20.8 per cent higher than it had been in 1968.[36] Unifarm Women sought to curb divorce through government-based educational and counselling programs designed to help couples work out their differences.[37] They believed that making wives equal partners in marriage would make divorce much less likely and would encourage couples to cooperate because they each held an equal vested interest in maintaining the farm or ranch. In keeping with their conservative values, partnership-based property reforms would also serve to uphold the family unit.

Both Unifarm Women and the CLCW recognized that federal divorce law reform was insufficient for establishing spousal partnership claims because property division was a provincial matter. Bolstered by experience obtained through long-term lobbying efforts and the recommendations from the recently completed Royal Commission on the Status of Women, the CLCW reported, on March 8, 1971, that the Alberta legislature had passed the following resolution:

> BE IT RESOLVED, that the Government of Alberta request the Institute of Law Research and Reform to study the feasibility of legislation which would provide that, upon the dissolution of the marriage, each party would have a right to an equal share in the assets accumulated during the marriage, otherwise than by gift or inheritance received by either spouse from outside sources.[38]

Thus, by the time the *Murdoch* case appeared in 1973, Unifarm Women and the CLCW had helped to slowly introduce partnership principles into some laws and had gained broader acceptance of these views. The key difference between the "partnership campaign" in the more recent period and first-wave lobbies is that women were framing their request as a share in "marital property" rather than as a share of their "husband's" property because they had increasingly come to view themselves as partners in a joint enterprise founded on equal labour.[39]

This history of campaigns to improve women's property rights made Unifarm Women and the CLCW receptive to Irene Murdoch's legal case. Reading from Murdoch's SCC transcript at the annual Women of Unifarm Convention in 1973, Betty Pedersen, President of Unifarm Women from 1969 to 1974, and the first Alberta member of the Canadian Advisory Council on the Status of Women, presented Irene Murdoch as a woman with whom they had much in common. Pedersen revealed that since seventeen-year-old Irene Nash's 1943 marriage to Alex Murdoch, she had worked outdoors alongside her husband, first as a hired hand, until they could afford their own small plot of land. The Murdochs expanded their ranch properties over the years by buying and selling plots of land until they acquired a substantial holding. Pedersen explained that the trial judge failed to find a partnership interest in the ranch for Irene Murdoch partly because the couple had never executed a formal partnership agreement. Pedersen then peered out at the crowd of rural women sitting in the audience before her and asked them a pointed question. "How many of you would have drawn up a legal partnership with your husband in the first throes of romance?"[40] Responding with laughter, the Unifarm Women clearly understood Pedersen's message. Without a written agreement acknowledging that they owned one-half of their property with their husbands, they knew they did not have any legal claim to an equal share of marital property. They were hardworking farm and ranch wives, but they were not true partners.

The Unifarm Women never abandoned the argument that wives, by virtue of their labour, were entitled to a one-half share of marital property. And it was in the language of partnership that they framed their resolution on the *Murdoch* case to the Alberta Provincial Cabinet within weeks of Pedersen's presentation. They wrote:

> As rural women we are seriously and justifiably alarmed at the Supreme Court of Canada decision (October 2, 1973) in the case of *Murdoch v. Murdoch*. We fear that this will set a legal precedent, and that other women in Canada will suffer as a consequence. As rural women who contribute in many ways to the building of a viable farm or ranch operation we feel that we have an indubitable right to a legal share in the assets of that operation. Therefore, we demand that upon the dissolution of a marriage, either by divorce or legal separation that assets accumulated during that marriage must be divided on a ½ and ½ basis.

The language of this resolution clearly echoed the "community of property" argument made by their predecessors in decades past. It also drew on their significant lobbying efforts and involvement with the Royal Commission on the Status of Women which had helped them to further identify and articulate partnership standards.

Patricia Krasinski, the CLCW's Citizenship Convenor, was also disheartened by Irene Murdoch's experience. After reading about Irene Murdoch in a *Time* magazine article, she decided to interview Murdoch personally to find out whether or not her story had been exaggerated. She drove to Turner Valley and over coffee with Murdoch, Krasinski discovered that "Florrie" (as friends called Irene Murdoch) had not embellished her story, and she allowed Krasinski to read the official SCC transcript of her trial. Krasinski learned that in addition to losing four court cases, Murdoch had been saddled with all costs including lawyers' fees and disbursements. Krasinski thought that this financial burden, coupled with Murdoch's legal loss, was unfair and unreasonable. Krasinski approached Joni (Margaret) Chorny, president of the CLCW, to set up a trust fund to help Murdoch pay her legal bills. At the next CLCW meeting, held on March 27, 1974, Krasinski announced the creation of the Irene Murdoch Trust fund, the aim of which was to "thank [Murdoch] from all women because her courage and tenacity have brought the unjustness of our laws on matrimonial property out into the open. And, lastly, the fund was a public gesture, a token of disapproval of the way the Supreme Court of Canada interpreted the law."[42]

The trust fund initiated by Krasinski may have helped some Canadian women to "find the women's movement."[43] Anne Enke argues that by the early 1970s many women had heard of the women's movement, but did not know where to locate it: the women's movement lacked a literal or physical location. Enke encourages scholars to consider "feminism" as including public physical spaces and non-traditional actors typically excluded from accounts focused on "radical" feminists.[44] This is especially pertinent when considering the feminist activities of rural farm women whose traditional values, including the preservation of marriage, and "conservative" stance would typically place them outside "feminist" parameters.[45]

Money sent to, and letters written in support of, the Murdoch trust fund provide some evidence of rural women's feminism. Many Alberta women wrote letters in support of Irene Murdoch, and contributed what they had: two women from rural Alberta apologized that they each had only $1.00 to give. Others, such as Mary Aitken, described the injustice of existing matrimonial law, arguing that "we must separate the equity which comes from affinity or kinship connection with the owner of property from that earned by the [unpaid] contributions made to the preservation and growth of property."[46] Aitken was speaking not only to the injustice suffered by Irene Murdoch, but also to the unfair patrilineal inheritance customs which, in her neighbour's case, witnessed the disposition of the family ranch to a disinterested son while completely omitting two daughters who had spent their lifetimes looking after the ranch. Some writers to the Murdoch trust fund poignantly identified how rural wives' labour differentiated them from urban wives. Farmer Sarah Rau wrote:

> The church makes no distinction between urban or rural dwellers in the marriage vows, where then does the court get the authority to proclaim that the 'usual DUTIES of a farm wife' are to castrate calves, ride bucking bronco, cook for hired men, and wash their dirty clothes, accept his beatings, summer-fallow, rake hay, pitch bales, keep books and whatever else he asks of her – does it follow that a farmer can divorce his wife on the grounds that she refuses to, or is unable to, perform this labour?[47]

Rau's words succinctly demonstrate the reality of the daily labour required from rural women in creating and maintaining a successful agricultural operation, and their frustration in being denied a legal claim to a fair share.

The Murdoch trust fund provided a forum for women outside the organized women's movement, and the letters opened and maintained a dialogue between rural wives and urban CLCW organizers. The Murdoch trust fund was even endorsed by the newly established Alberta Commission on Human Rights, which sent a letter to Ottawa asking for a revision of the SCC decision. Reflecting on the impact of the Murdoch trust fund, Krasinski wrote "the fund snowballed beyond all my wildest dreams. Letters and money have been pouring in from all over Canada. Sometimes it was a mystery to me how the news got spread; it must have been through the grapevine. Now, however, it has been taken up, not only by the press but by the Advisory Council on the Status of Women in Ottawa who have endorsed the fund and say that the Irene Murdoch case has become a symbol of the realities of Canadian matrimonial laws."[48] The Murdoch fund effectively mobilized grassroots interest in Irene Murdoch's case and provided ordinary women with a means of demonstrating their support.

Irene Murdoch's story was framed as a feminist message, but at tremendous personal cost to her. Suzanne Zwarun's 1983 *Chatelaine* article "Farm Wives 10 years after Irene Murdoch" presented Murdoch as a traditional, and by implication, outdated, farm wife who "still fail[s] to recognize" the inequities faced by Canadian farm women, in contrast to "modern" farm women determined "that every Canadian will one day understand that theirs is a career as important as any other."[49] Zwarun wrote:

> Irene Murdoch hasn't been heard from publicly since October 1976.... Murdoch answers the phone with the wariness of someone resigned to being ferreted out yet again and paraded in the merciless glare of publicity. The embittered Murdoch will likely never recover from the physical and psychological scars inflicted on her by a divorce that became a Canadian cause. She won't talk to the press.... When asked whether she at least feels a sense of accomplishment at the change her case set in motion, Murdoch says flatly: "I am sorry to have started it. It did a lot more harm than good." She foresees three-generation farms falling into the grasp of greedy teenage brides who might win half their husband's land in a divorce settlement. She fears farmers will turn away from marriage. "No husband wants to go through that."[50]

Zwarun's objective seems to have been to contrast Murdoch's legal experience and traditional values with the efforts of "modern" 1980s farm women to gain greater recognition and remuneration for their hard work. Zwarun's presentation of Murdoch as a conservative farm wife failed to understand or acknowledge Murdoch's personal partnership quest. Murdoch revealed that Zwarun's words had upset her; she believed that Zwarun had manipulated her words to suit her own agenda. With Krasinski's support she drafted a response to Zwarun's article. In a letter to the editor of *Chatelaine* published in May 1983, Murdoch, writing as re-married Irene Jespersen, replied:

> I resent the following passages that were quoted out of context by Su-zanne Zwarun: "I am sorry to have started it. It did a lot more harm than good." What I said was that I do not want to start it up again after 14 years. This is where it will do more harm than good. "Mrs. Murdoch foresees 3 generation farms falling into the grasp of greedy teenage brides who might win half their husband's land in a divorce settlement." This interpretation of my ideas makes no sense at all. My son may marry soon and I hope both will be able to share the farm someday. Since my divorce, what I have said over and over again is that I want to forget those eight miserable years that led up to it. I have a new life now and I want to forget the old. [51]

By the mid-1980s, Murdoch was clearly media-shy and media-weary. Fortunately, she had experienced the friendship and assistance offered by Krasinski, and fellow CLCW members Dorothy Groves and Joni Chorny, who maintained contact with her throughout the 1970s and early 1980s. They exchanged Christmas greetings, accompanied Murdoch to her lengthy lawyer appointments, and offered encouragement. In doing so, these influential women carried on a grassroots tradition of community support begun by their foremothers many decades past.

The grassroots efforts of Unifarm Women and the CLCW personalized Irene Murdoch's story and complicate historical understandings about the woman who came to represent a "feminist cause." Her legal strategy, carried out by lawyer Ernest Shymka, also offers insight into her motivations for pursuing a partnership claim. Irene Murdoch interviewed over a dozen Calgary-area lawyers before hiring Ernest Shymka to represent her.[52] Shymka, who held a sincere regard for Irene Murdoch's interests as a hard-working ranch woman, agreed to bring her partnership claim to the Alberta courts. He attributed his empathy for Irene Murdoch to his wife's feminism and because he valued his mother's active participation in his family's store-keeping business.[53] Les Duncan, Alex Murdoch's lawyer, attributes her "lawyer shopping" to the idea that "her advisors I don't think always agreed with her," thus insinuating that Irene Murdoch had difficulty finding a lawyer because she insisted on pursuing a partnership interest in the Murdoch ranch, rather than a divorce.[54] Duncan could not understand Murdoch's legal approach because the amended 1968 Divorce Act enabled petitioners to seek a lump sum payment, and he believed this was a stronger course of action for Irene Murdoch; however, lump sum payouts under the 1968 Divorce Act were entirely discretionary, and she would likely not have been compensated fairly for her contribution to the farm.[55]

More importantly, Irene Murdoch did not want to divorce her husband. Shymka recalled that "Mrs. Murdoch did not want a divorce. She wanted custody of her child who was then around 14 years old."[56] Shymka continued: "No matter what happened she doesn't want to hurt him."[57] Patricia Krasinski explained that Murdoch knew that the only law that gave her any interest in the property she considered half-hers was the Dower Act.[58] By separating from Alex Murdoch, Irene Murdoch could retain her dower rights, including the right to reside in the marital home until her death. If she sought a divorce, she lost this right.

Armed with the knowledge that Murdoch did not desire a divorce and motivated by his belief in the value of women's labour, Shymka presented Irene Murdoch's application for custody of their son, a judicial separation, and an equitable partnership interest in the Murdochs' ranch to the Alberta Court of Queen's Bench. In 1971, the court awarded Irene Murdoch a decree of judicial separation and a monthly alimony, but denied her partnership claim partly because he found as a fact that the money Irene Murdoch had received from her mother was considered a "loan" by Alex Murdoch. At the time, the law required evidence of a wife's direct monetary contribution to the husband's property acquisition before an equitable interest could be found. Further, neither Murdoch had ever filed a declaration of partnership under the Partnership Act, and as Judge Macdonald tellingly stated: "were I to declare that the plaintiff [Irene Murdoch] had an equitable interest in the farm lands and farm assets it would be tantamount to establishing a precedent that would give any farm or ranch wife a claim in partnership."[59] The court did not want to interfere with ancient, patriarchal concepts of land ownership.

Baffled by the loss, Shymka and Murdoch persevered.[60] Unlike other farm or ranch wives who had lost their applications at the court of first instance and then abandoned their claim, Irene Murdoch continued her application for a partnership interest at the appellate level.[61] The Alberta Supreme Court denied her application because Irene Murdoch was receiving alimony. The Supreme Court judges stated that their decision was based on trial judge Macdonald's rationale that the ranch holding needed to stay intact and undivided so that Alex Murdoch would have sufficient land so as to be able to keep up with the alimony payments. In advancing this line of reasoning the Supreme Court judges implicitly sanctioned a patriarchal assumption embedded in the common law that males were the rightful owners of land and property. Within this view of land ownership women's contributions were seen as those of unpaid helpmeets. As Lori Chambers states, "farms are occupational sites that have historically been profoundly shaped by the traditional belief that 'men farm, women help.'"[62] This view also reflected the archaic legal reality that the marital bond transformed the husband and wife into

one person—that person being the man. Under this scheme wives owed their husbands their physical services, including sex and labour, in return for care and protection.[63] Frustrated with the court's circular logic, Murdoch and Shymka made
their way to the Supreme Court of Canada.

At the Supreme Court of Canada, Shymka framed Murdoch's claim as a per-
centage-based interest in trust law rather than as an explicit partnership interest.
The majority decided against Murdoch on the basis that they could find no evidence of a resulting trust. Only Judge Laskin, in his dissenting judgment, was prepared to suggest Irene Murdoch's "extraordinary" labour and housekeeping might
substantiate a different form of constructive trust than was known to the law.[64]
Laskin found that Irene Murdoch's contribution of physical work to the maintenance and expansion of the ranch "can only be characterized as extraordinary."[65]
For five months of the year Irene Murdoch operated the ranch—single-handedly
doing all of the haying, branding, vaccinating of cattle, and other outside chores
while continuing to look after the home and the couple's son—while Alex Murdoch worked away from the ranch for a stock association.[66] All of this labour, in
Laskin's view, meant that Irene Murdoch could not be considered a dependent
wife owing "normal" housekeeping duties to her husband in return for his care
and protection under the marital bond.[67] Further, Laskin was also prepared to
find evidence of Irene Murdoch's financial contribution to the ranch acquisition
in the monies she had received from her mother in 1952. Significantly, Laskin's
reasoning did not extend to granting wives equal property division for services
they provided solely as wives and mothers. Laskin's requirement of "extraordinary" labour enraged some rural Albertan women who understood his words
as requiring more "ordinary" labour from farm wives than from city wives. Yet,
Laskin's dissent helped to create a new understanding of constructive trusts that
the Supreme Court of Canada would frame as "unjust enrichment" in 1975.[68]

Other than Laskin's dissent, the *Murdoch* case was quite unremarkable. It
was decided on the basis of current law, and accorded with legal precedent. According to Shymka, it was not until after word of Laskin's dissenting judgment
reached the ears of Toronto area feminists that the *Murdoch* case started on the
road to infamy.[69] Shymka, in fact, never viewed the *Murdoch* case as a landmark
case. Many years after the 1973 decision he continued to believe that if Murdoch
had been given even a small share of property, the case would not have made
the headlines.[70]

Yet reach the headlines it did. By 1973 Irene Murdoch was not the first ranch
woman to lose a claim at the hands of the law, yet her case inspired national comment and outrage. Mysty Clapton has suggested that there was something pivotal
about the *Murdoch* case that caused Canadians to pay attention. Clapton attributes the national interest to the power of Irene Murdoch's story as an "organizing

narrative" which women's groups could utilize to agitate for equal rights. Central to Clapton's argument is the idea that Murdoch's story "is exceptional because it occurred at a time when the public was increasingly aware of women's changing role in society and when society was eager to embrace past inequities."[71]

Certainly, the *Murdoch* case did take place at a pivotal time. The women's movement was well underway, and Canadian women had experienced some success in lobbying for greater awareness of women's rights. The hard-won 1967 Royal Commission on the Status of Women created a dialogue between and amongst Canadian women regarding many aspects of their lives, including family relations, employment rights, and female poverty. Unifarm Women, through Betty Pedersen's participation in the Royal Commission, were strongly involved in creating recommendations for women. They had provided resources for over forty provincial meetings on issues relevant to the status of women, with broad audiences including nurses, social workers, church group members, women's institutes, and student unions.[72] Based on their involvement with the Royal Commission, Unifarm Women commissioned a booklet, "Family Laws for Albertans," and held fourteen seminars across the province to help Alberta women become more familiar with family law issues.[73]

After the *Murdoch* case, the CLCW became involved with the Institute of Law Reform and Research, which proceeded to research property rights.[74] They asked Albertans for input on a wide range of issues. The final report was to be put before the legislature for consideration in creating new legislation. Under the report, they recommended a system of "deferred sharing" upon divorce. Deferred sharing meant:

> each spouse would during marriage be separate as to property and free to deal with it, though there would be safeguards against a spouse stripping himself or herself of property in order to defeat the claim of the other spouse. When the marriage ends or breaks down the couple would share the economic gains which they made during the marriage, either by a money payment or by a distribution of property. The law could require that the parties in every case share equally in the gains, or it could give the court some discretion to make a different distribution in exceptional cases.

Unifarm Women also presented a submission to the Institute of Law Research and Reform and agreed with the CLCW's recommendations.

Not everyone was outraged by the results of the *Murdoch* decision. Calgary lawyer Mary Hetherington could not understand the uproar over Murdoch's SCC loss, stating, "I can't understand the publicity that has been given the Murdoch case...what the public has failed to understand is that Irene Florence Murdoch only lost a case based on an application for half ownership in the farm.... The Nanton farm wife still has divorce settlement procedure open to her, in which she could be granted a substantial part of the farm."[75]

Hetherington's comment likely reflected her legal training and expertise, heavily substantiated by a belief in law as a system of justice, and in the value of legal precedent in maintaining the law. Yet, Hetherington's comment was negatively received by Calgary feminists, who stated that "Ms. Hetherington could not see the feminist viewpoint."[76] Krasinski believed that "lawyers are conservative people who don't like to rock the boat and prefer the status quo...action had to be taken by someone outside the law society. That is what I did."[77] Hetherington's comment also suggests why Irene Murdoch had difficulty finding a lawyer to represent her partnership claim. If, as the opinions of Les Duncan and Mary Hetherington indicate, the dominant legal approach would have been to seek a divorce and a lump sum payment, then certainly Shymka's willingness to pursue a partnership claim and judicial separation indicated his willingness to be persuaded by the validity of Irene Murdoch's partnership claim.

Alex Murdoch eventually initiated divorce proceedings, and in 1975 Judge Bowen of the Supreme Court granted Irene Murdoch a divorce settlement in the amount of about $65,000. Irene Murdoch's divorce lawyer, Henry Beaumont, had argued in court that Alex Murdoch's total assets were valued at $312,000 and that Irene Murdoch should receive a lump sum of $133,000. Les Duncan, on behalf of Alex Murdoch, argued that $15,000 was an appropriate settlement for Irene Murdoch.[78] Albertan women mourned this divorce settlement because Murdoch's lump sum settlement of $65,000 was equivalent to roughly one quarter of the total value of the marital assets. Further, the lawyers' arguments and the judge's decision underscored the vagaries inherent in a legal scheme dependent on "judicial discretion." The divorce settlement clearly indicated that despite the publicity incurred by the *Murdoch* decision of 1973 and the actions of the Unifarm Women and the CLCW, Alberta's legal system still did not see fit to recognize Murdoch's marriage as a partnership.

The divorce settlement provided further incentive for Unifarm Women and the CLCW to seek new provincial matrimonial property law. Unifarm Women continued its lobbying efforts by sending yearly resolutions to the Alberta legislature on the need for matrimonial reform and by supporting the Alberta Institute of Law Research and Reform. The CLCW likewise supported the Alberta Institute of Law Reform, and Krasinski helped to draft a position paper on matrimonial law reform.[79] Finally, in 1980, Alberta's new Matrimonial Property Act legislated the legal presumption that all property acquired during marriage would be subject to equal sharing upon marriage breakdown.[80]

It was not until 1973, when Irene Murdoch's SCC loss was splashed across Canadian newspaper headlines, that the time was ripe for re-evaluating the "partnership" debate. The place from which that debate emanated was Alberta, where the Unifarm Women and the CLCW had been grappling with partnership recommendations for well over fifty years. Examining the actions of these groups—in their relations with Irene Murdoch personally and in promoting her cause politically—suggests that these conservative women's groups were important participants in the 1970s women's movement. Localized analysis also provides a glimpse into some of the key personalities and women's organizations involved in the *Murdoch* case, including Irene Murdoch, her lawyer Ernest Shymka, opposing counsel Les Duncan, as well as Betty Pedersen of Unifarm and Patricia Krasinski from the Calgary Local Council of Women.

Concerned about the possibility of further appeals or costs issued to Irene Murdoch, the CLCW held onto her trust fund until September 12, 1979 when they unanimously decided, in their own words, that "the sums of money collected from across Canada be given to Irene Florence Murdoch."[81] In October of 1979 Krasinski, Groves, and Chorny drove to Turner Valley and presented Irene Murdoch with her cheque for $1805.91.[82] Murdoch, tired of being discussed in casual conversations and misquoted by journalists, quietly slipped out of sight, away from the public eye.[83]

NOTES

1   "Separated woman can't have share in husband's ranch, court says," *Globe and Mail*, October 3, 1973, 37.

2   Citing the court majority in *Murdoch v. Murdoch* (1974) 41 D.L.R. (3d) 367 (SCC), hereafter "*Murdoch*."

3   Most recently discussed by Mysty Clapton, "*Murdoch v. Murdoch*: The Organizing Narrative of Matrimonial Property Law Reform," *Canadian Journal of Women and Law*, 20 (2008): 197–230.

4   Legal Archives Society of Alberta [LASA], Vol. 19, File no. 154 (William Baskerville Gill).

5   Alimony was granted as a common-law remedy separate from divorce proceedings.

6   Bruce Ziff, *Principles of Property Law*, 2nd ed. (Toronto: Carswell, 1996), 198.

7   See for example, Catherine L. Cleverdon, *The Woman Suffrage Movement in Canada* (Toronto: University of Toronto Press, 1950; new ed. introduction by Ramsay Cook, 1974), 46; Carol Bacchi, "Divided Allegiances: The Responses of Farm and Labour Women to Suffrage," in *A Not Unreasonable Claim*, ed. Linda Kealey (Toronto: Women's Press, 1979), 89–107; Catherine Cavanaugh, "The Limitations of the Pioneering

Partnership: The Alberta Campaign for Homestead Dower, 1909–25," *Canadian Historical Review* 74, 2 (1993): 198–226.

8 Lori Chambers, "Women's Labour, Relationship Breakdown and Ownership of the Family Farm," *Canadian Journal of Law and Society*, 25, 1 (2010): 76.

9 Chris Clarkson, *Domestic Reforms: Political Visions and Family Regulation in British Columbia, 1862–1940* (Vancouver: UBC Press, 2007), 2.

10 Chambers, "Women's Labour," 78.

11 Sheila McManus, "Gender(ed) Tensions in the Work and Politics of Alberta Farm Women, 1905–29," in *Telling Tales: Essays in Western Women's History*, eds. Catherine Cavanaugh and Randi Warne (Vancouver: University of British Columbia Press, 2000), 138.

12 Cavanaugh, "The Limitations of the Pioneering Partnership," 187.

13 Ibid., 188.

14 Ibid., 190.

15 Ibid., 213.

16 Cavanaugh, "The Limitations of the Pioneering Partnership," 198; McManus, "Gender(ed) Tensions," 139.

17 Cavanaugh, "The Limitations of the Pioneering Partnership," 200.

18 McManus, "Gender(ed) Tensions," 139.

19 Cavanaugh, "The Limitations of the Pioneering Partnership," 207.

20 Margaret McCallum, "Prairie Women and the Struggle for a Dower Law, 1905–1920," *Prairie Forum* 18, 1 (Spring 1993): 19–34. Cavanaugh, "The Limitations of the Pioneering Partnership," 208. McCallum draws heavily on Cavanaugh in agreeing that this idea was simply too much for the time.

21 Glenbow Alberta Insitute [GAI], M1718, File 1, Document 3605 (Women of Unifarm).

22 GAI, M1718, File 1, Document 3605 (Women of Unifarm).

23 Numerous Canadian women's organizations participated in international campaigns to promote human rights after WWII, including the YWCA.

24 GAI M5341, file 59, "International Council of Women, I.C.W. Standing Committee on Laws and Suffrage, Plan of Work for 1960–1963," (CLCW), July 1960.

25 GAI, M8604, file 103 (Langford).

26 GAI, M5841, file 82, "Correspondence 1940–1943," (CLCW).

27 GAI, M8604, file 94 (Langford).

28 GAI, M8365, file 104, "Submission to the Prime Minister of Canada and Members of the Cabinet on The Report of the Royal Commission on the Status of Women," Women of Unifarm, March 10, 1972, 5–6.

29 FWUA was formed in 1949 with the amalgamation of the United Farmers of Alberta and the Alberta Farmers' Union to form the Farmers' Union of Alberta (FUA). Carrol Jaques, *Unifarm: A Story of Conflict and Change* (Calgary: University of Calgary Press, 2001), 161–162.

30 Jaques, *Unifarm*, 162.

31 GAI M5341, file 59, "International Council of Women, I.C.W. Standing Committee on Laws and Suffrage, Plan of Work for 1960–1963," (CLCW), July 1960.

32 GAI M5841, file 59, (CLCW), letter dated November 1960. This is not to say that the CLCW did not have its conservative elements, because it did. Between 1940 and 1942 the CLCW had a woman lawyer, Ruth Gorman, acting in the capacity of convenor of laws. As one of few women lawyers in Calgary, Gorman was familiar both with women's

issues and the inner workings of the law. Gorman was a very "conservative" woman lawyer—she did not, in fact, believe that women should be practising lawyers.

33   Jaques, *Unifarm*, 162.

34   GAI, M8604, file 94 (Langford).

35   In 1925 federal divorce law was amended to enable women, as well as men, to divorce on the grounds of simple adultery. Alison Prentice et al., *Canadian Women: A History,* 2nd ed (Toronto: Harcourt Brace, 1996), 147.

36   Bruce Ziff, "Recent Developments in Canadian Law: Marriage and Divorce," *Ottawa Law Review* 137 (1986): 121–210, at 137.

37   GAI M8365, file 105, "Submission to the Law Reform Commission of Canada in Regard to Working Paper 12 on Maintenance on Divorce by Women of Unifarm," September 12, 1975 (Women of Unifarm).

38   GAI M6696, file 4, "Text of Speech Given by Pat Wright," October 17, 1977 (Krasinski).

39   Cavanaugh, "The Limitations of the Pioneering Partnership," 208.

40   Provincial Archives of Alberta [PAA], PR 2003.0305/0239, undated audiotape "The Murdoch Case" (Women of Unifarm).

41   GAI M8604 file 32b, "Submission to the Provincial Cabinet by Women of Unifarm," November 28, 1973 (Langford).

42   GAI M6696, file 2, November, 1975, p. 2 (Krasinski). This is possibly from a speech to the Students' Union of the Univerity of Calgary.

43   Anne Enke, *Finding the Movement: Sexuality, Contested Space, and Feminist Activism* (Durham: Duke University Press, 2007.)

44   Ibid., 5.

45   Monda Halpern, *And on that farm he had a wife: Ontario Farm Women and Feminism, 1900–1970* (Montreal, McGill-Queen's University Press, 2001). Halpern argues that Ontario farm women's feminism was influenced by their experiences as outdoor labourers as well as inside homemakers.

46   GAI, M5841, file 286 (CLCW Clippings, 1972–1979).

47   GAI M6696, file 3, Sarah Rau authored an editorial featured in the *Calgary Herald* on August 22, 1974 (Krasinski).

48   GAI M6696, file 3, "Mrs. Murdoch and the Status of Women" (Krasinski)

49   Suzanne Zwarun, "Farm Wives 10 Years after Irene Murdoch," *Chatelaine,* (March 1983): 176.

50   Ibid., 176–7.

51   Irene Jespersen, Letter to the Editor, *Chatelaine* (May 1983): 192.

52   LASA Accession Number 2008019, "Oral History Project Interview with Les Duncan, interviewed by David Mittelstadt, September 21, 2006" (Duncan interview).

53   LASA, Accession Number 2009016, "Ernest Shymka Video," Senior Lawyers' meeting January 21, 2002. Shymka explained that his parents were store-keepers. He stated that women "played a very significant part in the matrimonial family," and recalled that his mother was "quite a businesswoman" (Shymka video).

54   LASA Oral History project, Duncan interview.

55   Ibid.

56   LASA, Shymka video.

57   Ibid.

58   GAI M6696, file 2, excerpt from a Students' Union brief, November 1975 (Krasinski).

59   *Murdoch v. Murdoch,* 1971 (AB Q.B.) CanLII 258.

60   LASA, Shymka video.

61   Mysty Clapton in "Murdoch v. Murdoch: The Organizing Narrative of Matrimonial Property Law Reform," at note 36 identifies three of these cases as: *Wesigerber v. Weisgerber,* [1969] 71 W.W.R. 461 (Sask QB), *Rooney v. Rooney,* [1969] 68 W.W.R. (Sask QB); and *Klutz v. Klutz* (1968) 2 DLR (3d) 332 (Sask QB).

62   Chambers, "Women's Labour," 76.

63   Ibid., 78.

64   Bruce Ziff, *Principles of Property Law,* 198.

65   *Murdoch v. Murdoch* SCC: 439

66   Ibid., 441

67   Chambers also discusses this idea in "Women's Labour," 82.

68   *Rathwell v. Rathwell ,* [1978], 2 S.C.R. 436, 1 E.T.R. 307, 1 R.F.L. (2d) 1, [1978] 2 W.W.R. 101, 83 D.L.R. (3d) 289. Very briefly, the principle of unjust enrichment was to prevent persons from gaining unfair financial rewards from another person's unremunerated labour.

69   LASA, Shymka video.

70   Ibid.

71   Clapton, "Murdoch v. Murdoch," 207.

72   GAI M8365, file 104 (Women of Unifarm).

73   GAI M8604, file 103 (Langford).

74   GAI M6696, file 4, "Some excerpts from Report #18 (Matrimonial Property) from the Institute of Law Research and Reform Issued in 1975" (Krasinski).

75   *Calgary Herald,* Sept. 1976 (a photocopied reproduction contained in the Krasinski fonds).

76   GAI M6696, file 3. This quote is taken from a handwritten note found on an undated clipping entitled "Options still open for Mrs. Murdoch" (Krasinski).

77   GAI M6696, file 5, letter to Women of the Year awards, August 13, 1979 (Krasinski).

78   Fred Haeseker, "Murdoch Ruling Reserved," *Calgary Herald,* September 30, 1976, 31.

79   GAI M6696, file 4, "Position Paper on Matrimonial Property," October 1974.

80   Matrimonial Property Act, R.S.A. 1980, c. M-9 (Krasinski).

81   GAI M6696, file 3, "Report to the Calgary Local Council of Women From the Irene Murdoch Fund Committee" (Krasinski).

82   Marj Norris, *A Leaven of Ladies: A History of the Calgary Local Council of Women* (Calgary: Detselig, 1995), 217.

83   I did not seek out Irene Jespersen (Murdoch) for an interview for ethical reasons. Archival documents as well as anecdotal information gained from informal conversations with Ernest Shymka convinced me that she is not interested in speaking about the *Murdoch* case.

EXAMINING THE FUTURE OF FIRST NATIONS AGRICULTURE BY EXPLORING THE IMPLICATIONS OF THE MANITOBA INDIAN AGRICULTURAL PROGRAM[1]

BRET NICKELS

A number of government policies and programs have contributed to the development of contemporary Aboriginal agriculture in Manitoba. One of those endeavours, and the principal subject of this study, is the federally funded Manitoba Indian Agricultural Program (MIAP), which operated from 1975 until 1993. MIAP was established to increase the number of First Nations farmers and on-reserve farm units by providing support, training, and technical assistance for First Nations farmers in Manitoba, making it a key component in the history of First Nations agriculture in Manitoba. MIAP's accomplishments and weaknesses can help us gain a deeper understanding of the problems and prospects facing First Nations agricultural development in Manitoba. An investigation of the program's history will also shed light on how the discontinuation of MIAP has affected contemporary First Nations agriculture in Manitoba.

A HISTORICAL OVERVIEW OF MIAP

In 1971, an inventory of reserve agriculture resources was undertaken by the federal and Manitoba governments to determine the potential for Aboriginal agriculture in the province. This analysis revealed the need to develop a First Nations agricultural program. Approximately twenty-six reserves were identified as being within the Manitoba agricultural zone. The total acreage in these reserve areas was 335,170 acres, of which 50 percent was considered to be of agricultural importance. However, less than 37 percent of this agricultural land was actually developed in 1971, and of that developed land only 40,126 acres were cultivated by Aboriginal farmers (the remainder was farmed by non-Aboriginal people).[2] Furthermore, there were only fifty-two self-supporting Manitoba Aboriginal farmers in 1971, earning an estimated $3,200 per farm unit. This was significantly below the 1972 Manitoba average of $14,225. MIAP also stated that "the average Indian farm production was around 11 percent of the provincial average" at this time. According to the MIAP, First Nations farmers, when compared to non-Aboriginal farmers, were mostly operating subsistence farms (based on the very low estimated earnings of $3,200 per First Nations farm unit) with little modern equipment and little access to credit. Section 89 of the Indian Act made it impossible for First Nations farmers to use property on reserve for security loans, meaning any credit would have to be based on a borrower's reputation.[3] As a result of this policy, few First Nations people were able to access loans and mortgages.

In February 1973, an official presentation of the proposed program was made to the minister of Indian Affairs, the Honourable Jean Chrétien, by the committee chairman. Consultation meetings were held in June of that year between senior officials of Indian Affairs, the Manitoba Indian Brotherhood, and the recently formed Manitoba Indian Agricultural Committee (MIAC), which was created to help form the MIAP. From these consultations came the agreement in principle for the program.[4]

The Manitoba Indian Agricultural Program was initiated on July 1, 1975. MIAP was first envisioned as a five-year program and aimed to provide Indian people with the means to help them gain greater economic prosperity through the planning and development of agricultural resources. To this end, the program's long-range goal was the creation of 300 viable farm units. The term "viable" was explained by one consultant as "a farm business, which will generate enough income to pay all operating expenses and other financial obligations, and provide a standard of living for the operator and his family comparable to the standard prevailing in the surrounding community.[5]

According to MIAP plans, The Department of Indian Affairs in Manitoba was to support MIAP in a variety of ways. An officer of Department of Indian and

Northern Development (DIAND) was to sit on the Board of Directors of MIAP. DIAND, in respect to the development of agriculture in Manitoba, shared MIAP's policy objectives, and was to provide MIAP with financial and policy support. With the exception of some continuing supervision of certain aspects of credit allocation, the role of DIAND was considered indirect. DIAND contributions were to be employed improving land on reserves used by First Nations farmers. DIAND contributions were also to be employed to execute and administer agricultural extension and training programs. These programs were intended to match or parallel federal/provincial programs such as Special ARDA—whose funds were to be applied to the improvement of farmlands on reserves, supporting activities such as brush clearing, breaking, and grazing land improvement—and federal programs like the Farm Credit Corporation, which was to provide long-term mortgage credit to assist First Nations farmers.[6]

In several ways, MIAP was a successful program. An evaluation of the first four years of MIAP was undertaken by P.M. Associates (1978), with a financial audit undertaken by Keith A. Shipou & Co. of Winnipeg. The evaluation and audit reported that the program spent some $1.24 million on land development compared to a budgeted $1.84 million. It was also reported by P.M. Associates that over 40,000 arable acres of crop and hay had been developed by 1978. The report also noted that some 10,842 acres previously leased by non-Aboriginals had been taken up by MIAP clients for a total of 50,842 acres, exceeding goals as set in 1975. Thus, during the first five years of MIAP (1975–1980) the program had achieved its objective with respect to arable land by 1978 and had exceeded those goals by 1980.[7]

In addition, P.M. Associates farm production figures reported that gross farm production had risen from $465,000 in 1975 to $3,000,000 in 1978 and would reach $4.0 million by 1980, exceeding the stated goal of $2.5 million set in 1975. The average gross income for First Nations farmers was $19,622 in 1978 (a rise of $6,872 from the 1971 figure of $12,750). This figure still represented almost half the Manitoba average of $36,000 and showed that the income gap between Manitoba's First Nations and non-Aboriginal farmers was far from the stated goal of 89 percent of the Manitoba average over the first five years first projected in 1975. However, MIAP had exceeded its goal of providing on-farm training to 200 First Nations farmers, having trained 229 individuals by 1980. MIAP only recorded 168 established farms by 1980, well short of the 1975 objective of 195 farms. There were also a total of 128 MIAP clients in 1978 (which would rise to 170 by 1980) and a total of 389 loans (totaling $4.3 million) to 168 farmers by 1980. In short, the 1986–87 Treasury Board submission states that, "In the 1975–80 period, MIAP met or exceeded all of its main objectives except the goal set for the number of farms to be established."[8] MIAP's new Five-Year Plan, developed in 1986, included the following objectives:

> Bring into production some 6,000 acres of arable land and 10,000 acres of pasture land (total 16,000 acres). To provide training in specified amounts: On the job—80 clients; on farm; 200 clients; workshop—1650 trainee days; other training 100 clients; Demonstration 90; Specialized training; 78 clients. To increase gross farm production to $14.4 from 350 farms. To increase gross income per farm unit to $48.6 from 21.0 in 1980. Increase the number of fully developed farms from 50 in 1980 to 185 in 1985.[9]

TABLE 1. A Comparison of 1971 Farm Figures, 1975 MIAP
Objectives and 1978 MIAP Achievements[10]

1971 MANITOBA AGRICULTURAL SURVEY FIGURES

Farm Production	$465,000
Farm Income	$3,200
Farm Units	52

1975 MIAP OBJECTIVES

Farm Production	$2,550,000
Farm Income	$12,750
Farm Units	195
Added Land Production	43,500 acres

1978 MIAP ACHIEVEMENTS

Farm Production	$3,000,000
Farm Income	$12,750
Farm Units	168
Added Land Production	50,842 acres

In 1983, a further evaluation of MIAP was conducted by Intergroup, which indicated that many of the 1980 objectives were not being met. A 1986–87 Treasury Board (1987) submission also stated, "in the 1980–85 period only the goals for increased acreage and training (except specialized) were met." Only 212 farms with a gross production of almost $5.0 million had occurred by 1985 (far below the 1980 goal of $14.4 million from 350 farms). The average gross farm income had reached only $23,400, rather than the projected $48,600 (though, once again, up significantly from the $12,750 in 1975). However, when compared to the overall Manitoba average of $57,507, MIAP concluded that "this would imply Indian production per farm was 36 percent of the Provincial average... thus indicating a need for improvement in productivity."[11] Instead of making up ground on non-Aboriginal farmers, it appeared that First Nations farms were falling further behind the Manitoba average. In addition, only eighty-seven farms were identified as being viable (meeting operating and capital costs plus providing basic income), not the 185 fully developed farms projected in 1980.

The Intergroup evaluation also showed that the majority of First Nations farms were not covering operating costs and were yielding a negative net return as low as -$4,800 in some cases. However, Intergroup also compared that figure to the non-Aboriginal Manitoba farmer and found the average Manitoba farm in 1980 was "experiencing even larger negative net returns, i.e. $32,000 in 1980."[12] Despite this, Intergroup stated,

> very few Manitoba Indian farms appear to be viable...it appears that, at most, 30 percent of MIAP-supported farms can be considered viable at present and many of these would be marginal. Support for the remaining 70 percent must be derived largely from off-farm income, loan arrears, drawing down of equity and social assistance. That 30 percent of farms are viable coincides with some program officials' subjective assessment. These assessments range from 20 percent up to 60 to 70 percent potentially viable in two or three years.[13]

On a positive note, Intergroup reported in 1983 that approximately 4,000 acres of cropland and 5,000 acres of cultivated hay and pasture had been made possible by MIAP contributions. This corresponded with the 1980–85 objectives to bring on some 6,000 acres of arable land and 10,000 acres of undeveloped pasturelands. By 1985, targets for developing cultivated land had been exceeded. It was reported that 85,000 acres of arable land had been added, far above the 16,000-acre goal set in 1980. In addition, advisory services and training was also seen as a bright spot in MIAP's 1980–85 achievements. The Treasury Board stated that, "goals were met in all cases except sub-goal in specialized training to graduate 41 new clients from the University of Manitoba with Agriculture Diploma. Five have graduated, 15 are enrolled."[14]

After the second mandate (1980–1985) ended, MIAP was extended only for one additional year instead of the previous five-year mandates. A management review was initiated based on the shortfall in program achievements during the 1980–1985 mandate period. The management review concluded that, in regard to most of the objectives, the program had fallen short of expectations. The review recommended developing a program plan for each year to 1990, as well as action plans for each program component. As a result, a number of new recommendations were made. Intergroup recommendations concluded that MIAP needed to concentrate its resources on existing clients with minimal new farms beyond the current 184. In addition, it recommended improved case-by-case monitoring and recording systems to include data from farms the day they entered the program, recording productivity, acreage, earnings, assets, net worth, loan performance, contribution rates, and cost per client. Finally, it recommended that Board members be prohibited from receiving contributions or entering into contracts, aside from employment, with the program to address conflict of interest issues.[15]

In 1986, MIAP obtained funding approval from the Treasury Board through to 1990. The funding was conditional upon MIAP meeting specific program goals each year as set by the Treasury Board. MIAP then developed a strategic plan through to 1990. One of the Treasury Board's requirements was to develop a database program. In addition, program objectives, according to MIAP, were to "increase Indian farmer productivity for the existing farms to $32,000 per farm by 1990, implying that Indian farmer productivity would be 45 percent of the provincial average by 1990...develop and maintain 250 fully developed farm units producing some $8,000,000 in annual sales...increase Indian control of cultivated lands to 100,000 acres by 1990."[16]

Further objectives were to increase the average farm size to 682 acres with a total value of Aboriginal farm assets to reach $14,117,050. Other objectives included developing "a client database on production and financial results; a training database on clients trained, training costs, and the application of training; annual training requirements, forecasts and plans as well as an assessment of training results for the program as a whole; and monitoring to ensure the program's objectives are met."[17] The 1985 MIAP program plan also addressed a number of fiscal concerns, stating "the amount of funding available for contributions has declined from $1,246,960 in 1980 to $445,637 in 1985 [but] farm investment requirements have increased significantly from program inception to the present time due to the diminished purchasing power of the dollar. To illustrate, a $60,000 contribution adjusted to 1985 dollars is worth $22,000. [Also] the loan fund has an arrears problem. The existing arrangement for joint DIAND/MIAP administration of the loan fund is complex and inefficient."[18]

Capitalization for a new separate loan fund designed to establish each farm with appropriate financial structures and to provide additional equity to the client so as to reduce interest costs was proposed. The plan called for a major change to the method of funding so that the program could use available resources to provide farm clients with sufficient levels of funding at interest costs commensurate with their abilities to pay.

As a result, a new entity called the Manitoba Indian Agricultural Development Corporation (MIADCo) was created in 1986 under the Companies Act of

Manitoba with MIAP as its only member. MIADCo was established to fully take over the MIAP loan fund portfolio and administer loan services separately. MIADCo's Board was appointed by the MIAP Board of Directors and included the Chairman of the MIAP Board, one individual with agricultural lending experience, and someone with a business and/or farming background. An office building was purchased in Winnipeg at 286 Smith St. MIADCo purchased a portion of the loan portfolio, and investigated possible investments in niche food products, such as rabbits, geese, and wild rice. In addition, the MIAP Board of Directors had begun reorganizing the program's structure in 1989. A new coordinating body called the Manitoba Aboriginal Resource Association (MARA) had established a committee to develop program plans for all its activities.

However, a report by Fossey and Cassie in 1993 concluded that MARA's service objectives as stated in the 1990 DPA Group Report were far from being realized. Instead of establishing 200 viable farm units, MARA recorded only 122 farm units. The 1990 service objectives also predicted overall gross sales of $10 million on the basis of a $50,000 per unit average, when the reality was a $3.5 million gross sales figure based on an average of gross sales per farm of $29,361. Furthermore, MARA, instead of developing 30 new enterprises as stated in the DPA Group (1990) list of objectives, had established only three new enterprises, one of which, Wapos Inc., had already gone out of business by 1993.[19]

By 1993, the federal government had a dim view of MIAP's perceived failures and decided that MIAP funding should be phased out. Its core funding was reallocated to support the Canadian Aboriginal Economic Development Strategy (CAEDS), highlighting a shift in Department priorities away from sectorial-based programming. CAEDS was introduced to end program and administrative duplication and create better coordination of program delivery. Furthermore, within the CAEDS framework, the prime objective was to strengthen Aboriginal financial and local development institutions so that they could act as delivery agents for the financial, technical, business, and employment services that were, at the time, delivered through a variety of government departments. As a result, existing programs such as MIAP were to be either reorganized or phased out. MIAP and its associated programs were phased out in 1993, with all outstanding loans taken over by Arthur Anderson Accounting. Loans were then taken over by Tribal Wi-Chi-Way-Win Capital Corporation (which became the premier lending institution for First Nations farmers), who purchased the MIAP debt.[20]

POST-MIAP

After the demise of MIAP, many of the MIAP farmers went bankrupt, resulting in the seizure of their equipment and buildings. Others were left with a sizable debt owed to Tribal Wi-Chi-Way-Win Capital Corporation. Many First Nations producers were "financially crippled by the demise of MIADCo due to the deterioration of their credit ratings caused by the elimination of MIADCo supports and the hike in the interest rates on outstanding loans."[21] As a result, "many of the farmers…were upset at the way their debts to MIADCo were handled. Some farmers commented that they believed that some farmers had received total write-offs, others received partial write-offs, some were able to re-negotiate more favourable conditions, while others were not given any of the above options."[22]

Some First Nations farmers were reported to be crippled by old debts that were restructured under the significantly higher interest rates, which ranged from three to four percentage points higher than those offered by conventional financing. Higher interest rates were felt to be necessary to offset loan default rates. Tribal Wi-Chi-Way-Win Corporation, which runs the First Nations Financial Corporation (FNFC) program, is a developmental lender that receives its capital from the federal government. Under the terms and conditions of its funding, it must cover all its own operating costs, including loan losses.[23]

Since the demise of MIAP, conditions for First Nations farmers have deteriorated. When compared to non-Aboriginal farmers in Manitoba, the situation for contemporary First Nations farmers has been quite dire. For instance, the average farm receipts for First Nations producers and the average farm size of First Nations producers is less than the average Manitoba farm operator. In addition to the problems involving access to capital, the lack of an appropriate land tenure policy on many reserves has limited or prohibited developments of First Nations farms. In addition, "current Aboriginal economic development programs are very limited for First Nations farmers to receive support to establish successful commercially viable farming operations. This is due to strict criteria being placed on job creation, incentive limits per applicant, equity and commercial financing requirements such as insufficient capital to compete with the non-Aboriginal agricultural sector. The current federal government is unwilling to provide tribal Wi-Chi-Way-Win and First Nations Farm Credit with the development capital and support for administering costs to adequately service the needs of First Nations farm clientele."[24]

The difficulties with acquiring credit, such as an inability to provide land as collateral, have relegated most individual on-reserve farming endeavours to small-scale, low-technology operations. This lack of capital and technical expertise—the provision of which was a hallmark of MARA and its subsidiaries—has made it difficult for reserve farmers to acquire the latest agricultural technology necessary for modern-day agriculture, relegating most First Nations farmers to subsistence farming. It can be concluded that without MIAP, reserve agriculture has taken a step backwards since 1993.

THE FUTURE OF FIRST NATIONS AGRICULTURE

A number of issues affect the future of First Nations agriculture in Manitoba. An adequate understanding of the strengths of First Nations agriculture can provide decision-makers with a clear path towards building an attainable vision for the future, while an accounting of the barriers will prevent future policy makers from repeating the negative outcomes of the post-MIAP period. The following section highlights the various strengths, barriers, and available opportunities for improved agricultural development among First Nations.

STRENGTHS

Currently, First Nations agriculture has a number of strengths that can be built and expanded upon. Many of these strengths flow from the past experiences of MIAP, which offer lessons for future First Nations agriculture and can serve as a platform for further agricultural development. While there were weaknesses in the program, an awareness of the history of MIAP, both its successes and its failures, can provide future policy makers with insight into what strategies will and what will not work, and what must be done to alleviate the difficulties facing any future agricultural programs. MIAP provided a number of individuals with the training needed to be agricultural producers. Many of these individuals are still working in the agricultural sector and their experience and expertise can help would-be producers attain future success.

In addition, there are strengths inherent in the present First Nations Elk and Bison Council (FNEB). The FNEB Council represents Status Indian Elk and Bison ranchers. It also provides educational assistance to producers wishing to become involved in elk or bison farming through workshops and supplementary materials. In addition, the Manitoba government, represented by the Minister of Natural Resources, has signed an agreement with the Assembly of Manitoba Chiefs (AMC) on behalf of the FNEB Council allowing the FNEB Council to capture wild elk for elk farming programs. The FNEB Council serves as an excellent model for "producers and would-be producers to get together and work cooperatively to develop and support a new commodity."[25] This model could work for other commodities, including herbal medicines. Economic opportunities also exist in livestock production, particularly since there is limited First Nations land suitable for cultivation and the land base is better suited for livestock production.[26]

Because of the Treaty Land Entitlement (TLE) process, First Nations have a potential land base from which to develop a larger agricultural sector. Southern TLE bands now have the financial resources required to purchase good quality agricultural lands adjacent to their communities. Thus, former difficulties securing an adequate land base for agriculture may be alleviated in the future thanks to TLE. This, in turn, would allow First Nations individuals to fully utilize their agricultural potential and could attract more First Nations individuals into the agricultural sector.[27]

The establishment of First Nations–controlled capital corporations, such as Tribal Wi-Chi-Way-Win in Manitoba, may be beneficial to the extent that decisions for funding economic development initiatives will become disentangled from the state. This has the potential to depoliticize the decisions surrounding financial support for economic development initiatives such as First Nations agriculture. First Nations capital corporations also help to create a level playing field within an arena that has been characterized as anything but level. Of course, the problems with borrowing through such high-interest entities will have to be addressed to make capital corporations useful to First Nations people, but nevertheless, the potential to help First Nations agriculture does exist in such corporate entities.[28]

BARRIERS

First Nations farmers face considerable challenges in an industry that historically stacked the rules against equal participation. Past government policies have led to significant barriers for First Nations farmers and the negative impacts can be seen today. There are currently "few specific government programs that address the problems of lack of capital and the need for technical expertise required for modern day First Nations agriculture."[29] Since the termination of MIAP, First Nations farmers have had difficulty acquiring credit, a reality which has relegated individual farming endeavours on reserves to mostly small-scale, low-technology operations. Technology transfer to potential and existing First Nations farmers has been too slow for them to stay abreast of the market pressures from consolidation and the "corporatization" of the agricultural industry. Without access to these new efficiency gains, it is impossible for First Nations farmers to compete. In addition, there are few sources of information and resources targeting First Nations farmers on escalating niche market opportunities within the agricultural industry, including technological innovations and farm management, and alternative agricultural products.

Current Aboriginal economic development programs are also very limited, making it difficult for First Nations farmers to receive support to establish successful commercially viable farming operations. This is due to strict job creation criteria imposed by Indian Affairs, incentive limits per applicant, equity and commercial financing requirements. First Nations training and employment programs do not place a high priority on agricultural training, and First Nations farmers are reluctant to utilize the training and extension services offered by the Province of Manitoba due to the lack of culturally appropriate programming.[30]

Further barriers can be found in the initial CAEDS strategy itself, and in later government programs, which follow the CAEDS model. CAEDS' requirement that business proposals be evaluated on the basis of potential profitability and likelihood of long-term economic success may "have the effect of sharpening class divisions within Aboriginal communities."[31] If the profit motive is to be the principal requirement to funding decisions, Aboriginal businesses, like their non-Aboriginal counterparts, will be under pressure to keep the wages of their work force low and resist efforts to unionize workers. This runs counter to the ideals of the Aboriginal working class, who see the improvement of wages and working conditions within First Nations–owned enterprises as paramount.[32] The emphasis on profitability for reserve agriculture also works against the idea of generating alternative forms of agricultural production, which are often not viewed as being potentially profitable. This policy requirement is particularly problematic for the northern reserves that do not have an obvious agricultural profit potential in traditional agricultural activities such as cattle, grain, forage, or swine.

Most First Nations governments do not see agriculture as the basis of a stable economy due to the lack of sufficient agricultural land.[33] As a result, agriculture is often considered to be a low priority for many First Nations leaders and government policy makers. The lack of an appropriate land tenure policy on many reserves severely limits or prohibits development of First Nations farms. The majority of First Nations farmers find themselves out on a limb regardless of whether they hold their land by traditional rights, Band Council Resolution, Certificate of Possession, or some other arrangement. The collective nature of First Nations land holdings also has a dampening effect on the ability of the individual farmer to obtain an adequate land base to develop a profit-bearing operation. In regards to this problem, some First Nations believe that profits gained through the use of such collective resources should be shared, a view which potentially undermines the motivation of the individual farmer.[34]

Along these lines, as Wien states, First Nations governments must develop effective institutions that are not based on the present Chief and Band system of governing. Strengthening the institutional capacity for economic development can have a positive effect on First Nations agriculture by creating a political environment that is safe, fair, and secure for development, and can attract confidence, commitment, and investment. Wien further contends that "political leaders do have an important role to play in economic development—for example, in setting long-term goals, identifying appropriate strategic directions, and in putting in place the institutional base for economic development—but that role should stop short of interference in the day-to-day operation of businesses or economic development organizations."[35]

Wien suggests that, unlike the present Indian Act–imposed Band system of governing, institutions need to operate at arm's length from the political leadership in terms of their day-to-day operations. Band interference (and indifference) is a problem that affects the growth of agriculture in some First Nations communities. Wien argues that if the way Bands are governed does not change, then institutional capacity for economic development will be unlikely to occur, which has dire consequences for First Nations agriculture.

The difficulties engendered by the termination of MIAP have left a sour taste in the mouths of many present-day First Nations farmers. A number of farmers are wary of any new government-sponsored programs. This kind of thinking, though understandable, could make it difficult for any new program to be initiated, due to suspicion, uncertainty, and mistrust by the present First Nations farmer populace.

The historical development of First Nations agriculture is another important barrier. For instance, "history has shown that in farming areas in Western Canada it has taken 3 to 4 generations to develop successful viable farms with good farm managers and innovative operators. Prejudicial historic policies, which decimated early First Nations agricultural attempts, have significantly reduced the number of inter-generational farming families on-reserve."[36]

This historical development illustrates how government policy was instrumental in limiting the number of First Nations farmers.[37] As a result, there are few present-day First Nations farmers who can offer their experience, knowledge, and wisdom to help others who wish to take up farming. Therefore, there are few role models available to young or potential First Nations farmers. In addition, many potential First Nations farmers may be apprehensive of undertaking agriculture as a pursuit due to the problems experienced by many of the MIAP farmers.

The lack of a collective voice to raise issues and share concerns is another threat to First Nations agriculture. In the past, MIAP, despite its problems in this area, had filled this role. Today, many First Nations farmers feel isolated and lack an effective lobby to raise attention to their issues with government, the general public, or in the media. Aboriginal organizations such as the AMC or many of the Tribal Councils have not always been interested in taking up this role, though the Indian Agriculture Council of Manitoba (formed in 2006) has been supported by the Southern Chiefs Organization. As a result, a lack of cooperation and partnership among First Nations farmers themselves has existed since the demise of MIAP.[38]

OPPORTUNITIES FOR DEVELOPMENT

For First Nations to develop an agricultural economic sector, the limited potential that does exist must be exploited. Firstly, there is an opportunity to increase the number of Manitoba First Nations farms to 276 from the approximately less than 100 farms today.[39] This figure is based on existing First Nations reserve land usage of 116,791 acres, with a further potential of 100,000 acres of new agricultural lands under the TLE process, and applying the average Manitoba farm acreage size of 784 acres. Romanow, Bear and Associates also project that the annual gross farm receipt potential for First Nations farms can be $33.6 million (276 First Nations farm units at $121,809 average Manitoba farm receipts). To reach this potential, they state that the total average farm capital required to create and maintain 276 competitive First Nations farm units is in the range of $144 million.[40]

The relatively new Indian Agricultural Council of Manitoba (IACM), formed in 2006, also represents an opportunity. This First Nations initiative, with an elected Board of Directors, has resolved through resolution to "undertake an extensive review and analysis of current agriculture, federal, provincial and private sector programs currently available to both First Nation and non-First Nation producers." In addition, IACM has boldly resolved to reinstate the MIAP program and that it be "administered through Indian and Northern Affairs Canada, Manitoba Region, and that Indian and Northern Affairs...commit new and substantial dollars to said program."[41] However, the federal government, through Agriculture and Agri-food Canada (AAFC), has only responded with a 2007 policy report based on a series of regional discussion workshops with First Nations and Aboriginal producers across Canada.[42] These discussions offered a forum for Aboriginal producers to express their views on key issues and challenges that hinder their participation in agriculture. According to the document, "the ultimate goal is to increase the capacity of the department to engage with Aboriginal producers and communities for successful implementation of AAFC programs and services."[43] For the Aboriginal community, the intended outcome is to increase Aboriginal involvement in the agricultural sector and to develop Aboriginal capacity through education and awareness. However, Indian Affairs has not responded to this report as of this writing.

Other opportunities that ought to be explored include alternative medicinal agriculture and niche food products. The current interest of the general population in herbal therapies and medicines provides First Nations with an excellent opportunity to enter the industry with considerable expertise. First Nations people have been collecting, preparing, and using herbal remedies for many centuries, and there is room in the market place for the development and marketing of Indigenous medicines. Also, based on the soil classification of reserve land, it would appear that the land is more suitable to livestock than grain production, particularly to developing alternative niche livestock markets such as bison and elk. Both animals are indigenous to North America and are culturally connected to First Nations peoples and suitable for land on the reserve.

First Nations agricultural economic development played a prominent role in the recommendations of the Royal Commission on Aboriginal Peoples (RCAP), released in 1996. The RCAP made several recommendations for First Nations agriculture, including eliminating Aboriginal economic development strategies (such as CAEDS and other related programs which impede equitable access by Métis farmers and Aboriginal farmers), restoring funding to Aboriginal organizations and related programs such as MIAP, allowing and supporting Band Councils to undertake changes in land tenure and land use so as to develop efficient, viable Aboriginal farms and ranches, and implementing and advancing viable education and training programs to develop Aboriginal capacity in the agricultural sector.[44]

The main thrust behind the RCAP report with respect to agriculture is that First Nations people have historically suffered significant disadvantages in trying to set up agricultural operations.[44] Whereas government policies for non-Aboriginal farmers were designed to be supportive, government policies for First Nations farmers have had the opposite effect. These recommendations, if advanced by the government, would go a long way to correct some of these disadvantages and offer new opportunities for First Nations farmers.[45]

Hopeful expectations for the future have been reinforced in the official federal government's response to RCAP. The statements made in this document emphasize a vision for "strong, healthy communities and new relationships founded on mutual respect, with responsible, transparent, accountable, sustainable governance structures and institutions."[46] In order to implement this vision, the government highlighted four strategic initiatives: renewing the partnerships, strengthening Aboriginal Governance, developing a new fiscal relationship and supporting strong communities, people, and economies. Subsequent government documents, such as the 2000–2001 report on Plans and Priorities, and the 2007 Agriculture and Agri-Foods policy report, emphasize a similar vision.

MIAP: FINAL COMMENTS

Despite some weaknesses, MIAP, as a program to assist First Nations agriculture, can be considered a success, particularly when compared to the lack of specific First Nations agricultural programs available since MIAP's demise. Though it has been shown that MIAP did not achieve all its goals or objectives in many of its strategic initiatives, without MIAP First Nations agriculture has suffered a great deal. MIAP's problems originated from a failed government policy, which included a lack of commitment for adequate funding, long-term dedicated programming, the lack of emphasis on farmer education and advisory services, particularly in its last years of operation, as well as inadequate safeguards against conflict of interest. MIAP's other problems originated from a lack of commitment from First Nations governments and organizations, particularly in the support of First Nations agriculture and the settlement of land tenure issues. Of course, First Nations agriculture would never have succeeded under MIAP without addressing the issue of new land for new farmers and established ones who wished to expand their farms. Perhaps the settlement of land claims and TLE settlements will correct this problem that most First Nations communities with agricultural potential have experienced from the MIAP era well into contemporary times.

Despite its problems, MIAP did have a number of successes. Chief among these successes is that First Nations farmers have greater achievements during the MIAP period when compared to the contemporary situation. In the MIAP era, more farmers harvested more produce from more land and received more income from farming than they do today. MIAP farmers also were able to spread their awareness of the potential for farming to other prospective farmers—in doing so, they acted as role models for the entire potential First Nations agricultural industry. Most important, however, is the fact that MIAP can be used as a blueprint for any future agricultural policies in First Nations communities. Future policy makers have the advantage of using MIAP as an example of the potential of First Nations agriculture. In viewing the weaknesses and strengths of MIAP, policy makers can build on the successes and prevent a repeat of the problems. In this way, MIAP, as an historical example of government policy, can be used to help formulate future policies toward First Nations agriculture. Perhaps future policies and strategies, using the experience of MIAP as a framework, will help to establish a sound First Nations farming sector that will be able to operate on an equal basis with the non-Aboriginal sector.

NOTES

1   This chapter is a modified excerpt from my doctoral dissertation: Bret Nickels, "A Field of Dreams: The Story of the Manitoba Indian Agricultural Program" (PhD diss., University of Manitoba, 2003).

2   DPA Group, *Evaluation of the Manitoba Indian Agricultural Program—Final Report* (Vancouver: DPA Group, 990), 9.

3   *Manitoba Indian Agricultural Program* (Winnipeg: MIAP, 1985), 13–14.

4   Girman and Associates, *Swampy Cree Tribal Economic Development Planning Conference* (Winnipeg: Girman and Associates, 1989), 4.

5   Treasury Board, *Treasury Board Submission to Extend MIAP* (Hull: Treasury Board, 1986), 14; Intergroup, *Manitoba Indian Agricultural Program: Program and Performance Evaluation* (Winnipeg: Intergroup Consulting Economists, 1983), 1; MIAP, 3.

6   MIAP, 3–5.

7   Includes figures from P.M. Associates, *MIAP Evaluation Study—1975–1980* (Winnipeg: P.M. Associates, 1981), 3; MIAP, 5.

8   P.M. Associates, *MIAP Evaluation Study*, 6–8; Intergroup, Program and Performance Evaluation, 12–13; MIAP, 15.

9   P.M. Associates, *MIAP Evaluation Study*, 6–10.

10 All numbers from: DPA Group, *Final Report*.

11 Intergroup, *Program and Performance Evaluation*, 49.

12 Ibid., 50.

13 Treasury Board, *Treasury Board Submission to Extend MIAP*, 13.

14 MIAP, 11.

15 Includes figures from Intergroup, Program and Performance Evaluations, 50; MIAP, xx.

16 DPA Group, *Final Report*, 9.

17 MIAP, 59.

18 DPA Group, *Final Report,* 2.

19 Peat, Marwick, Stevenson and Kellog Consultants, *Project Report: A Profile of the First Nations Agricultural Sector"* (Winnipeg: INAC Report, 1993); DPA Group, *Final Report,* 2–3.

20 Treasury Board, *Treasury Board Submission to Extend MIAP*: 12–13; Peat et al., *Project Report,* 4.

21 Romanow, Bear and Associates, *Manitoba First Nations Agricultural Analysis and Strategy: Final Report* (Winnipeg: Romanow, Bear and Associates, 2000), 53.

22 Romanow et al., *Manitoba First Nations Agricultural Analysis*, 60.

23 Ibid., 60–61.

24 Ibid., 52–53.

25 Ibid., 50.

26 Ibid., 1–20; Symbion Consultants, *Economic Impact on the Manitoba Economy Deriving from the Expenditure of Funds Acquired as Partial Fulfillment of TLE* (Winnipeg: Symbion Consultants for the Manitoba Treaty Land Entitlement Committee, 1995), 12; Southern Chiefs Organization, *Indian Agricultural Council of Manitoba Holds Successful Forum*, South Wind, 2007.

27 Symbion, *Economic Impact on the Manitoba Economy,* 11.

28 T. Wotherspoon and V. Satzewich, *First Nations: Race, Class and Gender Relations* (Scarborough, Nelson Canada, 1993).

29   Interview with Daryl Bear, President of the Indian Agricultural Council of Manitoba, April 22, 2007.

30   Ibid.; Romanow et al., *Manitoba First Nations Agricultural Analysis*.

31   Wotherspoon and Satzewich, *First Nations*, 260.

32   Douglas Daniels, "The Coming Crisis in the Aboriginal Rights Movement: From Colonialism to Neocolonialism to Renaissance," *Native Studies Review* 2, 2 (1986): 97–115.

33   Romanow et al., *Manitoba First Nations Agricultural Analysis*.

34   Ibid., 53.

35   F. Wien, *Nine Steps to Rebuild Aboriginal Economies: Recommendations of the RCAP Report* (Toronto: Cando-Royal Band Symposium on Economic Development, 1997), 21.

36   Romanow et al., *Manitoba First Nations Agricultural Analysis*, 52.

37   See Sarah Carter, *Lost Harvests: Prairie Indian Reserve Farmers and Government Policy* (Montreal: McGill-Queen's University Press, 1993).

38   Romanow et al., *Manitoba First Nations Agricultural Analysis*; Interview with Daryl Bear, April 2007.

39   Ibid.

40   Romanow et al., *Manitoba First Nations Agricultural Analysis*.

41   Southern Chiefs Organization, "Indian Agricultural Council of Manitoba Holds Successful Forum," 1.

42   Agriculture and Agri-food Canada, *Next generation of Agriculture and Agri-Food Policy: Report on Aboriginal Discussion Workshops National Report"* (Ottawa: Agri-food Canada , 2007).

43   Ibid.

44   Royal Commission on Aboriginal Peoples (RCAP), *For Seven Generations* (Ottawa: Minister of Supply and Services, 1996).

45   Ibid., 75.

46   Indian and Northern Affairs Canada, *Gathering Strength; Canada's Aboriginal Action Plan* (Ottawa: Indian and Northern Affairs Canada, 1997).

ON THE TRAIL OF
THE MARCH WEST
THE NWMP IN WESTERN CANADIAN
HISTORICAL MEMORY

AMANDA NETTELBECK AND ROBERT FOSTER

INTRODUCTION

The role of the North West Mounted Police (NWMP) in facilitating the "peaceful occupation" of the North-West Territories is so pervasive in Canadian national iconography it needs no introduction.[1] For non-Canadians, the iconic status of this colonial police force provides a singular example of how an arm of government—more often regarded elsewhere in the world with anti-authoritarian suspicion—forms the centrepiece of a narrative of peaceful national foundation. The starting point for this national narrative is the March West, which the newly established mounted police force undertook from southern Manitoba in the autumn of 1874. From that historic march arises the cherished story of the arrival of law and order in western Canada, whereby the NWMP conquered the lawless frontier not through force but through the powers of peaceful negotiation and the respect they commanded amongst First Nation peoples of the prairie lands. "Law and Order Heads West"; "the establishment of law and order in our Dominion"; "peace and progress"; "justice and civility": these are some of the repeated phrases through which the arrival of the NWMP in the North-West Territories is remembered along the historic trail of the March West through southwestern Canada, and which commemorate their role in helping to build the modern nation.

This mythic image of the NWMP has come under some stress in recent decades with the rise of a critical historical scholarship on the role of the NWMP as agents of colonial governance whose tasks entailed the suppression of First Nations' cultural autonomy.[2] This critical historiography emphasizes the importance of the NWMP to Ottawa's intention to develop agricultural and industrial economies in the North-West Territories through land settlement, a process that required ensuring First Nations compliance with Canadian sovereignty. Since its officers held magisterial powers, the force could function as a self-contained instrument of the Queen's law without reference to distant authorities in Ottawa, enabling it to implement the government's Indian policy with "benevolent despotism."[3] The NWMP's contribution in facilitating the treaties that were signed with First Nations of the western territories through the 1870s has traditionally been constructed as part of the force's peacemaking role. More recently, historians have argued that the treaties were the starting point from which First Nation sovereignty gave way to a longer era of "oppression, land theft and starvation."[4]

The NWMP strengthened the leverage of their legal authority by pressing senior First Nations men to police their own people.[5] This strategy proved to be successful in policing Aboriginal peoples who were subject to treaties, and was expanded with the introduction from the mid-1880s of "native scouts" as attachments to NWMP patrols. Scouts were considered particularly useful to police in being able to travel easily within the country, and although they played a mediating role between police and First Nations—the most famed instance in Canadian historical memory being Jerry Potts—less central to the national mythology is the fact that scouts also served to police their own people, particularly in providing information as to movements on the reserves.[6]

By the 1880s, policing tasks became more explicitly tied to persuading First Nations peoples to settle on reserves, backed, when needed, by forcible removal. The granting or withholding of rations was one strategy employed by the government to facilitate this process, administered by the mounted police in cooperation with the Department of Indian Affairs.[7] For the remainder of the nineteenth century, as Sarah Carter puts it, a government policy to "supervise and monitor the movements and activities of reserve people" was pursued "with great vigor."[8] The NWMP played a vital role in the fulfillment of this policy. It could be said that this was no more than an extension of the NWMP's original task to bring the protection of the Queen's law to the First Nations peoples of the North West, since the protective function of the law was conditional on their enforced obedience to the legal authority of the new nation state.

The NWMP, then, are at the centre of two potentially competing narratives of national origin: one geared around their role as bringers of peace and good government to the North West, and the other around their role as a colonial instrument of Aboriginal surveillance and containment. This paper seeks to examine how much these potentially competing narratives of nation-building are visible in the public forums of historical memory across western Canada that commemorate the NWMP's original March West and their role in the North-West Territories over the decades to come. In examining the regional markers and memories of the March West, this chapter considers not just the role given to the NWMP in the national story of Canada's "gentle occupation," but more particularly whether and how that national mythology varies in its regional expressions.

COMMEMORATING THE NATION

The commemoration of national foundational moments constitutes a central aspect of the "sites of memory," to use Pierre Nora's famous phrase, that define the current age of concern with the role of history in shaping concepts of national identity. Over the past several decades and across Western democracies globally, Nora notes, the question of how societies relate to the past has moved squarely into the foreground as we witness a revived interest in national history at the same time as we witness the recovery of once-repressed or minority histories.[9] In response, a growing body of scholarship has examined the social and political implications of how the national past is remembered, and the purposes it serves in the public domain.[10] This is as true of Canada as it is of other western democracies that have seen an unprecedented expansion in the realm of public history, at the same time as a national re-examination of the past in terms of recognizing and reconciling with once-marginalized histories.[11] In this respect, heritage sites and commemorative events that speak to narratives of national foundation are particularly relevant, as they constitute a particular form of public history-making, one that relies upon the symbolic power of central moments in the past as being emblematic of national consciousness.

The March West of the NWMP can be regarded as one such central moment in the making of Canadian national consciousness. At the national level, it has a tangible "site of memory" at the RCMP Heritage Centre in Regina, which serves as Canada's centralized institution for the history and ongoing legacy of the world's most loved police force. The NWMP headquarters moved to Regina in 1882 and, more than a century later, RCMP recruits are still trained at the Academy there. Opened in May 2007, the Heritage Centre aims, its visitor brochure states, "to share the RCMP story with the world" as "a great Canadian story."[12] Exhibits on the history of Canada's mounted police at the Heritage Centre are structured chronologically from the NWMP's establishment in 1873 and its history over time to its seamless transformation into a contemporary police force. An exhibit dedicated to the work of the NWMP in the North-West Territories, *Maintaining Law and Order in the West*, is primarily a material collection of NWMP photographs and artefacts. A set of summarizing panels reminds us that the NWMP force was based on the Royal Irish Constabulary, "famed for its competence and fairness," and that its tasks were "to establish friendly relations with the Indigenous peoples, enforce Canadian authority, pave the way for settlers, and maintain law and order on the frontier." As the RCMP's official site of remembering, the Heritage Centre is understandably geared towards a touristic eye, whereby a familiar national story is told—and sold in myriad forms of merchandise at the Centre's shop—for the world's visitors.

If the RCMP Heritage Centre is the official forum for the collection and display of NWMP history, the March West re-enactment in 1999 was its lived expression. The re-enactment of foundational moments forms an integral part of commemorative history-making in that it makes history broadly accessible by condensing complex historical processes into symbolic scenes.[13] As a commemoration of the 125th anniversary of the March West, the 1999 re-enactment held nationally symbolic significance in bringing back to life "the treacherous journey that brought peace and order to Canada's prairies."[14] Over two and a half months, from 8 May to 24 July, some 200 riders, including members of the contemporary police force as well as civilian participants, followed in the path of the NWMP's original trek in a journey that took them from Fort Dufferin in southern Manitoba to Fort Saskatchewan in Alberta. The March West re-enactment created an opportunity to relive, both across the nation and across western Canada's regional communities, the story of a force formed "to establish friendly relations with the Aboriginal Peoples and to maintain the peace as settlers arrived."[15] From this original achievement, the re-enactment brochure states, arose the remembered achievement of the mounted police in "forging the nation that exists today." Some contemporary members of the RCMP who had participated in the re-enactment afterwards described how moving it had been to take part in an event where the police were, in contrast to their everyday roles as urban law enforcers, remembered and welcomed as peacekeepers and protectors.[16] One RCMP member who participated recalled how in the small towns they passed through, children would run up to the riders for an autograph.[17] Along the route, families joined the march for part of the way, some dressed in period costume. A local from Boissevain in southern Manitoba described how she and her family, dressed as nineteenth-century settlers, had hitched horses to a wagon and accompanied the march to the next town: for her, the March West re-enactment had engaged the whole community, and was a means of expressing community identity.[18] In these terms, the re-enactment of the March West was a great success in celebrating western Canada's pride in its NWMP history, come again to life. The trek's progress was recorded in a documentary film, and detailed in a commemorative book which traces the spirit of the contemporary RCMP back to "the men of the Great March."[19]

Not everyone remembered the NWMP's achievements in such positive terms, however. Responding to the RCMP's news release of the re-enactment in May 1999, an anonymous commentator noted that this re-enactment of "peace and order" could be seen instead as a re-enactment of invasion, and wryly observed that the history of colonization offered "nothing to celebrate."[20] Although this observation provides a glimpse of an alternative perspective in which the March West symbolizes a history of colonial occupation, it does so in the face of a much more powerful national narrative which regards this foundational event as the point of origin for a history of peace and progress.

While commemorative events such as the March West re-enactment will inevitably hold a symbolic role in their representation of national history, perspectives on national history do of course demonstrate shifts as an index of changing social and political climates, and may also vary from region to region, shaped by more specific networks of place. How then is the story of the NWMP's March West told at regional sites across western Canada, and how much do those sites articulate with the iconic national narrative about the March West and the nation-building role of the NWMP?

REGIONAL MARKERS OF THE MARCH WEST

Fort Dufferin, in southern Manitoba, was the starting point of the March West where, in 1874, the police recruits undertook three weeks of training before their long trek across the prairie lands. Now a quiet historic site on the muddy banks of the Red River set amidst a thicket of elms, it marks the beginning of the Boundary Trail Heritage Region. A sign welcoming visitors to the Boundary Trail Heritage Region carries an image that can be seen along the paved roads that now more or less follow the 49th parallel marked out by the North American Boundary Commission in 1873. Celebrating as it does two historic treks, the image depicts William Hallet, Chief Scout for the Boundary Commission, alongside G.A. French, first Commissioner of the NWMP and leader of the March West. As the starting point of the March West, the Fort Dufferin historic site focuses less upon the police force's acclaimed peacekeeping or law-bringing role after its arrival in the North-West Territories, and more upon its task of nation-building. A memorial plaque near the front gate informs the visitor that the "newly delineated boundary paved the way for settlement and resource development in the Canadian West." Although within a decade the arrival of the railway would "blaze a new path across the vast prairie," the old trail serves as an important reminder of the first march towards Canadian sovereignty and an emblem of "our pioneer heritage." Another sign near the entrance states that the NWMP force was formed to secure Canadian sovereignty: with the opening of the American west and the risk of American expansion, "it was time to send a message that Manitoba and the Northwest belonged to Canada!"

The story of the March West, as it is told at the Fort Dufferin historic site, is fundamentally a Genesis story of Canadian sovereignty. A visitor's guide brochure describes in more detail how this point of national foundation was defined by three groups who "changed the Canadian west." The first of these are the men of the Boundary Commission who marked out the long line of the 49th parallel. The second are the men in Red Serge, who were "sent to the frontier to maintain law and order as settlers arrived, and to establish friendly relations with the First Nations." The last are the settlers who followed "with little more than dreams of owning their own land."[21]

Amongst a series of photographic panels that dot the grassy footpaths around Fort Dufferin, one shows a gathered group of thirty Métis scouts—the "49th Rangers"—who travelled in advance of the Boundary Commission "to negotiate with the First Nations and to establish storage depots." This is the only reference at the historic site to the Métis, who supported the westward push as scouts and negotiators; there is no visible record of the First Nations peoples with whom they would mediate. A full-wall mural on a site building, painted in 2007, features as its centrepiece a NWMP officer astride his horse. To his left is the police camp as it can be imagined at Fort Dufferin in 1874, and from his right approaches a steamer that will bring settlers along the Red River in readiness for their journey west. In the right-hand corner is a silhouette of the future pioneers, for whose lives in the west the NWMP would pave the way. This history, the mural's title tells us, is "A History of Firsts." Curiously absent is any reference to the First Nations people upon whose acquiescence Canadian sovereignty would ultimately depend.

HISTORY IN MURALS

Travelling west from Fort Dufferin along the route of the Boundary Trail Heritage Region, the historic story of the March West is everywhere evident in murals that adorn the walls of buildings in country towns north of the Canadian border, and that celebrate both the specificity of the town's history and the national narrative of the opening up of the west. In other contexts, scholars have examined the function of murals as a dynamic form of political practice as well as a symbolic expression of place and identity, one that both reflects and determines the ways in which the history of place can be understood.[22] Boissevain, in southern Manitoba, lies just north of the original NWMP trail and is famous for its murals. On the wall of the Redcoat Inn, located on the eastern edge of town, a large mural tells the story of the March West from G.A. French's record. French's 1884 account of the March West provides a parable of foundation of the Canadian west, told through hardships encountered and overcome. In the Redcoat Inn's mural, the top left-hand corner illustrates the thunderstorm which, in French's account, nearly blew away the police camp; in the top right-hand corner is the forest fire which similarly threatened the safety of the riders west. Such hardships have served over time to strengthen the mythic potential of the NWMP's achievement, a mythic potential discerned early on by French himself when he reported on the trek at its end: "Day after day on the march, night after night on picquet or guard, and working at high pressure during four months from daylight until dark, and too frequently after dark, with little rest, not even on the day sacred to rest, the Force ever pushed onward.... The fact of horses and oxen dying for want of food never disheartened or stopped them, but pushing on, on foot, with dogged determination, they carried through the service required of them."[23]

The role of the NWMP in "paving the way," despite the hardships they faced on their journey, takes centre stage in the mural, with the image of the redcoats riding west followed by a wagon train of pioneers. This story is one that is nationally familiar, but in this iteration it also includes a regionally specific reference. In the bottom left-hand corner sits a retired officer of the NWMP, his dress uniform draped beside him. The named journal he holds tells us that he is G.A. French himself, now an old man, and from it he reads to a young recruit who listens intently at his feet. The young recruit, a memorial plaque nearby tells us, is Dominick French, great-grandson of G.A. French, who had joined the redcoats "after hearing the stories of his great-grandfather's adventures" and who had served for a time in Boissevain. The story of the March West is foundational at the national level, and in this mural, a personal connection renders it locally meaningful.

Through the southern belt of Manitoba, Saskatchewan, and Alberta, most towns display public murals, and most of them feature the NWMP's March West. These murals offer localized expressions of the NWMP story that are both regionally specific and nationally generic: it is a story that can be locally claimed, but that still remains shared across the nation. The largest mural in southwestern Canada covers a community sports centre wall in Fort Macleod, Alberta: painted in 1992, it was created to celebrate the town's 100th year of incorporation. To one side an "Indian Brave" stands alongside Chief Crowfoot and an Indigenous camp. To the other is the eponymous mounted redcoat, seated next to Colonel Macleod and the famous interpreter and guide Jerry Potts. These nationally familiar scenes of the pre-settler west frame an extended "photo album" of the town's own historical highlights.

In murals across Canada's southwest, other kinds of local references enrich the national tale. Pictorial histories of the region's oil or wheat industry are painted alongside a well-known triptych of figures: mounted redcoats at the centre, framed by the First Nations on one side and the arriving settlers on the other. In this repeated triptych, the NWMP represents the hinge that brings together a passing world of ancient tradition and a dawning one of modernity; it is the mounted police force's place in historical memory to mediate peacefully between these worlds. On a mural at Maple Creek, Saskatchewan, a Mountie standing beside an Aboriginal man fulfils his historical role as "friend of the Indian"; another depicts the NWMP at Fort Walsh while Indians camp safely nearby, witnesses to a wagon train that bring settlers to the west, while overhead a steam train, symbol of the near future, flies surreally through the clouds. Some murals also contain a hint of melancholy for a lost Aboriginal past: at the far left of one mural at Maple Creek is the portrait of a chief, his headdress trailing behind to frame a future of settlement in which, presumably, he is not destined to take a part. Towns take pride in their murals. A printed brochure and map of Boissevain's nineteen murals tells us that all had been commissioned by the town council. As the murals have weathered they have been restored, ensuring the story they tell is not lost to succeeding generations.

At Calgary International Airport, near the base of the Rockies where the NWMP ended their westward push, one can see another historical mural, or rather a smaller version of the original that was damaged when the new terminal was opened in 1977. The scene depicts a group of settlers travelling in covered wagons to their new home on the Bow River. From their hill-top vantage point the settlers behold a vision of the future city of Calgary, illuminated in a shaft of light emanating from a cloud above. Within the cloud is a group of key histori-cal figures who appear like angels standing guard over the future: framing the group are the Reverend John McDougall and Father Lacombe, who travelled to Alberta as missionaries and are remembered for their work in establishing friendship with the First Nations; to the left is Colonel James Macleod, founda-tional figure of the NWMP; in the centre, Chief Crowfoot shakes hands with an early settler. The plaque accompanying the mural tells us that the cloud forma-tions depict the outline of Canada and the British Isles. The mural depicts the apotheosis of this foundational group: having made the west safe and peaceful, they have ascended to heaven.

MATERIAL HISTORY

If murals across western Canada tell a remarkably consistent kind of foundational narrative, the historical memory of the March West has more material expression in the several forts which once formed the base of police operations in southwestern Canada, and which are now open to the public as historical sites. Each of these former forts held a significant strategic role in policing the border with the United States. As the starvation era increasingly affected First

Nations groups from the mid 1870s, the police forts became important locations for the distribution of vital rations and for the management of the policing patrols, which undertook surveillance of First Nation peoples with the aim of suppressing cross-border traffic and inter-clan horse stealing.[24] At strategic locations along the boundary, for instance, "look-out" posts were established which would prevent the sale of ammunition to First Nation refugees from across the border, and in the words of Commissioner James Macleod, "to give information as to their movements."[25] Even from the early years of the NWMP's presence in the west, the goal of establishing friendly relations with the First Nations would become combined with the task, as Commissioner James Macleod understood it, to "keep them in check."[26] By 1880, a mood of discontent fuelled by starvation amongst the First Nation populations moved Macleod's successor Commissioner Irvine to consider that more police power was required to handle this potentially "dangerous class."[27] A critical historiography of the NWMP suggests that within a few years of its arrival, the role of the NWMP on the western frontier became geared less towards the task of peaceful mediation between First Nations and the Canadian government, and more towards coercive strategies in making First Nations peoples compliant with the Queen's law and Ottawa's Indian Policy.[28] At the historic sites that mark the NWMP's former forts, how much of this strategic policing role is evident?

On the route from the east, the first westward fort the visitor reaches is Fort Walsh in Saskatchewan. Named after its commanding officer Superintendent James Morrow Walsh—now primarily remembered for his friendship with the refugee Sioux leader Sitting Bull—Fort Walsh was the NWMP headquarters between 1878 and 1882. Once linked in communication to Ottawa only by the Fort Benton Trail, it is now part of the "Old Forts Trail" and a National Historic Site administered by Parks Canada. Situated about fifty kilometres southwest of Maple Creek, it sits strategically in the lee of a range of hills that rise from the prairies. The contemporary fort is a reconstruction of the original square palisade made of hand-hewn tree trunks. Around the perimeter of the compound are reproductions of the stables, officers' quarters, troopers' dormitory, and kitchen, and near the centre flies the Maple Leaf flag.[29] Beside it squats a field artillery piece capable, if need arose, of enforcing it.

On arrival at Fort Walsh, visitors today first view a short documentary film in the interpretive centre. It tells the story of how the NWMP force was established, and of how its presence in the west was triggered by the Cypress Hills massacre of 1873, in which some two dozen Assiniboine people were murdered by wolf hunters. This remains a familiar starting point of the national myth of the NWMP, whereby the force marched west to bring law to a lawless frontier and to protect Aboriginal peoples from any further such atrocities.

This historical memory of the NWMP's foundational purpose forms the basis of a positive national myth which appears to be little diminished by the more critical argument of some historians that the NWMP was primarily formed to fulfil Ottawa's determination to bring the North-West Territories within its jurisdiction and so gain access to the region's vast economic potential.[30]

Although the documentary film that introduces the visitor to Fort Walsh presents a nationally familiar story of NWMP origins, the interpretative centre offers a less mythic, more critically engaged story of the NWMP—one that speaks directly to the particular history of the immediate region. Panel displays describe the sometimes-fraught relations of that part of the western frontier, and the interactions of diverse groups that "were not always peaceful." The installations describe the complex roles the NWMP performed. As part of the task of establishing Canadian sovereignty in the region, the police "acted as customs and excise agents and border guards. They acted as quarantine agents and brand inspectors. They established mail routes and other communications infrastructure. They arrested whiskey traders and enforced the various criminal statutes of the day.... Should circumstances require, they were trained to fight." In short, they represented "both the civil and the military authority in the West."[31]

One of the policing roles examined at the interpretative centre was the challenging task of implementing controversial aspects of the government's Indian Policy in an era of starvation and rising discontent in the west. The brochure accompanying the Fort Walsh interpretative centre notes: "The years Fort Walsh existed, 1875–1883, were a period of tremendous struggle and misery for everyone and the Cypress Hills region staged some of its saddest scenes."[32] Fort Walsh was also at the heart of the legendary story of Sitting Bull and the Sioux who sought refuge from the US cavalry on Canadian soil after defeating General Custer in 1876 at the Battle of Little Big Horn. Although Canada's part in providing sanctuary to the Sioux and the famed friendship between Sitting Bull and James Morrow Walsh are key aspects of popular Canadian mythology, the Fort Walsh interpretative centre offers, in more critical depth, the story of the "long diplomatic nightmare" that this history entailed, including Ottawa's three-year effort, eventually successful, to remove the Sioux from Canadian territory and induce them to return to the United States.

From the interpretative centre, visitors are driven to the reconstructed Fort compound itself, now an immersive style of museum that revitalizes the past into living history. In contrast to the traditional museum, which serves as a re-pository of the past, the emphasis here is on recreating a sense of place and time in ways that invite identification with history as lived experience.[33] Visitors to the Fort can experience the lived conditions of mounted police life on the prairies, to the point of participating in a court hearing from a list of cases tried at the Fort and recorded in the Magistrate's colonial reports. Receiving sentences for such crimes as trading whiskey to the "Indians," contemporary visitors can be reminded, if they wish to think of it, of the magisterial powers that gave the NWMP their authority as a virtually self-contained instrument of Canadian law on the western frontier.

Further west, at the historic town of Fort Macleod in southern Alberta, the history of the NWMP is remembered at the Fort Museum, a latter-day reconstruction near the site of the original fort established under Assistant Commissioner James Macleod. Here, as a text panel near the entrance informs us, "visitors can experience what it was like to live at a NWMP post and explore the influence the NWMP had on the settlement of Western Canada." Unlike at Fort Walsh, however, there is little sign of a critical engagement with the specific history of the NWMP in the region. The historical memory of the NWMP at Fort Macleod is broadly geared toward relating the wider national story of the police force as "one of Canada's most recognised symbols," primarily as symbols of the arrival of law, order, and peace in the North-West Territories. The museum's Tradition in Scarlet exhibit room is filtered through the figure of Macleod himself, whose local significance is ensured by the fact that the town takes his name. Macleod's intention, a text panel tells us, "was that firm and cordial relations alone would prevail, that honesty and perseverance would be the watchwords of the force, and that the native peoples could be afforded justice and fair play."

The regional relevance of the NWMP story and its impact upon this part of western Canada is intertwined with other exhibits of regional significance, including the Ranching Gallery, which tells the story of the cattle industry in the Fort Macleod area, the Centennial Gallery, which displays the decorative art of the region's First Nations peoples, and the Cultural Gallery, which highlights the broader history of southern Alberta. After visiting the museum's exhibits, visitors can stay to experience the famed NWMP Musical Ride, which is performed daily through the summer months.

Further west from Fort Macleod is the historic town of Fort Steele, British Columbia. Fort Steele's prospects as a thriving mining town in the late-nineteenth century were short-lived. When the Canadian Pacific Railway bypassed it in 1898 in favour of nearby Cranbrook its fortunes waned, and by the mid-twentieth century it was little more than a ghost town. It is now reinvigorated as an historic site where visitors can stroll through its reconstructed streets, mingle with one-time "residents" in period costume, and participate in the life of a colonial township. Before its life as a town, Fort Steele's origins were as a police post, established there in 1887 for just under a year by Superintendent Sam Steele in response to an uprising by the Ktunaxa people. A reserve had been laid out for the Ktunaxa in 1884 on St. Mary's River, but conflict over land use led to rising tension between ranching investors and the Ktunaxa when Chief Isadore forcibly removed two of his men from gaol in 1887.

The larger history of inter-cultural tensions underlying this event are not described in great detail at the contemporary historic site of Fort Steele, though the outcomes are summarized on a plaque outside the former police buildings: "The police presence led Chief Isadore to relinquish his claims and retire to the reserve. Within a year order had been imposed, leaving the area open for development, and the police post was abandoned." Nearby, a text panel featuring photographs of Chief Isadore and Superintendent Sam Steele tell the same story in somewhat more conciliatory terms: "The combination of Steele's diplomacy and Chief Isadore's wisdom peacefully diffused the tensions," and by the time the NWMP left the district the following year, a "mutual respect had grown between the Ktunaxa and the red coats."[34] Not far from Fort Steele, the imposing building of the former St. Eugene Mission—now a First Nation–owned hotel and casino complex and home to the Ktunaxa Interpretative Centre—provides an alternative glimpse into the future of the reserve-bound Ktunaxa people in the years following the NWMP presence, and the institutionalized life from 1912 of Ktunaxa children at the residential school.

PARALLEL PERSPECTIVES

In the vast majority of popular sites relating to the historical memory of the March West and the NWMP's role in "making" western Canada, First Nation histories and personalities appear alongside those of the NWMP as part of an enduring story of cross-cultural negotiation and mutual respect. Rarely does a First Nation perspective on the arrival and role of the NWMP provide an actual alternative to this nationally powerful narrative. An attempt to do so is visible in two exhibitions at the Glenbow Museum in Calgary: *Mavericks: An Incorrigible History of Alberta* and *Nitsitapiisinni: Our Way of Life*. A history of the Mounties forms one part of the *Mavericks* exhibition, and is represented through parallel perspectives. On the one hand, the NWMP story emerges in terms familiar within the national mythology, emphasizing the hardships the force encountered on its westward march and its role in establishing law and order on the frontier. A diorama of a NWMP encampment includes a darkened tent which, when illuminated, casts the silhouette of a young recruit who relates events of the March West. A display on the foundational figure of James Macleod tells how he "meted out tough but fair justice" on the western frontier, and "embodied the larger-than-life myth of the Mounties." Most entertainingly, a "Great March West" board game sits on display, inviting players to throw a dice and join the NWMP on their long trek west— depending on how the dice falls, players can participate in the different challenges the police faced on their route from Fort Dufferin.

Alongside this well-known narrative of the March West is "A First Nations Perspective," which does not override the mythic story but runs parallel to it. A panel titled "The North-West Mounted Police" relates how, when the force first arrived in Blackfoot territory, they were invited to stay for the winter: "They never left. At first our people thought the Redcoats were helping us...but soon [they] began enforcing their own laws." Another panel describes how the NWMP became "the symbol of the great changes that were coming to our territory":

> We waited for them to learn about us and learn the proper way of co-existing with us.... Some of the police were good men who shared food with us when no bison could be found. Others...did not respect us or our ways.... The police brought laws from the East. The Indian Act, passed by the Canadian government in 1876, placed our lives under the rule of Indian Agents. Our ceremonies were banned. Our travel was restricted. The NWMP enforced these rules.[35]

Next door to the *Mavericks* exhibition is the *Nitsitapiisinni: Our Way of Life* gallery, which opened in 2001 as the outcome of a long collaboration between Alberta's First Nations communities and the Glenbow Museum. A fundamental aim of the gallery's development was to shift the traditional museum focus on objects and artifacts to an emphasis on specific social relationships, experiences and stories.[36] While the *Mavericks* exhibition includes "A First Nations Perspective" on the impact of the NWMP's arrival, the *Nitsitapiisinni: Our Way of Life* gallery tells the story of post-contact life entirely from a First Nations perspective. Its exhibits relate how traditional religious ceremonies were banned, access to traditional lands was lost, and treaties dishonoured as First Nations were subjected to the oppressive policies of the government's Indian Act. The ongoing effects of these policies of the past are commented upon in a display on Treaty 7, the signing of which was overseen by NWMP Commissioner James Macleod in 1877, with the statement: "We do not believe that the governments have ever met their obligations to the treaties."[37]

CONCLUSION

Despite the emergence of a critical Canadian historiography in recent decades which details the role of the NWMP in suppressing First Nations people's autonomy on the western frontier in the course of securing Canadian sovereignty, the public historical memory of the NWMP across western Canada appears to remain overwhelmingly that of building peaceful relations with the First Nations as an integral aspect of establishing "law and order" in the west. At one level there is clear justification for this: the NWMP did enlist negotiating powers rather than force in their implementation of the Queen's law, unlike the United

States military not far to the south, whose contribution to the unfolding history of an explicitly violent frontier has helped to create a different kind of foundational mythology in American national consciousness. Yet despite this contrast with the making of the west in the United States, there seems to be little engagement in the public historical sphere with the ways in which, as Andrew Graybill has put it, Canada's frontier policing history helped to facilitate a thorough conquest of First Nations peoples by the end of the nineteenth century.[38]

That this should be so is perhaps a sign of the practical factors that shape the heritage sector broadly. Reflecting on the changing nature of heritage policy in Canada over the past three decades, Frits Pannokoek argues that market conditions more than community debate has driven the ways that historical understanding is shaped, often leaving little room to "commemorate the marginalized."[39] Yet the benign national image of the NWMP also prevails because, more than their role as peacekeepers and negotiators with First Nations peoples, they play a central role in Canadian historical memory as founding fathers. In the range of historic sites that commemorate the March West across western Canada, the police are the figures who mediate between the pre-settler world and the world to come— precursors to the settlers who would build a life on the land and the railway that would define it as modern. In so far as this view of the NWMP's role in opening up the west shows regional variations along the former route of the March West, it does so for the most part in ways that confirm rather than challenge the national mythology of gentle occupation. Exceptions are the interpretative centre at Fort Walsh and the exhibitions at the Glenbow Museum, which not only point out the often difficult, mundane tasks of a colonial police force, but also offer more critically detailed histories of the impact and consequences of the arrival of the NWMP for the region's First Nations peoples. On the whole, however— from road markers to murals to museums—regional historic sites tend to own the national narrative of the NWMP in locally significant ways rather than to challenge its essentially familiar terms.

As Daniel Francis notes in *National Dreams*, the persistence of national myths entails some forgetting, and "what we choose to forget tells as much about us as what we choose to remember."[40] In an age of anxiety when the familiar is under siege, he argues, such national myths serve to inspire a sense of reassurance by providing a thread of continuity between the past and the present. At the same time, inevitably, they serve to obscure the less-reassuring undercurrents of national history.[41] With few exceptions, the sites of memory relating to the path of the NWMP across western Canada suggest that remembering the role of this colonial police force in the foundation of Canadian sovereignty entails a forgetting or disremembering of its more nuanced roles as an instrument of colonial governance.

NOTES

1   Ken Coates, "The Gentle Occupation: The Settlement and the Dispossession of the First Nations" in *Indigenous Peoples: Rights in Australia, Canada & New Zealand*, ed. Paul Haverman (Auckland: Oxford University Press, 1999), 141.

2   See, for instance, Lorne Brown and Caroline Brown, *An Unauthorized History of the RCMP* (Toronto: James Lorimer and Company, 1973); John Tobias, "Protection, Civilization, Assimilation: An Outline History of Canada's Indian Policy," *Western Canadian Journal of Anthropology* 6, 2 (1976): 13–30; R.C. Macleod, *The North-West Mounted Police and Law Enforcement, 1873–1905* (Toronto: University of Toronto Press, 1976); Katherine Petipas, *Severing the Ties that Bind: Government Repression of Indigenous Religious Ceremonies on the Prairies* (Winnipeg: University of Manitoba Press, 1994); Vic Satzewich, "'Where's the beef?': Cattle Killing, Rations Policy and First Nations' 'Criminality' in Southern Alberta, 1892–1895," *Journal of Historical Sociology* 9 (1996): 188–212; Brian Hubner, "Horse Stealing and the Borderline: The NWMP and the Control of Indian Movement, 1874–1900" in *The Mounted Police and Prairie Society, 1873–1919* ed. W.M. Baker (Regina: University of Regina, Canadian Plains Research Center, 1998), 53–70; John Jennings, "Policemen and Poachers: Indian Relations on the Ranching Frontier" in *The Mounted Police and Prairie Society, 1873–1919*, 41–51; Sarah Carter, *Aboriginal People and Colonizers of Western Canada to 1900* (Toronto: University of Toronto Press, 1999); Roderick Martin, "The North-West Mounted Police and Frontier Justice 1874-1898" (PhD Diss., University of Calgary, 2005); Andrew Graybill, *Policing the Great Plains: Rangers, Mounties, and the North American Frontier, 1875–1910* (Lincoln: University of Nebraska Press, 2007).

3   Macleod, *The North-West Mounted Police*, 22.

4   Syd Harring, "'There seemed to be no recognized law': Canadian Law and the Prairie First Nations" in *Laws and Societies in the Canadian Prairie West*, eds. L. Knafla and J. Swainger (Vancouver: University of British Columbia Press, 2005), 92.

5   For instance, Commissioner's annual report of 1877, republished in *Opening up the West: Official Reports to Parliament of the Activities of the Royal North-West Mounted Police Force 1874–1881* (Toronto: Coles Publishing, 1973).

6   See, for instance, the annual report of P.R. Neale, Appendix E to Commissioner's annual report of 1887, republished in *Opening up the West*.

7   Commissioner's annual report of 1884, republished in *Opening up the West*.

8   Carter, *Aboriginal People*, 161.

9   Pierre Nora, "Reasons for the Current Upsurge in Memory," *Transit* (April 2002). http://www.eurozine.com/articles/2002-04-19-nora-en.html.

10 For instance, John Bodnar, *Remaking America: Public Memory, Commemoration and Patriotism in the 20th Century* (Princeton, NJ: Princeton University Press, 1992); Roy Rosenzweig and D. Thelen, *The Presence of the Past: Popular Uses of History in American Life* (New York: Columbia University Press, 1998); Alon Confino, *Germany as a Culture of Remembrance* (Chapel Hill: University of North Carolina Press, 2006); Margaret Conrad, et al, "Canadians and their Pasts: An Exploration in Historical Consciousness" in *Public History in Canada*, special issue of *The Public Historian* 31, 1 (2009).

11 Lyle Dick, "Public History in Canada: An Introduction" in *Public History in Canada*, special issue of *The Public Historian* 31, 1 (2009): 7; Veronica Strong-Boag, "Experts on Our Own Lives: Commemorating Canada at the Beginning of the Twenty-First Century" in *Public History in Canada*, special issue of *The Public Historian* 31, 1 (2009): 49.

12   RCMP Heritage Centre visitor brochure. http://www.rcmpheritagecentre.com (accessed 1 April 2010).

13   For instance Vanessa Agnew, "What is Re-enactment?"*Criticism* 46, 3 (2004); Stephen Gapps, "Performing the Past: A Cultural History of Historical Re-enactments" (PhD diss., Sydney University of Technology, 2002).

14   RCMP press release, 3 May 1999, http://www.mailarchive.com/nativenews@mlists.net/msg02504.html (accessed 1 April 2010).

15   RCMP March West re-enactment brochure, summer 1999, no publishing details.

16   Conversation with authors.

17   Brian Bergman, "RCMP Recreates Historic March," *The Canadian Encyclopaedia*. www.thecanadianencyclopedia.com/index.cfm (accessed 1 April 2010).

18   Conversation with authors.

19   Fred Stenson, *RCMP: The March West 1873–1999* (Ontario: GAPC Entertainment, 1999), Postscript.

20   "RCMP Re-enact Invasion aka 'Peace and Order,'" anonymous submission, "Settlers in Support of Indigenous Sovereignty," 7 May 1999. http://www.mailarchive.com/nativenews@mlists.net/msg02504.html (accessed 1 April 2010).

21   Points West Trail brochure, no publishing details.

22   See for instance Neil Jarman, "Painting Landscapes: The Place of Murals in the Symbolic Construction of Urban Space," http://cain.ulst.ac.uk/bibdbs/murals/jarman. htm (accessed 1 April 2010); Bill Rolston, *Politics and Painting: Murals and Conflict in Northern Ireland* (Cranbury, NJ: Associated University Presses, 1991).

23   Journal of G.A. French, republished in *Opening up the West*, 27.

24   Hubner, "Horse Stealing and the Borderline," 55-68

25   Commissioner's annual report of 1877, republished in *Opening up the West*.

26   Ibid.

27   Commissioner's annual report of 1881, republished in *Opening up the West*.

28   For instance, Carter, *Aboriginal People*, 129; Graybill, *Policing the Great Plains*, 4.

29   Although the national flag is a familiar aspect of historical sites commemorating national origins, an original flag at the Fort would of course have been the Union Jack.

30   For instance, Brown and Brown, *An Unauthorized History of the RCMP*, 11.

31   Fort Walsh National Historic Site of Canada brochure, Parks Canada, no publishing details.

32   Ibid.

33   Kevin Walsh, *The Representation of the Past: Museums and Heritage in the Post-modern World* (London and New York: Routledge, 1992), 105–110.

34   Explanatory panel, historic site of Fort Steele (visited August 2009); see also http://www.fortsteele.ca.

35   Explanatory panel, *Mavericks: An Incorrigible History of Alberta* exhibition, Glenbow Museum (visited August 2009); see also http://www.glenbow.org/mavericks/.

36   Cara Krmpotich and David Anderson, "Collaborative Exhibitions and Visitor Reactions: The Case of *Nitsitapiisinni: Our Way of Life*," *Curator* 48, no. 4 (2005): 386.

37   Explanatory panel, *Nitsitapiisinni: Our Way of Life* Blackfoot Gallery (visited August 2009); see also http://www.glenbow.org/blackfoot/.

38 Graybill, *Policing the Great Plains*, 58–59.

39 Frits Pannokoek, "Canada's Historic Sites: Reflections on a Quarter Century 1980–2005" in *Public History in Canada*, special issue of *The Public Historian* 31, 1 (2009): 74–75.

40 Daniel Francis, *National Dreams: Myth, Memory and Canadian History* (Vancouver: Arsenal Pulp Press, 1997), 11.

41 Ibid., 172–173.

PREVENTING THE LOSS OF IMPORTED LABOUR
TRAINS, MIGRANTS, AND THE DEVELOPMENT OF THE CANADIAN WEST,[1] 1896—1932

LISA CHILTON

The Canadian West was, in part, the result of aggressive state initiatives. From the systematic separation of First Nations peoples from their lands and traditional lifestyles to the establishment of an outrageously expensive transportation system, the colonization of western Canada involved substantial state investment. Peopling the Prairies and British Columbia with white newcomers of European origin was a key component of federal politicians' plans for Canada's national development. After Confederation, land-based incentives in the form of homesteads were designed to attract farming families to the Canadian prairies, and then to hold them there. But settlers were quick to communicate to local, regional, and federal government officials that the lives of men and women situated in rural areas were just too difficult for most who tried to make a living from farming. Keenly aware of the challenges faced by the Prairies' rural settlers, immigration agents watched with dismay as an endless stream of disgruntled newcomers moved to Canada's urban centres or south to the United States in search of an easier existence.

One of the many grievances communicated to government officials by settlers in the West during the late nineteenth and early twentieth centuries was that it was exceptionally difficult to find and keep adequate waged labour.[2] As a result of serious public pressure, the recruitment of male farm hands and female domestic servants became a top immigration priority for federal state authorities by the early 1890s. Various programs were implemented to entice prospective emigrants of specific age, health, work experience, and ethnic credentials to sign up for migration to the West.[3] Immigrants thus slated for work as labourers on farms east of Ontario were considered valuable commodities by the government bodies that recruited them. Once in transit, these migrants were expected to stick to their original travel plans, regardless of any incentives they might have encountered en route to do otherwise. Efforts to undermine the state's investment in the western settlement of these labourers were typically understood by state officials to be unjustifiable on any grounds. The government's stake in this migration gave state employees the right to overrule various central Canadian interest groups and the migrants themselves concerning their ultimate destinations.

In their efforts to control the movement of working-class immigrants, the Canadian immigration department had willing allies. Despite the fact that the federal government and the Canadian Pacific and Canadian National Railways' (CPR/CNR) managers were motivated by fundamentally different relationships to immigrants and immigration, the railways frequently acted like a branch of the state in their interactions with government-recruited farm labourers and domestic servants.[4] Porters, conductors, and railway security personnel helped state-employed conductresses, interpreters, and immigration agents to police the movements of working-class immigrants.[5]

This chapter will examine some of the political dynamics of organized settlement in the Canadian West through an exploration of the combined efforts of Canadian federal agents and CNR/CPR railway officials to ensure that immigrants who left Europe or the British Isles with the stated intention of working as labourers somewhere west of Ontario actually reached their specified destinations. The case studies drawn upon here highlight tensions between Canada's Anglo-centric nation builders and the aspirations of individuals connected to other ethnic networks. In order to put the activities of the railway and state employees into context, this chapter begins with a brief overview of the system of immigrant care and distribution established by the Canadian government over the course of the nineteenth and early twentieth centuries. The chapter then outlines a sample of situations where the state's efforts to compel immigrants to keep moving westwards resulted in conflict. I conclude with some preliminary thoughts about the significance of these findings for our understanding of state efforts to develop the West.

As early as the 1840s, the government bodies responsible for matters relating to immigration began to put in place a system whereby migrants' movements would be carefully managed and assessed. This system was designed to ensure that the immigrants' early experiences in Canada would contribute to their successful integration into their host communities, and to make it possible for the government to gain information about obstacles to achieving satisfactory rates of immigration in the future. Government officials were sensitive to the ways in which negative commentary about immigrants' initial experiences on Canadian soil could affect attitudes towards immigration in the sending societies. For this reason, the primary stated aim behind the government's establishment of an extensive system of in-transit immigrant supervision was to provide support in order to create the right impression. As one memorandum on the subject made clear, "this branch of work is considered one of the most important in connection with the Immigration Service, as the importance of pleasing the new settler by his first reception in the country and locating him to his satisfaction cannot be overestimated. Very often his first report is alone sufficient to encourage or discourage settlement."[6]

Because trains featured so prominently in migrants' journeys and because train travel in its own right could be a serious trial at the best of times, the federal government and transportation companies employed conductresses and interpreters to provide newcomers with on-board assistance any time numbers seemed to warrant this cost. It was these state employees' responsibility to "look to the comfort and safe journey of the new settlers," to see that the train cars were "properly heated and lighted and not overcrowded." They were expected to communicate with train conductors about the condition of toilet facilities, find medical assistance in times of need, and manage the migrants' appropriate dispersal at the end of their voyages.[7]

A review of correspondence between state officials and railway managers provides a wide range of examples of this sort of support. Two examples are given here to provide a sense of the various ways in which representatives of the state and of the railway companies were willing to intervene in the travel experiences of train passengers. The first example relates to food. Immigrants travelling large distances across Canada by train were reliant upon instantly accessible sources of food, either from station and train restaurants or small-scale vendors for their sustenance while in transit. After their transatlantic journey, fresh food supplies were essential. Of course, there were always enterprising individuals around who saw the immigrants' urgent need to secure food as a personal financial opportunity. Federal and local government agents worked with railway officials to ensure that all reports of inflated prices and poor food quality were investigated and, where necessary, dealt with. Reports by state-employed train conductresses in the spring of 1928 that someone was selling bread to immigrants outside of the Toronto railway station at extortive rates generated a serious hunt for the offending party involving railway and station employees, government officials, various bread vendors, and managers at Toronto's largest bakeries.[8] While the correspondence among officials about the practices of food vendors frequently conveyed racist and class-based prejudices, their attempts to regulate the price and quality of foodstuffs were evidently well received by the migrants themselves.

The second example relates to government and railway officials' efforts to ensure the psychological comfort of in-transit immigrants. Of all of the different immigrants sought during immigration drives, the most carefully managed on their cross-country journey was the single British woman destined to work as a domestic servant in the Dominion. The fact that the demand for domestic servants of a British background always outstripped the available supply was combined in the minds of government officials with racist and gender-based concerns relating to the women's safety to justify an extensive, multi-faceted program of recruitment and care of this particular class of migrants.[9] In order that these women would feel comfortable in transit, government agents and railway employees were expected to go to great lengths to ensure that they would not be offended by the behaviour of other-ethnic travellers on the trains. Whenever possible, British women were given their own compartments on the trains and separate areas within which to wait at transfer stations. When numbers did not warrant separate spaces for these immigrants, their conductresses attempted to secure an empty buffer zone around them in their carriages so that they would have to mingle with the "foreigners" as little as possible.[10]

As the latter example suggests, the care that state and railway officials provided for immigrants in transit was not evenly distributed. The provision of a comfortable travel environment for one group of immigrants could significantly undermine the comfort of others. In this case, migrants other than the British domestics received less space, or were forced to move, for the pleasure of the more privileged chaperoned women. This example also highlights the policing involved in caring for these migrants—not only were other train travellers monitored and managed in terms of their behaviour around the chaperoned female migrants, but the migrant women themselves were observed, assessed, and disciplined for behaviour considered socially inappropriate. As Marianna Valverde and Barbara Roberts have shown, the in-transit care of migrants became an important element in a state system that would deport thousands of immigrants during the early decades of the twentieth century.[11] There were many aspects of the state's program of care for migrants in transit that the migrants would rather have done without.

The politics of immigrant distribution within Canada regularly taxed federal state officials, who were expected to respond to the needs of a wide variety of interested parties. The primary concern of the immigration department might have been to see large numbers of appropriate immigrants settled in the West, but federal politicians and bureaucrats were well aware that they ignored the concerns of central Canadians at their peril. They were sensitive to the animosity that existed in Ontario and Quebec concerning these provinces' substantial financial contributions toward the development of western Canada. They were also highly conscious of the demand that existed in the eastern parts of the Dominion for domestic servants and some categories of male waged labourers.[12] As a lengthy memorandum by an astute high commissioner writing in the early 1890s explained, any program designed to recruit domestic servants only for the West was likely to arouse the jealousy of the older provinces. It would thus be politic to at least gesture toward a distribution program that included some central Canadian destinations.[13] The tensions raised in central Canada around the state's financial support of settlement in the West were matched by rural-urban tensions of a similar nature. In a period when settled Canadians and immigrants alike were increasingly oriented towards migration into the nation's urban centres, the immigration department saw its responsibility as first and foremost to prop up agricultural areas through targeted immigration programs.[14] Yet prospective employers in urban centres regularly voiced their disapproval of the biases toward rural Canada in immigration policies, and they used a variety of means to tap into the labour pool established through government programs.

The correspondence generated around one of the many short-lived programs to bring domestic servants into agricultural areas east of Ontario demonstrates some of these competing demands and resulting tensions. In 1898 Mrs. Livingston, a woman well-experienced in immigration work, was employed to recruit and chaperone a large party of Scottish emigrant women to the Prairies. Almost immediately, Livingston became embroiled in distribution-related controversy. Recruitment proved to be more difficult than anticipated, and so the number of servants available for self-identified prospective employers was seriously restricted. William McCreary, the commissioner of immigration at Winnipeg, wrote to the deputy minister of the interior, James Smart, to complain: "From your letters of instruction as well as a conversation had with you, I inferred that the object was to supply the farmers with help, but I fear that Mrs. Livingston having had so many letters from personal friends in the cities and towns she has been obliged to depart somewhat from the original intention."[15] McCreary's concerns were well-founded—Livingston had indeed been lobbied hard by various city-dwelling homeowners looking for domestic help. But prospective employers in western urban centres were hardly the only cause of the party's attrition; before these immigrants even arrived in Canada, several had been slated for the private residences of influential politicians and bureaucrats located in Montreal and Ottawa.[16]

As this case shows, immigration officials were determined to direct the movements of immigrants as far as possible. In instances where a financial investment had been made—in the form of bonuses to independent immigration agents or in the form of subsidized travel—they believed that the migrants had contracted themselves to settle according to state directives. The origins of these sorts of assertions on the part of state authorities, together with the collusion of transportation companies to encourage migrants' compliance, can be seen as early as the 1840s.[17] However, this understanding of the obligations of migrants to go to specific destinations, and the right of the state and collaborating businesses to act coercively to achieve these ends became more entrenched during the Sifton era, when the state invested more heavily into immigrant recruitment programs. They became central to the state's relationship with immigrants during the second half of the 1920s, when the Railways Agreement was in place.[18]

The example of Livingston's chaperoned party of servants highlights another theme that runs through the correspondence relating to the state's efforts to determine immigrants' settlement patterns: from the moment that migrants representing desired employable labour started out on their travels to and across Canada, they became of interest to various parties who sought to affect their choice of destination. In this particular case it was the friends and superiors of their chaperone who sought to redirect the migrants. In the cases discussed below, interested parties attempted to circumvent the state's employees completely. Drawing upon past personal relationships and like-ethnic associations and identities, these individuals sought rather to communicate directly with the migrants themselves about alternative destination possibilities.

The Canadian state, in collaboration with railway officials, constituted a forceful (though not always effective) influence on migrants' decisions about whether or not to settle in the Canadian West. In theory, every immigrant was supposed to be kept under the constant watch of a state official until his or her successful integration into Canadian society had been achieved. The standard justification for this supervision was benevolent, but in reality there was a significant coercive edge to the in-transit management of migrants. State officials and railway managers endeavoured to force all lower-class immigrants to behave according to prescribed codes of conduct and to follow the travel plans laid out for them in advance of their arrival on Canadian soil. Their efforts were frequently thwarted by immigrants who had had alternative plans from the beginning or who were encouraged to change their plans by people they met along the way.

The major urban centres that migrants heading west might pass through in central Canada were considered special sites of trouble by the various officials charged with ensuring that immigrants reached their destinations. As the busiest of the railway transfer points, Montreal was typically responsible for the immigration officials' most serious headaches. Not only was the volume of traffic higher there than anywhere else, but the design of Bonaventure Station was such that it was exceedingly difficult to keep immigrants isolated from the general public. As M.V. Burnham of the Women's Branch of the Department of Immigration and Colonization noted in a letter to F.C. Blair, the agents charged with ensuring that immigrants did not disappear while waiting to be transferred to a west-bound train faced a herculean task at this station. She described how matrons assigned to specific parties of immigrant women tried to confine their charges to an upstairs waiting room, where they would "stand guard" until it was time to board the next train. On one occasion, she wrote, "there were three woman officers in the station...who had all they could do to control the situation and to prevent relatives and so-called friends from interfering."[19] As far as the government officials were concerned, it was preferable that migrants in transit interacted with no-one they might consider a friend, be they bona fide blood relations or not. On occasions when such interactions were sanctioned, the agents made it clear that permission to do so was not automatic, but should be considered a special favour—perhaps a reward for behaviour that indicated that the immigrant might be trusted.[20]

It was clear to immigration officials that railway stations were impossible locations to control. There was too much movement, too much activity, and too much to watch for to be able to control all interactions between immigrants and members of the public. Of particular concern in cities like Montreal and Toronto were people who claimed that they were representatives of transportation companies or ethnic organizations. Individuals who attempted to gain access to the immigrants on this basis were carefully scrutinized by state and railway employees alike, who combined information to determine the legitimacy of all such representations. One of the conductresses' reports on the movement of a party of immigrants neatly encapsulates the challenges that individuals in the business of receiving and working with immigrants from their own ethnic communities faced when trying to navigate the official system of immigrant care so that they could interact with newcomers. "Among the persons who met the train," the conductress wrote, was Mr Leptich, "who is interested in the passengers from the Holland American and other Lines. He has opened the Globe Travelling Office, 1070 Union Ave, Lanc. 6319 and intends to have an Employment Office there. He also runs a boarding house at this address. He states that he is an Officer in the Deutsche Gesselshaft [sic], the German Club Harmonia and the Swiss Canadian Fund." Leptich's careful provision of details about his identity and professional connections were not sufficient to convince Mr. Bain, an officer working in the CNR's Investigation Department. According to the conductress' report, Mr. Leptich was unlikely to be allowed on the station platform again, as Mr. Bain "does not think that he should be treated as a bona fide steamship Agent."[21]

In April 1930, the efforts of government and railway authorities to protect immigrants from members of the general public at the railway station in Toronto nearly sparked a riot. According to the report submitted by one of the chaperones, Miss Chase, her "alien" immigrant charges were all transferred from their train to the Immigration Waiting Room under guard, "as men from the city were trying to entice them out." Some of the immigrants made the mistake of alerting Chase to the fact that they desired to change their minds about going west—a move that resulted in increased security. They had "begged" her "to let them go," as they had friends or relatives in Kitchener or Toronto and wished to stay with them rather than continuing on as they were expected to do. Chase noted that she had explained to the immigrants "that they must keep the contract," and this advice was supported by a priest who had volunteered on the spot to assist her. "No girls escaped from the waiting room, but only because I was there every minute and had a detective with me," wrote Chase. "As the crowd of men [at the station] grew so dense and annoying a number were arrested and set off in a patrol wagon." According to Chase, this had a "salutary effect on the remainder." Yet some of the immigrants still managed to get away from their guards. After having been placed on the west-bound train and put under the guard of CNR policemen, six women managed to disembark and melt away into the crowd only ten minutes before the train's departure. "No official would believe it possible," Chase recalled, "but I re-checked and counted and convinced them." Because of the exceptionally determined challenges to the conductress' authority experienced in this instance, the CNR's Chief Investigating Officer, Mr. Hamilton, escorted the immigrants from Toronto to Sudbury, after which a police officer patrolled the train until it passed Capreol.[22]

As far as immigration authorities were concerned, immigrants' desires to congregate with people of like ethnicity were highly problematic and needed to be strongly discouraged.[23] Single women who demonstrated a strong inclination to travel with men of their own ethnicity rather than stay with their chaperoned parties of women of various ethnic backgrounds were represented in the official correspondence as "trouble." From the perspective of the chaperones, such behaviour clearly indicated evidence of loose morals.[24] This perspective was not held by all members of the immigration service; there were some who understood the problem as one that was not necessarily linked to moral deviance. A memorandum written by the assistant deputy minister of immigration and colonization in 1930 demonstrates a more insightful understanding of the larger picture, though he too was concerned with how to ensure a greater degree of immigrant compliance. "We are well aware of the trouble that the conductresses have in getting parties of domestics through to the West," he wrote. "It is quite a common thing to lose a number of girls between the ocean port and Winnipeg but these girls are not lost in the ordinary sense of the word but merely take advantage of the break in the rail journey to leave the train and join relatives or friends in Eastern Canada or sometimes the United States." He considered the various efforts that had been made to "provide a remedy" unlikely to be successful as things stood at that time. "If we had the co-operation of the young women themselves, that is to say, if they wanted to be protected, we would have no trouble but when they want to get away...it is very difficult to prevent losses en route."[25] When one considers the fact that the women assigned to chaperoned parties of mixed ethnicity were sometimes travelling on the same train as siblings or close friends from back home, that they did not necessarily speak English, and that they would have been feeling a wide range of emotions about leaving home, it is astonishing that the chaperones had any success at all in their efforts to keep unwilling immigrants in their parties. .

While major urban centres in Quebec and Ontario provided special challenges for the immigration agents and railway employees responsible for keeping their charges on a direct path to the West, there were also losses reported on the presumably benign route between Ottawa or Toronto and Winnipeg. Sioux Lookout, Nakina, Hearst, and Cochrane—relatively rough, undeveloped stops along the way to Manitoba—became sites of intense immigration policing in the 1920s. The correspondence among immigration and railway officials relating to the "theft" of immigrants at these locations is fascinating for what it reveals about these officials' attitudes about these communities, their inhabitants of East European origin, and the relationship between the state and immigrants in transit. One of the conductresses' reports, which was quoted and embellished freely by her superiors, lays out the basic situation:

> At Sioux Lookout on July 24th, when I was passing through en route to Winnipeg, with a Special train, Letitia and Megantic passengers, a foreign woman came to the train, and began talking to my foreign girls. I recognized her at once as a woman who got two of my passengers off but not away, early this spring. I have seen her several times since, but her attempts were not successful.

> I watched her carefully and when she saw the police were also watching, she left[.] Two hours later she returned dressed in a different costume, and with a small child, but seeing she had no chance left at once.

> The following information I received from the Police and a reputable man. Her name is Poletka (or sounds so when pronounced) she keeps

a lodging house (of sorts). Her star lodger was arrested last week for boot-legging, and the Provincial Police told me in confidence that they were raiding her house shortly. Her husband also frequents the train and gets men off. He is a small, well dressed man of the slick type, has been in Canada seventeen years and not naturalized.[26]

Other conductresses had also reported experiencing problems in the way of un-invited visitors who had tried to convince immigrants to get off the train at their stations. A thorough investigation ensued, which led to the information that the woman named in the above-quoted report was in fact a Mrs. Plytka, whose husband (the "slick" male) worked at the CNR roundhouse. The investigators discovered that other "foreigners" had also tried to talk with the immigrants. For example, "Mrs. N. Rodroski, formerly a Ukrainian school-teacher...admit-ted that she frequently had had conversations with immigrants, but denied that she had ever persuaded any to leave the train." Likewise, Mrs. J. Anderson and Mrs. Z. Hancharuk were implicated in the efforts of Sioux Lookout's residents' efforts to increase their population with East European immigrants destined for settlements further west. Although the local constable testified that these various individuals were respectable members of his community, the higher state authorities and their railway associates maintained a firm stance. The im-plicated men and women "were warned that their activities in interfering with immigrants must stop, or otherwise drastic action would be instituted."[27] It is worth noting that a year later, reports were still being filed which complained that Sioux Lookout operatives—likely the Plytkas—were still active, and that they regularly endeavoured to use disguises to get past the immigrants' guards.[28] Clearly, the residents of Sioux Lookout were not thoroughly cowed by the state's threat of force.

It is not clear what these immigrants were told about their rights and obliga-tions in relation to the Department of Immigration upon their departure from Europe. The sources are vague regarding whether the state actually had the pow-er to compel them to stay on track to their predetermined destinations in the West and it is not clear whether signed contracts were involved. Evidence sug-gests that immigration authorities and their associates working for the railways generally had to rely upon their ability to cajole, bluff, and bully the immigrants travelling under their supervision, although the power to initiate deportation proceedings would have served as a useful tool in instances where more serious concerns about immigrant intransigence were raised.

For those who worked under the direction of federal state officials, the rail-way was supposed to be merely a means by which migrants were transported directly from Canada's eastern ports to pre-determined destinations in the West. By contrast, these migratory journeys opened up interesting possibilities for new immigrants in transit that, if explored, involved collaboration with people of like ethnic background in opposition to Canadian state authorities. As the examples outlined above suggest, there was no one typical immigrant experience of train travel during the periods of most intense state supervision. Some of the differences in experience can be explained in terms of the particularities of the system of care that the state put in place. For example, men who wished to leave the train prematurely found it relatively easy to do so. There was far more supervision of female migrants, because the added concern about women's safety—as understood by middle-class bureaucrats and reformers—served to justify increased resources put toward their control. But there were also variations in the attitudes of the immigrants themselves. Some migrants were apparently content to disembark according to state officials' orders, whereas others energetically resisted the state's determination of their itinerary. An individual's gender, ethnicity, and social connections (or lack thereof) with people in the communities through which he or she passed were only some of the many possible reasons for differences in perspective and experience.

Histories of the Canadian West have emphasized the active parts played by various levels of the Canadian government in the post-Confederation settlement of the region. The state invested heavily in immigration and in the infrastructure that would help to keep those immigrants on-site. Case studies ranging from explorations of African American efforts to settle in the region to works on the history of immigration and labour radicalism show that the state was actively involved in discouraging and removing newcomers to the Prairies who were considered undesirable.[29] An examination of the cases explored in this paper contributes to our understanding of how the state endeavoured to shape the West through a combination of investment and coercion. It highlights the complexities of immigrant agency in the face of state regulation, and the clash between the state's vision for the West and the immigrants' understandings of their own place in Canadian society and its economy.

NOTES

1 While some of what I have to say below relates to most of the Canadian West, this paper is really about the Prairies rather than British Columbia.

2 Library and Archives Canada (hereafter LAC), RG 76, Vol. 113, File 22787, Part 1 (Roll C4776), To Hon John Carling, Minister of Agriculture, from Geo H Campbell Ottawa, 15 Dec 1891.

3 For example: see Valerie Knowles' discussion of the turn-of-the-twentieth century North Atlantic Trading Company immigration program, a clandestine operation whereby shipping companies received higher than usual bonuses for bona fide agricultural settlers. *Strangers at Our Gates: Canadian Immigration Policy, 1840–2006*, rev. ed. (Toronto: Dundurn Press, 2007), 92–3. See also Donald Avery's discussion of the Railways Agreement (1925–1929) in *'Dangerous Foreigners': European Immigrant Workers and Labour Radicalism in Canada, 1896–1932* (Toronto: McClelland and Stewart, 1979), 99–112. For information concerning the recruitment of domestic servants see Lisa Chilton, *Agents of Empire: The Migration of Single British Women to Canada and Australia, 1860–1930* (Toronto: University of Toronto Press, 2007).

4 Avery, *Dangerous Foreigners*, 99–112; Gerald Friesen, *The Canadian Prairies: A History* (Toronto: University of Toronto Press, 1987), especially Chapter 8.

5 In all of the correspondence among officials working with immigrants, the managers of the railways were clear about their desire to assist the federal government's representatives in any way possible to "safe-guard the movement" of any immigrants considered the state's charges. LAC RG 76, Vol. 139, File 33175, Part 1, letter from J. Black, CNR, to A. L. Jolliffe, Department of Immigration and Colonization, 7 November 1928. It was clearly in the railway's best interests to do so. The Railways Agreement stipulated that immigrants imported under this agreement would be repatriated at the expense of the railway corporation in the event that he or she had not settled in the West within a year of their arrival. Avery, 100–101.

6 LAC, RG 76, Vol. 139, File 33175, Part 1 "Memorandum for the Minister," Department of the Interior, 17 June 1899.

7 Ibid.

8 LAC, RG 76, Vol 139, File 33175, Part 1, see correspondence during spring 1928.

9 Marilyn Barber, *Immigrant Domestic Servants in Canada* (Ottawa: Canadian Historical Association, 1991); Chilton, *Agents of Empire*; Rebecca Mancuso, "'This is our work': The Women's Division of the Canadian Department of Immigration and Colonization, 1919–1938" (PhD diss., McGill University, 1999); Barbara Roberts, "'A Work of Empire': Canadian Reformers and British Female Immigration," in *A Not Unreasonable Claim: Women and Reform in Canada, 1880s–1920s*, ed. Linda Kealey (Toronto: University of Toronto Press, 1979).

10 Lisa Chilton, "Travelling Colonist: British emigration and the construction of Anglo-Canadian privilege," in *Empire, Identity and Migration in the British World*, eds. Andrew S. Thompson and Kent Fedorowich (Manchester: Manchester University Press, 2013).

11 Barbara Roberts, *Whence They Came: Deportation from Canada, 1900–1935* (Ottawa: University of Ottawa Press, 1988); Mariana Valverde, *The Age of Light, Soap, and Water: Moral Reform in English Canada, 1885–1925* (Toronto: McClelland and Stewart, 1991).

12 Roberts, "A Work of Empire"; Marilyn Barber, "The Women Ontario Welcomed: Immigrant Domestics for Ontario Homes, 1870–1930," *Ontario History* 72 (September 1980): 155-166; Marilyn Barber, "Sunny Ontario for British Girls," in *Looking into My Sister's Eyes: An Exploration in Women's History*, ed. Jean Burnet (Toronto: Multicultural History Society of Ontario, 1986); Marilyn Barber, "The Servant Problem in Manitoba, 1896–1930," in *First Days, Fighting Days: Women in Manitoba History*

(Regina: Canadian Plains Research Center, University of Regina, 1987); David Gouter, *Guarding the Gates: The Canadian Labour Movement and Immigration, 1872–1934* (Toronto: University of British Columbia Press, 2007).

13   LAC, RG 76, Vol. 113, 1893. File 22787, Part 1 (Roll C4776), Extract of a letter from the High Commissioner dated April 7.

14   A particularly good discussion of these issues may be found in chapters 3, 4, and 5 of Ninette Kelley and Michael Trebilcock, *The Making of the Mosaic: A History of Canadian Immigration Policy* (Toronto: University of Toronto Press, 1998).

15   LAC, File 22787, Part 1 (Roll C4776), William F. McCreary, Commissioner of Immigration, Winnipeg, 31 May 1898, to James A. Smart, Deputy Minister of the Interior.

16   LAC, File 22787, Part 1 (Roll C4776), Murray to James A. Smart, Deputy Minister of the Interior, Ottawa, 4 June 1898. These servants were to go to the homes of Clifford Sifton, James A. Smart, and the Hon Mr. Fisher. This incident was hardly unique; organized groups of domestic servant immigrants regularly lost their most experienced members to influential politicians, bureaucrats, etc. For other examples, see Chilton, Chapter 5: "Welcoming Women: Reception Work in Canada and Australia," in *Agents of Empire*.

17   Lisa Chilton, "Managing Migrants in Toronto, 1820–1880," *Canadian Historical Review*, 92:2 (June 2011): 231–62.

18   The Railways Agreement (1925–1929) established the right of the railway companies to recruit immigrants in parts of Europe that previously had been designated "undesirable." For details, see Avery, *Dangerous Foreigners*, 99–103; Knowles, *Strangers at Our Gates*, 141–2.

19   LAC, RG 76, Vol. 139, File 33175, Part 1, Memorandum from M. V. Burnham, Supervisor, Women's Branch of the Immigration Department, to Frederick C. Blair, 14 November 1928.

20   See, for example, the discussion concerning immigrant Miss Chalka Olin, who was allowed to visit with her brother and his friend, closely watched by one of the immigration agents at Montreal. LAC, RG 76, Vol. 139, File 33175, Part 1, Report by Miss Greg to M. V. Burnham, 29 January 1929.

21   LAC, RG 76, Vol. 139, File 33175, Part 1, Report by Miss Greg to M. V. Burnham, 29 January 1929.

22   Extract from Train Conductress' Report, Miss Chase, 12 April 1930. For a period after this incident the immigrants were guarded so closely that it was impossible for them to acquire food while at the station. See Assistant Deputy Minister, Department of Immigration and Colonization, to J S McGowan, Dept of Colonization, CNR, 28 April 1930. Both documents in LAC, RG 76, Vol 139, File 33175, Part 1.

23   As Kelley and Trebilcock note in relation to Ukrainians, immigration agents instructed to prevent ethnic group settlements usually failed, "for the agents were unable to persuade new immigrants that it was best for them to settle in areas distant from their compatriots." Kelly and Trebilcock, *Making the Mosaic*, 131.

24   See, for example, the case of Hilda Buchholz, described in an extract from Miss McKenney's Train Conductress' Report, Conducted to Toronto "Dresden," 2 March 1930. LAC, RG 76, Vol. 139, File 33175, Part 1.

25   LAC, RG 76, Vol. 139, File 33175, Part 1, Assistant Deputy Minister, Memo, 26 April 1930.

26   LAC, RG 76, Vol. 139, File 33175, Part 1, Millicent Chase, Conductress, to A.S.M. Bullock, 28 July 1928.

27   LAC, RG 76, Vol. 139, File 33175, Part 1, W.J. Black, CNR, to A.L. Jolliffe, Dept of Immigration and Colonization, 7 November 1928.

28   LAC, RG 76, Vol. 139, File 33175, Part 1. See the extract from Millicent Chase's report and M.V. Burnham's letter to W.J. Black, 3 May 1929.

29   See Knowles, *Strangers at our Gates*, 117–9, on the efforts of the federal government to exclude Black Americans from the region and Avery, *Dangerous Foreigners,* on efforts to ensure that all communists and potential disseminators of pro-union politics would be barred or deported.

RAILWAYS, RACISM, AND CHINESENESS ON THE PRAIRIES[1]

ALISON R. MARSHALL

The historical terrain of railway infrastructure—the main and branch lines, the telegraph poles built alongside the tracks, the stations and cars—both fixed and enabled the transcendence of stereotypical Chinese-Canadian identities.[2] It also provided the framework out of which Chinese-Canadian settlements grew. This paper focuses on the Prairies, from the late 1870s when settlement began to the period around 1947—the year that the fourth and final version of the Chinese Immigration Act (first enacted in 1885) was repealed, all Chinese Canadians were able to vote, and Chinese women and families left behind could begin coming to Canada.

Winnipeg, Manitoba was the transportation centre of Canada and the prairie headquarters of Chinese political and voluntary organizations. This chapter draws heavily on life stories of Chinese Canadians who, at some point in their lives, resided in Winnipeg and lived in the shadows of mainstream society.[3] While the number of Chinese Canadians who settled in Winnipeg and later on the Prairies is relatively low, almost everyone I interviewed during this research program had lived in the city at some point, if only briefly. Many Chinese, en route from either Montreal or Vancouver, changed trains in Winnipeg, visited the immigration hall, and, while waiting for eastbound trains to arrive, visited the city's well-stocked Chinatown, which was a short walk from the Canadian Pacific Railway (CPR) station. Some Chinese travellers decided to stay in Winnipeg.

In the paragraphs that follow I attempt to understand the impact of railways on ordinary and more powerful Chinese residents. In the case of powerful merchant-class Chinese, railways were, in the words of Lisa Lowe, "cross-race and cross-national projects to change the existing power, the current hegemony."[4] Railway work, travel, and networks helped Chinese men, seen as low-class minority bachelors, break down some of the barriers that prevented their acceptance by white society. The same was not true for all Chinese—for women, labourers, Chinese missionaries and ministers limited by their gender and incomes, railway networks, personnel and coaches presented conditions that inflamed and fixed racist attitudes.

Railways were built by early foreign labourers, many of whom were of Chinese origin. Most of these Chinese labourers, who resided in BC, were not given the status of citizen.[5] Some of them were allowed to reside in Canada after the rail lines were completed, but none of the Chinese labourers were invited to the last strike ceremony in November 1885 that celebrated the completion of the first phase of the CPR's transcontinental railway. That Chinese labour, Chinatown settlement patterns, and identity were defined by the railway is not a novel idea. It is well known that over 17,000 Chinese came to Canada to work on the railroad in 1881, and that many died in the process. The work was hard and Chinese were paid little. James Carmichael, who was travelling from Montreal to Victoria in the 1880s, remarked on the Chinese workers he saw as he travelled through the beautiful Fraser Valley, "This whole section is very beautiful, as the mountains are wooded in some places from base to summit. All the workmen you see along the line are Chinamen—melancholy-faced, plaited-haired, low stunted looking Chinamen—some of them the ugliest looking mortals I ever looked at, but for men doing hard railway work, unusually clean looking."[6] Chinese men were known not only by the racist term "Chinaman" but also by other pejorative monikers such as coolies (Mandarin: *kuli*), a term that predated migration to Canada and railroad work but literally meant bitter (or *ku*) strength (or *li*) and became quickly associated with the railway. The term "chink" referred to the sound of Chinese men swinging their picks to build its tracks. It became loosely applied to the Chinese cooks who made the food for the gangs of railway workers and to the men who worked in coal mines, canneries, or in market gardens. It also came to be associated with the men who finished their railway contracts and gambled on a life operating a washing shop or café under harsh conditions in small-town prairie Canada.

In 1885, the year of the completion of the first phase of the construction of the CPR's transcontinental main line, Canada enacted the first version of the Chinese Immigration Act that was designed to keep Chinese from emigrating to and working in Canada. Although Chinese were at first deterred by the poll tax of fifty dollars, eventually they started to emigrate to Canada in large numbers, again. Many Chinese initially settled in British Columbia and then travelled east along the new lines and settled in small prairie cities, towns, and villages, where they opened businesses. Some bought lots from the Canadian Pacific Railway and others rented space to operate train station laundries, cafés, and dry goods shops on Railway avenues throughout the Prairies. By the 1890s at least one Chinese business had been established in most places that could be reached by railway lines in Manitoba. By 1911, the same was true in Saskatchewan.[7] Through repeated associations with rail travel and the construction of the railways, Chinese came to be known in negative ways—not only as "coolie" and "chink," but also as "celestial," "bachelor," "laundryman," "Chinaman," and "prostitute."

RACISM

People got onto trains (or were put onto them "in bonds" or in boxes)[8] at various stations across the country in Vancouver, Lethbridge, Calgary, Regina, and other places, bringing with them different kinds and degrees of racism. In this way, railways disseminated racist attitudes and behaviours. But new rail technology also enabled Chinese to redefine themselves in societies just being conceived and mitigate discrimination, to some extent. Train travel was an adventure—you boarded trains and sometimes shared a coach with itinerant salesmen, wealthy British travellers, performers, or someone from the labouring class. Train travel was a white British domain defined by workers of chiefly British stock, values, and customs such as kettles and teapots on board for British travellers and train conductors. Yet the experience also provided an opportunity for the mixing of cultures, cross-cultural communication, and even understanding during the many hours seatmates spent talking and possibly sharing food. Train travel enabled the most powerful and affluent Chinese men, when allowed to share first-class cars, to break into the highest ranks of Canadian society.

Railways and stations enabled Chinese men to be mobile and to move away from places where there were large Chinatowns and ghettos, economic competition, and racism. A small number of Chinese men moved to the Canadian Prairies. People on the Canadian Prairies were generally less hostile toward Chinese immigrants than those who lived elsewhere in Canada, with Manitoba being the least hostile and parts of Saskatchewan being the most.[9] In Manitoba, people were modest and fairly accepting of newcomers who were different; freedom and an entrepreneurial spirit characterized Alberta and its welcoming attitude.[10] Saskatchewan was different. Chinese could not vote and for a time could not employ white women. Here, settler identities had to conform to more polarized stereotypes—assimilated or traditional Chinese.

Saskatchewan-born Chinese Canadians were repeatedly warned to participate, conform, and not make trouble. Racism was more severe in Saskatchewan, I suspect, because Chinese men had settled there almost two decades after they had settled in Manitoba. While Saskatchewan's Chinese population was still negligible in 1900, in the ten years that followed large numbers of Chinese men moved to Saskatchewan's villages, towns, and cities. By 1911 Census data shows that the number of Chinese in Saskatchewan had exceeded the number of Chinese in Manitoba.[11] Discussions with research participants born during the exclusion era (1923/4–1947) suggested that Chinese women were more negatively regarded by dominant society and generally associated with a lack of propriety or prostitution. While Chinese-born and Chinese-Canadian women were scarce in most provinces, they were more numerous in Saskatchewan. Thus, the rapid influx of large numbers of young Chinese men—unattached to families, churches, or elders—to a large number of locations, and the comparatively high number of Saskatchewan Chinese women, may have led to an increase in racism. Racism was made worse by the misplaced fear that white women could be harmed by the ubiquitous and unattached young Chinese man.[12]

Chinese populations were small, and were presumed to pose less of a threat to white labour on the Canadian Prairies. The ethnic makeup of a place may have played a role, too. Several prairie towns had large non-British, European settlements: Esterhazy, Saskatchewan had a large Hungarian population, Dauphin, Manitoba had a strong Ukrainian background, and towns such as Baldur, Manitoba had a sizeable Icelandic population. The harsh conditions of prairie life also made the cultivation of good human relationships essential. Winter on the Prairies generally lasted from November to April, and people needed each other during the coldest months. These six months were spent indoors and in the company of others. For this reason, people on the Prairies welcomed newcomers into their community with greater frequency than those living in British Columbia where mild winters, moderate climates, and stunning landscapes drew one's attention away from people and toward nature.[13]

THE IMPACT OF RAILWAY EXPERIENCES ON CHINESE LIVES

Mobility and new technologies like rail travel dislodged fixed impressions of difference and enabled the more powerful Chinese leaders to make use of railway networks to build intercultural bridges between Chinese and non-Chinese society, and to create multiple overlapping identities for themselves. Chinese community leaders used railway networks to break down cultural stereotypes and fixed ideas linking race, class, and appearance (but not gender), and to reinvent cultural spaces for their own use. While the new networks and matrices used by dominant Chinese successfully transformed and reinvented large-scale white dominant social perceptions and spaces, they nevertheless were constrained by the need for margins where those who by nature of gender, connectedness, and economic status resided. To some extent, elite Chinese used power and networks to create difference between themselves and those without money or connections.[14]

In order to understand the ways in which railway networks and train travel shifted the understanding of Chineseness, I examine a range of accounts of Chinese labourers, and those belonging to dominant Chinese society. What this data reveals is a more complicated picture of the railway's impact on the private—or, in the words of Erving Goffman, "back-stage"—lives of men from different parts of Chinese society.[15] Chinese dramatic performers, coal miners, loggers, and laundry workers relied on the branch and main lines to move from one job or performance to the next. Low-paid Chinese missionary workers and ministers travelled by train, visiting cafés and laundries throughout most of the Prairies and the rest of Canada. There were wealthier, powerful Chinese who were interpreters, ticket agents, activists, politicians, and community leaders with economic, social, political, and cultural capital due in part to modern train technology. And there were Chinese women on trains, of course. Chinese women travelled from China and Vancouver to the Prairies to join new husbands or to live in Winnipeg at girls' homes where they might be able to find a good merchant husband.

Although many Chinese remained in Canada after the railroad was completed and some settled on the Prairies, others had to return home. But Chinese kept coming to Canada. They sailed from Hong Kong to Vancouver, a trip that took about four weeks. When they arrived in Vancouver, they disembarked and reported to the Immigration Hall where (after 1903, and if they did not have merchant or other special status) they had to pay the $500 head tax. Chinese were subjected to medical examinations, and had to have their hearing and eyes checked. A clerk would examine their papers, compare their appearance to their immigration photograph, and note (after 1910) their final Canadian destination on the General Register of Chinese Immigration. From there, Chinese would be corralled into the CPR detention hall, and sometimes detained. This experience was an especially traumatic and life-changing experience for women. Some daughters of early Chinese-Canadian women remarked on a mother's detainment, sometimes for as long as five weeks. Male contract workers travelling through Canada on their way to New York, Boston, Cuba, Mexico, Trinidad, or South America to work in factories and on plantations travelled in special secure cars, sometimes in chains and with bodyguards. The men were referred to in newspaper articles as "Chinamen travelling in bond." Early settlers described these cars as having screens on the windows. The doors on either side were locked so that none of the men who signed contracts could escape. Guards were posted outside the doors. CPR Immigration officials arranged for Chinese grocers to provide Chinese foods including sausage, cured fish, tofu, and Chinese vegetables to the men on the journey. Each of the cars also had a stove so the men could prepare a hot Chinese meal.

Detainment was followed by a long ride to what was often a small prairie town in a third-class car. A Chinese-Canadian female passenger would likely have been the only woman of her own ethnicity riding on the train, and many people would have assumed she was a prostitute. One boy, now an elderly gentleman, suggested that this stereotype prevailed even in the 1950s. When he first emigrated to Canada from Hong Kong, he travelled with his sister, and a few other Chinese boys, by train to the Prairies. At one point during the trip two railway workers came up to him and his friends, and began talking to them. They were friendly enough but they were swearing in Chinese, which was offensive to his sister, still a young girl. He knew the men would not have sworn in the presence of a white girl. He sternly told the men not to use this language in front of a lady. They laughed and walked away.[16]

The railway reinforced the assumption that all Chinese women were heathen prostitutes and bachelors "Chinamen," if male. Until the 1920s and '30s, accounts often referred to large "herd-like" numbers of Chinese passengers with disparaging language, suggestive of their inhumanity. Large groups of Chinese on trains were a threat—in the mid-1890s Laura Johnstone described the costumes and behaviour of forty-five "Chinamen" who shared her waiting room, presumably in British Columbia:

> At one end of the waiting-room forty-five Chinamen were standing or sitting over their baggage, refugees from the United States, waiting for the express to convey them to Vancouver. I afterwards saw several more, standing, as if in an ecstasy, round a barrel of apples in front of a fruiterer's shop in Main Street, Winnipeg. Their costume, which was exactly alike, was a Yankee modification of the Chinese labourer's dress; and they seemed well supplied with dollars. Canada will not have them, except in British Columbia, where they are admitted on a payment of about £50 a head, so they are passed on, in bond as it were, from the United States, whence they have been expelled.[17]

In 1900, 145 Chinese male travellers in bond were documented in Brandon. Here Chinese passengers were referred to as "Celestials", a term that was occasionally used throughout North America and in Australia, among other places, to allude to the somewhat primitive religious and political importance of the celestial realm in Chinese culture. *The Brandon Sun* noted: "A special train conveying one hundred and forty-five Chinamen from Vancouver, where they were landed direct from their native country, bound for Montreal en route to Boston and New York, passed through Brandon just before twelve o'clock last night. The Celestials were all in bond."[18]

Train conductress reports provide an important window into life on Canadian trains. The reports contain correspondence from passengers who were shocked by a train's unsanitary conditions and lack of water or food. They tell about the problems people encountered when they wanted to buy fruit, milk, or meals for the journey. They also reported complaints when passengers were patronizing the better and cheaper Chinese-run station restaurants, and not the officially sanctioned British-run lunchrooms and dining cars. These reports emphasized the need for racial segregation—white British passengers, especially young females, risked racial contamination during train travel. British passengers did not like sharing cars with "Russians, Czechs, the scum of Europe and Chinese."[19] Chinese passengers were to be contained in special cars, or Immigrant Specials. Conductresses asked that when British girls shared cars with Chinese that, at the very least, the compartments be curtained off. But even the conductresses who were charged with the care of immigrant passengers[20] had difficulties justifying passenger complaints about Chinese passengers: "As the immigration authorities appreciate, the movement of less than special car parties of Chinese presents difficulties. While they are not objectionable in their habits and usually quiet and well behaved, it is recognized that a number of occidental passengers object to riding in the same car with them. We believe, however, we can keep risk of serious complaint down to a minimum by keeping Chinese out of cars occupied by women immigrant passengers [of British descent usually]."[21] Train conductress reports also stressed the privileging of Victorian food customs on board. Passengers and conductresses complained about the lack of access to "fire," tea kettles, dishes, and utensils to make tea: "You know the old country people love their cup of tea, and they can drink many, many cups of it journeying from Quebec to Vancouver."[22]

MERCHANTS AND MINISTERS ON THE TRAIN

Until 1920, when many affluent young Chinese men purchased an automobile to use for travel, labouring and merchant-class Chinese travelled by train. Chinese men got off the train at various prairie villages, towns, and cities along the way. Train stations became the points of entry into and exit from nascent Chinese communities, and as such came to define the boundaries of Chinese clan territory. Laundries, cafes, groceries, tea houses, and other urban businesses opened in and around the stations, eventually defining the blocks of streets and avenues known as Chinatown. Dominant Chinese society recognized that the railway station was the key entry point into Chinese markets and worked hard to control access to it. Until the 1950s, the Lees and the Wongs posted representatives at the larger train stations to ensure that only those from their families could settle and open businesses there.

Other accounts of train travel show that the Chinese moving through Canada were not just labourers who lived and worked in one place, or women mistaken as prostitutes reuniting with or joining husbands. Chinese politicians travelled along Canadian Pacific Railway and Canadian National Railway lines as well. Newspapers sent their reporters to wander through the cars of stopped trains at CPR stations to interview and write about the nationality of "oriental" passengers. The Chinese immigrant was interesting and exotic to local readers who knew a little about the history of the Boxer Rebellion and the uprisings that led to the fall of the Qing dynasty in late 1911. On Saturday, April 14, 1900, *The Daily Sun* reported on a Chinese diplomat in one of the cars of a stopped train:

> Ting Tee Chung Whung passed through the city on Thursday evening's train en route to China from New York. A *Sun* reporter tried to get the gentleman to enter into a conversation, but he did not seem inclined to talk for publication. His fellow passengers however, volunteered the information that the Chinaman was a member of the Chinese legation at New York, and had been out here for three years. He had been recalled by the emperor but no one on the train seemed to know why. A large crowd was at the depot in New York to see him off. He is traveling alone and has plenty of money. He said he had enjoyed his stay in America very much but thought the Americans and their customs were not as good as those of his own country. He was dressed in the most elaborate style in a cloak ornamental with yellow dragons here and there a red or green monstrosity of Chinese design.[23]

This Chinese diplomat must have been a grand sight on the train, in his brightly coloured cloak with strange dragons and designs. The way he dressed and behaved was in stark contrast to that of the humble western Manitoban laundryman. The diplomat represented the other hidden and more "Chinese" side of the western Manitoban identity. Like this early diplomat who was returning home after a three-year assignment in New York, early settlers to western Manitoba longed for their native customs.

Sun Yatsen—the man credited with ending the last Chinese dynasty and known to Chinese throughout the world as the father of China—and other Chinese Nationalist League (KMT/Zhongguo Guomindang) dignitaries were among those who shared first-class cars to move across the nation. Sun Yatsen came to Canada three times: first, in July 1897, then in February 1910 and finally, from January to April, 1911. As his great-grandson recalled: "Sun widely travelled from coast to coast by train in both the United States and Canada raising funds amongst overseas Chinese communities in order to support his revolution. Practically every major overseas Chinese community in North America was visited by Sun. Sun often described himself as a vagabond without a home."[24] Chinese revolutionary leaders in Canada convinced Sun Yatsen to make a stop in Winnipeg after he spoke in Vancouver in January 1911. They met Sun at the CPR station near Chinatown and acted as his bodyguards, along with the ones he brought with him, as he toured the city, held fundraising meetings, and gave political speeches. Sun Yatsen made stops in other places in addition to Winnipeg. Old-timers across the Prairies reminisce, for example, about how Sun Yatsen visited Saskatoon, too. Another prominent Chinese figure, Hu Shi, in Canada for a conference in Banff, travelled by train to Winnipeg in August 1933 and gave a speech at the KMT office in Chinatown.[25]

Chinese prairie organization leaders made use of railway networks to promote nationalism and Chinese culture: the Chinese Freemasons, the Chinese United League (Tongmeng hui, which formed around 1905 and merged with the KMT after 1912), and the loosely organized Chinese Dramatic Society appear to be the earliest active groups. Leaders arranged for the transportation of goods that were needed for community celebrations during Chinese New Year, the Moon Festival, and for the grave customs observed in the spring and autumn. Railways moved boxcars filled with incense, spirit money, firecrackers, and Chinese foods and medicines from Vancouver to Chinatowns throughout the country. In the early 1920s, Chinese Dramatic Society prairie members used the railway to convince prairie nationalist leaders that they were strongly anti-Communist. Being itinerant performers, most Chinese performers did not belong to either a political party or to a church group. But in 1920s Winnipeg and Edmonton, where a lack of political membership meant one became targeted by the *de facto* Chinese government in Canada, Chinese Dramatic performers used the railway to prove their patriotic spirit. Boxes of rifles were smuggled across the American border into Canada and over to Guangzhou, China via Hong Kong by the men so that they could avoid being labelled as communists. In doing so, they demonstrated their support for the nationalists in the fight against "treasonous rebels." In 1924, both the Winnipeg and Edmonton Chinese Dramatic clubhouses were awarded first class silver medals as evidence of their superior contribution.[26] The Winnipeg certificate is still proudly displayed on the Chinese Dramatic clubhouse wall.

Well-connected Chinese men who spoke good English reaped the benefits of new rail technology by augmenting their already considerable salaries with part-time work. The Canadian National Railways would issue train passes to men who were hired as Chinese passenger agents. These Chinese passenger agents were responsible for certain regions of Canada—for instance, for the territory between Ontario and Quebec, and between Manitoba and Ontario. Having the title "Chinese Representative of the Canadian National Railways" brought with it many benefits, such as season tickets to Exhibitions organized and hosted by the railways. Chinese Railway representatives were often shipping agents for other railways, too, such as American President Lines.[27] One of the most noteworthy early Chinese merchants on the Prairies was Frank Chan, who was a Sun Life and Wawanesa Insurance agent serving Chinese living in Manitoba, Saskatchewan, and northern Ontario until his untimely death from meningitis in 1952. Frank held the part-time position of Canadian Pacific Railway interpreter and ticket agent as well, and listed the dormitory where he lived as his ticket agent address. In May 1940, Frank acted as translator for Chinese travelling in bond through Winnipeg, as noted in the *Winnipeg Free Press*: "There were three passengers aboard three cars of bonded Chinese from Hong Kong, who passed through Winnipeg Wednesday night, en route to New York and the British West Indies over Canadian Pacific lines. Frank Chan acted as interpreter.[28]

Chinese merchants travelled for leisure as well. Happy Dong was a restaurant owner and operator in small Saskatchewan and Manitoba towns for almost four decades. Until the late 1920s, when Happy purchased a car, he made a monthly 400-kilometre trip to Winnipeg's Chinatown to buy supplies and socialize. Like other loyal Chinese nationalists on the Prairies (party membership was voluntary but expected), he attended meetings at Chinese Nationalist League offices in the vicinity of King Street and Alexander Avenue in Winnipeg. Several times a month he travelled over 200 kilometres to Brandon, where he was part-owner of restaurants. By the 1940s, Happy had also purchased a home near Brandon's small Chinatown on 12th Street, although he still lived in a small Saskatchewan town. He had a small bedroom above his restaurant where he slept when he was not serving customers, cooking, or baking pies. When he was not working or travelling to Winnipeg or to Brandon by train, he could be found in a town near to his own supporting the local hockey team, which he sponsored.

Happy took longer trips as well. He travelled first class on the train in a sleeper car, and visited friends, notably George Gardiner, fourth premier of Saskatchewan and federal minister of agriculture, in Toronto, Ottawa, and New York City. Happy certainly was not the only Chinese immigrant who travelled for leisure. Chinese merchants throughout North America travelled for leisure. Donald Eng, a close friend who lived in New Jersey, provided Happy with his train itinerary when he visited England. George Dong and Parkie Gao sent Happy postcards summarizing their travel by rail. Travelling along the main railway lines was described in Chinese correspondence with great flourish as "flying into the station."

The accounts of Happy's travels, Frank's role as ticket agent and interpreter, travelling politicians, and the transportation of firearms present a more intimate view of Chinese lived experiences, emergent power structures, and the ways in which Chinese made use of the railway's white cultural spaces. These accounts focus, for the most part, on those men who had become powerful in part because of networks, hubs, and relationships forged by railway technology and construction. Beyond this frame were many less privileged Chinese settlers who travelled by train.

The last part of this paper examines the lived experiences of an important Chinese Canadian family. More than most Chinese families of the time, this family's life was defined by the railways. Ma Seung (1870–1951), the fifth son of a southern Chinese farming family, had intended to emigrate to the United States where an elder sister had married. When his ship docked in the Victoria harbour in 1892 he disembarked there instead. Four years later and after much hardship, Ma Seung converted to Christianity and was baptized by the Presbyterian mission in Cumberland, BC. Showing great promise, Ma Seung was soon sent to Canton, China, where he attended a Christian college and received a theological education. By January 1900, newly married Ma Seung returned to begin his career as a Chinese mission worker, first in Victoria from 1900 to 1907, then in Cumberland from 1907 to 1917, and finally in Winnipeg, Manitoba from 1917 to 1935. Most of Ma Seung's more than thirty-five years in Canada were spent on the railway branch and main lines as an itinerant minister who was responsible for the care and conversion of Chinese living in Winnipeg as well as the smaller prairie cities and towns. Ma Seung's sons Peter and George also conducted what they referred to as "missionary chataquas" in many small prairie communities. In a 1921 report, eldest son Peter noted:

> Following instructions given in the letter, I left the Conference on July 6th arriving at Souris that afternoon. Next day I began my work. From Souris I went on the CPR to Brandon, Oak Lake, Elkhorn, Virden; then on the C.N.R. to Hartney. From Hartney I went to Napinka and Melita, and then along the Napinka-Winnipeg line to Plum Coulee stopping at Deloraine, Boissevain, Ninga, Killarney, Cartwright, Crystal City, Pilot Mound, Manitou, Morden and Winkler. From Plum Coulee, I went north to Carman, stopping at Roland on the way. After leaving Carman, I visited Elm Creek, Rathwell, Treherne, Holland, Cypress River, and Glenboro, returning to Winnipeg via Boissevain, visiting in all 27 towns.[29]

Having received an advanced Chinese and Christian education, Ma Seung could read, write, and speak English with a fluency rarely encountered in Chinese communities. As a man who had dedicated his life to the work of the church and the

Presbyterian mission, Ma Seung had not desired the life of a powerful or wealthy Chinese merchant. But I do not think that Ma Seung anticipated the suffering or financial difficulties he would have to endure, the letter-writing campaigns that had to be undertaken for reimbursement, or the small bean-sprout factory his wife opened in order to house, feed, and clothe their family. Ma Seung's correspondence clearly indicates that Chinese-Canadian mission workers and ministers lived under a shadow of severe discrimination. While Ma Seung was often instructed to travel to prairie cities like Calgary and Edmonton by train, the Presbyterian board was unwilling to pay his expenses, or even give him the half-fare mission worker's certificate to prove his identity. On one occasion in 1924, Ma Seung described his harsh treatment on the train to the Presbyterian board: "Going from Calgary to Edmonton that was a lot of trouble between the conductor and I because I was unable to show him the half fare certificate and I didn't get to Edmonton until after a series of quarrels with him…he even threatened to put me off. Because of these troubles I was afraid that the same trouble might happen so I didn't stop at Saskatoon, Regina, etc., but went straight home."[30] Writing these letters must have been very embarrassing for Ma Seung.

The Presbyterian mission board appeared to hold Chinese missionary workers in low regard. They considered Chinese food to be simple and therefore cheaper than Western food. Ma Seung, when challenged on his accounting of expenses, went out of his way to document and compare the equal costs of both Chinese and Western tastes, subtly exposing the racism in such comments. Chinese missionary workers were expected to ask their friends and acquaintances who ran cafés and laundries (and who had meagre incomes) to feed them and give them lodging for a night. When these men visited places where the Chinese community was unfamiliar, they paid their own expenses.

If life for Ma Seung was hard, life for Ma Sheung's wife, Young Honglin, (1880–1972), was much worse. She came to Canada with him at the age of twenty, first living in Victoria, where racism was intense. Next she resided in Cumberland in a home where the roof leaked, and she and her children were confined to Chinatown's segregated life. At the peak of her adult life, she moved to Winnipeg, where her husband was often away in China or on another trip by train to visit small Chinese prairie communities. Her arm hurt in the winter from stoking the coal furnace, she missed her family in China, and the family was poor. Young Honglin's bean sprouts–growing business became so successful that she began selling her crop to local restaurants, using the income to help pay for her first son's university education. On top of her home business, and to the neglect of her housework, Honglin started a sewing class and organized and hosted an annual mothers' picnic for Chinese women in the community in the 1920s and 1930s.

Soon, Honglin had opened her home to Chinese girls born in BC who wished to travel to Winnipeg by train and meet a good merchant husband.

Ma Seung and Honglin moved their four sons to Winnipeg, Manitoba where they hoped the boys would have a better education. Three of the boys attended University of Manitoba. While their father and mother had lived on the edges of dominant white and Chinese society—for most of their lives with very little money—life was much better for their sons, all of whom earned post-graduate degrees. First and fourth sons Peter and Jacque became doctors, third son George obtained a PhD in pharmacy from Columbia University, and second son Andrew earned a master of science degree in electrical engineering from the University of Manitoba in 1927. Andrew's first job upon graduation from university was for the Canadian Pacific Railway in Winnipeg. Andrew remained at that job until he returned to China with his family in the mid-1930s, where he also was employed by a railway company.[31]

A focus on trains and railway networks redirects our attention away from old positioned sightings of the static and stereotypical "coolie," "chink," "bachelor," "laundryman" and "Chinaman." The transcontinental railway line that was completed in 1885 enabled thousands of Chinese Canadians to move away from British Columbia and make a new life elsewhere. In many ways, Chinese settlements grew up, around, and out of the railway stations that dotted the Prairies. Where Chinese individuals were welcomed, accepted, and sometimes embraced, they remained, and many of their descendants still live in those small towns and cities today. Large numbers of early Chinese Canadians, however, left Saskatchewan.

By examining the various ways that Chinese lives intersected with the railway, we are able to have a better appreciation of the range of Canadian experiences. Some Chinese Canadians were cosmopolitan power-brokers who flourished because of networks, charisma, or English proficiency. They used skill, privilege, and new technologies such as the railway (and later, automobiles) to position themselves inside the acceptable realms of white society and to keep, either intentionally or unintentionally, those labourers, women, and other lower-class Chinese on the margins. They were welcomed by new prairie communities because they had the means to make use of new technology and networks. For those marginalized Chinese, the experience with railway employees, travel, and work was much more negative. Trains offered a medium for dominance, and racism, and occasionally resistance, or liberation on the Canadian Prairies.

NOTES

1   The research presented here is part of a multi-year research program to investigate Chinese Canadian prairie settlement and is funded by The Social Sciences and Humanities Research Council of Canada. I am also grateful to Brandon University and The Rural Development Institute for their generous support, and to research assistants Coco Kao, Li Chunwei, Sarah Ramsden, and Kristopher Keen.

2   The history of Canadian railway construction and operations is beyond the scope of this paper. In my research I have come across references to Chinese passengers and workers on the Canadian Pacific Railway and the Canadian National Railway. I am aware that the prairies were served by many more railway companies, including the Canadian Northern Railway, the Grand Trunk Pacific Railway, the Winnipeg Great Northern Railway, and the Lake Manitoba Railway, among others.

3   I rely on mixed methods to conduct research. As an anthropologist, I conduct fieldwork consisting of semi-structured interviewing, and sometimes the use of surveys. I also do participant-observation research, which in the case of Chinese Canadian settlement oral history collection, means spending between an hour and several days with the people I interview. I have been interviewing Chinese Canadians, collecting their oral histories, photographs, and documents for seven years. While the focus of my research is the Canadian prairies, I have met with and interviewed hundreds of people in British Columbia, Alberta, Saskatchewan, Manitoba, Ontario, and Quebec between the ages of eighteen and ninety-nine. The research presented in this paper is the result of interviews conducted with Chinese Canadians born between 1912 and 1930. I combine this ethnographic (anthropological) approach with historical research relying on Chinese and English materials that document the period 1890 to 1950. The majority of these documentary materials have been given to me by research participants and are not available in archives.

4   Lisa Lowe, "Heterogeneity, Hybridity, Multiplicity: Marking Asian American Differences," in *Theorizing Diaspora: A Reader*, eds. Jana Evans Braziel and Anita Mannur (Malden: Blackwell, 2003), 139–140.

5   British Columbia denied Chinese residents the provincial right to vote from 1872 (and in subsequent acts in 1902, 1908, and 1939) to 1947. According to the 1900 Dominion Elections Act, a provincial loss of voting rights automatically meant a federal loss of voting rights. The only other province where Chinese were denied the right to vote was Saskatchewan. Under Saskatchewan provincial law Chinese were denied the provincial right to vote from 1909 to 1947.

6   Peel 1718: Carmichael, James (1835–1908). A holiday trip: Montreal to Victoria and return via the Canadian Pacific Railway, midsummer 1888. [Montreal: Canadian Pacific Railway], 1888. July 6, 1888, 23.

7   The General Register of Chinese Immigration from 1910 to 1949 listed 112 Saskatchewan destinations where Chinese settled. This was roughly the same number of destinations listed in the Register for British Columbia. Local histories and Census data show that Chinese men and women settled in many more Saskatchewan destinations than those which were indicated on the Register. See Alison Marshall, *Affective Regimes: Religion, Racism and Gender and the making of Prairie Canada* (Vancouver: UBC Press, forthcoming).

8   Chinese bodies were carried to ports on CPR rail lines and then shipped to China. The transportation was often financed and/or organized by Chinese voluntary organizations. Peel 4915: David Blythe Hanna, as told to Arthur Hawkes, *Trains of recollection: Drawn from fifty years of railway service in Scotland and Canada* (Toronto: Macmillan, 1924).

9 In 1977, Frank Quo noted in a government report that people on the Canadian Prairies were less hostile toward Chinese immigrants than those who lived elsewhere in Canada. These observations were confirmed in a recent interview with Jacque Mar (1912-2011), the 99-year-old son of Winnipeg's first Chinese minister. A resident of Winnipeg, Manitoba from 1917 to 1936, he remarked that his family had moved away from British Columbia because of racism and a desire for the boys' quality education. Jacque's father Ma Seung, being an itinerant minister from 1900 to 1935, had travelled to many prairie cities and towns and had noticed that Manitoba was more welcoming than other places. While in Victoria and Cumberland, British Columbia, the family had not been able to interact with non-Chinese people; in Manitoba the family had friends who in the words of Jacque were "white, black and yellow." See also Quo F. Quei, 1977 "Chinese Immigrants in the Prairies." Preliminary Report Submitted to the Minister of the Secretary of State. Simon Fraser University; Alison R. Marshall, *The Way of the Bachelor* (Vancouver: University of British Columbia Press, 2011), 8–10; and Alison R. Marshall, *Affective Regimes* (Vancouver: UBC Press, forthcoming).

10 See Marshall, *The Way of the Bachelor*, and Jared J. Wesley, *Code Politics: Campaigns and Cultures on the Canadian Prairies* (Vancouver: University of British Columbia Press, 2011). I examine this subject in greater detail in Alison R. Marshall, *In the Service of Our Friends: How Networks Made the Fabric of Chinese Prairie Canada* (Vancouver: UBC Press, forthcoming).

11 1911 Census data.

12 Saskatchewan's Chinese population was comparatively small, but these Canadians lived under a more severe shadow of discrimination, similar to those who lived in British Columbia. Census data, though largely unreliable, shows general trends. In the 1901 Census, a small number of Chinese resided in Saskatchewan, in contrast to 209 Chinese in Manitoba. Ten years later more than 950 Chinese indicated residence in Saskatchewan on the 1911 Census versus 885 in Manitoba. By the 1921 Census, the Chinese population in Saskatchewan was double the number of those who appeared to be living in Manitoba.

Between 1910 and 1923, 613 Chinese Canadians who had paid the head tax indicated on the General Register of Chinese Immigration that they intended to settle in Saskatchewan. In contrast, only 592 individuals indicated that they would settle in Manitoba. As in Manitoba, most new Chinese settlers to Saskatchewan were males between 11 and 20 years old with the youngest newcomers arriving at the age of 8. Chinese settled in just 28 Manitoban villages, towns, and cities, compared to the 112 Saskatchewan ones.

13 I am grateful to Kate Zimmerman, who made this observation about British Columbia life and sociality. This observation is anecdotally confirmed by more than five Chinese Canadians born during the exclusion era who had lived in both the prairie provinces and in British Columbia.

14 I draw heavily here on the work of Rita Dhamoon and her examination of the many ways that power makes difference. See Rita Dhamoon, *Identity/Difference Politics: How Difference Is Produced and Why It Matters* (Vancouver: University of British Columbia Press, 2009).

15 Erving Goffman, *The Presentation of Self in Everyday Life* (New York: Doubleday, 1959).

16 Interview with research participant born during the 1920s.

17 Catherine Laura Johnstone, *Winter and Summer Excursions in Canada* (London: Digby, Long and Co, 1894), 4.

18 *Brandon Daily Sun*, September 28, 1910, 8.

19 Library and Archives Canada (hereafter LAC), RG 76, vol. 140, page 309, file 33175, vol. 3 1927–1933, *Conductress Report: Miss Burnham*, August 20, 1928.

20   I would like to thank Lisa Chilton, who generously suggested that I obtain copies of the conductress reports from Library and Archives Canada. These reports provide an important window into Chinese experiences on the train.

21   LAC, RG 76, vol. 140, file 33175, vol. 3, 1927–1933, *Letter to Lady-in-Charge, Queen Mary's Coronation Hostel*, October 6, 1928.

22   LAC, RG 76, vol. 140, file 33175, vol. 3, 1927–1933, *Letter from Margaret Lewis*, October 3, 1930.

23   *The Daily Sun*, Brandon, Saturday, April 14, 1900, 2.

24   Correspondence by e-mail dated 22 June 2009, with Charles Wong, great grandson of Sun Yatsen.

25   "Dr. Hu Shih Urges Fellow Chinese To Have Patience," *Winnipeg Free Press*, Friday, August 4, 1933, 1.

26   Participation Observation Fieldwork, Winnipeg, Manitoba.

27   LAC. MG 30, File: *Ernest Mark Scrapbook 1* 51–100, Series D219.

28   *Winnipeg Free Press*, May 9, 1940.

29   "Report of the Chinese Work in Villages and Towns of Manitoba July/August 1921," Peter Mar, to the Members of the Presbytery of Winnipeg, Manitoba. Ma Seung Fonds.

30   Ma Seung Fonds (private collection).

31   Many Chinese Canadians living on the prairies were employed by the railway in various capacities. King Wong resided with his wife in Radville, Saskatchewan until about 1923. A Canadian National Railway employee, he laboured in the roundhouse. See Radville Laurier Historical Society, *Radville-Laurier: The Yesteryears* (Altona, MB: Friesen Printers, 1983), 772.

TRAINS, TEXT, AND TIME
THE EMIGRATION OF CANADIAN MENNONITES TO LATIN AMERICA,1922—1948

ROYDEN LOEWEN

This essay recounts a set of rather unique train rides leaving rather than entering western Canada. They are the travels of approximately 10,000 Mennonites who left western Canada in the mid-1920s and late 1940s for rural settlements in Mexico and Paraguay. The emigration of the 1920s followed 1916 and 1917 school legislations in Manitoba and Saskatchewan, respectively, which compelled children to attend English-language, publicly inspected schools. The smaller "echo migration" of the late '40s occurred after the introduction of war-time patriotic exercises in schools and urbanization threatened the Mennonites' rural, pacifist ways.

Trains played a major role in these migrations. The Mexico-bound settlers of the 1920s chartered dozens of complete trains, taking passengers, machinery, household goods, and livestock; most departed from Gretna, Manitoba and headed south or southwest to El Paso, Texas, from where migrants proceeded south to Chihuahua City and then west to the small road siding of San Antonio (later Cuauhtémoc) in the Bustillos Valley of the northeastern Sierra Madre after being reloaded on to Mexican trains. A smaller group of Mexico-bound settlers left from Rosthern, Saskatchewan via chartered trains to El Paso, continuing through Chihuahua State to Nuevo Ideal in Durango State. Other migrants to Paraguay left from Niverville, Manitoba on smaller chartered trains (as they took no livestock and few household goods) or on regularly scheduled trains via Minneapolis, Chicago, and Cleveland to New York. Here migrants boarded ocean-going vessels for the lengthy voyage to Buenos Aires, Argentina, from whence they proceeded by riverboat up the Paraná and Paraguay Rivers, passed Asunción and went north almost to Brazil to the river port of Puerto Casado. From here they headed west into the heart of the Paraguayan Chaco by narrow-gauged company train and ox cart. The migrants to Paraguay in the 1940s also took chartered trains to the east; leaving Saskatoon and picking up additional passengers in Winnipeg, they continued to Montreal. From there they sailed via Buenos Aires to Asunción, and then travelled by trains into East Paraguay. The final legs of the trip were taken by cargo truck and ox cart.[1]

Descriptions of the train travel vary depending on which route one took and therefore which country's trains are described. In studying these various descriptions, however, it becomes apparent that the experience of train travel does not differ much from the experience on other forms of transportation, be it the back of a cargo truck, on an ocean liner or riverboat, or even on an airplane—all technologies of migration of the 1920s and '40s. What does matter is the medium in which a particular train story is told. The reason seems to be that references to trains relate not so much to the technology itself, but to the effect of this particular technology on habits of time and space. In the telling of fundamental changes to time and space brought about by train travel, it especially mattered if the story was related by the medium of diary, memoir, letter, or oral history.

These media suggest that the Mennonite train travellers viewed time in multi-linear ways, with a strong sense of the present as located in a continuum of the past and future—even the afterlife—and as related to abstract ideas of tradition or progress. Simply put, the diarist had an especially strong sense of the "present," which isolated the day and compellingly juxtaposed it to "yesterday" and "tomorrow," thus structuring a world in flux and paying special attention to distance covered, speed, fleeting images of the exotic other along the way, and to the restructuring of "Mennonite" community within the cars of the train.[2] The letter announced the important events—those pertaining to life-cycle and life-shaping moments—of the immediate past, the week and month; it recounted the especially poignant moments of departure at train stations in the old Canadian homeland and the arrival at the strange "other" end. Memoirs written years after the trips spoke of teleological design, revealing an attempt to detach oneself from quotidian concern and evaluate a lifetime, especially with ideas of eternity in mind; in this instance, the train took on ontological significance as it carried people to a "promised land," a territory of "salvation." Finally, oral history stories recounted memories of a yesteryear, an epoch ago, a moment two generations earlier. These stories related train travel with reference to a momentous time, but in quaint and even quixotic language; they were anecdotal, stories told casually by the elderly about their childhood. It was as if each medium related train travel with a unique perspective, enveloping it with a distinctive sense of time.

This linkage of train and text with time, however, was intersected by other constructions of time that seemed especially relevant to migrants and the Mennonite train-riding migrants in particular. The diaries especially recounted new time imperatives, reflecting a demarcation between agrarian and industrial time, not unrelated to E.P. Thompson's comparison of time when seen as "natural in a farm community" and a "time-discipline" that is "imposed" by technologized imperative. In the migrant diary's depiction of uprooting and resettling, these two cultures of time were not sequential but interwoven, moving from one to the other and back to the former.[3] The letters describing train travel spoke not only of recent events, but did so by reaching for a common vocabulary of time; here time was conceptualized with reference to epochs, especially those of the pre- and post-migration periods. The memoirs looked backward, too, but reflected Pierre Bourdieu's idea of the "forthcoming," described by one recent study as a conceptualization of it "not only as a future" but a compelling sense that a life was meaningful only as a collective and teleologically oriented struggle. Memoirs helped "people make sense of the current state of affairs" and certainly authenticated the sense of sacrifice sectarian Mennonites felt they were making in the south.[4] The oral history stories also scan backward over a lifetime, but construct a romanticized yesteryear built on what the anthropologist Michael Jackson dubs a "site of selfhood," one narrowly centred on the subjective "I" and created at the moment of the interview. Because storytelling arises from "one's strategic struggle to…synthesize oneself as a subject in a world that simultaneously subjugates one to other ends," it relates the travel experience to quotidian minutiae.[5]

The train, then, takes on different meaning depending on the concept of "time" with which a particular train narrative is constructed. Reflecting this argument, this essay moves spatially rather than chronologically, transitioning from the quotidian text (the diary) to the weekly or monthly text (the letter) to the epochal text (the memoir) to the life course text (the oral history).

THE DIARY: THE TRAIN AS AN IMPOSITION OF INDUSTRIAL TIME, 1948

The selected diary of train travel here is one kept by a female migrant, self-identified as "Frau Isaac F. Bergen" of Rosthern, Saskatchewan, who in 1948 migrated to East Paraguay with her family of ten children and husband by train, but also travelled by ocean liner, riverboat, cargo truck, and ox cart.[6] Bergen's published diary begins on 16 June 1948 with these words: "Late in the evening, as we had finished packing at our old place, we drove to…Johann Klassens' to bid them farewell." The Bergens took leave of neighbours, relatives, and church members over the next week. Finally, on June 21 they travelled from Rosthern to Saskatoon, and at once located the railway station and the chartered train that would take them to Montreal. Father and the boys spent the final night in the train, while Mrs. Bergen and the girls stayed in the apartment of Aunt Susie, an unmarried sister working in the city.[7]

More than anything else, the imperatives of train travel alter the familiar, agrarian world of the Bergens. The train dictates that time is suddenly recast, turned into a series of impositions; the words "must" and "need" and "should" now take over Bergen's vocabulary. In addition, space is recast as the train narrative becomes intersected with descriptions of new places. On the morning of June 22, after taking breakfast at a Mennonite home in Saskatoon, Bergen "soon…had to pack up…as the Isaac Hildebrands were there to take us to the train station." Here loved ones from the Mennonite farm districts had assembled and at "one o'clock the train finally departed." Even though Bergen was delighted to discover an oven and washing facility on the train (allowing the resumption of domestic routine), overwhelmingly time now was measured by distance: Yorkton by night-fall, Gladstone at the first dawn, Winnipeg at noon. "Train time" was always an imperative: in Winnipeg father and "*Ohm* Jacob" disembarked to purchase food, but then as the "train was supposed to depart all the men were back except for father and *Ohm* Jacob; Aunt Sarah and I were deeply worried, and truly the train began to depart." Worry ended only at the next stop when, surprisingly, "father and *Ohm* Jacob appeared in our car," having caught up with the charter on a regularly scheduled train.[8]

The train did allow for a semblance of the familiar, cohesive community. Bergen writes that along the way the Saskatchewan travellers left their cars "to introduce themselves to the people from Manitoba" in their cars, and vice versa. She was delighted when "Uncle Jacob Elias suddenly dropped by to visit us with his two daughters." But always the familiar was interrupted by the exotic. By the time the Mennonite train reached Port Arthur, Bergen "had seen a lot, including frightening images, such as the time another train suddenly overtook us and passed us by." A full night of fast travel later, Bergen noticed a new and strange society as the people in "the city we came to...we could see, were French." The trip ended with passage through a somewhat frightening "one mile long tunnel," requiring that "they had to turn on the lights" in the cars.[9]

Significantly, the diary presents the train in no different terms than that of the ship that followed. The ocean voyage brought a similar range of imperatives and exotica. At the seaport in Quebec the travellers were told they could only board with the clothes they could wear and only as a complete family. To that end, the Bergens embarked wearing as many jackets each as possible and in order: "father went ahead, then all the [ten] children, and then, me, at the end." On board, the Bergens faced more disruptions of familiar domestic space and time. For the night Frau Bergen, the girls and small boys were separated from father and the "big boys"; in the morning they were summoned precisely "at six o'clock" and told to "make our beds." Meals could not be taken until the English command "it's time for the second sitting"; even then, it was always "hurry up, eat, or we will remove the food."[10] The very passage of time and space seemed imposed by announcements from the loudspeakers; on June 28 Bergen writes that "we are supposed to be adjacent to New York, but land is no longer in sight," and on July 9 they were informed that "at 1 o'clock we passed over the equator." Over the course of the journey, time was also measured by the fleeting images of the unusual: on June 30 it was groups "of little fish that fly off from the water"; on July 3 in Trinidad "little negroes" peddling "large oranges, grapefruit and bananas"; on July 13, a day out of Rio de Janeiro, the sighting of "approximately 13 ships." The ocean voyage ended on a Sunday in Buenos Aires, except that it "didn't seem like a Sunday" as a command that "we would have to disembark very soon" was followed by a stress-filled re-embarking on a riverboat for the trip up the Paraguay River.[11]

At this point Bergen's diary incrementally returns to communitarian familiarity, albeit in increasingly primitive conditions, documenting the reversal of progress and eventually the return to agrarian time. The riverboat was overcrowded and its toilets and kitchen dank and dirty; as Bergen noted, "in Low German we would say 'prost.' " The transition to train travel in Asunción was related in a seamless narrative of time imperatives, descriptions of the new land, and hints of refashioned communitarianism. The train into the East Paraguay jungle was crude and rough, and only a sense of community made it palatable; on the train, for example, Bergen was comforted by "Aunt Derk Klassen...a good mother and grandmother." The final sections of the lengthy trip—by cargo truck, ox cart, and on foot—slowed down the race through time and space. Bergen could bear the rough road by truck to Colonia Independencia, for it "was closer to our land" and it was a German-speaking community with plenty of fruit and familiar food. Another truck trip to Caaguazú was followed by a final day of travel by ox cart. And then the Bergens walked the entire night till 4 a.m., when they arrived at the newly grounded Sommerfeld Colony; six hours later, at 10 a.m., on December 18, they arrived at their village lot in newly named Waldheim, literally, "forest home."[12] Here at a place with "grass taller than my head" and not far from "clear, wonderful water," Bergen "spread a blanket on the ground and we ate lunch." By evening, three tents had been set up and the family retired, "exhausted." Time slowed as agraria resumed with a series of familiar tasks—washing, cooking, visiting, and securing shelter.[13]

The trains in this narrative—the one from Rosthern to Montreal, and the one from Asunción to Independencia—were in their nature a little different than the other modes of transportation. Each was marked by observations of the strange and unusual, each dictated an inherent disruption to domestic routine, and each marked the quick passage of time, offering a modicum of reconstructed community along the way.

THE LETTER: TRAIN STATIONS AS SITES OF TRANSITION IN A TRANSCULTURAL WORLD: 1922

If the daily diary marked the significance of the train for its ability to disrupt quotidian rhythms and hurtle farm families through space, the letters composed days, a week, or even a month after a train trip saw its significance in strikingly different terms. Letters describing train travel were almost always by definition written by those witnessing weighty moments of departures and arrivals, or those travellers who had experienced both. Dozens of such letters describing the 1920s migration to Mexico were published in a German-language newspaper, the *Steinbach Post*, a bi-weekly that quickly ascended from a local to a transnational medium during the migration. The letters, written by ordinary subscribers, seemed focused on moments of commencement and completion. One from March 1922 announced the departure of the very first train to Mexico and spoke of broken social ties: "On the 1st of March the first train with Old Colony Mennonite emigrants left for Mexico. This occurs only with a great deal of pain, especially when one thinks of leaving all that one loves and taking bid from so many loving friends."[14] Other letters, such as one from October 1922, spoke of the hope of new settlement: "Concerning the migration to Mexico one can report that between 18 and 20 families have ordered [rail] cars for themselves so that they can leave on November 8 and by this time next winter will be happily living there."[15] Usually the reports held very precise information. The specific denominational label of one group of migrants was important to the writer of a November 1922 letter from Altona, Manitoba: on "Saturday the 11th a train left again from Altona with a group of immigrants for Mexico. These, however, were not Old Colonists, but Sommerfelders."[16] The specific identity of immigrants was important to a January 1923 writer from Gouldtown, Saskatchewan; he set out to "provide the names of the emigrants, as perhaps it might interest some folks," and then listed twenty-eight families and explained, "these have loaded together a total of 17 [rail] cars with 3 cars reserved for the colonists themselves."[17]

Soon, too, came letters reporting on the arrival of these chartered trains in Mexico. A few were written by Mennonites already in Mexico; one by an Abram Rempel noted the arrival in the border town of Juárez of a train, including five passenger cars: "[They were] full of Mennonites, large and small, old and young...all showing happy faces that they have finally arrived in Mexico.... And these 5 passenger cars were attached to an endless row of freight cars, I think there were over 30, with horses, cows, dogs, cats, geese and chickens and all loaded with all possible types of cultivation equipment and household goods.... The whole train offered up quite a treasure and represented for Mexico no little matter. After completing their official formalities they will continue their trip, leaving at 10 p.m. for San Antonio [later named Cuauhtémoc]."[18]

Those who wrote about traversing of the American Midwest described the trip itself in almost clinical terms, a time in between, linking two nodes in a transcultural world. What they did emphasize was not the trip itself, but the weighty moments of departure and arrival. Rev. Abram Görtzen of Morse, Saskatchewan filed the following letter in July 1923:

> We left for Mexico on 16 December 1922 from Herbert and Morse, Saskatchewan; 27 families with 17 freight cars. The trip took us somewhat over 11 days. We arrived at our destination...on the morning of December 28; the trip seemed slow, but God be thanks, everything went well. As we arrived we praised our heavenly shepherd by the singing of Song # 679 from the Old Songbook and then we began the unloading. By 2 p.m. everything was unloaded. The railroad company was very accommodating and allowed us three freight cars in which we could live as long as we wished. From there the long process of settling on the land began.[19]

Just as the 1922 move to Mexico became a central concern in letters published in the *Steinbach Post*, so too did the 1926 move to Paraguay. And just as letters from Mexico made short shrift of the trip itself, so too did those from Paraguay once they began appearing in the *Post* in April 1927, three full months after the migrants arrived at their southern destination. The first letters reported the late December 1926 arrival at Puerto Casado, the outpost on the Paraguay River, 400 kilometres north of Asunción and still 200 kilometres from the proposed settlement site west of the river in the Paraguayan Chaco. These first letters emphasized safe arrival at Puerto Casado and described immense difficulty at the river port. The trip itself—the train to New York, the voyage to Buenos Aires, the 1,000-kilometre riverboat trip north, past Asunción—was described in simple terms. In his April 1927 letter, A.A. Bergen noted the trip as a "very long" one that resulted in "much illness, of which I too was not spared." Perhaps the "wonders on the trip were remarkable," he noted, "but none of it interested me, and I gave no room for such thoughts." In fact, he was certain that "on the next trip I want to take in a hot air balloon, as more misfortune I cannot endure."[20]

Once the migrants moved inland, their letters emphasized the start of permanent settlement in the Chaco and not the 200-kilometre trip from the riverport. True, there were statements about the arduous twelve-day trip inland, the first ninety kilometres covered by narrow-gauge company rail, the last seventy by ox cart. In one letter published on 17 September 1927 the writer noted cursorily that the "little train has it very busy; oftentimes it takes three groups a week out" into the Chaco.[21] Fuller descriptions, however, were reserved for the points of embarking and disembarking. For letter writers, these were the points of the newsworthy events.

THE MEMOIR: TRAINS AS
DIVINE INSTRUMENT, 1922 AND 1926

A series of memoirs—some seemingly written with the help of a diary, others published as lengthy submissions to the *Steinbach Post*—describe in detail these various trips from western Canada. Unlike the diary and letters, the memoirs conceived of the relocation in religious terms, and the trains as divine instruments securing teleological promise. Typically written by an elderly or middle-aged person well after the event, the memoirs placed the migration within the narrative of a lifetime, and infused it with religious symbolism that assumed an eternal afterlife. In each case the backward glancing occurred with an intended affect of what will come, the anticipation of a "forthcoming" of cosmological significance.

The first of two memoirs examined was serialized in the *Steinbach Post* in 1946 by forty-two-year-old Jacob D. Harder of Weidenfeld, Paraguay. Significantly, it was penned a full two decades after the 1926 event and was written not only to describe the journey for the curious, but to attest to the trip's wider, cultural meaning. Harder chose his beginning without equivocation: "For a long time I've had the idea to write something about my life, but haven't had time; yet I've decided to write something about the migration from Canada to Paraguay and hope that the readers will overlook my many mistakes. My memories go way back, yes to Canada, and begin when I was only 23 years old." Before offering further detail, Harder reached for higher meaning: "the reason our forefathers allowed themselves to be separated from their [old] homeland was this, because of their faith." Only then did he commence the story, telling how on the day of departure a friend drove the family by sleigh to the railroad station in Niverville, Manitoba, and did so in a -30 degree snowstorm. Harder moved quickly to the actual departure, describing in romantic German terms how the locomotive lurched forward with "pfiff" and a shower of sparks, and with smoke stack belching it went "zisch, zisch, zisch, ever farther southward."[22]

Poetic vocabulary, both secular and sacred, is interwoven with the text. Harder noted that the immigrants left Niverville "without any jubilation, just quiet conversation in Low German, a din mixed with the constant hum of the wheels under the cars." Their trip eastward to New York bore sacred meaning: "day and night the train raced on with us, poor worms, over water and mountains." Those very vistas reminded him twenty years later "how great God is and that God himself had said as he made the world, 'see, it is very good....'" Leaving "the Canadian train" in New York marked a solemn moment: "all eyes looked up and there stood the ship of our voyage, which we were to board, with father, mother, grandparents, etc."[23]

Like the diary, the memoir made little differentiation between train and ship. The memoir moved seamlessly from one mode of transportation to another. If trains travelled too fast, ships rocked too ceaselessly, causing Harder to describe seasickness with an English phrase: "a little sick, but not in the legs, only in the belly." If trains brought moments of fear, so did the ship, a time Harder described in biblical language: the expanse of the ocean, for example, gave thought to many a parent, he noted, "to the biblical stories of the Apostle Paul being shipwrecked on the Mediterranean."[24] For the memoirist, the train travel, as well as the ocean voyage, was always more than simple relocation, it was a moment infused with deep significance.

The second memoir was written in the early 1960s, some four decades after the event it described—the 1922 trip of the immigrants to Mexico. The author, an Old Colony Mennonite minister residing in Mexico, Rev. Isaak Dyck, had outlined the background to the emigration in the first volume of the memoir, and he did so by employing overtly religious language, suggesting that the difficult decision to leave militaristic and assimilative but well-to-do Canada was nothing less than an act of religious faithfulness, a "suffering with Christ." The second volume described the emigration itself, and the settlement in Mexico was similarly anchored to religious symbolism. Indeed the description of the train trip was presented with almost foreboding vocabulary.[25] Taking leave of loved ones at the border town of Gretna, Manitoba had been difficult enough, but what followed was nothing short of frightening. Dyck's description of the train trip itself commenced with a description of the crossing of the American Midwest, and just after the emigrant group had cleared United States customs at Neche, North Dakota:

> The train began to double its speed and only seemed to go faster and faster.... We raced into the black night accompanied by the horrific noise of the two large locomotives. We were so afraid and anxious because of the high speed, the women especially, that we decided to talk to the engineer to see if they could slow the trains down, because we didn't want to end up in a serious accident.... His casual response was that the train was not our responsibility and in any case they were in a race with the other railroad companies to see who could make it Mexico the quickest. And so we realized we had no other option but to put our trust in God.[26]

The arrival at El Paso, Texas, just four days later was met by Dyck with the relief—"oh how thankful we were to God and the engineer when we arrived." But other apprehensions followed. "At this point we had to transfer to another train, a fact of which we were not previously aware…. And at once a feeling of fear swept over us, for once we entered Mexico it was as if we were the children of Israel," trembling as they did when they first entered Canaan, the ancient "promised land," albeit one filled with hostile forces.[27] And then, while it was good that "our new train in Mexico travelled much more slowly than the previous one" in the United States, new fears arose at each stop as "Mexicans surrounded our train because they had never before seen Mennonites." It made Dyck and his fellow passengers feel very "uncomfortable, for we had never seen such dark people…. These were to be our neighbours…. O how strange and unfamiliar everything was." Then, as "we left the border town Juárez, about 20 heavily armed men boarded our train…as was the custom to protect us from hijackers. But [their presence] caused fear and timidity among our women and children."[28] Eventually the soldiers turned out "to be very friendly and benevolent," allowing them to "grow accustomed to our new companions."[29] But then other apprehensions followed: from the vantage point of the train, the landscape of the U.S. with its "winter wheat standing in splendid green" now was replaced by the semi-arid Chihuahua landscape in which "everything appeared to be dead…the grass was totally dry, the cattle were skinny," and so "we had to remind ourselves that [according to Psalm 74] it was God who set [things so]… that each land possesses its own character."[30] This sense of trust again gave way to "more anxiety and sadness" upon arriving in Chihuahua City:

> The [railyard workers] began separating our train into two…because the rest of the trip was too treacherous for the train to make in its present state. We would have to travel over high mountains and through deep valleys, across high bridges, and there was no way that the long train could make it. And so the passenger cars were separated from the cattle and freight cars, and the latter train was hooked up to two locomotives. This aroused no small amount of worry and served as motivating force for us to entreat the Lord to lead us safely to our destination.[31]

The final leg of train travel was also the most fearful: "we drove through a dark tunnel" certain "that the mountain was going to collapse on top of us."[32] Then while crossing one mountain range the grade became "so steep that even after the engine had exerted all of its steam power, it still could not make it all the way up, so we were stuck near the top for a while." At this point "many women came to where Bishop Franz Loewen and I were seated and confessed that they had not prayed enough in preparation for this important journey and it was because of them that we were having all these difficulties."[33] But Dyck thought to himself, "how can one sell oil to another when one's lamp is almost dry and about to go out." His only comfort at this moment was the poem which spoke of "the journey to blessed eternity [as] all the more difficult."[34] At dawn the train finally made it through the mountains, and Dyck was relieved to see that the freight train had made it to "our new home, the village of San Antonio, thankful and praising the Lord." A final encounter with the train turned Dyck dour once again. Upon arriving, the tired and apprehensive migrants were met by "railroad officials [who] sternly informed us that we had [but] two days to empty our cars."[35] A new round of uncertainty began. The whole affair with the train had reminded Dyck that the only certainty in life was that in this world the true pilgrim would need to "suffer alongside Christ." Ironically, the technological wonder of modern train travel had brought the Mennonite emigrants to a place in northern Mexico from which they could contest all that which was modern.

THE ORAL HISTORY MEMORY: TRAINS AS SITES OF YOUTHFUL INNOCENCE

The final medium under consideration is the oral history narrative. In this study it is also the text constructed at a moment furthest removed from the event of relocation. In an oral history project undertaken in 1979, a Canadian graduate student, Ronald Sawatsky, interviewed two dozen Mennonites who had "returned" from Mexico to Canada, settling in southern Ontario.[36] Sawatsky's primary interest was integration into 1970s-era Canada, but the interviews with the more elderly participants (that is, those participants born in Canada) include questions about the migration from western Canada fifty to sixty years earlier. Sometimes Sawatsky's questions pertained specifically to the train trip from prairie Canada to Mexico in the 1920s. The oral text produced, recorded with a tape recorder, was fundamentally different than the memoir, even though both were created a long time after the remembered event. The memoir written in a moment of contemplation and for public consumption presented the train trips with teleological significance; the oral history text was produced within a private conversation, in the company of a stranger, for the purposes of producing an archival holding. There were no sweeping statements of the wider significance of the train travel.

Most importantly, the elderly migrants, in recalling childhood, also recalled a child's perspective. That perspective, similar to the outlook of the letter-writers, recalled poignant moments of departure and arrival. But a child's life is more circumscribed than an adult's and memories necessarily relate to that which the child sees and experiences at those points. Maria Voth, born in 1910 in Didsbury, Alberta, and twelve years of age when her family emigrated, was the oldest of Sawatsky's oral history participants and had the most vivid memories of the adults on the trip. Voth recalled travelling from Saskatchewan where her family lived in 1922 to visit "my step-grandfather [who] was still alive and we stayed there for several days.... When the train came we took it. Got on there... at Easter."[37] She also possessed prominent adult-centred memories of the arrival in Mexico:

> [Upon arriving] in El Paso we had to wait for a long time, something was going on but children can't catch everything. I don't know why. But my grandfather was a minister.... *Ohm* Isaak Giesbrecht. He got sick there. They planned to hold a church service there but he got sick so he couldn't lead it.... [Then, in Chihuahua state] halfway [to our final place of settlement] there we had to [disembark and] sleep on the ground in the mountains in a strange place. I can still clearly remember that. We had to use horse-drawn vehicles, through the mountains, my sister and I, also my mother and youngest brother. It was just us four. The others were in cars.... I can't remember that we were afraid. We finally arrived at our destination, Santa Clara. That's its name.[38]

By coincidence and without prodding by the interviewer, each of the other interviewees, all somewhat younger than Maria, had faint memories not so much of people or places, but of animals they saw from the train, or animals encountered just before or just after the train trip. Cornelius Peters, born in 1913 in Hague, Saskatchewan, did recall the moment of departure from Gretna, Manitoba when he was ten with reference to adults: the train "started off very slowly and a lot of people walked with the train." But in his description of the train itself, he quickly moved from people to animals: there were "47 cars on that train," but there were "many fewer passenger cars than livestock transport cars" as the Mennonites "took horses and cows" and even "dogs and cats."[39] Anna Peters, born in 1915 near Gretna, Manitoba, also recalled the departure at age seven in 1922. True, her strongest memory was that during "the last evening in Manitoba when we were waiting for the train.... I was very thirsty; I'll never forget that," but Anna's only other memory included the daily moment when the train stopped and she went "with my father...when he tended to the animals...[in] the livestock car."[40]

Other interviewees who were even younger than Anna and Cornelius in 1922 had singular memories of these animals. Heinrich Voth had two memories of arriving in Mexico when he was nine: the first was of "one family's horses, big horses for those days," bolting when they were unloaded from the train, breaking "the halters and the rope" and galloping "east.... [So] glad to get off that train; Mexicans were sent after the horses on their horses; [and] they brought [the runaways] back." Voth also recalled the dogs they brought with them. Arriving on the open fields of Valle Bustillos may have been "difficult for my parents" but for "my cousin and me, once we were off the train, we both had a dog...and we played with them, walking barefoot on that dry Mexican grass. Oi-yoi-yoi."[41] Peter Giesbrecht, born in 1917 near Gretna, Manitoba, was seven when his family moved to Mexico in 1923. He had a single memory of Canada and it too related to animals: how "my uncles rode on a sleigh pulled by dogs in winter." Similarly his two memories of the train trip through the American Midwest was animal-centred: he recalled how "I and my father went into the livestock cars and attended to the animals"; and how "our dogs" which had been brought along from Manitoba "tried to jump from the train" and "some ran back" to Manitoba, in fact "I heard that they made it back to Manitoba."[42] Corny Friesen, born near Winkler, Manitoba in 1919 was only four when his family moved in 1923 and his single memory of the migration was "the dogs they brought with them...that interested me." [43]

Ironically perhaps, the text produced the longest time since the train trip turned attention not to day, month, lifetime, or eternity, but to fragmentary moments of the quotidian. More so than the diary, letter, or memoir, the oral history text turned attention from the meaning of the train trip to the experiential, and from an attempt to create any kind of coherent narrative to the circumscribed moment.

CONCLUSION

The travels of western Canadian Mennonite emigrants in the 1920s and 1940s took them on one of several extensive train trips: to northern Mexico across the vast American Midwest, to the eastern ports, to Montreal, or to New York. For all travellers the trains were imposing, representing the technology that uprooted them from western Canada and placed them on the way to strange lands in faraway places. But the nature of the train travel varied from country to country, from one migration to another. The U.S. and Canadian trains were faster and cleaner than those in Mexico or Paraguay. The chartered trains allowed for greater degrees of familiarity than those taken on regularly scheduled lines.

The greatest differences, however, lay not in the types of trains, but in the perspectives shaped by specific texts that were employed in the telling of the trips. Train travel was never merely a matter of crossing space, but of reordering time. The train took the Mennonite settler from close-knit agrarian communities at Swift Current, Hague, and Rosthern (Saskatchewan), and from Winkler, Altona, Gretna, and Steinbach (Manitoba), and thrust them into the mid-western U.S., the eastern seaboard, or central Canada before sending them into Mexico or to ships heading for South America. The meaning of this train-propelled uprooting and reordering of time depended not so much on just which train one took, as on the medium with which the story was told.

Diaries recording train travel noted the manner in which the quotidian imperative of yielding to nature's cycle gave way to a new technologically driven imperative on daily life. The letter revealed a consciousness of significant events—those that compelled the letter to be written in the first instance—and thus focused on departures and arrivals, encapsulated with the common vocabulary of sweeping epochs, especially of pre- and post-migration. The memoir created a narrative of a lifetime or life-altering event, and thus the train trips here were cast in teleological language granting them cosmological and even eternal meaning, a text set within a context of the forthcoming. Memories recorded in oral history projects may have been the longest in the making, but given the conversational style of the discourse, were perhaps the most hastily constructed. And conjuring up long-past childhoods, they rendered train travel with the most minute details, referencing memories with the perspectives of one's immediate milieu; for the child the strange technology of the train was anchored with the memory of the most familiar, parents and grandparents for some, but the farm animal for most.

The travellers from western Canada, as do travellers everywhere, clearly cultivated concepts of time to order their uprooted lives, giving meaning to them as they were lived in a space in flux and in a changing world. And, as for all travellers, time was relative. Ideas of time reflected the difference between the traveller and non-traveller. They also changed as the migrants moved from one world to another. But they especially differed depending on the particular manner in which the travelling was considered. It was as if different media of communication solicited different perspectives that produced a multi-linearity of the present.[44] The trains that took the Mennonite emigrants from western Canada didn't merely move a people spatially, they also introduced them to a complex constellation of time constructions. And just which particular construction of time prevailed depended on the particular text employed to tell the story.

NOTES

1   For standard accounts of these migrations see entries for Mexico and Paraguay, *Global Anabaptist Mennonite Encyclopedia Online*, www.gameo.org, accessed 18 January 2013. Edgar Stoesz, *Like a Mustard Seed* (Harrisonburg: Herald Press, 2008); Calvin Redekop, *The Old Colony Mennonites* (Baltimore: Johns Hopkins Press, 1969); Harry Leonard Sawatsky, *They Sought a Country: Mennonite Colonization in Mexico* (Berkeley: University of California Press, 1971); Abe Warkentin, *Strangers and Pilgrims* (Steinbach, MB: 1987).

2   See Robert Fothergill, *Private Chronicles: A Study of Private Diaries* (London: Oxford University Press, 1974).

3   E.P. Thompson, "Time, Work-Discipline and Industrial Capitalism," *Past and Present* 38 (1967): 58, 90; for a critique of Thompson's view see Mark M. Smith, "Old South Time in Comparative Perspective," *American Historical Review* 101, 5 (1996): 1432–1469.

4   Quoted from his book *Pascalian Meditations* (Cambridge: Polity Press, 2000) in Anna Sofia Hedberg, *Outside World: Cohesion and Deviation among Old Colony Mennonites in Bolivia* (Uppsala: Uppsala Universitet, 2007), 28.

5   Michael Jackson, Introduction, *Politics of Storytelling: Violence, Transgression and Intersubjectivity* (Copenhagen: Museum Tusculanum, 2002), 13.

6   Frau Isaac F. Bergen, "Reisebericht der Frau Isaak F. Bergen," in *Unsere Reise Nach Paraguay, 1948*, ed. Jacob H. Sawatsky (Sommerfeld: Paraguay, self-published, 2004), 20–37.

7   Ibid., 21.

8   Ibid.

9   Ibid.

10   Ibid., 22.

11   Ibid., 23–25.

12   Ibid., 29–30.

13   Ibid., 30.

14   *Steinbach Post*, 8 March 1922.

15   Ibid., 18 October 1922.

16   Ibid., 15 November 1922.

17   Ibid., 3 January 1923.

18   Ibid., 25 May 1924.

19   Ibid., 11 July 1923.

20   Ibid., 20 April 1927.

21   Ibid., 4 September 1927.

22   Ibid., 7 August 1946.

23   Ibid.

24   Ibid.

25   Isaak M. Dyck, "Emigration from Canada to Mexico, Year 1922," trans. Robyn Dyck Sneath, unpublished manuscript in possession of author. This book was published most recently as *Die Auswanderung der Reinlaender Mennoniten Gemeinde von Kanada nach Mexiko 1970* (Cuauhtémoc: Imprenta Colonial, 1993).

26   Ibid.

27   Ibid.

28   Ibid.

29   Ibid.
30   Ibid.
31   Ibid.
32   Ibid.
33   Ibid.
34   Ibid.
35   Ibid.
36   Mennonite Archives of Ontario, tape-recorded interviews by Ronald Sawatsky, Mennonite Archives of Ontario. Interviews translated and transcribed by Kerry L. Fast; hard copies in possession of author.
37   Ibid.
38   Ibid.
39   Ibid.
40   Ibid.
41   Ibid.
42   Ibid.
43   Ibid.
44   Jacques Derrida, *Margins of Philosophy* (Chicago: University of Chicago Press, 1982), 34.

HOME AWAY FROM HOME?
THE DIASPORA IN CANADA AND THE ZIMBABWEAN FUNERAL

JOYCE M. CHADYA

I began this paper musing over a conversation I had overheard on a combi (public transport) in Harare, Zimbabwe. Two women who were returning from a funeral were talking—as Zimbabwean women usually do—about what they had heard and seen at the funeral. I could not help but listen, as the women had to talk loudly over the din of the combi engine. An elderly woman had passed away, they said. Her children "*vakaparira nepasi* [were all over the world]." One was in New Zealand, two in Australia, and another one in Canada. The two women admired the deceased, for God had blessed her with "diaspora children." The mourners and sympathizers had gathered at the deceased's Zengeza home, extended by the "diaspora children," and stayed overnight eating and drinking food bought by the "diaspora children."[1] The following day after breakfast, they were told to disperse until further notice as arrangements were being made for the "diaspora children" to come back home. The funeral would resume once the children had arrived. "Obviously," one of the women concluded with admiration, the dead woman was going to have a "grand funeral, what with all her 'diaspora children'!"

The more I pondered about this conversation the more I began to contemplate how the "diasporanization" of millions of Zimbabweans has affected one of the most fundamental social practices in any society—the mourning and burials of family members, in this case those left in the original homeland. The idea for this paper was, thus, initiated. Being a member of the Zimbabwean diaspora[2] myself, living in Winnipeg, I chose Winnipeg as the primary focus of my study. However, my conversations with the Zimbabwean diasporans in other western countries confirmed that, except for certain Canadian peculiarities, they also shared similar experiences of the Zimbabwean deathscape (the terrain of death: mourning and burial) of family members in the original homeland.[3]

Large-scale emigration to Canada by Zimbabweans is a recent phenomenon. It was instigated by the economic and political calamity now generally referred to as the Zimbabwe Crisis[4] in scholarly idiom. The crisis, which began in the 1990s, became a major defining moment in Zimbabwean emigration, as an unprecedented number of over 4 million Zimbabweans (out of a total population of about 13 million) left the country since the mid-1990s. Some went to neighbouring countries in southern Africa as economic and political refugees. Others, however, went to far-flung countries like the United Kingdom, the United States, Canada, Australia, and New Zealand in a move some Zimbabweans have called the "empire striking back," in reference to this reversal of the direction of migration that prevailed during the colonial period.

Because of its relative newness, the study of the Zimbabwean diasporans is still in its budding stages, with most of the studies devoted to the diasporans in the UK and South Africa, the epicentres of Zimbabwean diaspora destinations.[5] Scholars on the Zimbabwean diaspora, however, have largely focused their studies on the role played by the diaspora in providing an economic lifeline to Zimbabwe, employment opportunities for (and the health of) the diaspora, and immigration, identity, and citizenship status in receiving countries.[6] One issue that has not been effectively examined is the diaspora's experience of mourning and death. The lone scholarly work that I came across, by Beacon Mbiba, examines how the Zimbabwean diaspora in Britain deals with death and mourning of one of their own. He establishes that the British Zimbabwean diaspora has a strong preference to be buried at "home" in Zimbabwe.[7] Shifting the angle of vision, I explore the Canadian-Zimbabwean diaspora's experience of death in the city of Winnipeg, with a special focus on the death of family members in the original homeland. I do so within the framework that sees death as an inextricable component of social experience. This chapter draws on oral histories and conversations with the Zimbabwean diaspora residing in Winnipeg, Manitoba, Canada, but it is also based on the Zimbabwean diaspora in other locations in Canada and the global north as well as Zimbabweans who live within Zimbabwe. The interviews were carried out between 2008 and 2011.

Exploring the experience of death of family left behind by the Canadian Zimbabwean diaspora provides us with an insight into issues of identity and belonging which have a direct bearing on the transnational relationships that develop between the Zimbabwean diaspora in Canada and family in Zimbabwe. This sense of belonging manifested itself through regular remittances to family members in Zimbabwe, economic investment at home, marrying Zimbabwean spouses in Canada/the West or "importing" spouses from Zimbabwe, return visits and even participation in transnational social/cultural events in Zimbabwe such as funerals—either by having funeral wakes in Canada, remitting money for funeral expenses and/or travelling to Zimbabwe to attend funerals. Additionally, this sense of belonging is also evinced in the diaspora's continued reference to Zimbabwe as *kumusha*—home. When I asked Nyengererai, one of my informants, if Zimbabwe is the home, what then is Canada, she did not hesitate to answer: "a home away from home."[8] This is not surprising, as it echoes the strong attachment to countries of origin by other first-generation immigrants from elsewhere.[9] It was from Nyengererai that I borrowed the title of this paper. The question mark serves to accommodate the shifting attitudes by the Zimbabwean diaspora as they begin to invest by buying properties in the receiving countries.

Canadian-Zimbabwean diasporans' perception of themselves as belonging to Zimbabwe, as suggested by my informants, generates a sense of obligations on the part of the diasporans and expectations—entitlements, even—by family in Zimbabwe. These kinds of relationships have, in some cases, created both appreciation and umbrage that emanate from receiving the help or not receiving enough (or anything at all), respectively. Looking at the Zimbabwean diaspora's experience of death of family in Zimbabwe also provides us with a window through which to observe some of the transported memories/customs. For the Zimbabwean diaspora, the transportation of memories is two-way. Their response to social situations like death is shaped by their socialization in Zimbabwe. Conversely, when they go to Zimbabwe for funerals they also bring with them their experiences of western funerals. Sometimes this has generated conflict between generations, as the elderly who regard themselves as custodians of culture question the new ways of conducting funerals. I argue, however, that this is nothing new. Funerals and burials have always been dynamic, especially whenever there has been a significant socio-economic shift. Although diasporan-sent foreign currency made possible major transformations in some basic features of Zimbabwean funeral paraphernalia—funeral food, dressing, and etiquette, the kind of casket one is buried in, and the use of funeral homes for burial—these changes had been underway since independence, albeit in the realm of the privileged educated, economic, and political elite.

In Zimbabwe, the term diaspora is used exclusively for those who emigrated to western countries.[10] Thus the identity comes loaded with connotations. In particular, the diasporans are perceived as people who live in countries of "infinite possibilities and easy riches accessible to all" and that, as the diasporans, they are "loaded with money" and are, therefore, "your go-to-guys" where financial needs are concerned. While this identity has persisted in Zimbabwe, individual circumstances and changes over time have not been taken into account.

One's immigration status and class, for example, affect the diasporans' ability to help their families. As shall be demonstrated below, some Zimbabweans holding "*rese rese*" jobs (literally any kind of job but specifically refers to menial jobs) discovered the hard way that "if your social security number starts with a nine," meaning a temporary work permit/refugee status, or if one has a refused refugee status, they can be underpaid or passed over in terms of promotion.[11] Such people's ability to respond to deaths in Zimbabwe monetarily is therefore compromised. Likewise, having families in the diaspora can affect how much disposable income one has. In addition, the dollarization of the Zimbabwean economy in 2009 changed the fortunes of the diasporans, as it became more expensive to support family in Zimbabwe in general, and funerals in particular. Indeed, newspapers and my informants in Zimbabwe talked about how some diasporans have changed from "saviours to confidence tricksters"[12] since the introduction of the "greenback" which eroded their financial power.

HISTORICAL BACKGROUND

Zimbabweans have had a moderately long history of emigration. The first wave of emigration from Rhodesia, colonial Zimbabwe, was in response to the labour needs of South African mines at the turn of the nineteenth century. As part of the Witwatersrand Native Labour Association recruitment system or as individuals in clandestine emigration, Zimbabweans migrated to better-paying South African mines until the 1930s.[13] This was followed by the politically induced decolonization emigration from the 1960s until independence in 1980.

There were two distinct groups in this phase. First were Africans—principally men—fleeing from political repression, oppression, imminent arrest, imprisonment and/or detention, and the insecurity wrought by the liberation war including conscription.[14] Although a majority went into neighbouring independent African countries, some went overseas, especially to Britain and the US because of the colonial and lingo ties respectively. Many who went overseas were the educated elite who ended up enrolling in universities.[15] An overwhelming majority of them returned to Zimbabwe at independence.

The second group was composed of white Rhodesians who emigrated between the mid-1970s and 1980. Tens of thousands crossed the border into white South Africa, fleeing from the escalating liberation war and its attendant insecurity. They also wanted to protect their sons from conscription into the Rhodesian army. Also, with majority rule becoming imminent, they did not want to be under a black government and thus they "voted with their feet."[16] The first post-colonial emigration began with the ZANU PF/ZAPU[17] political struggles that led to state-sanctioned and state-perpetrated *Gukurahundi* violence and massacre of 20,000

Ndebeles between 1983 and 1987.[18] While some fled largely into neighbouring countries in the southern African region, others emigrated overseas.

The latest (and perhaps biggest) emigration by Zimbabweans started in the mid- to late-1990s due to political instability and repression on one hand, and an economic collapse of gigantic magnitude on the other.[19] A number of factors intertwined to produce the economic collapse, among which were state welfarism of the 1980s[20] and gross mismanagement of the economy. The adoption of the "one size fits all" structural adjustment program as an economic recovery panacea in the early 1990s accelerated the economic deterioration.[21] Social services provision disintegrated. Most companies closed down or relocated into neighbouring countries leading to the retrenching of thousands of workers. In 2008, unemployment was over 85 percent.

By 1999 there were commodity shortages ranging from food to fuel, as well as severe electric power cuts and water rationing, among other socio-economic woes. To boot, the country experienced world-record inflation, reaching 230 million percent by December 2008.[22] The political repression—particularly since the 1999 arrival of a formidable opposition party (Movement for Democratic Change—MDC) on the political scene—left many young people in the opposition party. Those who deplored the violence across the parties had only two options—conform to "Mugabeism" or flee from the country.[23] White farm invasions, quietly endorsed by the state beginning in late 1998, only exacerbated an already dire situation.[24] In a nutshell, the economy collapsed and the political climate was harsh. Accordingly, an overwhelming majority of the Zimbabwean diaspora are either political refugees, economic migrants, or both.[25]

The Zimbabwe Crisis–induced diaspora has a number of striking features. First, and as demonstrated above, the numbers are unprecedented. Second is the multiplicity of their destinations creating Zimbabwean diasporans in countries outside the historical colonial ties (UK) or traditional destinations such as the USA, to countries such as Canada, New Zealand, Australia, and elsewhere, including the Middle East. As one interviewee put it, "Now there is hardly any country on earth where you cannot find one or two Zimbabweans."[26] Third, the Zimbabwean diaspora are now emigrating for indefinite periods and, more or less, on a permanent basis as evidenced by property investments and acquisition of citizenship in destination countries. Fourth, the demographics shifted—prior to the 1990s, a vast majority of the emigrants were male, but the 1990s and 2000s saw husbands moving with their wives and children as well an increasing number of single women emigrating. Previously, leaving wives and children in Zimbabwe without applying for citizenship in destination countries suggested Zimbabwe was the base to which male migrants always returned. However, bringing them to new countries suggests the base is shifting. Finally, while prior to the 1990s

Zimbabweans who emigrated were largely the educated/professional elite, from the late 1990s it was more of a mixed bag ranging from infants, grade school children, young people in higher education to highly educated/professional people and some adults with little to no educational or professional qualifications.

While statistics for Zimbabweans who immigrated into Canada are not available, my estimate is that they are in the tens of thousands. So why did they choose Canada as their destination? African emigration to countries with which they have no colonial ties—like Canada—began, even before Zimbabwe attained majority rule, in the 1970s after the independence euphoria across the continent had died down.[27] By then it had dawned that most African governments had failed to deliver on their promises.[28] Some Zimbabweans chose Canada as a destination specifically because it was one of the fifty-four members of the Commonwealth in the late 1990s, and so Zimbabweans had a sense of connection with the country, especially the shared history of colonization and the linguistic advantage of the use of English. As Commonwealth members, Zimbabweans did not need visas to enter Canada, at least until 2001, when immigration laws became more restrictive against Zimbabweans. Thus, it was much easier to get into Canada, unlike other western countries, like the US. As well, with the Zimbabwe crisis deepening, Zimbabweans became "aware of Canada's respect of its obligations towards refugees"[29] and began emigrating to Canada. While Zimbabwean immigration started as a trickle, by 2000 Canada had become one of the most popular western destinations. The numbers increased in the next year when Zimbabweans rushed to beat the 2001 introduction of visa requirements for Zimbabweans visiting Canada.[30] The period between 1998 and 2001 became the biggest wave of Zimbabwean immigration.[31] After 2001, Zimbabwean immigration receded to a trickle, consisting largely of highly professional people who found it easy to get work permits and permanent residency and by those who were assisted by family already resident in Canada.

Another large wave of Zimbabwean immigration into Canada took place between December 2002 and July 23, 2009, under the Canada-US Safe Third Party Agreement. Under this Agreement, any people seeking refugee status had to do so in the first country they entered—that is, either in the US or in Canada—unless they qualified for an exemption. The provisions of the Immigration and Refugee Protection Regulations meant Canada "could declare a temporary suspension of removals [commonly called a moratorium] to countries where there is a generalized risk to the entire civilian population, as a result of armed conflict, environmental disaster or other temporary or generalized situation."[32] Because of the political violence in the country, Zimbabwe was among countries that qualified for a moratorium in 2002. It was under this moratorium exemption that thousands of Zimbabweans who had lived in the US for several years, but whose visas had expired and had thus gone "underground" or had a refused refugee status, moved to Canada between 2002 and 2009. However, in July 2009, Canada revoked Zimbabwe's moratorium status.[33] Thus from 2009 Zimbabwean immigration into Canada yet again reverted to a dribble. These were the circumstances under which a large number of Zimbabweans settled in Canada. An overwhelming majority of the diaspora in Canada was born in Zimbabwe and has very strong ties to their country of origin. This attachment has been greatly facilitated by a transformation in telecommunications, travel, and ways of remitting money. Paul T. Zeleza succinctly explained the importance of this communication revolution to the African diaspora thus: "[It] compresses the spatial and temporal distances between home and abroad, offers contemporary diasporas unprecedented opportunities to be transnational and transcultural, to be people of multiple worlds and faculties, perpetually translocated, physically and culturally, between several countries or several continents. They are also able to retain ties to Africa in ways that were not possible to earlier generations of African diasporas."[34]

In Zimbabwe, this communication transformation in the form of cellphones, the Internet and *bureaux de change* facilitated communication between the diaspora and Zimbabwe. Cellphones have become so ubiquitous in Zimbabwe that people refer to them as *asina irombe,* roughly translated as something that one must be extremely poor to not have.[35] Undeniably, cellphone calls and texting are the main means of communication used between Zimbabwe and the diaspora. In addition, the Internet has made possible email, chat rooms, Facebook, and Skype communication. In a country where a large majority of Zimbabweans do not have computers and/or access to Internet networks at home, Internet cafes (since the 1990s) have been central in facilitating communication. The Internet was also used by the diaspora to remit cash through underground money-transfer schemes and to buy petrol and food online for family at home at the height of basic commodity shortages.[36] All these items are essential at funerals. *Bureaux de change* and other money-wiring companies made it possible to send money instantly.[37] During the years of crisis, 1998–2008, a number of Zimbabwean diasporans also ran informal (and, technically, illegal) money-transfer services. The communication revolution, therefore, made it possible for the Zimbabwean diasporans in Canada and elsewhere to be kept abreast of sickness and death in the family back home, remit money, and participate in funerals and burial even from a distance.

RECEIVING THE "BAD NEWS"

The most common way that has been used to transmit messages of death from Zimbabwe is the phone. For the elderly, it is absolutely essential to make sure that all family members get the news of death because in Shona cosmology those who have not been informed *"vanoona mashura*—they will have mysterious/ weird experiences."[38] Here are two examples to that effect. Janet, in her late fifties, recounted how her body was weak the whole day. She could not even get out of bed. Later in the evening she heard her father had passed away. Retrospectively she understood why she had been weak.[39] Silas had an even more bizarre experience when his father passed away. His manager called him into his office and told him they did not have his social insurance number—after working for the same company for three years. He therefore had to stop working. The following day, the day he had received the call about his mother's death, the manager informed him they had found it—it was their mistake! He was immediately reinstated.[40] Not all of my informants went through such experiences though.

To make sure the news gets to the intended person in Canada, families in Zimbabwe use all kinds of communication at their disposal—phoning, texting and emailing—sometimes all at once. Twenty-eight-year-old Tashinga, for example, came to Canada in 2001 at eighteen years. When she was twenty-one, her father passed away. For the six months her father was seriously ill with leukemia, her family did not tell her the extent of the illness, but simply said he was not feeling well. Many mothers, like Tashinga's, worry about telling their children about illness at home, especially when the children are young, and worse, do not have the social network of relatives to comfort and commiserate with them. When her father eventually passed away, her family called her apartment, but she had left for school. So they left a voice message on her phone as well as sending an email. It was the email that she saw first: "Can you believe it? I saw the message when I was in the computer lab where a bunch of other students were working. It was such a huge shock that I just collapsed on the chair and sobbed. My friends had to help me, as I was an emotional wreck."[41] They took her back to her apartment. Her classmates, friends, and workmates raised enough money for her air ticket and she left for Zimbabwe two days later. She was able to see her father buried.

When the Zimbabwean diasporans have a sick relative, a phone call with a Zimbabwean caller ID can be unsettling. Memory's mother, for instance, had been diagnosed with stage four breast cancer. Whenever her caller ID showed a Zimbabwean phone number, Memory answered the phone with the dreaded question, *"Kwakanaka here?*—Is everything okay?" as she expected to hear "bad news" any day.[42] So she answered the phone wanting to know, but dreading to hear, what the call was about. "Every time I was told that my mother was okay, I had a sigh of relief." She was eventually told about her death when she least expected it.

In another example, Florence received the call about her mother's death from her younger brother, who was seventeen at the time: "He was trying very hard to have a light conversation but I could tell something was off. I asked him, 'Steven, everything okay? You do not sound yourself.' He just broke down and in between sobs told me that Mama's sugar level had spiked and she died in her sleep. I fought back my tears and steadied my voice. I had to be strong to console him. I only started crying after the call. You begin to ask, no matter how much you help them financially, whether it was the right decision to settle here."[43]

For Viola, the death was of her six-year-old daughter she had left behind in the care of her sister in 2001. The daughter came back from school one day complaining that she was sick. By evening she was fast deteriorating and the family took her to an upscale hospital in Harare. They called Viola on the way to the hospital: "I stayed by the phone, praying fervently. I called in sick and ten hours later my brother-in-law called, 'It was meningitis. The doctors did all they could, but...' I threw the phone down and screamed. I left her when she was a year old. For five years all I had was hearing her voice on the phone and her pictures sent via email! She was the reason I worked so hard. I just hope she did not feel abandoned."[44]

I heard many harrowing stories of the Zimbabwean diasporans receiving news of death of family members in Zimbabwe on the phone. Most, especially women, immediately begin crying on the phone while the other person at the end of the line in Zimbabwe is also crying:

I was crying for so many reasons. The loss of my father and not being there when he was sick. I think that was the hardest part. Yes, I always sent some money for his hospital bills and other needs, and I called very frequently but that wasn't enough for me. I heard he always asked when I was coming home. I also cried because I could not go to Zimbabwe to mourn the parent we had lost together with my siblings. I could not afford to go. I cried for my mother. Who was going to console her in all this? Is living here really worth missing those precious moments of saying goodbye to your parent? You know how important daughters are in parent-care in our culture.[45]

Feelings of guilt for "not being there," of abandonment of one's parents or children are common under normal circumstances, but the diasporans' guilt is heightened in moments of death.

News of death in Zimbabwe always generates a flow of money from the diasporans to Zimbabwe whether they end up going or not. Like other Africans, the Zimbabwean diasporan is expected to carry most of the funeral costs, in particular those of parents or children.[46] The money remitted to Zimbabwe is needed to pay for the mortuary fees, funeral food—all mourners are fed by the deceased's family—transporting the cadaver from the mortuary to the house where it lies in state overnight as well as to transport the corpse and the mourners to the cemetery. The money is usually sent to a trusted person, as there are known cases where the money was misused and/or substandard caskets were bought and the change was "pocketed."

Interestingly, the relationship between the Zimbabwean diaspora and family in Zimbabwe echoes the colonial-induced relationship between town and country in colonial Zimbabwe. On one hand, Canada plays the role of colonial urban and mining centres—places of employment and opportunity. On the other hand, Zimbabwe is the periphery, the place where people seeking opportunities originated from—much like the colonial reserves where Africans were confined during the colonial period. Denied the right to urban tenure, the majority of colonial Zimbabwean Africans were forced to see the reserve as home. Accordingly, bodies of those who died in the city were ferried home. Africans also had to travel to the rural areas for funerals of kin whenever time and funds permitted. In the event that they could not take time off, they sent some money, usually with bus conductors, to help alleviate the funeral costs.[47]

After remitting funeral money, the diasporans have to make a decision: Do they go to Zimbabwe or not? If they do, when would be the most convenient time? The decision has to be made quickly, as it affects burial plans in Zimbabwe. Burial goes ahead if diasporans cannot travel to Zimbabwe for the funeral, or is postponed until the diasporans have arrived, as is revealed in the story at the beginning of this paper. But postponing burial is only feasible when someone dies in places where mortuaries exists—otherwise burial is immediate. For those who cannot go (and those who can only go at a later date), close friends and/or family organize a "wake" for the deceased in the diaspora's Canadian locality.

WITH THEM IN SPIRIT:
WAKES FOR FAMILY MEMBERS WHO DIE IN ZIMBABWE

The Zimbabwean diaspora have imported some of their cultural memories into Canada. Most significant of these is the notion of a funeral as a communal social event where friends and family meet to commiserate. Consequently, whenever a member of the diaspora receives news of the death of close family members they inform other Africans and friends in general, and Zimbabweans in particular, via email or phone calls. These friends are also informed of the date and time for commiseration at the bereaved's residence. Those who cannot attend on the specific day can visit the bereaved any other time as individuals or they can pass on their condolences over the phone. On the chosen day there might be thirty or more people, depending on the social networks of the bereaved and/or the time and day of the week. In addition to commiseration, this visitation is also a display of the community's Africanness that is emblematic of what most of them will experience, at one point or another, as those left behind in Africa, especially parents, pass on.

Although the Zimbabwean culture shapes the way the diaspora in Canada conduct wakes for Zimbabwean relatives, ultimately those wakes are reshaped by the Canadian social environment. For instance, instead of the bereaved family providing and preparing all the food for mourners as is done in Zimbabwe, women from the Zimbabwean community prepare food (usually Zimbabwean dishes) to take to the "funeral," potluck style.

As part of their effort to console the bereaved, Zimbabweans, like many other Africans in the diaspora, show their sympathy by spending time with the bereaved family, carrying on light conversation, singing church hymns, and praying. At some point the bereaved person/family says something in memory, and to celebrate the life, of the deceased. Then food is served, after which people stay a little longer and then disperse. Sometimes when mourners know of the time of a burial they gather for a vigil, singing and praying, the night before the burial at the bereaved's residence.[48] They always disperse by midnight, especially when it is during the week.[49]

While Zimbabweans try to maintain, as much as circumstances in Canada allow, the Zimbabwean traditional funerary practices, many find the experience somewhat alienating. Think about Janet, whose father passed away in 2009. She could not go to Zimbabwe to mourn with the rest of her family. The Zimbabwean community and other Africans in Winnipeg gathered at her apartment to commiserate with her. Without the corpse, the tangible certainty represented by the actual body that accompanies mourning in Zimbabwe, she found it estranging and weird to have a "funeral" and mourn a loss known only through the abstraction of words. "He was the first close member of my family to die since I left Zimbabwe nine years ago. I understood he had died but I guess it hadn't sunk in yet. I felt I had to go home to have closure."[50] So Janet, who is in her fifties, worked for five months, taking three jobs, and saved enough money for an airline ticket. She went to Zimbabwe in time for the *nyaradzo*, the memorial service that is usually held after about one month, but in this case had been postponed at Janet's request.

Other than having a corpse-less wake, Janet was frustrated by the fact that she had to bottle her emotions inside and mourn quietly like a *murungu* (white person). Zimbabweans, like other Africans, have very emotional and expressive funeral customs where they openly display their sorrow through keening and elegies while some more dramatic mourners throw themselves to the ground. This is particularly true of women. In the rural areas of Zimbabwe women going to attend a funeral start keening long before reaching the bereaved's homestead, while in urban centres keening, which is a little subdued, usually starts upon entering the house of the bereaved. Wailing at funerals is so important that after funerals people, mostly women, compare notes about who cried the most, who cried little, who didn't cry, or who had "crocodile tears."[51]

While funerals in Zimbabwe are accompanied by emotional crying, singing, clapping, and vigorous dancing—practices generally culturally specific to sub-Saharan Africa—in Canada, mainstream society has a totally different approach to mourning, and such displays of emotion are interpreted differently. In 2005, Netsai was asked by the police to ask her guests "to keep it down," as her neighbours had complained of the noise emanating from her apartment when friends and acquaintances had gathered to sympathize with her on the passing of her father. "I was told I was disturbing the peace," and infringing on her neighbours' rights. That was despite her having informed her neighbours. Thus, "behaving like the Romans when you are in their country," as Janet put it, meant changing the ways of mourning.[52] Keening has to be eschewed and singing subdued. In Winnipeg and the rest of Canada, the wooden floors of many apartment buildings and houses mean that the sound from dancing feet is significantly amplified. Yet the dancing and singing are meant to ease the grief. The western social environment in general, and the Canadian one in particular, is so alienating that one Zimbabwean elderly woman visiting her daughter did not even need to be told that she could not weep loudly when she heard news that her sister's daughter had passed away in Zimbabwe.[53] Without going through the traditional processes of mourning, therefore, some Zimbabweans only feel closure when they eventually go to Zimbabwe for the funeral, or even later to give their beloved a fitting and respectful farewell. Even if they go to Zimbabwe days, weeks, or months after burial, social decorum dictates that they mourn like the person has just died.[54]

One of the funerary customs carried over from Zimbabwe by the diaspora is the donation of *chema* "funeral money" to the bereaved family by those who come to pass on their condolences. In Zimbabwe, funeral money is usually used to buy food for the mourners. In Canada, however, what it is used for is up to the recipient. Some send the money to their families in Zimbabwe as funeral money donated by friends in Canada, while others use it towards an air ticket to travel to Zimbabwe.[55] How much one donates is up to an individual's discretion. The relationship between the bereaved person and the sympathizers is important in determining how much one donates. The size of the support network the bereaved has ultimately determines how much one gets as funeral money. Individual donations of up to $100 are common. In towns with very strong Zimbabwean associations members make monthly contributions, and their associations also act as "burial societies" which disburse a substantial amount to bereaved members.[56] Depending on one's social networks, funeral money can amount to thousands of dollars—conversely, it can be insignificant. It is a testimony to the sizable amount of money that Zimbabweans can contribute as funeral money that one woman in a big Canadian city used the "death" of her father as a money-making opportunity. She announced her father had passed away and Zimbabweans quickly responded by contributing funeral money, only to discover that the father had been dead for more than a year.[57]

GOING HOME FOR THE FUNERAL

The ideal response by Zimbabwean diasporans to the death of close family members in Zimbabwe is to go to Zimbabwe to pay their last respects at the same time as the rest of the family. But whether one goes to Zimbabwe or not invariably depends on intertwining factors and circumstances. These include the diasporans' immigration status in Canada, work considerations, the availability of money for travel to Zimbabwe, and the relationship of the deceased to the diasporan.

The immigration status of Zimbabweans in Canada has a huge bearing on their ability to travel outside the country. Zimbabweans with valid documentation—citizenship, residency certificates, or work permits—can easily travel in and out of Canada. However, those with a refugee status—that is, those who were accepted into Canada as people fleeing from political persecution in Zimbabwe—cannot. Going back to Zimbabwe when the country is still under the same regime they ran away from implies that their life was not in that much danger in the first place. Consequently, going to Zimbabwe would have serious ramifications, including the nullification of their refugee status.[58] Another category of Zimbabweans who cannot travel back is those living in "limbo"—Zimbabweans who have been denied a refugee status in Canada but have not been deported. Between 2000 and 2005, for instance, 745 Zimbabweans had a refused refugee status. Such people, therefore, live in a legally indeterminate state with no right to appeal. According to the Canadian Council for Refugees, "living in limbo has profound impacts on people from moratorium countries, affecting virtually every aspect of their lives." One such Zimbabwean refused refugee status, who has been in Canada since 2001, had lost his sense of belonging by 2005. He perceived himself as a *citizen of nowhere*: "I don't know where I am. I am not in Canada, I am not in my country, I am not anywhere."[59] Going to Zimbabwe to attend a funeral was, therefore, out of the question for such Zimbabweans.

Nevertheless, having valid papers does not necessarily mean that Zimbabweans can go to attend funerals in Zimbabwe. For most there are other hurdles—for instance, the nature of one's work and time can be huge constraints on travelling. Those with temporary jobs for which they can get paid only when they show up for work find it hard to take time off. A week or more off work would have negative financial implications or, even worse, could mean losing one's job.[60] One woman who had been a professional in Zimbabwe "experienced deskilling" when she settled in Canada. She now holds a temporary health-care job. She remarked, "I do not have a permanent job. So when I do not go to work I do not get paid. What do you do when you have bills to pay and children to feed? Much as I wanted to attend my mother's funeral, it did not make economic sense. So I did not go." She went on to add, "Remember, other financial commitments to family in Zimbabwe that you are responsible for do not stop because there is a funeral. You know how it is. You have to weigh your choices."[61] For some, swapping shifts with workmates is the only way to make it possible to travel. Professional Zimbabweans reported that they get only a few days off work to attend funerals, thereby making it hard to travel the 26,000 kilometre round trip to Zimbabwe. With no direct flights between Canada and Zimbabwe, the return trip takes anywhere from three to five days.[62]

The cost of travelling to Zimbabwe is another major hindrance. Tickets bought for emergency travelling were upwards of $4,000 in 2010, a prohibitive figure for most people—including professionals. This is aggravated by the fact that, in the event of going, one also needs to carry a substantial amount of money for funeral expenses, as diasporan breadwinners are expected to shoulder most, if not all, of the costs in a context of high unemployment in the country. Those who earn low wages are particularly distressed by the cost of travel. In interviews carried out by the Canadian Council for Refugees, for example, many Zimbabwean refugees complained of the low wages they earned and tied this to their status as refused refugees. "I will never get a raise; I am looked down upon as a 'refugee.' In theory we should get the same rights as other employees, but we don't," griped one. "If my social insurance number starts with a nine, they know they can take advantage of me because this is my only means of surviving," complained another.[63] Raising money to travel to Zimbabwe is, therefore, a daunting task for most of the Zimbabwean diaspora. My discussions with informants revealed that many Zimbabweans in Canada, professional or otherwise, usually choose, or are forced by circumstances, to attend a "funeral" in Zimbabwe long after the deceased had been buried to fulfill the cultural politesse as well as to get closure.

The concerns raised above also mean that Zimbabweans in Canada cannot attend funerals for every member of their immediate and extended family as dictated by the norm.[64] They are forced to rank funerals according to the familial bond they had with the deceased. Thus, there are must-attend funerals, there are some for which one simply makes a financial contribution, and then there are others one can simply ignore. This strategy became more crucial in the light of increasing mortality due to the HIV/AIDS pandemic from the late 1990s and the 2008–2010 cholera epidemic.[65] The general unsaid canon is that, other factors permitting, it is obligatory to attend and carry the expenses for funerals for the diasporan's parents and children. Diasporans' parents are ordinarily retirees whose pension was eroded, and whose funeral policies were rendered worthless, by a world-record hyper-inflation during the Zimbabwe crisis, or they might be poor peasants who had used all their resources to "bank in [their] children" by sending them to school as security for old age.[66] In any case, African ideology impels adult children to look after their parents (including burying them). The adage *"Chirere chigokurerawo mangwana"*—literally, "take good care of your [children] so that they take care of you tomorrow"—represents both ideology and practice. It is not surprising, therefore, that Thomas, whose father abandoned his mother and three other siblings when they were little, refused to be responsible for his father's funeral in 2009.[67]

Marjorie, who settled in Winnipeg as a refugee in 2007 after several years in the US, informed me that she had received funeral calls and requests for financial assistance "left, right, and centre." While initially she used to "pander" to such requests, she has since begun to assign "hierarchies" to the requests. For funerals of distant extended kin, she just remits about US fifty dollars in funeral money. The closer she is to the deceased, the more she sends. She ended the interview by asking a rhetorical question, "How did they manage before I came here?"[68] For twenty-seven-year-old Paul, the physical distance between Zimbabwe and Canada facilitated emotional distance such that he stopped sending money to the extended family altogether except those he was very close to. "Gone are the days when you can give anyone and everyone money. *Unoseenzera mahara* [otherwise you won't have anything to show for your labour]."[69] Fafi, who has been in Canada since 2000, received a phone call informing her of an extended relative who had died. She immediately called to pass her condolences to her immediate family in Zimbabwe only to find out that some relatives in Zimbabwe had not yet been informed. "Do you know why they called me first?" she asked without waiting for the answer. "They want me to send some money. I cannot do it anymore. I just don't have the money—I am overextending myself as it is."[70] But she sent the money anyway.

Response to funeral phone calls is gendered, with women as mothers, daughters, sisters, and cousins responding to these phone calls faster than men. Not surprisingly, this is in conformity with the general gender expectations of Zimbabweans. Even in Zimbabwe, men find it easier to wiggle out of attending funerals than women.[71]

Sometimes the funeral financial commitments are so many within a short period of time that some Zimbabwean diasporans have come up with coping mechanisms. Some have come up with their own version of the Verizon wireless commercial when they receive such calls, "I cannot hear you. I am sorry I am losing you. Hello, hello…and the line goes dead," quipped Danai, laughing and adding "*kuseka nhamo kunge rugare*—I am laughing but it's not a joke at all."[72] "Sometimes, I just tell them that I will call them back but I never do on the pretext that I could not get through," said Timothy.[73] Some simply ignore the call, thanks to caller ID which enables them to ignore calls but listen to the voice message.[74] Thus they can ignore certain requests while accommodating others. Predictably, such coping mechanisms are highly gendered male.

Deciding to go to Zimbabwe often means that the burial of the deceased has to be delayed. With some families having siblings scattered all over the world, burial might be delayed for up to a month. In that case, family and friends who customarily gather for the wake, at the house of the bereaved until burial, are told to go back to their homes until further notice, as experienced by the two mourners mentioned at the beginning of this paper. That way the deceased family can cut the costs of feeding mourners as well as providing them with accommodation. It is not always possible to delay burial. Some parents live in the rural areas far from hospitals, with no access to mortuaries, and the cadaver cannot be kept unrefrigerated for more than one night. In those circumstances, by the time the diasporan arrives in Zimbabwe the deceased was buried—as was the case with Pedzisai's aunt, the surrogate mother who looked after Pedzisai when her mother passed away when she was only two years old.[75]

Where the deceased is kept in a mortuary, the diasporans typically assume the mortuary bill.[76] However, high HIV/AIDS mortality (killing about 3,000 people every week in the early to mid-2000s), severe state financial constraints culminating into consistent electric power cuts, and failure to procure necessary morgue chemicals inadvertently affected the operation of state mortuaries. The mortuaries' carrying capacity was exceeded several-fold at a time when power cuts meant cadavers could not be kept in a frozen state. In fact, up to 2008, Zimbabwean newspapers were awash with stories of over-stacked mortuaries that were hardly working.[77] Corpses in such mortuaries ran the risk of decomposing. Some families in Beitbridge, Zimbabwe's southern border town, ingeniously adapted by temporarily "exporting" cadavers to morgues across the border to Musina, a border town on the South African side, where they were kept until burial.[78] In larger cities, some families coped by moving cadavers into privately run, prestigious but expensive mortuaries which had diesel-generated power. Indeed, diaspora-remitted money for funerals contributed to the flourishing of the funeral industry at a time when most industries were folding.[79]

THE ZIMBABWEAN DIASPORA AND THE SHIFTING ZIMBABWEAN DEATHSCAPE

Since the Zimbabwean Crisis, remittances from the diaspora have precipitated a shift on many facets of the Zimbabwean deathscape. One such aspect is the use of funeral parlours by Africans. Long seen as part of the western culture and, therefore, a preserve for whites and a few "moneyed" blacks until the 1990s, diaspora remittances have made it possible for many former working-class or peasant families to suddenly afford to commodify death by not only buying expensive caskets but by professionalizing and commercializing death care and burial as well. A "new middle class" not tied to production or service thus emerged, and its existence trampled the old maxim that one's status in life was carried over into death. The use of funeral parlours and expensive caskets in burying the dead—once left to close kin—became commonplace. Such funerals at once transformed death customs from being a sorrowful occasion into something to be admired while also being perceived as a symbol of "progress" and a mark of *kuvigwa zvakanaka*—a funeral conducted admirably.

Families with a member in the diaspora wanted to "exhibit" their "prosperity" by the eminence of the casket (the more expensive the better) and having a funeral home and a professional undertaker prepare and bury the deceased, much to the financial burden of the diasporans.[80] Buying an expensive casket and hiring funeral parlour services became one of the "exhibitions" for a parent with a child in the diaspora. Otherwise mourners and sympathizers have been known to leave funerals remarking, "*Kacasket kacho! Ungamboti vane mwana ari kudiaspora*—the poor quality of the casket [oh my goodness]! Who would believe that they have a child in the diaspora?"[81] In some cases the diasporans have been forced to "conform and fit the bill."[82] In the process, death rituals previously confined to domestic spaces were being slowly shifted into the very impersonal and industrial-like funeral parlours.

Although the diasporans have helped their families give their loved ones a decent burial, financial dependency has negatively affected the relationship between the younger generations who have moved into Canada and the older generations in Zimbabwe. In fact, the dependency on the diasporans has truncated the customary deference that is given to seniors, lending credence to a saying among Zimbabweans that "*Ane mari ndiye mukuru*—the one who has money makes the decisions/is accorded more respect." Traditionally senior patriarchs— fathers, uncles, and older brothers, the custodians of culture—made decisions about how the funeral was to be conducted and they also handled the traditional funerary rites. They had the power to define certain things as *chinyakare* (traditional) and thus sanctify them with cultural legitimacy—an indispensable asset for controlling the younger generations who are supposedly not well-steeped in *chinyakare*. However, urbanization, Christianity, and westernization had been slowly eroding some aspects of *chinyakare* funerary traditions. Moreover, the Zimbabwean economic crisis had made most of the poor seniors superfluous, as poverty forced some of them to listen to the younger diasporans with money.

This over-dependency on the diaspora for money thus created power struggles, resentment, and ill feeling. Consider Tonderai, a thirty-year-old unmarried, professional man who settled in Winnipeg in 2003. His father passed away in 2008. With his father dead, his uncle (father's junior brother) was automatically supposed to preside over Tonderai's father's funeral arrangements. However, Tonderai had his own ideas about how things were supposed to be done. His uncle ended up confronting him as he reminded him, "Tonderai, you are still a young boy with milk on his nose [denoting a nursing infant and therefore infantilizing him]. Some of these things you should let us, the elders, lead you. You are being disrespectful because you think money is everything. You still need your elders no matter how much money you have." Tonderai, however, thought his uncle was taking advantage of his seniority to control Tonderai and his siblings and, as the oldest child, he felt obliged to protect his and his siblings' interests. He told the uncle, "If you want to do things your way then you should pay for the funeral," and that effectively silenced the poor uncle.[83]

Tonderai was emboldened by, and took advantage of, the power he had gained in the diaspora. The younger uncles who had a bone to pick with the senior patriarch due to his overbearing authority also buoyed him—they also figured it paid to be in Tonderai's good standing for future financial gain. Thus, due to his diaspora-earned money and his social status as a diasporan, Tonderai was able to usurp power from his uncle. Although power struggles and conflicts had always existed between generations, the diaspora phenomenon is taking such conflict and power struggle to new heights. Tonderai's uncle was so aggrieved that he could not resist the urge to tell him off: "You have to be grateful to Mugabe [the Zimbabwean president whose policies forced him out of the country]. Otherwise without diaspora you would be nothing."[84]

In a different but similar example, Danai, a twenty-nine-year-old woman who has lived in Canada since 2001, asked her uncles and brothers in Zimbabwe to delay interring her father until she arrived:

> They simply said it was impossible. They could not send mourners who had travelled long distances back before burial. He was buried a day before I arrived. Some members of the family later told me that one uncle [who directed the funeral] had said that they could not postpone the burial because of a girl-child. I was furious although I did not confront him. It was tricky because I was planning on going to Zimbabwe the following year to get married [for her fiancé to pay the bridewealth]. Now with my father dead, it meant that the same uncle and my brothers were going to preside over my marriage proceedings.[85]

Tonderai and Danai's responses were immersed in the traditional generational and gender relations among the Shona, where the elders police familial hierarchies. But Tonderai was already asserting his role as an emerging patriarch, while for Danai female politesse, subordination, and deference dictated that she suffer silently because of fear of being ostracized with potential negative ramifications for her in the future. But while gender played into the different reactions that Tonderai and Danai received from their families, there are many other examples where uncles took into consideration the opinions of their nephews and where uncles gladly waited for the arrival of nieces in the diaspora. Like in other epochs of economic change, social conflicts between the younger generations and the elderly were always in the offing as new economic opportunities ushered in more autonomy and decision-making powers for the young.

Cultural dislocation, shock, and clashes occur when diasporans bring their children who were born and raised in Canada or their non-African Canadian spouses to funerals. One couple took their two daughters (ages twelve and fifteen) to Zimbabwe to mourn their paternal grandmother. Their father explained: "They frowned at the dramatic exhibition of emotion where mourners arrived keening at the top of their lungs while others threw themselves to the ground [African gesticulations of sorrow]. They made comments later which made me realize I had not quite understood the extent of their cultural disarticulation. It was quite sad. Here in Canada they are not perceived as Canadians, as evidenced by the oft-asked question, 'When are you guys going back?' while in Zimbabwe all relatives were referring to them as 'Canadians' or more generally *madiaspora* [the Diasporans]." The second generation of Zimbabwean-Canadians find themselves estranged from their parents' cultural past, including the funeral rituals they had never experienced and did not, therefore, understand. "At the same time," the father lamented, "they are not quite familiar with Canadian [read: Western] burial customs other than the rudimentary stuff they know from watching TV. It's a generation with an identity crisis," he concluded.[86]

Cultural disarticulation is also experienced by Canadian spouses of Zimbabwean men and women who go to funerals in Zimbabwe. In what Peter described as an "epic case of cultural misunderstanding," he took his wife, Meghan, to his mother's funeral in Zimbabwe. The burial went well. The day after the burial family members gathered to dispose of Peter's mother's possessions as prescribed by custom. Among these effects were some clothes that Meghan had bought for her mother-in-law. While Peter had informed her what was going on, she could not understand why she was not given anything when in actual fact she had bought some of the clothes which were being distributed. So "without talking to anyone she stood up, walked to the pile where her mother-in-law's clothes were and picked up all the clothes she had bought, hissing, 'You selfish people. When we are in Canada you call all the time asking for money. I come here and you do not have the courtesy to give me anything.' "[87] But Meghan had failed to grasp the "sacrosanctness" of the occasion and misconstrued the meaning of the practice. Culture dictates that the effects of any deceased woman, mothers-in-law included, cannot be given to anyone but her natal family. Thus Meghan had felt slighted out of ignorance. Peter had to apologize to his family for his wife's behaviour.

Zimbabweans in the diaspora have also contributed to unabashed visual displays of funerary commoditization, rampant funerary consumerism—what elderly Zimbabweans have called "lavish funerals" where "mourners eat and drink as if they are at a party."[88] James Tsuro, in his sixties, told me of one funeral paid for by a Zimbabwean soccer player based in the UK: "They hired Rooney's [a high-end catering company] which brought a huge tent, chairs, and plenty of food and drinks. People ate and drank until they were full. In fact anybody in the neighbourhood who wanted came for free food. The food tasted so good it was like food at a wedding party."[89]

While Zimbabweans generally expect children to give their parents a decent funeral, the extravagance flew in the face of elderly Africans' sense that funerals should be modest. Traditionally, funerals are supposed to be sombre: "Funeral food is meant to keep body and soul together rather than to be enjoyed. In fact some of the people closest to the deceased are so grief-stricken that they can't eat at all. But *madiaspora* [diasporans] are organizing funerals in such a way as to show off. There are families that have three or more people in the diaspora so they have the money. Sometimes you wonder whether they feel the loss at all."[90]

Many elderly people see such flaunting of money in the form of funeral food as being imprudent and ostentatious, for "why would anyone hire a catering company as if they are at a wedding?"[91] Some elders were critical of some of the young people in the diaspora who never really cared for their parents but spent thousands of dollars on their funerals. Although the elders' concerns about over-the-top funerals are, in some cases, valid, they are also working with a selective memory, as they "forget" that, for time immemorial, better-off Africans always provided better food for mourners—even among peasants. For instance, one of the traditional food requirements at an adult's funeral is that the bereaved family slaughter an ox for funeral meat—the poorer ones had to make do with a goat, which meant less meat for the mourners. Thus good and plentiful food affirmed the bereaved family's status while for the poor, their poverty was mirrored in poor/less food consumed at a funeral.

While the diasporans import their cultural memories into Canada, the reverse trend is discernible, especially among younger diasporans. Their exposure to, and exportation of, aspects of western funeral practices to Zimbabwe has hastened a shift in funeral clothing in Zimbabwe. I say hastened because the dress code has been slowly shifting from mournful simplicity to fancy clothing due to the exposure to western, especially American, funeral dressing represented on television and film. Many of my informants also pointed out that diasporan women, in particular, do not show much emotion anymore. I asked why that was and John ventured an explanation: "It's probably the makeup. If they cry it will be smudged all over their faces." Kizito, however, thought it was because women quickly change and behave like *varungu*. "I heard one say she won't mourn like a peasant after staying abroad for so long."[92]

The dress code at funerals has changed, especially among the diasporans and those who are better off. Traditionally, mourners did not get dressed to be noticed at funerals. According to one sixty-seven-year-old ambuya Mutanda, twenty years ago most Zimbabwean women slipped into "decent long dresses, head covers and *mazambia* [cloth wrapped around a woman's body from the waist down]" to go to funerals. In fact, custom compelled the widow to take no bath until her spouse's corpse was buried. But now "women dress to kill," especially on the burial day. "If you see them in their fancy black dresses, pantyhose, high heels, hats even, you would think they are going to a party," she said with derision.[93] Those with western influence and the money to buy trendy clothing dress in black from head to toe. They also wear a lace covering their face complete with makeup and impressive hairdos. Many elders feel it is downright disrespectful to care how one looks to that extent when in mourning. Senior women's disparagement of the young diasporan and better-off Zimbabwean women also stem from their loss of power over them. Still, the commercialization of Zimbabwean funerals has not reached West African proportions, where the grandiosity of food, funeral fashions, and professional entertainment has been taken to new heights and has created a new industry in its own right. The amount of funeral money one donates is even publicly announced in Ghana and Nigeria.[94]

The conspicuous consumption at Zimbabwean funerals has extended to the use of cameras and video cameras at funerals. The diaspora uses video cameras to capture the funeral for the benefit of family members who cannot attend—so that the loss only known through the abstraction of language could be more tangible—and also for posterity. Seniors in Zimbabwe see the use of video cameras as totally out of place, untraditional. When Monica was shooting a video during her mother's burial, her maternal uncle pulled her aside and asked her what she was doing. "You are taking this solemn moment to shoot a film?" For him the video camera was being used in ways that were radically different from what he thought was appropriate respectability, and he took offence.[95] "Your mother must be turning in her box [casket] even before she is buried! You know that is not part of our culture."[96] But Monica explained that it was important to film the burial so that her children and siblings who were not able to attend the funeral can watch how their mother was buried and thus provide something that could help with the emotional acceptance of the loss. But as Pierre Bourdieu has concisely argued, taste classifies the classified as much as it classifies the classifier.[97] As much as Monica's uncle was appalled by his niece's untraditional taste, in Monica's perception, his taste of anti-modernity in turn marked him as a traditionalist, an SRB—someone with a Strong Rural Background.[98]

When contrasted with other parts of Africa, Zimbabwe is still lagging behind as far as funeral consumerism is concerned. Among other funeral consumptions, video cameras, hired entertainers, expensive caskets and impressive clothing have long become part of the funerary culture in West Africa. Kwame Arhin's study on the Akan of Ghana illustrates that funerals have become spaces to parade the status of the bereaved family. In Nigeria, Joan Omoruyi has shown that funeral programs have been used as indicators of the socio-economic status of the deceased.[99] The information on the program includes a picture of the deceased, names and sobriquets, date and place of birth and death, educational institutions attended with dates and certificates obtained, date of marriage and name of spouse and survivors.[100]

While some seniors in Zimbabwe oppose this "western way" of behaviour at funerals, the diasporans' argument, summed up by Jonathan, is that "this is the last time I am spending money on my parent. Let me do what I can in appreciation of everything they have done for me. It's not about showing off at all. Some of the people who complain—it's only because they do not have the means to do that for their loved ones."[101] There are also some open-minded kin who support the diasporans' efforts. In Monica's case above, her other uncles came to her defence: "*Ko ndizvo zvava kuitwaka. Zvichamboshamisa here*? [This is how it is being done nowadays. It is not such a taboo anymore.] Watch the national TV and you will see videos of the burial of government ministers being aired."[102] But for Monica's older uncle, that was for the politicians—not ordinary people like his sister. These different takes on funerary dos and don'ts make us privy to some of the social changes that are taking place at funerals. Where elders feel that funeral decorum is slipping away, they try to remonstrate with young people. The power to define certain practices as traditional bequeath them with cultural authenticity which becomes an asset in such exchanges. Needless to say, the younger generations argue, beyond the earshot of the elders, "What has culture got to do with it? Way back when video cameras were not used at funerals because we did not have them. But things are changing."[103] While these kinds of generational differences and struggles are forever ongoing, they are heightened in moments of socio-economic crises such as the one Zimbabwe is confronting right now.

Perhaps I should be careful not to paint my canvas with very broad brush-strokes because, as much as there are conflicting moments between the Zimbabwean Canadian diasporans and the elders at funerals back in Zimbabwe, there are many moments of harmony and cooperation that have brought the diasporans tears of gratitude. Many diasporans told me of how uncles, aunts, and other relatives stepped up to the plate and helped in this period of sorrow. Tinaye, a refused refugee who could not go to Zimbabwe when her mother passed away in 2005, had nothing but gratitude for her extended family. "My parents had two children. One already passed away so now it's just me. I just sent money and my extended family did everything amicably. Everybody I called sang praises for my uncles."[104] The diasporans also acknowledge that cooperation is important because most of the younger generations are not familiar with burial rituals—hence the elders' input and guidance is absolutely crucial.

But like news in the media, the good stories do not always make headlines—they might not even make it into the bulletin. What my informants remembered most were those moments of discord which have been imprinted on their minds. While some diasporans understand why some family members have to ask for financial assistance, the fact that poverty has made some Zimbabweans not-so-honest in their dealings with the diasporans has not helped either.[105]

Whether they attend the funerals in Zimbabwe or simply send money to help with funerary costs, the Zimbabwean diasporans in Canada have provided a lifeline that extends to the grave. Money from fathers and mothers, sons and daughters, brothers and sisters, cousins and even friends has made it possible to give some of the deceased a decent burial—the ultimate dignity that all Zimbabweans hope for—during a period of socio-economic and political turmoil. However, not all people in Zimbabwe have a diaspora connection, as evidenced by the fact that some poor families have no choice but to divest themselves of the responsibility of burying their dead relatives, forcing the state to give a pauper's burial to thousands of bodies abandoned in Zimbabwean government hospital morgues.[106]

CONCLUSION

One of the most difficult moments for the Zimbabwean diaspora in Canada is when family members in Zimbabwe die. Zimbabwean funerals are customarily perceived as spaces where family (both nuclear and extended), friends, and the community gather for familial and community rejuvenation as well as to express grief for and pay last respects to the deceased. Those who remain behind in Zimbabwe are, by and large, bound to attend family funerals, as they are encompassed by pressures and solidarity of the familial group. As well, death has always been a unifying power for the extended family in Zimbabwe and it always helped to aver people's commitment to the sanctity of human life. However, the diasporanization of a quarter of the population has, to a large extent, capsized these conventions and expectations. The diasporans' immigration status, distance, the time and cost of travel, and work commitments have facilitated the loosening and/or overturning of the constraints of custom, obligation, and conscience for some. Whether one ends up going to Zimbabwe for a funeral or not, diaspora-earned funeral money has played a crucial role in maintaining the connection between the Zimbabwean diasporans and relatives who have remained in the original homeland. Evidence gathered for this chapter has demonstrated that death and mourning for the Zimbabwean Canadian diasporans in Winnipeg and elsewhere in Canada has its continuities and shifts defined by culture, history, and conditions that vary over time and space. The evidence also demonstrated that the funeral social scene in Zimbabwe is a practice in flux, forever adapting to different socio-economic conditions including, most recently, the diasporans produced by crisis.

NOTES

1   Most of the houses in low-income Harare and Chitungwiza cities were built by the state, the city council, and private companies, and these were later sold to individuals. At the very beginning these core-houses had two, three, four, or five rooms, depending on the area. Families which could afford later extended these original houses to make bigger and better-looking houses. Most of the poor working-class families could not afford to extend these houses until their children emigrated to the diaspora.

2   By Zimbabwean diasporans I am referring to Zimbabweans who have emigrated to other countries but still have a strong social and material connection to, and a collective memory of, Zimbabwe. See Peter Kivisto, "Theorizing Transnational Immigration: A Critical Review of Current Factors," *Ethnic and Racial Studies* 24 (2001): 549–577.

3   Bodies of Zimbabweans who died in Canada have been repatriated even when the people had attained Canadian citizenship. Beacon Mbiba had the same findings for the UK Zimbabwean diaspora. See Beacon Mbiba, "Burial at Home? Dealing with Death in the Diaspora and Harare," in *Zimbabwe's New Diaspora: Displacement and the Cultural Politics of Survival*, eds. JoAnn McGregor and Ranka Primorac (New York: Berghahn Books, 2010), 144–163.

4   The Zimbabwe Crisis refers to the period between 1998 and 2008 when the country was undergoing political and socio-economic crises. See Brian Raftopolous, "The Crisis in Zimbabwe, 1998–2008," in *Becoming Zimbabwe: A History from the Pre-Colonial Period to 2008*, eds. Brian Raftopolous and Alois Mlambo (Harare: Weaver Press, 2009). The Zimbabwe Crisis notwithstanding, the late twentieth century has been characterized as the "age of migration" across the globe. See, S. Castles and M. Miller, *The Age of Migration: International Population Movements in the Modern World* (Basingstoke: Palgrave Macmillan, 2003); *New African Diasporas*, ed. Khalid Koser (New York: Routledge, 2003).

5   See, within a rapidly growing scholarship McGregor and Primorac, *Zimbabwe's New Diaspora;* Daniel Pasura, "Gendering the Diaspora: Zimbabwean Migrants in Britain," *African Diaspora* 1, 2 (2008): 86–109; JoAnn McGregor, "'Joining the BBC (British Bottom Cleaners)': Zimbabwean Migrants and the UK Care Industry," *Journal of Ethnic and Migration Studies* 33, 5 (2007): 801–824; Beacon Mbiba, "Zimbabwe's Global Citizens in 'Harare North': Some Observations," in *Skinning the Skunk, Facing Zimbabwean Futures,* eds. M. Palmberg and Ranka Primorac (Uppsala: Nordiska Afrikainstitutet, 2005), 26–38; Rudo Gaidzanwa, *Voting with Their Feet: Migrant Zimbabwean Nurses and Doctors in the Era of Structural Adjustment"* (Uppsala: Nordiska Afrikainstitutet, 1999), 111, 91; International Organization for Migration, "The Development Potential of Zimbabweans in the Diaspora," *IOM Migration Research Studies* 17 (Geneva: International Organization for Migration, 2005); Human Rights Watch, *Neighbours in Need: Zimbabweans Seeking Refuge in South Africa* (New York: Human Rights Watch, 2008); *Zimbabwe's Exodus: Crisis, Migration, Survival,* eds. Jonathan Crush and Daniel Tevera (Cape Town: Southern African Migration Program, 2010); Terence O. Ranger, "The Narratives and Counter Narratives of Zimbabwean Asylum: Female Voices," *Third World Quarterly* 26, 3 (2005): 405–421; JoAnn McGregor, "Abject Spaces, Transnational Calculations: Zimbabweans in Britain Navigating Work, Class and Law," *Transaction of the Institute of British Geographers* 33, 4 (2008): 466–482.

6   Gaidzanwa, *Voting with their Feet,* 91; International Organization for Migration, *The Development Potential of Zimbabweans in the Diaspora;* Human Rights Watch, *Neighbours in Need;* Crush and Tavera, *Zimbabwe's Exodus;* Ranger, "The Narratives and Counter Narratives of Zimbabwean Asylum"; McGregor, "Abject Spaces, Transnational Calculations."

7   Beacon Mbiba, "Burial at Home? Dealing with Death in the Diaspora and Harare," in *Zimbabwe's New Diaspora,* 144–163.

8   Interview with Nyengererai, Winnipeg, 17 April 2010. Nyengererai came to Canada in 2001 but the rest of her family are in Zimbabwe. To protect the identity of my informants, I will use pseudonyms for all interviewees.

9   See for example, Uvana Djuric, "The Croatian Diaspora in North America: Identity, Ethnic Solidarity and the Formation of a 'Transnational National Community,' " *International Journal of Politics, Culture and Society* 17, 1 (2003): 113–130.

10 Those who settled in South Africa, for instance, are simply referred to descriptively as "those who went to South Africa," while in South Africa itself, they are called *makwerekwere,* or blabbers, who speak incomprehensibly. See James Muzondidya, "*Makwerekwere:* Migration and Identity among Zimbabweans in South Africa," in *Zimbabwe's New Diaspora,* 37–58.

11 The Canadian Council for Refugees, "Lives on Hold: Nationals of Moratoria Countries Living in Limbo," Montreal, July 2005, http://www.ccrweb.ca/livesonhold.pdf, accessed July 18, 2011.

12 Ropafadzo Mapimhidze, "Diaspora Dollar Dries Up for many Zimbabwean Families," *News dzeZimbabwe,* May 13, 2011. Dollarization means the Zimbabwean diaspora in Canada has to remit US dollars to Zimbabwe.

13 See, among others, Charles van Onselen, *Chibaro: African Mine Labour in Southern Rhodesia, 1900–1933* (London: Pluto Press, 1973).

14 See Peter Godwin and Ian Hancock, *Rhodesians Never Die: The Impact of War and Political Change on White Rhodesia 1970–80* (Harare: Baobab Books, 1994).

15 See Alois Mlambo, "Student Protest and State Reaction in Colonial Rhodesia: The 1973 *Chimukwembe* Demonstration at the University of Rhodesia," *Journal of Southern African Studies* 21, 3 (1995): 473–490.

16 See Alois Mlambo, "A History of Migration to 1990," in *Zimbabwe's Exodus.*

17 ZANU PF stands for Zimbabwe African National Union Patriotic Front, the ruling party in Zimbabwe since independence (1980) to February 2009. ZAPU stands for Zimbabwe African People's Union, the major opposition party in Zimbabwe between 1980 and 1987, when a unity agreement led to the "swallowing up" of ZAPU by ZANU PF.

18 *Gukurahundi* is Shona for the first rains of the summer season which wash away the chaff from the last agricultural season. But in this case it refers to the "anti-dissident" campaign by the Mugabe regime against the Ndebele (one of the two major ethnic groups in Zimbabwe). See Catholic Commission for Justice and Peace in Zimbabwe (CCJP), "*Gukurahundi* in Zimbabwe: A Report into the Disturbances in Matebeleland and the Midlands, 1980–1988, Zimbabwe" (Zimbabwe: April 1999).

19 Some scholars have begun to describe Zimbabwe as a failed state. See Myron Echenberg, "Zimbabwe, Portrait of Cholera in a Failed State," in *Africa in the Time of Cholera: A History of Pandemics from 1817 to the Present* (Cambridge: Cambridge University Press, 2011), 163–174.

20 Between 1980 and 1990, the Mugabe regime provided free education and health services to the entire nation. Partly because of that, Zimbabwe has the highest literacy rate on the continent. However, after 1990, IMF later advised the country to cut education subsidies. See Ranger, "The Narratives and Counter Narratives of Zimbabwean Asylum," 407.

21 So-called because the IMF has been "giving the same medicine" with strings attached to ailing third world economies. See M. Rodwan Abouharb, *Human Rights and Structural Adjustment* (Cambridge: Cambridge University Press, 2007). For more on the impact of the economic structural adjustment program in Zimbabwe see Alois Mlambo, *The Economic Adjustment Programme: The Case of Zimbabwe, 1990–1995* (Harare: University of Zimbabwe Publication, 1987).

22 Raftopolous, "The Crisis in Zimbabwe," 203.

23 See Bjorn Lindgren, "The Green Bombers of Salisbury: Elections and Political Violence in Zimbabwe," *Anthropology Today* 19, 2 (2003): 6–10.

24 James Muzondidya, "Jambanja: Ideological Ambiguities in the Politics of Land and Resource Ownership in Zimbabwe, *Journal of Southern African Studies* 33, 2 (June 2007): 325–341.

25 For an account of the late 1990s emigration from Zimbabwe see A. Bloch, *The Development of Zimbabweans in the Diaspora* (London: Institute of International Migration, 2005); Gaidzanwa, *Voting with their Feet*; Lovemore Zinyama, "International Migration and Zimbabwe: An Overview," in *Zimbabweans who Move: Perspective on International Migration*, eds. D. Tevera and Lovemore Zinyama (Cape Town: Southern African Migration Project, 2002).

26 While this was probably an exaggeration, it remains true that for the first time Zimbabwean emigration was cast in a wider area. Interview with Zororo, 7 July 2010, Winnipeg.

27 Zimbabwe achieved majority rule status in 1980

28 Emmanuel Akyeampong, "Africa in the Diaspora: The Diaspora in Africa," *African Affairs* 99 (2000): 183–215. The post-colonial immigration of Africans into Canada definitely contributed to more visibility of blacks on the Canadian map. In 1981 the Canadian African population stood at 101,700 and then it increased to 114,800 in 1986 and 166,200 in 1991. Paul Tiyambe Zeleza, "Rewriting the African Diaspora: Beyond the Black Atlantic," *African Affairs* 104, 414 (2005): 35–68. Obviously, the relatively relaxed immigration policy in the 1990s, the Rwandan genocide of 1994 as well immigrants from other African hot spots witnessed an exponential increase in immigrants from Africa since 1991.

29 Canadian Council for Refugees, "Lives on Hold."

30   From December 2001, Canada required Zimbabweans to have visas to enter the country. I am not sure whether Canada's decision to impose visa requirements was a rejoinder to a large influx of Zimbabweans in the years leading to 2001 or whether it was in response to the suspension of Zimbabwe from the Commonwealth in 2001 and its subsequent withdrawal from the "Commonwealth Club" in 2003. See "Commonwealth News Release: Zimbabwe's Withdrawal from the Commonwealth, 12 December 2003. http://www.thecommonwealth.org/Templates/Internal.asp?NodeID=35505, accessed 18 July 2011.

31   The number of Zimbabweans in Canada remained greatly lower than those in the UK or the USA. This is probably because Zimbabweans generally did not have a history of emigrating to Canada unlike the UK and US, the first countries of choice. See James C. Hathaway, *The Rights of Refugees under International Law* (Cambridge: Cambridge University Press, 2005).

32   See Immigration and Refugee Protection Regulation 230 (1).

33   This was probably because of the inclusive government that had been forged between the ruling ZANU PF party and the opposition MDC, after which the country was considered stable. See Amnesty International, "The Human Rights of Refugees," http://www.amnesty.ca/refugee/Canada.php, accessed 21 July 2011; See also, "Canada-US Safe Third Country Agreement," http://www.cic.gc.ca/english/department/laws-policy/menu-safethird.asp.

34   Zeleza, "Rewriting the African Diaspora."

35   This is a phrase that is not easily translated into English. The phrase can also be about chastizing those who are not trendy. Cellphones became more affordable in the late 1990s. Tendai, a Zimbabwean diasporan in Canada since 2001, told me, with some amusement, that his mother answered his call when she was weeding her corn field in the "back of beyond" rural Chivi. Interview with Tendai, Winnipeg, 21 April 2010.

36   Mukuru.com for instance, was a website one could use to send money to Zimbabwe, or buy fuel and/or groceries for family in Zimbabwe. See, http://mukuru.com/zimbabwe?g clid=CHO3srukp60CFQzHKgodvBcAWg

37   The diaspora deposited money (usually US dollars/UK pounds) into these individuals' bank accounts. By the end of the day, the Zimbabwean equivalent would be deposited in the recipient's bank account in Zimbabwe.

38   I must say though that this translation does not do justice to the phrase. Interview with Mr and Mrs Matengu, Seke, Chitungwiza, 13 November 2008. Probably in their late sixties, this couple informed me that some of the strange and unexpected experiences might include being verbally abused by someone for no apparent reason or almost being overrun by a car on a pedestrian crossing. "It's just something that will make you ask, what is happening, and then you know I am going to hear something bad. So to avoid *mashura* made families make a serious effort to inform all relatives of a death in the family."

39   Interview with Janet, Winnipeg, 27 August 2010.

40   Telephone interview with Silas, Vancouver, 28 June 2010.

41   Interview with Tashinga, Toronto, 8 May 2011.

42   Interview with Memory, Steinbach, 17 June 2010. Zimbabweans invariably refer to news of death as "bad news."

43   Telephone interview with Florence, 11 January 2010. She lives in Lethbridge, Alberta.

44   Interview with Viola, Winnipeg, 11 June 2010.

45   Telephone interview with Loveness, Sudbury, 27 July 2010.

46   See for example, Sjaak van der Geest, "Funerals for the Living: Conversations with Elderly People in Kwahu, Ghana," *African Studies Review* 43, 3 (2000): 103–129; Marleen

de Witte, "Money and Death: Funeral Business in Asante, Ghana," *Africa: Journal of the International African Institute*, 73, 4 (2003): 531–559.

47 For an examination of colonial Harare's funerary practices, see Joyce M. Chadya, "Segregation to the Cemetery: African Funerary Practices in colonial Harare," in progress.

48 Interview with Memory, 13 August 2010.

49 Because Zimbabwe is seven hours (summer) or eight hours (winter) ahead of Winnipeg's Central Time Zone, burial actually takes place while the diasporans in Canada are sleeping or early in the morning, Canadian time.

50 Interview with Janet, Winnipeg, 27 August 2010.

51 Ibid.

52 Interview with Netsai, Medicine Hat, 21 August 2010.

53 Interview with Patricia, Winnipeg, 9 July 2009. Patricia was a senior woman in her sixties. She had come to visit her daughter and son-in-law who live in Winnipeg.

54 Interview with Janet, Winnipeg, 27 August 2010.

55 This was confirmed by several of my informants.

56 Burial societies were/are one of the strategies used by poorly paid African workers (for whom there were no official funeral policies during the colonial period or who, in independent Zimbabwe, could not afford official funeral policies) in Zimbabwean urban and mining centres to raise money for funeral expenses. The Zimbabwean diasporans fell back on long-established coping mechanisms used by migrant labour in Zimbabwe. See N.P. Hall, "Self-Reliance in Practice: A Study of Burial Societies in Harare, Zimbabwe," *Journal of Social Development in Africa* 2 (1987): 2, 49–71. The Zimbabwean Canadian Burial Society based in Ontario, for instance, was started in 2007. Members pay monthly subscriptions of $20 per month and receive $500 from the society in the event of a death of a close family member (that is, a parent, child, or sibling).

57 I heard this story from a conversation with a friend's relatives who had visited Winnipeg, 1 July 2011. Sjaak van der Geest points out that in West Africa funerals have become sites for making money, love making, and courtship. See van der Geest, "Funerals for the Living," 113.

58 See also McGregor, "Abject Spaces, Transnational Calculations." Zimbabwean newspapers have highlighted the plight of children of the diasporans whose parents cannot return to the country because of their refugee status and yet they also cannot bring over their children because of that same status. See for example, "The Silent Victims of the Country's Economic Collapse," *The Standard*, 17 June 2007.

59 Canadian Council for Refugees, "Lives on Hold," 7.

60 Interview with Janet, Winnipeg, 27 August 2010.

61 Interview with Tarisai, Winnipeg, 11 August 2010. Tarisai is a single mother of three who emigrated from Zimbabwe when she was in her thirties. She lives with her three children. Many Zimbabweans in the diaspora are also financially responsible for their parents, young siblings who are still in school/college, and nephews and nieces who are HIV/AIDS orphans.

62 Among such professionals are doctors, nurses, those in managerial positions, and even professors. Those travelling to Zimbabwe have to fly via the US, Europe, or the Middle East, usually with a total of three stopovers.

63 Canadian Council for Refugees, "Lives on Hold," 9.

64 That said, economic hardships within Zimbabwe have also meant that even those Zimbabweans in Zimbabwe are being selective of which funerals they attend. See Joyce

M. Chadya, "Where the Dead Queued for Fuel" in Tina Mai Chen and David Churchill, eds., "Historical Materialism," in progress.

65 Look for another forthcoming article by Joyce M. Chadya tentatively entitled "Death in the Time of Cholera, Zimbabwe 2008–2010," forthcoming. See also Muchaparara Musemwa, "From Sunshine City to a Landscape of Disaster: The Politics of Water, Sanitation and Disease in Harare, Zimbabwe, 1980–2009," *Journal of Developing Societies* 26, 2 (2010): 165–206; Mark Nyandoro, "Historical Overview of the Cholera Outbreak in Zimbabwe, 2008–2009," *Journal of Contemporary History* 36, 1 (2011): 154–174.

66 "Banking in my children," is an expression used by Zimbabweans who use most of their resources to send their children to school in the hope that they, in turn, would look after them. Unfortunately, since the economic collapse, school, college, and university leavers are finding it hard to secure employment.

67 Telephone interview with Thomas, 12 August 2010.

68 Interview with Majorie, Winnipeg, 27 June 2010.

69 Telephone interview with Paul, Yellowknife, 10 February 2011.

70 Interview with Fafi (Tafadzwa), Winnipeg, 17 July 2010.

71 See Chadya, "Where the Dead Queue for Fuel."

72 Interview with Danai, Winnipeg, 17 January 2010. Danai is the only one in his family who is in the diaspora so it is not surprising that he feels overwhelmed by requests from Zimbabwe.

73 Interview with Timothy, who has been in Canada since 2002. According to Timothy he hardly ever receives a call from Zimbabwe without being asked for money.

74 Telephone interview with Susan, Quebec City, 23 August 2010.

75 Telephone interview with Pedzisai, Fort MacMurray, 19 August 2010.

76 It must be noted, however, that there are families which have been doing very well despite the decimated Zimbabwean economy and thus are able to shoulder mortuary bills. Some of them fall within the rubric of the so-called "new money" that was accrued because of the Crisis.

77 Newspapers throughout the Zimbabwe Crisis period are saturated with news of overloaded and hardly functioning government hospital mortuaries forcing families which could afford to take the bodies to private-run mortuaries which are more expensive. See "Mass Burial to Ease Pressure on Mortuaries," *The Zimbabwean*, 13 May 2009, http://www.theZimbabwean.co.uk/news/21142/mass-burial-to-ease-pressure-on-mortuariies-.html, accessed 30 July 2011; Alex Duval Smith, "AIDS Deaths Overwhelms Zimbabwe's Mortuaries," *The Independent* 10 February 2000 http://www.independent.co.uk/news/world/AFrica/aids-deaths-overwhelm-zimbabwe's-mortuaries-726980.html, accessed 30 July 2011; See also Joyce M. Chadya, "No Rest for the Dead: The Zimbabwe Crisis and the Mortuary Industry," forthcoming.

78 Some newspapers also reported the use of ox-drawn ambulances as there was no money to repair broken ones. "Zimbabwe's Dead 'Cross Over' to South Africa," *Zimonline*, 11 October 2005, http://www.reliefweb.int/node/187442, accessed 20 July 2011.

79 Chadya, "No Rest for the Dead." Nyaradzo Funeral Services, for instance, was started in May 2003, http://www.nyaradzofs.co.zw/abtus.html, accessed 19 July 2011; Nuffield Funeral Home started operating on 1 March 2008 http://www.nuffieldfuneralhome.com/, accessed 3 June 2011. Some funeral homes have moved into border towns in neighbouring countries to capture business both from home in Zimbabwe as well as to serve Zimbabweans living abroad. See http://afrol.com/articles/19657, accessed 11 June 2011.

80 Telephone interview with Mandipa, Brandon, 10 May 2011. This was corroborated by many of my informants who made the same observations.

81 Interview with Cecilia, Glen View, Harare, 11 October 2008.

82 Interview with Chandakupa, Winnipeg, 12 June 2010.

83 Interview with Tonderai, Winnipeg, 26 March 2010.

84 Ibid.

85 Interview with Danai, Ottawa, 6 May 2010.

86 Interview with Zororo, Winnipeg, 30 May 2010.

87 Interview with Peter, Toronto, 26 February 2010.

88 Interview with Mr and Mrs Matengu, Chitungwiza, 11 December 2008.

89 Interview with James Ndoro, Chitungwiza, 17 November 2010.

90 Interview with Mr Tomani, Glen View, Harare, 30 November 2010.

91 Interview with James Ndoro, Chitungwiza, 17 November 2010.

92 Telephone interview with John, Calgary, 7 May 2010.

93 Interview with Ambuya Mutanda, Mbare, Harare, 3 December 2010. Ambuya literally means grandmother in Shona, but it can be used to refer to any senior woman.

94 See for instance, Marleen de Witte, "Money and Death: Funeral Business in Asante, Ghana," *Africa: Journal of the International African Institute* 73, 4 (2003): 531–559.

95 In West Africa, video cameras at funerals have long been in use. See Kwame Archin, "The Economic Implications of Transformations in Akan Funeral Rites," *Africa: Journal of the International African Institute* 64, 3 (1994): 307–322.

96 Interview with Monica, Toronto, 7 May 2011.

97 Pierre Bourdieu, *Distinction: A Social Critique of the Judgement of Taste*, trans. Richard Nice (Cambridge: Massachusetts: Harvard University Press, 1987).

98 A description used by young Harareans to refer to someone who has "traditional" tendencies in the way they dress, behave, think, or their diet.

99 Archin, "The Economic Implications of Transformations in Akan Funeral Rites," 307–322.

100 Joan Omoruyi, "Nigerian Funeral Programmes: An Unexplored Source of Information," *Africa: Journal of the International African Institute* 58, 4 (1988): 466–469.

101 Telephone interview with Jonathan, Lethbridge, Alberta, 15 February 2010.

102 Interview with Monica, Toronto, 7 May 2011.

103 Ibid.

104 Interview with Tinaye, Winnipeg, 13 June 2011.

105 There is a welter of stories of how the diasporans' hard-earned money meant for construction of diasporans' houses in Zimbabwe, for school fees, or the upkeep of parents has been fleeced by family members.

106 See "Unclaimed Bodies Get Pauper's Burial," *The Herald*, 28 May 2009; "68 Get a Pauper's Burial," *The Herald*, 15 November 2006; Stanley Karombo, "Decent Burials Beyond the Means of Majority," *Interpress New Agency*, 26 July 2004, http://www. ipsnews.net/africa/interna.asp?idnews=24789, accessed 27 May 2011.

THE IMPORTANCE OF PLACE
OR, WHY WE'RE NOT POST-PRAIRIE

ALISON CALDER

Prairie literature writers and scholars were amazingly successful at establishing prairie literature as a field of study in a very short time. It was only in the 1970s and early 1980s that "prairie literature" became recognized as a *thing*, with enough critical mass to carry anthologies, courses, publishing houses, and writing careers.[1] It would now be odd for a Canadian literature survey course not to include at least one or two prairie books, though often still bracketed off in a "prairie" section. Writers from the prairies like Guy Vanderhaeghe, David Bergen, Miriam Toews, Joan Thomas, Fred Stenson, Sandra Birdsell, Margaret Sweatman, and Andrew Davidson regularly receive national and international recognition: their work wins awards, makes the bestseller lists, and is the subject of book club discussions. So why, then, is prairie literature studies a disappearing field?

It makes me sad to ask this question, but the field is in trouble. The 2010 Place and Replace conference, jointly sponsored by the Western Canadian Studies Association and the St. John's College Prairies Conference, featured sixty-eight presentations, only eight of which were on literature. For comparison's sake, the 2001 St. John's College Prairies Conference featured twenty-nine papers on literature, while the 2004 conference featured twenty-one. The publishing record is also diminishing: while there have been several collections of critical essays, all but one based on the St. John's College Prairies Conferences,[2] no monograph on prairie literature was published between Deborah Keahey's 1998 *Making It Home*, and Jenny Kerber's *Writing in Dust: Reading the Prairie Environmentally* from 2010.[3] The publication of Kerber's book highlights its exceptional status. As Dennis Cooley wrote in 2008, "there was a surge of statements from 1973 to 1989. One wonders: where now are the new statements?"[4] We can posit many reasons for this dearth of scholarship, such as the institutional conflation of

Canadian and postcolonial literary studies, which has meant that scholars have drifted into a sexier internationalism and away from a supposedly more staid regionalism. Or, we could think of the retirement of senior colleagues and the steadily increasing workload for junior faculty, which has meant that time for research decreases radically even as administrative expectations about research productivity grow. We can also cite circumstances like the federal Conservative government's radical slashing of funding to established Canadian Studies programs in Europe, which has meant that Canadian authors can no longer promote their work at universities abroad, and that our European colleagues no longer have the funding required to do their work. But, frankly, these are all excuses. The reason for the fading away of prairie literary studies is contained within the terms by which the field has defined itself. The good news is, I hope, that it is not too late to change those terms.

Gerry Friesen famously announced in 1998 that the prairies do not exist.[5] I think he is right, and I want to extend his statement even further, to say that the prairie has never existed, at least in the way that we think it has: as a given, as the way things are, as "the great prairie fact" (to use Robert Thacker's title). The land has always existed in various forms, but we understand that land through the stories that we tell about it, and "prairie" is a story that European settler/colonizers brought with them. This story, based on the extraction of wealth, displaced the earlier, various stories of Aboriginal peoples, who also used the land, albeit differently. The prairie story is inextricably linked to agriculture and propels (and is propelled by) colonization in ongoing ways. A story is an active thing: as historians show us repeatedly, the past is continually reenacted in the present. When prairie literature was established as a field, it was this prairie story, colonial in nature, which defined its terms. "Prairie literature" emerged as a field of study centred on representations of the traumatic experiences of white, largely male settlers.[6] Over and over, we see represented in the canon narratives of settlement and agriculture. A confrontation with the land is the point of narrative origin: how to make a new place home, and how then to deal with the changes that modernity brings to that home are the recurring themes. Later, this battle became defined in explicitly language-centred terms: how can writers express this new place in an imported language, one that was developed in far-off lands and which disenfranchises them at every turn? These are worthy questions. I am not saying that they ought not to be asked. But looking at these twin linchpins of prairie literary studies—depiction of the physical encounter with the landscape and dramatization of the linguistic encounter with it—we can see that the field is already setting itself up to implode.

There are a number of problems in traditional prairie literary studies that have already been talked about.[7] One problem that has not been talked about, but that eclipses all others, is that there is no way that Aboriginal people can be accommodated in this agri-centric definition of prairie literature. They are not immigrants and Indigenous languages are not imported. When Aboriginal authors write in English, a whole set of other challenges come into view. Thus, texts by Aboriginal authors are already excluded from participating in the "important" issues explored in prairie writing. The history of Aboriginal people's relationship to agriculture is fraught as, of course, colonial agriculture was explicitly used against them.[8] The exclusion and displacement of Aboriginal people is built into an agri-centric system from the very beginning: it is structurally impossible for the critical field as it is to accommodate them. Aboriginal characters and issues do exist in many early "prairie" texts, though their presence is often occluded or oblique. In W.O. Mitchell's canonical novel *Who Has Seen the Wind*, for example, the streets of the town are named Blackfoot and Riel, though there are no Aboriginal characters identified in the text.[9] The street names reveal an alternate, older history: one that predates the town and points to a colonial violence that is the foundation for the seemingly natural prairie that generates the novel's affective power. Discussions of the text that focus only on Brian's decision to become a "dirt doctor" to help people be better farmers miss the opportunity to look instead at alternative ways of relating to the land that are encoded in the text: instead of "how might we do agriculture better," the question might be reframed as: "how else, in addition to agriculture, could we be conceiving of our relation to this space?" Critical emphasis on the white male settler's confrontation with a hostile environment has had a kind of cumulative effect over the years. Writings by Aboriginal authors are rarely included in critical studies of prairie texts, although the field of Aboriginal literary studies is rapidly growing.[10] More tellingly, scholars of prairie Aboriginal literature seem to be self-selecting away from the "prairie literature" category. Certainly, representation by and of Aboriginal authors and scholars has always been shockingly low at the St. John's College Prairies Conference. This is partly because the subjectivity of both author and critic that is assumed in prairie literary scholarship is white. One can also ask why indeed scholars of Aboriginal literature would want to work within a critical framework that simply is not appropriate to the texts. Since many Aboriginal authors and scholars seek to decolonize prairie spaces through their writings, adopting a critical methodology that takes the colonial project for granted—generally approving it as a good thing—presents obvious problems. So, my argument here is that colonialism is built into the foundational terms of prairie literary studies, and that the scholarship itself, done unreflectingly, is a form of colonizing practice.

Another reason for the implosion of prairie literary studies is that the conceptual framework for the field has such difficulty dealing with the present. As

Jenny Kerber points out, critically emphasizing texts that pit "prairie" against modernity, with "prairie" always losing, naturalizes the "idea of the prairies as a region unable to co-exist with the transformative forces of modernity."[11] Because the field is so much focused on the originary struggle with the landscape, in physical and linguistic terms, it seems increasingly irrelevant to diverse urban populations who may have been born here, may be recent immigrants, may have little connection to an agricultural landscape, or little connection to a settler history. The landscape they may be struggling to articulate is likely not an agricultural one: it can be urban, or it can be virtual. Present-day prairie dwellers are likely to engage with the environment in terms of recreation or aesthetics rather than economics. Traditional models can seem both obsolete and confining, easy to parody and reject.

In the past ten years or so, some prairie writers and critics, myself included, have urged the development of a new way of looking at writings from the prairies. It is understood by many artists that there has been a fundamental shift in cultural practice on the prairie, and that new ways of representing prairie culture need to be articulated. We see new artistic conversations about prairie identity as writers and visual artists try to articulate their experiences. From these conversations comes the start of new vocabularies that are at this point provisional, and under continual negotiation. One suggestion, appearing in two recent anthologies, is that we are now "post-prairie": meaning that we used to be prairie, and now we are not. I want to look at what is implied in this suggestion, and then explain why I'm not sure that this is the best way to think about where we are now.

The term "post-prairie" first came up in the book *Post-Prairie: An Anthology of New Poetry* edited by Jon Paul Fiorentino and Robert Kroetsch. It also appears in the title of *Scratching the Surface: The Post-Prairie Landscape*, an anthology of critical-creative writings and visual art that was curated by Steve Matijcio. The visual art had been exhibited at Winnipeg's Plug In Institute of Contemporary Art from September to November of 2007; the writings were commissioned following the show, and the book was published in 2008. There are differences between the anthologies, but both share the conviction that "prairie" is over: it is no longer a good framework for thinking about this place, and is being replaced by something that is substantially different. As Fiorentino writes in the introduction to *Post-Prairie*, "Robert Kroetsch and I wanted to document and celebrate the poetry of the prairie as it is being written now, in the new century. We soon discovered that the prairie was missing, or perhaps the prairie had become unrecognizably present in this new work. The poets we have gathered here... are speaking in new voices, and their 'home place' of the prairie has become less unified, more urban, technologically adept, and theoretically informed."[12]

Key in Fiorentino's remarks throughout the Introduction is the idea of the "new," an idea linked with rejecting the historically based, traditional images of the prairie that are identified with "the rural, the wheat field and the grain elevator."[13] There are a number of provocative things about this introduction; in particular, the way Fiorentino continually emphasizes newness, while Kroetsch continually emphasizes connection, saying things like "Shit, we old dogs knew that on day one."[14] When pressed by Kroetsch to identify the influences on this new writing, Fiorentino suggests a number of texts, both critical and creative, by authors from within and without the prairie region. He figures the inspiration for the new post-prairie as literary and linguistic, not geographic: "post-prairie" in this case means a rupture from the past, a separation from a rural environment that is agricultural in focus, and distinct from the worlds of technology and theory.

We've gotten away from the struggle with the landscape, but now the prairie as a *place* seems irrelevant. New writing is that in which the prairie is "missing," or "unrecognizably present," phrases that mean significantly different things. The double meaning of "present" as both place (here) and time (this instant) points to a crucial conflation of geography with history. In fact, I think it's not too much of a stretch to say that here, place = rural = past, and the present is a kind of unrooted urban space that is radically disconnected from this past. The construction of this urban prairie present as post-prairie is plausible only if we allow the prairie to be defined within these terms: as incompatible with either modernity or postmodernity, as irretrievably located in a vanished and obsolete rural landscape. Why we would accept these limitations is puzzling. But if the history of the agricultural prairie is the history of colonialism, does it then follow that, in the post-prairie, colonialism is over, and we are now all starting fresh, on a field that is as level as, well, the now-vanished prairie? Certainly the work of poets like Rosanna Deerchild, Marvin Francis, and Duncan Mercredi, all included in Kroetsch and Fiorentino's anthology, speaks directly against that idea. When Deerchild writes that "red skins/white skins remain in sequenced order" in her poem "This Is a Small Northern Town," she is explicitly making the point that historical processes continue, and that for her, the past is all too recognizable.[15] The face of colonial practice, grain elevators and wheat fields, may have changed, but the underlying structures remain in place, as do their effects. Like colonization, decolonization is a long-term project, one that requires seeing the past in the present and understanding the ways that power can shape-shift to perpetuate itself in many guises.

So far this essay has stressed two main points: that the mechanism of colonization is at the heart of traditional prairie literary studies; and that the vocabulary of "post-prairie" has the potential to sever links with the past that need to be maintained in order to understand the present prairie. Annette Lapointe's novel *Stolen* illustrates one version of a present prairie that might, on first glance, appear unrecognizable. *Stolen*, published in 2006, is a novel, not poetry, but it provides an interesting example of what is definitely a "new" prairie. The protagonist, Rowan, lives on a farm outside of Saskatoon, but he makes his money by selling drugs and stolen merchandise, not wheat. He is thoroughly into technology: he builds robots, rewires alarm systems, and constructs and destroys sophisticated electronic circuitry. When we first meet him, he is out in the bush, burying a body that "could be a deer."[16] This is a post-modern prairie: not a "fact," but an unstable site, hollowed out by potash mining and capable of hiding just about anything. The nuclear family is marked by madness and incest; the fragmented community is made up of different tribes (farmers, ranchers, druggies, hippies, skateboarders, geeks). There's no such thing as a rural/urban split: Rowan is back and forth to Saskatoon regularly, to the university or to McDonald's. He also ranges further afield: to Ile-a-la-Crosse in northern Saskatchewan, to British Columbia, to Detroit. Geography is not limiting for Rowan. The real division is between actual and virtual worlds: "He's discovered there are two worlds out here. The one he recognized first is scattered, nearly empty. One person every two miles, hunkered in the prairie, close and surrounded by the rusting hulks of machinery and the shells of mobile homes. Thinly connected by wires and never filled. The world he found more recently is crowded. When Rowan was a teenager, the universe shrank to the size of a fifteen-inch monitor, and it's impossibly full."[17]

Though Rowan continually distinguishes between the place he lives (the prairie) and the place he does things (online), the novel presents over and over the spectacle of interpolation. Boundaries of all kinds—national, provincial, physical—are crossed and blurred. Rowan's queerness extends this fluidity as we see him in sexual encounters with both men and women. The novel's opening pages set up the permeability of the region, as radio waves, the Internet, and crystal meth circulate freely between spaces. At the same time as we see these things entering the region, we see people, goods, and ideas moving out of it and back again, creating a kind of exchange that, I would argue, changes both spaces. "The internet made all the difference in what Rowan does," says the text, and it's tempting to think of this wired prairie as something that is separate from place, that could happen anywhere.[18] But the novel also insists on the *here*-ness of this new, globalized and wired space: it is not free-floating, but touches down in specific sites. The description of Rowan's full, online world continues: this world is full of "information, but also stuff. Old books, machine parts, dinnerware, used clothes. Processors and RAM sticks. Glass and oxidized metal and plastic. Chemicals in vials and pails. Not all of it's wanted in Canada or the U.S., but it's all currency somewhere. Raw and contaminated metal breaks down in the trees around [Rowan's] house."[19]

Globalization happens in specific sites: place matters. The endless circulation of goods and money happens in different places in different ways, and it is those local sites, here the trees around Rowan's house, where these forces are negotiated. It is a different thing to be in a farmhouse outside of Saskatoon than it is to be in Saskatoon, or in Vancouver, or New York, or Beijing. In *Stolen*, location matters, though recognizable terms like "rural" and "urban" no longer apply. Race also matters: the world is different in this novel if you are white than if you are Aboriginal. When the unnamed Cree girl pawns her jingle dress, she does so because she is hungry and poor. When Rowan buys it from the pawnshop for $300 so that he can sell it online for thousands of dollars, he does so legally, but the transaction is represented as being clearly exploitative. Though Rowan declares that "all [she has] to do is put me up a couple of times and we're even," it is obvious that no relationship is equal when one side gets to define all the terms.[20] We see that this inequality is not individual, but systemic:

> The Indian things that sell for pocket change here are worth big money in the States, and more in Europe. A beaded moosehide jacket sells for a hundred and fifty dollars in Battleford; it goes for eighteen hundred in Chicago (American dollars, which are still worth more and getting easier to convert without a physical trip to the bank). He sold a chicken dancer outfit once, online, to a woman who paid three thousand dollars for it. She took it to New York and sold it in some gallery for twenty thousand, and sent him a picture of the cheque.[21]

There are layers of exploitation here. Rowan may not be the biggest villain, but he still profits from an ongoing process of colonization, as the inheritor of race-based privilege.

While the world in *Stolen* may be post-modern, it is not post-prairie: it is the prairie itself that is post-modern. It is neither "missing" nor "unrecognizably present." In fact, it may be more recognizable than we commonly allow. Rowan keeps the things he steals in granaries and he depends on foreign or international markets to buy his goods. This is familiar ground to anyone versed in classic prairie fiction, like R.J.C. Stead's 1926 novel *Grain*, which is very much about the intersection of local and global economies, and which also features forbidden love, the fracturing of the nuclear family, and a protagonist who is fascinated with technology. *Stolen* is also very much about houses and horses, in ways that present a fascinating complication of the traditional prairie literary and critical dichotomy. So the concept of "post-prairie-ness," articulated as a rupture with the past and a representation of an "unrecognizable present,"

175

just does not work with this novel. If we must hang on to the "post-prairie" idea, then I suggest a more useful articulation may be that made by Kroetsch in his Foreword to *Scratching the Surface*: "This is not to say that the prairie has disappeared. Rather, these artists and writers and filmmakers have undergone transformations in their lives and in their concepts, and those transformations are responsive to the continuing transformations of the prairie itself. Landscape and artist are involved in an exchange that is one of elaborating complexities."[22] Rather than linking the prairie to a rural past that is finished, Kroetsch's formulation allows for the understanding of "prairie" as a process that is continually under negotiation, inhabiting the present, and capable of changing and being changed. The past, in other words, is still with us, for better and worse.

What is at stake here? To say that we are post-prairie, that we used to be something and now we are not, to define ourselves in terms of rupture from the past and from our immediate environments, is to refuse to see the ways in which we have come to hold the positions that we do. The prairie story is one of colonization, and this story is ongoing, reproduced on buses, in malls, on small-town Main Streets, and in universities. Defining ourselves only in terms of "newness" is an evasion of responsibility. To see the present as unrecognizable is to ignore the choices that have led us to this point. Environmental degradation and social inequality are not inevitable. What happens if we define ourselves in terms of continuity instead of rupture? In terms of prairie literary study, I suggest we see the possibility of recognizing within literature and criticism connections to the past that can be helpful or damaging. I want to return to the idea that traditional prairie literary studies are built on an assumption of white subjectivity that supports an agri-centric methodology that fundamentally disallows the involvement of Aboriginal scholars and texts. Scholars of prairie literature need to recognize our participation in that system. If we think of the trajectory of the field in terms of rupture with past practice, then we can proceed as if those problems of exclusion are gone. But if we think of the field in terms of continuity, then we may be more likely to see colonizing structures as they reproduce themselves even in our "new" work. And by thinking in terms of continuity and transformation, process rather than product, we also assume the responsibility for making what might be some real changes. Recognizing the prairie story for what it is—an ongoing story, rather than an inert fact—grants us the kind of agency that might be able to save our field and, ideally and idealistically, intervene in public space in meaningful ways. The "raw and contaminated metal" breaking down among the trees around Rowan's house in Annette Lapointe's novel *Stolen* came from somewhere, and it is going somewhere—somewhere that we live. Hanging on to the idea of place allows us to look at where we actually are and what our responses might be to globalization and social change.

NOTES

1 Edward McCourt's study *The Canadian West in Fiction* (Toronto: Ryerson Press, 1949) had been published in 1949, of course, but it was not until Laurie Ricou's *Vertical Man/ Horizontal World: Man and Landscape in Canadian Prairie Fiction* (Vancouver: UBC Press, 1973) and Dick Harrison's *Unnamed Country: The Study for a Canadian Prairie Fiction* (Edmonton: University of Alberta Press, 1977) appeared that the field gained real critical weight.

2 I am here thinking of *Toward Defining the Prairies*, ed. Robert Wardhaugh (Winnipeg: University of Manitoba Press, 2001) and *The Prairies Lost and Found*, ed. Len Kuffert (Winnipeg: St. John's College Press, 2007), both of which are composed of papers from St. John's College Prairies Conferences; *History, Literature and the Writing of the Canadian Prairies*, eds. Alison Calder and Robert Wardhaugh (Winnipeg: University of Manitoba Press, 2005) which was conceived of at a St. John's College Prairie conference, but did not include conference material; and *West of Eden: Essays on Canadian Prairie Literature*, ed. Sue Sorensen (Winnipeg: CMU Press, 2008), which was generated independently.

3 S. Leigh Matthews, *Looking Back: Canadian Women's Prairie Memoirs and Intersections of Culture, History, and Identity* (Calgary: University of Calgary Press, 2010) points to definitional problems within critical treatment of "prairie writing." Prairie writing, as a critical field, traditionally excludes memoir, concentrating almost exclusively on fiction and poetry, with drama making rare appearances. Memoirs seem to be considered "history," not literature, a standing challenged by the recent appearances of such major texts as Sharon Butala's *The Perfection of the Morning* (Toronto: HarperCollins, 1995), Trevor Herriot's *River in a Dry Land: A Prairie Passage* (Toronto: Macfarlane, Walter, and Ross, 2002) and Warren Cariou's *Lake of the Prairies* (Toronto: Doubleday, 2002). Looking over Matthews's index shows that this critical separation between "history" and "literature" is maintained, as she cites no literary criticism. I do not intend this as a criticism of Matthews—it's not her fault that the literary criticism is not useful—rather, I want to emphasize the power of the definition to establish critical and conceptual boundaries, and the critical opportunities that can open up if these boundaries are reconceived. That there is no crossover between the fields inhibits growth in each.

4 Dennis Cooley, "The Critical Reception of Canadian Prairie Literature, from Grove to Keahey" in *West of Eden*, 47.

5 Gerald Friesen, "Defining the Prairies: or, Why the Prairies don't Exist" in *Toward Defining the Prairies*, 13–28.

6 I want to clarify here that I mean that it is the critical field that centres on these preoccupations, not necessarily the literature itself. A prairie literature canon that placed texts like Nellie McClung's *Sowing Seeds in Danny* (Toronto: William Briggs, 1908), Douglas Durkin's *The Magpie* (Toronto: University of Toronto Press, 1974 [1923]), Christine van der Mark's *In Due Season* (Toronto: Oxford University Press, 1947), and Vera Lysenko's *Yellow Boots* (Edmonton: NeWest, 1992 [1954]) at the centre would look much different.

7 I am thinking specifically of the critical and creative work that Aritha van Herk in particular has done to introduce a discussion of women into a very masculinized Western academic space.

8 I would like to distinguish between agriculture as it was practised by Aboriginal peoples as part of their traditional cultures, and agriculture as it was later imposed on them by the federal government. See Sarah A. Carter, *Lost Harvests: Prairie Indian Reserve Farmers and Government Policy* (Montreal and Kingston: McGill-Queens, 1993) for a discussion of this issue.

9 W.O. Mitchell, *Who Has Seen the Wind* (Toronto: McClelland and Stewart, 2001).

10 In fact, the explosion of Aboriginal writing and publishing in Manitoba today mirrors in many ways the explosion of regional writing and publishing that took place across western Canada generally in the 1970s. These regional anthologies and publishing houses were largely established as a means of resisting an Ontario-centred literary power that marginalized writing from the prairies and sought to control the ways in which the region was represented. These publishing houses, like Turnstone, Coteau, and NeWest, are now firmly established with a degree of literary power of their own. It is interesting to speculate about their relationship with the new Aboriginal writing and publishing: given regional presses' roots in resistance to assimilation, is it not possible that the upsurge in Aboriginal writing and publishing could be rooted in similar resistance?

11 Jenny Kerber, *Writing in Dust: Reading the Prairie Environmentally* (Waterloo: Wilfrid Laurier University Press, 2010), 10.

12 *Post-Prairie*, eds. Jon Paul Fiorento and Robert Kroetsch (Vancouver: Talon Books, 2005), 9.

13 Ibid.

14 There is an interesting conflict between generations of critics here.

15 Rosanna Deerchild, "This Is a Small Northern Town," *Post Prairie*, 46.

16 Annette Lapointe, *Stolen* (Vancouver: Anvil Press, 2006), 13.

17 Ibid., 18.

18 Ibid., 17.

19 Ibid., 18.

20 Ibid., 39.

21 Ibid., 34.

22 Robert Kroetsch, "'Foreword,' in *Scratching the Surface: The Post-Prairie Landscape*, ed. Steven Matijcio (Winnipeg: Plug In Editions, 2008), 7.

FOR THE LOVE OF PLACE
——NOT JUST ANY PLACE
SELECTED METIS WRITINGS

EMMA LAROCQUE

This essay has an express purpose of exuding orality, with the objective of raising awareness about Metis love of land, or of landedness. As such, I am approaching the discussion more from a literary and creative approach. I am of course aware that any mention of the Metis can bring up any number of issues from pretty much any number of disciplines. I will not try to address these multi-faceted issues which can involve historical, constitutional, social and ethnographic questions. My discussion here is obviously quite exploratory, and I have taken some poetic liberties with style and organization.

While the displacement and dispossession of the Red River Metis is more or less a well-known historical fact within academia (and to a lesser extent, in the wider community), ironically rarely is the theme of place associated with the Metis. By place I mean more than geographical location or mapping, though all that is included; by "place" I mean more like attachment, rootedness, groundedness, materiality. Familial-ity. Home. Homelands. A particular and unique land area in this country where we carry out body and home-stitching everydayness. A place where we live. And go to work from. Or in. A place where we come to know the ways and voices of family and neighbours. A place where we become familiar with pots and pans, woodpiles and water pails. Or computers and iPods. A garden we tend. Blueberry meadows we work or rest in, meadows surrounded in sunlight streaming through poplars and birch. A place where we dream. Yes there was the Red River and that was and is a place. To be sure a very significant place. But Red River has been so over-politicized that we can barely recognize it as a real place where real people practised their everyday ways of life and liveli-hoods. What did Riel eat?

Let me put this matter of place in another way. People in western Canada, and especially Manitoba, know about the Red River Metis. Or should. Everyone knows that Riel defended Metis interests and died for the Metis cause. And ev-eryone knows the prairie Metis (or a handful of them) took a sort of last stand at Batoche, put up a good fight but lost.[1]

And everyone knows the other Canadian story—the sanitized school story—the pioneer version of how the coureurs de bois, or the voyageurs in early fur-trade times, sang and joshed their way up and down the St. Lawrence, portaging their way into the interior. Strapping, jovial "halfbreed" men who seemed to be forever paddling.

Another theme of halfbreed wanderings is to be found in Norma Bailey's Daughters of the Country series produced by the National Film Board. In the third film, titled *Places Not Our Own*, there is a scene where a Metis family is travelling by horse and wagon. It is sometime in the Depression. It is somewhere in the Prairies. Here the Metis are the prairie gypsies—apparently homeless and with no specific place to go.[2] And where did Morag's Metis lover in Margaret Laurence's *The Diviners* live? Where does he come from? Where does he go? Like an apparition, he fades in and out of Morag's life.[3] Whether the Metis are presented as portaging minstrels, prairie gypsies or inconstant lovers, popular culture has romanticized and perpetuated the myth of Metis as roaming tran-sients with little or no sense of rootedness to homes and lands, to homelands.[4]

Yet everyone knows the Metis fiddler. Or the Metis fighter. And the Me-tis martyr. But who knows the people? Who knows where they played their fiddles? Who really knows why they fought, or why they sacrificed their lives? Who knows who the Metis are and what they love and hold dear? Who knows where they have lived—or where they live now? Who knows how they felt or how they feel now about being displaced, then replaced? And today—where are their places? How do they live in those places? What do they feel about these places? Or that one place?

Of course, I am not going to answer these questions or issues. I raise them poetically rather than ethnographically. Here I only have time to offer vignettes of thoughts from several Metis writers and to highlight those facets and issues which often get neglected in film, literature, and other popular productions, but even in critical discussions. Generally, critical attention to Metis writers focus on socio-economic and identity issues.[5] Here I take three well-known Metis—Maria Campbell, Marilyn Dumont, and Greg Scofield—who clearly express their profound attachments to home and landedness. I turn first to Maria Campbell, who in *Halfbreed* (1973) offers considerable cultural information tracing Metis life from the Metis Resistance era of the late 1800s to her own era of the 1950s–70s from which she wrote the memoir. Maria Campbell is of Cree/Scottish Metis Nation ancestry from Saskatchewan. Her parents raised her and her siblings with Metis material culture as well as Metis values. It is not incidental that Maria begins her facts of biography with this: "I should tell you about our home now before I go any further."[6] She then proceeds to describe their "two-roomed large hewed log house," detailing their homemade tables and chairs, beds and hay-filled canvas mattresses, the hammock that babies swung from, the huge black wood stove in the kitchen, the medicines and herbs that hung on the walls, the wide planks of floors scoured evenly white with lye soap, and so forth. I am sure it was with tears of love that she reminisced: "The kitchen and living room were combined into one of the most beautiful rooms I have ever known."[7] Clearly, these tangible everyday objects remain a cultural palate of warm memory and strong attachment from which Maria Campbell has written and lived.

In a very short non-fiction piece called "The Gift,"[8] Alberta Metis writer Marilyn Dumont writes about watching her father revisit and linger over a beloved spot of land he had long ago lost. This land, located in northeastern Alberta, had been given to him as a wedding gift by his father—but he and his wife (Marilyn's parents) were unable to keep it due to the Depression in the 1930s. Many years later Marilyn and her aging father climb up a hill to see—and to say a final goodbye—to this place. Before leaving this ancestral high ground, Marilyn watches with pain as her father "tucked some blades of grass and twigs into his wallet." She describes her own reaction: "My thoughts raced. I wanted to take something too. Something to say I'd been here. My eyes searched in the grass. A light flickered. I picked up a brown piece of glass. The heavy broken bottom of a jug. I didn't know what I'd do with it. It didn't matter; I gripped it against me."[9] This fact-based story is another very moving testament to Metis attachment to place, in this case a parcel of land. Not just any land. But a very site-specific, family-significant, and much-loved place. It is excruciatingly difficult to lose places we love. As Marilyn Dumont puts it: "Who knows what it's like to leave, to give up a piece of land? If you do, it might haunt you forever, follow you til you come back."[10]

Many Metis—not all, but altogether too many—have been forced in some way or other to leave their special places. In this sense, there is some truth to the image of the Metis as prairie gypsies, but this should be seen as a consequence of displacement—not as a cultural or individual trait to be romanticized. The sad fact is that many Metis cannot come back to their places of origin due to urban and industrial encroachments, or outright dispossession by either federal or provincial laws and actions. But even this reality does not erase the Metis love of home, kin, or community. Some have had to adopt symbolic places that hold great significance. One such place is Batoche. In his autobiography *Thunder Through My Veins* (1999), Metis poet Gregory Scofield titles one chapter "Pekewe, Pekewe" ("Come Home, Come Home" in Cree). He had come home to Saskatchewan, to the prairies, to what he calls his roots. After a very long and troubled and confused youth, Gregory had finally discovered Batoche—on one hand a historic place of sacrifice, loss, and pain, but for him, a new place of peace and belonging. A place, a people, a culture that he could identify as his very own.[11] These prairie writers, each work reflecting a different period of time, nonetheless experienced some form of uprootedness in their personal and community lives—yet each is deeply rooted to particular histories, places, geographies, and families. To be sure, there are many differences between these writers (age, gender, experience, and genre among them), yet one constant stands out—a strong identification with placeness. Landedness for the Metis remains an unbroken bond.

My father used to say we are nothing without land. Rarely did my gentle father make such categorical pronouncements. He was born at the turn of the twentieth century in northeastern Alberta, his roots coming directly through the Red River Metis of the 1870s–90s. Bapa was a hard-working man forced by colonial history to raise his family in a road allowance section of land he never got to own. "We are nothing without land." It took me some time to realize the full profundity of his statement. He was not just talking about legal ownership of property—although land and resource rights, of course, remain an unfinished business for the Metis, certainly for the Red River Metis. My father (and mother), who never had the means to own property, had a philosophy and praxis about land that was far greater than capitalist notions of land as real estate commodity. Metis writers reflect and express what Metis peoples know and feel—that they are deeply, ancestrally, Indigenously, and fundamentally rooted to their lands and families. To my Metis parents land represented identity, culture, self-sufficiency, and independence. Landedness also meant family, home life, kin, and community. Landedness is purposeful; it gives meaning to language and life.

For all our efforts to explain our identity and our epistemic world views in relation to land and place, stereotypes and ignorance about the Metis persist. I come back to the beginning. I have just spoken to the well-known and perhaps worn-out old stereotypes. Earlier in my research I had been struck by the portrayals of Metis as alienated loners who insert into Native or white lives without context or belonging. Like Billy Jack in the movie *Billy Jack*. Sometimes they were romanticized. Like Morag's lover in *The Diviners*. Often they were demonized. Historians and novelists alike presented metis as volatile males splintered between the chasms of civilization and savagery.[12] These should be old stereotypes, yet have these rather classic images changed? I am not so sure. I have noticed that some

Native American writers and academics make no distinction between individuals who are half-white/half-Indian, and those Metis Nation peoples of western Canada who formed a distinct ethnic culture and community.[13] The more recent post-colonial emphasis on hybridity or border-crossing, useful concepts in some contexts, can serve to further obscure Metis national identity and culture and, in turn, Metis land and resource entitlements.[14] But even in Canada we still have films, poems, stories and books, titles and academic treatments that tend to focus on Metis homelessness, identity crises, marginalization, or an in-betweenness. Of course, there is some sad truth to these images. The Red River Metis did lose their beloved lands in the Red River, and about 83 percent of this population were forced to relocate and many could not find a new place or new homelands.[15] If they did, they would face other dragons such as the "scrip" that the federal government gave as poor compensation for Metis claims, the Gatling gun at Batoche, provincial confiscations of traplines through Natural Resource laws, or the oil sands in northeastern Alberta. To name but a few. And notwithstanding the somewhat recent Powley Supreme Court Decision (2003) that recognized specific Metis harvesting rights,[16] neither the provincial nor federal governments are anywhere near fulfilling the Canadian constitution—that is, of actualizing Metis land and resource rights as Aboriginal peoples. But despite all these historic pressures, Metis managed to stay together and even to develop strong communities in central and northern parts of the prairie provinces, many along road allowances. The Metis Nation story is a remarkable feat of survival and cultural tenacity. For despite all the succession of losses and obstacles, there are thousands of Metis Nation families and individuals across western Canada who live lives quite similar to those of "ordinary Canadians." That is, they have homes—maybe even "homelands"—and culturally cohesive and functioning family lives with meaningful occupations. Without in any way seeking to minimize those Metis who have suffered much personal and cultural dislocation, some of us Metis have had to say "hey—not all of us were stolen or fostered, not all of us suffered identity crises (even despite huge obstacles) and not all of us had to look for homes and places." Historians and literary critics now need to refocus and enlarge their portrayals and treatment of Metis peoples, issues, and themes. I say this to draw attention to our rootedness, to our integrated identity as Metis Nation peoples. To our love of our lands.

Love of land does not depend on property ownership (though that certainly should be a right that Metis have). My family still owns no lands. But long before the province of Alberta was established, long before Confederation was arranged, my paternal and maternal Plains and Woodlands Cree/Metis ancestors filled these lands by use and love of the land. Like other Red River Metis Nation peoples of their generation, my parents knew every nook and cranny of lands stretching hundreds of miles within their areas. My brothers—along with others of our generation and their children—still know, occupy and use these lands. Metis scholars, and writers and poets such as Maria Campbell, Marilyn Dumont and Greg Scofield carry the nooks and crannies in their hearts. As do I. I end with Marilyn Dumont's poem "not just a platform for my dance":

This land is not
just a place to set my house my car my fence

This land is not
just a plot to bury my dead my seed

This land is
my tongue my eyes my mouth

This headstrong grass and relenting willow
these flat-footed fields and applauding leaves
these frank winds and electric sky

are my prayer
they are my medicine
and they become my song

this land is not just a platform for my dance[17]

NOTES

1   I am referring to the Northwest Metis Resistance at the Battle of Batoche in 1885 where some 250 Metis men fought some 900 Canadian Militia troops. The Metis took a last stand to protect their lands against imperial forces. See Walter Hildebrandt, "The Battle of Batoche" in *The Western Métis: Profile of a People*, ed. Patrick C. Douad (Regina: Canadian Plains Research Center, 2007). See also *1885 and After: Native Society in Transition*, eds. F. Laurie Barron and James B. Waldram (Regina: Canadian Plains Research Center, 1986).

2   *Places Not Our Own*, directed by Derek Mazur (National Film Board, 1986), available online at http://www.nfb.ca/film/places_not_our_own, accessed 6 October 2011.

3   Margaret Laurence, *The Diviners* (Toronto: McClelland and Stewart, 1974).

4   I am not suggesting that we confine any Indigenous group, including the Red River Metis, to the sort of rootedness that freezes them to the past which would keep them "in their place" so that colonizers can gaze or segregate them. For an interesting discussion on the uses and abuses of notions of "roots" see Renate Eigenbrod, *Travelling Knowledges: Positioning the Im/Migrant Reader of Aboriginal Literatures in Canada* (Winnipeg: University of Manitoba Press, 2005), especially the chapter on "The Rhetoric of Mobility."

5   For example, see Kateri Damm, "Dispelling and Telling: Speaking Native Realities in Maria Campbell's *Halfbreed* and Beatrice Culleton's *In Search of April Raintree*" in *Looking at the Words of Our People*, ed. Jeannette Armstrong (Penticton: Theytus Books, 1993): 93–114. For a more post-colonial reading see Helen Hoy, *How Should I Read These? Native Women Writers in Canada* (Toronto: University of Toronto Press, 2001).

6   Maria Campbell, *Halfbreed* (Toronto: McClelland and Stewart, 1973), 16.

7   Ibid., 17.

8   Marilyn Dumont, "The Gift" in *Writing The Circle: Native Women of Western Canada– An Anthology*, eds. Jeanne Perreault and Sylvia Vance (Edmonton: NeWest Press, 1990), 44–46.

9   Ibid., 46.

10   Ibid., 44.

11   Gregory Scofield, *Thunder Through my Veins: Memories of a Metis Childhood* (Toronto: HarperCollins, 1999).

12   Emma LaRocque, "The Metis in English Canadian Literature," *Canadian Journal of Native Studies* 3, 1 (1983): 85–94.

13   Native American writer and academic Elizabeth Cook-Lynn in *Why I Can't Read Wallace Stegner and Other Essays* (Madison, WI: University of Wisconsin Press, 1996) takes a very troubling view of "Métis" as halfbreed individuals who threaten Native "tribal" identity. There is no mention or appreciation of the Red River Metis as Indigenous with Indigenous identity. See also Julia D. Harrison's treatment of the Metis as people in between in her book *Métis: People Between Two Worlds* (Vancouver: Douglas and McIntyre, 1985).

14   For further explorations of these issues, see Emma LaRocque, "Native Identity and the Métis: *Otehpayimsuak* Peoples" in *A Passion for Identity: Canadian Studies for the 21st Century*, eds. David Taras and B. Rasporich (Toronto: Nelson Thomson, 2001), 381–400; Emma LaRocque, "Reflections on Cultural Continuity Through Aboriginal Women's Writings" in *Restoring The Balance: First Nations Women, Community and Culture*, eds. Gail Gutherie Valaskakis, Madeleine Dion Stout and Eric Guimond (Winnipeg: University of Manitoba Press, 2009), 149–174; Emma LaRocque, *When the Other is Me: Native Resistance Discourse* (Winnipeg: University of Manitoba Press, 2010).

15   See Joe Sawchuk, Patricia Sawchuk, Terry Ferguson and Metis Association of Alberta, *Metis Land Rights in Alberta: A Political History* (Edmonton: Metis Association of Alberta, 1981). See also Canada, *Report of the Royal Commission on Aboriginal Peoples* (1996), Volume 4, Chapter 5 on "Metis Perspectives," 198–386, found at http://www.collectionscanada.gc.ca/webarchives/20071115053257/http://www.ainc-inac.gc.ca/ch/rcap/sg/sgmm_e.html, accessed 10 April 2012. See also D.N. Sprague, *Canada and the Métis, 1869-1885* (Waterloo: Wilfrid Laurier University Press, 1988), Chapter 3.

16   R. *v.* Powley, [2003] 2 S.C.R. 207, 2003 SCC 43, found at http://www.canlii.org/en/ca/scc/doc/2003/2003scc43/2003scc43.html, accessed 5 October 2011. Also see the recent Manitoba Metis Federation vs. Canada decision at http://scc.lexum.org/decisia-scc-csc/scc-csc/scc-csc/en/item/12888/index.do," accessed 25 March 2012.

17   Marilyn Dumont, *A Really Good Brown Girl* (London, ON: Brick Books, 1996), 46.

LITTLE UKRAINE ON THE PRAIRIE
"BABA" IN ENGLISH-LANGUAGE UKRAINIAN-CANADIAN LITERATURE

LINDY LEDOHOWSKI

"Ethnic patterns," according to Wsevolod Isajiw, "even if completely torn out of their original social and cultural context, become symbols of one's roots," so that "through [an] ancestral time dimension one can, at least symbolically, experience belonging."[1] His idea that belonging can be located in the ethnic symbolism of the past tells only half the story; the other half belongs to space, particularly what Sneja Gunew refers to as "spatial entitlement," or a sense of belonging to a particular place.[2] In the context of English-language Ukrainian Canadian writing, this combination of the past with a place blends to make a heady identity elixir, one not without a strange taste.

Ethnic identity, or the experience of belonging, arising from a "home" precisely coded as Ukrainian-hyphen-Canadian, appears in much Ukrainian Canadian English-language literature through the coupling of symbolic references to perogies, babas, folk songs, and big Ukrainian weddings with a prairie landscape as a place of ethnic belonging.[3] Because Cold War Ukraine was a closed locale—one difficult, if not impossible, to visit during much of the twentieth century—contemporary Ukrainian Canadian writers began to take their images of Ukraine's culture, history, language, literature, and politics and write them on the Canadian prairie as a substitute for "their original social and cultural context," Ukraine itself. In his seminal essay on home, J. Douglas Porteous reminds us that "although a psychic space, home is usually identified with a particular physical space,"[4] and for many Ukrainian Canadians, a prairie landscape offers a place onto which they can project the "psychic space" of Ukraine as a lost ethnic home. This chapter examines this construction of "Ukrainian-ness" and "prairie-ness" in literary texts, because the nexus where the contested concepts of home, Ukrainian Canadian-ness, and the prairie meet creates a particular kind of Andersonian "imagined community" at the subnational, ethno-cultural level.

Postcolonial theorist Rosemary Marangoly George tells us that "twentieth century literature in English is not so concerned with drawing allegories of nation as with the search for viable homes for viable selves,"[5] and contemporary Ukrainian Canadian literature—of both the twentieth and twenty-first centuries—searches for ways of making the Canadian prairie operate as a viable replacement home to substitute for a lost and inaccessible Ukraine itself. In her introduction to the 1987 reprinting of *All of Baba's Children*, on the tenth anniversary of its first publication, Myrna Kostash writes, "I had been insisting that ethnicity was one thing, having to do with this time and this Canadian place, nationalism another having to do with Europe and history, and that the latter were not my affair. I was willing, even eager, to engage in the construction of neo-Galician prairie identity, but I was emphatically not prepared to take up the baggage of the Ukrainian nation."[6]

Kostash explicitly states that her ethnicity arises not just from "this Canadian place," but specifically the Canadian prairie place; her interest lies in a "neo-Galician prairie identity," not one that finds its origin in Ukraine, inviting us to interrogate the connection between Ukrainian-ness and prairie-ness in a public imaginary. What does this "neo-Galician prairie identity" look like?

The literature suggests that it is particularly interested in Ukrainian peasant folk culture of a previous era as its main expression. Scholars of this literature write about "an entire genre of Ukrainian-Canadian pioneer stories"[7] that are "historical narratives that sentimentalize or romanticize the bygone days of early immigration and settlement."[8] Critics have agreed upon some defining features of this pioneering narrative: first, a focus on "the undeniable hardship that these pioneers endured"; second, "an emphasis on hard work"; third, a construction of the "Ukrainian farmer [as] imbued with a certain nobility of character"; an attention to characters who "are sanctified as forefathers engaged in a noble pursuit"; a "reliance upon biographical material and alleged socio-historical truth"; and finally "the overwhelming use of first-person narration."[9] This focus on the lost, and somehow more simple and satisfying, days of early immigration is a dominant thematic of the literature.[10] The corpus of literature that contributes to this genre "simultaneously perpetuates a narrative of progress that constructs Ukrainian immigrants and their children as innately amenable to hard work; as willing to assimilate to Canadian culture while retaining some aspects of their ethnic identity; and as successful, ultimately, in ascending the social and economic hierarchies of the multicultural society they helped build."[11]

Both literary critics and historians have provided reasons for the proliferation of this prairie pioneer myth as a particularly persistent articulation of Ukrainian-ness in a Canadian context. Some simply point to the verifiable facts behind Ukrainian immigration to Canada at the turn of the last century. Given the significant numbers of Ukrainian immigrants who arrived on the prairies seeking ten-dollar homesteads, Sonia Mycak understands the dominance of this pioneering motif in the literature to represent the desire of a hitherto silenced and marginalized community to tell its story.[12] Mycak's view foregrounds the historical reality of Ukrainian immigration to the Canadian prairie. In contrast, Kostash suggests that the continued construction of Ukrainian Canadians as part of an "imagined community" of ethnic homesteaders appearing as "colourful, dancing, *horilka*-tippling hunkies recently arrived from a wheat farm in Saskatchewan" is preferable to the more sinister conceptions of Ukrainian Canadians as Nazi sympathizers or anti-Semites; in her words, "compared to these stigmatizations, the fun-loving bumpkin is almost lovable."[13]

Another strategic reason has been suggested for the adoption of such an image of this ethno-cultural group: namely, that as similar pioneer myths are at the heart of many settler-invader identities, we should not be surprised to see Ukrainian Canadian writers claiming their place through manual labour on the land. Think here of the last two lines of Margaret Atwood's poem "Death of a Young Son by Drowning" as the young immigrant mother buries her stillborn child, she says, "I planted him in this country / like a flag."[14] Ukrainian Canadian pioneer stories present death and sacrifice as a claiming of place. Thus, these stories fit into a general trend of asserting legitimacy by claiming a kind of baptism through suffering as a way of claiming one's legitimate space on a landscape. Related to this general claim is a more specific one about the timing of this kind of national assertion. By the 1970s and 1980s, debates in Canada arose in response to the Royal Commission on Bilingualism and Biculturalism that contributed to its evolution from a document codifying the bilingual and bicultural nature of Canada into one articulating a formal recognition of federal multiculturalism. Using the pioneer story, Ukrainian Canadians could write themselves into Canadian history as a "third force" to counter the two founding nations' model that dominated those early discussions.[15] Historian Frances Swyripa convincingly argues that Ukrainian Canadian "myth makers were driven by the desire for a tidy and satisfying picture of the past that promoted the goal of recognition for their group as a legitimate and valuable actor on the Canadian stage. The result was a founding fathers myth erected on the peasant pioneers: in their backbreaking toil and sacrifice to introduce the prairie and parkland to the plough and to exploit mining and forest frontiers so that Canada could be great, lay Ukrainians' right to full partnership in Confederation."[16] She makes it clear that there were very real political gains to be made by constructing Ukrainian Canadian-ness as synonymous with a pioneering forefather mythology, thus creating a legitimate space for Ukrainian Canadians within the larger Canadian polity.

Even as much of the corpus of English-language Ukrainian Canadian literature developed this genre of pioneering stories—lionizing a Ukrainian émigré past as essential to the Canadian nation-building project—other authors recognized some of the problems inherent in this type of myth-making. For instance, Helen Potrebenko's feminist rewriting of the typical Ukrainian pioneering tale, her 1989 "A Different Story," which Mycak reads "as a parody of the myth of the glorified pioneer,"[17] and her 1977 study *No Streets of Gold* seek to show darker sides of the pioneering experience to undercut its dominance in the literature. Further, Lisa Grekul rejects these homesteading stories as offering nothing more than a "hackneyed prairie pioneer myth." She specifically sets her own Ukrainian Canadian coming-of-age novel not in the pioneer era, but "in the multicultural heyday of the 1980s and early 1990s," calling it a story "shaped as much by humour as by hardship."[18] Even though writers such as Potrebenko and Grekul attempt to engage critically with the celebratory mythology of the pioneering era, they still set their stories in the Canadian prairie. They are not alone. In addition to the ever-increasing genre of contemporary Ukrainian Canadian texts set in a historical homesteading era, such as Shandi Mitchell's widely acclaimed 2009 novel *Under This Unbroken Sky* or Yuri Kupchenko's Cossack cowboy 1989 epic *The Horseman of Shandro Crossing*, Ukrainian Canadian authors often set their contemporary narratives in the prairie provinces, such as Daria Salamon's popular "chick lit" 2008 novel *The Prairie Bridesmaid* or Orest Talpash's sweeping family epic, *Rybalski's Son*, also from 2008. The trend of seeing "Ukrainian-ness" and "prairie-ness" as somehow interconnected persists.

The trend of reading Ukrainian Canadian texts as representing socio-historical facts about Ukrainian settlement and life on the prairies, and the connection linking the author and subject matter, remains dominant. Analyzed not so much as creative fiction but more as ethnographic documents creating "generic confusion," blending together the fictive with "social history, personal memoirs, historical fiction, biography, [and] autobiography," critics conflate the literature and the history of Ukrainians in Canada.[19] And this history is that which most Canadians (of Ukrainian descent or not) still see as synonymous with homesteading on the Canadian prairie. Janice Kulyk Keefer points this out when she laments that for a "Canadian reading public" Ukraine—the country, its history, politics, and culture—means "only *borshch* and cabbage rolls, vast and shining wheat fields."[20] While some voices—Potrebenko's, Grekul's, and Kulyk Keefer's among them—reject overly simplified folk culture versions of Ukrainian-ness in Canada, there persists a reading of these texts as "less provocative than predictable" in their portrayal and reaffirmation of "the centrality of the pioneer era in the Ukrainian-Canadian imaginary."[21] I argue, however, that even in the earliest examples of this pioneering story, the "underlying, but unmistakable sense of nostalgia for what [Ukrainian Canadians] see as a simpler time and place, a nobler way of life,"[22] is complicated by an underlying ambivalence and discomfort with the forced assimilation and loss of culture that shaped the experience of immigration to Canada by those early homesteaders. In looking closely at these texts, we find the literature expressing more than a desire to express a silenced history, more than a desire to claim a legitimate space within the Canadian national narrative, and more than a desire to present a non-threatening cultural symbol. Grekul suggests that Ukrainian Canadian authors feel frustrated with multiculturalism as offering "too little encouragement too late."[23] I argue that this frustration is embodied in the ever-present "baba" figure in Ukrainian Canadian texts set on the Canadian prairie. The baba is a figure that elicits feelings of both nostalgia and frustration. She represents the desire to belong as much as feelings of non-belonging, particularly in her relationships with her Canadian-born granddaughters.

The tendency to read these texts as offering little more than an overly simplistic linking of Ukrainian-ness to prairie-ness fails to reckon with the prairie space as anything other than a blank page onto which specific ethnic fantasies can be written. Gerald Friesen challenges the idea of prairie emptiness with his assertion that "the West has taken a new shape in recent decades," a shape informed as much by economic and social ties as by the myth of the empty landscape.[24] Likewise, the interpretation of stock symbolic references, particularly the "Ukrainian grandma figure, the saintly 'baba,' "[25] in reference to a stable "home" on a fetishized empty prairie, uncritically replicates the traditional positioning of home as a stable, feminized space, ignoring the work of feminist theorists who argue that envisioning stable, female homes reproduces limiting binary constructions of knowledge that do not account for multiple perspectives.[26] While this literature has been read and understood as signalling a desire for a clear and coherent articulation of a stable and acceptable, even "lovable," ethnic identity as "Ukrainian Canadian," located in a specific place and rooted in land and matrilineal families, I contend that this body of literature complicates this simplistic picture. Often the literature problematizes home and place, and plays with ethnicity and identity in ways that indicate a much greater discomfort with Ukrainian-ness in Canada than a celebration of it as something fixed and folksy. In particular, the figurations of baba in this literature are often much more nuanced than merely representing a typical matriarchal figure embodying hearth and home in the most traditional manner.

Swyripa offers important observations about the dominance of women in Ukrainian Canadian literature, categorizing them into two groups: Nasha Meri and Katie on the one hand, and baba on the other. In Swyripa's words: "Nasha Meri and Katie—together they symbolized the Ukrainian immigrant girl in young womanhood and her Canadian-born sister testing the freedoms and attractions of the new country."[27] Nasha Meri and Katie often appear Canadianized, and distanced from their Ukrainian roots.[28] Their counterpoint appears in the traditional baba, "the revered pioneer grandmother," who holds tight to and preserves Ukrainian folk culture for Ukrainian Canada.[29] In her survey of ethnic prairie symbols, Swyripa calls the "much loved *baba* (grandmother)" a "popular grassroots incarnation" of Ukrainian Canadian-ness, and points out that the folk and culinary arts over which she is the undoubted mistress have become the symbols, monuments, and handicrafts of a Ukrainian Canadian identity on the prairie. She writes that baba as a symbol is "Neither beautiful and feminine nor conforming to the settlement-era stereotype of the Ukrainian peasant woman as submissive and downtrodden, *baba* [...] personified [a] Ukrainian peasant heritage, even endearing traits once branded foreign and inferior."[30] Poet Andrew Suknaski made a similar comment in 1979 when discussing ethnicity and writing in Canada. He states: "*baba* demythologizes our long-standing belief that the man was the head of the household in those days. In fact, *baba* was the god and the head of the household."[31] This kind of powerful baba appears in the literature more often than the saccharine, "revered," and "saintly" figure that critics so often discuss. In my reading of the genre of Ukrainian Canadian pioneer stories, as well as those set in the contemporary prairie, the babas are more complex and sometimes more angry than they are usually given credit for being. More importantly, her interactions with her Nasha Meri and Katie granddaughters demonstrate that these protagonists are not merely "guilty of rejecting traditional restraints and values, and of succumbing to the vulgar and superficial in the Canadian lifestyle," as Swyripa characterizes them.[32] Rather, the authors create young, female protagonists engaged in complex cultural and personal negotiations with their babas.

Let us begin first by looking at the figure of baba in the novel that is often considered the first in this genre of backward-looking Ukrainian pioneering tales, Vera Lysenko's *Yellow Boots*. First published in 1954, *Yellow Boots* is credited as the first English-language novel written by a Canadian of Ukrainian descent.[33] It tells Lilli Landash's story: as the daughter of Ukrainian immigrants, Lilli experiences a harsh life on a prairie farm as the victim of a tyrannical and patriarchal father. Ultimately, she leaves her ethnic, rural surroundings and becomes a renowned singer. Lysenko sets her novel in 1929, more than twenty years prior to her writing, and paints a picture of a Ukrainian Canadian peasantry whose culture includes rich musical traditions. Lysenko writes this novel, in part, to create a kind of memorial to what she views as the lost Ukrainian culture of immigrants settling across the Canadian prairie. In the foreword to the book, she writes that her "story of a girl's search for music is offered as a reminder of their lost inheritance, and to preserve for them something of the old beauty."[34] From the beginning, cultural preservation motivates her. According to Carolyn Redl, many early ethnic writers worked to preserve elements of their ethnic identity; she even cites Lysenko's *Yellow Boots* as an example of this preservation and presentation mode of ethnic writing.[35] While some critics read this novel as a feminist, proto-multiculturalist text,[36] Grekul disagrees, arguing that Lilli's story articulates an ethnic compromise wherein Lilli's Ukrainian Canadian-ness becomes nothing more than "simply a costume she will wear on stage," as her femininity and ethnicity become assimilated into a dominant, masculinist, and Anglo-normative Canadian culture. While these critics may disagree about the implications of Lilli's story as that of a Ukrainian Canadian girl from the prairies who achieves mainstream success as a pan-ethnic folk singer, they agree on the focus of both Lilli and her mother as the embodiments of the feminized Ukrainian subject.[37] Tamara Palmer Seiler goes so far as to suggest that Lysenko's novel creates in Lilli a protagonist who appears as "a new world embodiment of the ancient female earth goddess," one who possesses the "power of a nurturing and holistic female vision,"[38] a notion which calls to mind Marian Rubchak's work on feminine symbolism in contemporary Ukraine. In her analysis of the appearance of *Berehynia*, a combined figure of female youth and the "ancient 'hearth mother,'" Rubchak suggests that "the archaic hearth mother" functions as an enduring symbol in Ukraine and, in her words, "female centrality remains lodged as an idea in the Ukrainian psyche."[39] Yet Lysenko does more than demonstrate the connection between ethnic Ukrainian-ness and femaleness through Lilli's relationship to her mother and to the prairie landscape her mother clings to; she also complicates this idea that culture operates as a matrilineal inheritance through the grandmother figure.

Alexandra Kryvoruchka suggests that this baba operates as "a folk poet who passes on the stories of days gone by," and sees her as one more example of the general notion that in this book "the retention of Ukrainian culture is carried out by the women."[40] Mycak shares this attitude, and sees the grandmother figure in this novel possessing the simple function of perpetuating Ukrainian culture and passing it on to Lilli.[41] There is, however, more to this baba and her relationship with Lilli than that. This baba first appears in the second chapter of the book cooking the feast for the anticipated funeral for Lilli that never materializes, because, against all odds, the girl survives her childhood fever and cheats death. In this scene, her grandmother is not a simple, "saintly" figure of a mythologized "hearth mother," but a proactive and powerful force in the home. Lysenko writes: "Granny was casting wax into water and murmuring incantations. She was convinced that some evil thing had caused the girl's illness and that the wax would take the shape of this evil and drive it from the girl."[42]

As the rest of the family sits vigil over the sick child—professional mourners already wailing, the mother already sewing a shroud, and the father anxious to get back to his fields—Lilli's grandmother works her spells and magic to save the child from death: "Granny, imperturbable in the midst of the tumult, now stepped in to take charge of the situation. From the bags around her waist, she had taken an herb and was now scattering it over the bed of the girl, murmuring an incantation.... The old lady stood with a crafty smile upon her face. 'I have fooled the Old Robber,' she triumphed. From the oven she extracted a brick, wrapped it in grey flannel and placed it under the girl's feet. 'She sleeps.' "[43]

Lysenko offers us a baba more aligned with witchcraft than specific Ukrainian culture. She is referred to as "Granny" rather than baba, and her use of spells, wax, herbs, and incantations are elements of pagan folk medicine that can certainly be associated with Ukrainian peasant culture, but that can also just as easily be associated with women's alternative folk practices with no specific ethnic element. Even when Granny tells her granddaughter stories, Lysenko characterizes these stories as creating an "enchantment" and writes "Granny could enter the child's world of fantasy and create something new and beautiful out of scraps, whether of cloth, food or words."[44] It is false, therefore, to see in grandmother nothing more than a "folk poet" who embodies the Ukrainian peasant culture that she bestows upon her granddaughter. In their collaborative analysis of witches in contemporary culture, Silvia Bovenschen, Jeannine Blackwell, Johanna Moore, and Beth Weckmueller write: "witch mythology mediates between the historical and the empirical witch, at the juncture between the femininity syndrome and aggressive self-representation. In popular myth, witches stand side by side with the ancient mother goddesses."[45] In this iteration, Granny Yefrosina is both specifically Ukrainian—like a *Berehynia*—but also just another figure within a larger "witch mythology." She is, therefore, a much more complicated figure than a simple repository "of the old beauty," as Lysenko may have intended.

Importantly, "witch mythology" has long connected the figure of the witch to gendered dissent. "When women began to deliberately assume the witch role," for instance, "they were in no way behaving as spontaneously and arbitrarily as it may appear."[46] Lilli's grandmother casts her spells, saving the child from death, and lures Lilli into a world of fantasy, introducing the girl to the folk arts that will inform her career as a singer, in the context of resistance to blind adherence to cultural practices. Lilli's mother and father await her death, replete with an outward projection of all the expected cultural norms and practices, but her grandmother rejects these and busily casts her spells. Far from being a simple repository of Ukrainian-ness on a peasant prairie homestead, this grandmother figure implies that power also resides in resistance to cultural norms and expectations.

However, Lysenko presents for Lilli a cautionary tale about female resistance. The true witch character in the book, Tamara, is expunged from the text in the most macabre fashion. Lilli's village bands together in a mob and kills Tamara one night, a murder that Larry Warwaruk echoes in his 1998 book *The Ukrainian Wedding,* where Marusia, the town's provocative and sensual figure of natural magic and allure—like Tamara—is found murdered. These murdered women represent the risk to the protagonist of being associated with witchcraft or dissent through sexuality. Tamara's face is "full of the sensuality one sees in beautiful women who have grown up in primitive surroundings," and her voice is "delicate." In Lilli's mind, Tamara is linked to witches throughout the ages.[47] Unlike Granny Yefrosina, whose witchcraft is stripped of sexuality ("neither beautiful [nor] feminine," to use Swyripa's words), Tamara's version is threatening and ultimately expunged as a result of the townspeople viewing her as an eroticized danger. As the community gathers to plan the lynching of the unfortunate Tamara, one of the widows, as "homely as a potato," delivers the "most telling charge" against Tamara, claiming that she "cast a spell" on the woman's husband, driving him to suicide.[48] The homeliness of the widow contrasts with Tamara's beauty and sensuality, and after this final charge against Tamara is made, the villagers head out into the dark night towards Tamara's home, which is burned to the ground—either by her own hand or the mob itself. The novel leaves the assignation of responsibility ambiguous.

Immediately after Tamara's death, the novel reintroduces Granny Yefrosina. The juxtaposition of the death of the sensual witch with the one whose face is "smocked with wrinkles" reinforces the connection between these two women.[49] Once again, on this visit Lilli's grandmother is cast as a natural healer, a good witch. She treats a cut on Lilli's foot and feeds her husband "a herbal concoction" for his mysterious ailment.[50] At the end of this chapter, "Granny, bristling with bossiness, apt to mischief, teeming with legend as a bee with honey," dies.[51] Lysenko removes both witch figures—Tamara and baba—from the novel. With their deaths, Lilli begins her process of leaving the farm and moving to the city to become first a labourer and then a famous folk singer. Thus, baba appears less as a figure intimately connected with the landscape—operating as the wellspring of cultural specificity on the prairie—and more of an ambivalent figure vis-à-vis Ukrainian-ness. In this novel, she is more associated with the dissident and the aberrant than with the traditional and the sacred, and her death represents not necessarily a lost culture or lost way of life, but rather the inability for Lilli to move into mainstream culture and still accommodate this seemingly atypical grandmother figure and even less so her more sexualized younger version. Lysenko cannot seemingly reconcile either "safe" dissidence (through baba) or "dangerous" dissidence (through Tamara) for her protagonist, and kills both witch figures—characters representing female power and/or resistance.

Enoch Padolsky creates a linear trajectory from *Yellow Boots* and Illia Kiriak's epic *Sons of the Soil*, which was translated into English from Ukrainian in 1959, right through to more contemporary Ukrainian Canadian writings.[52] Scholars of ethnic minority writing in Canada have long documented the growing number of ethnic or minority literatures in Canada in the post-war era, and Ukrainian Canadian literature is most often seen in this context.[53] The pioneering stories that emerged in the latter half of the twentieth century can be understood through the explanations offered by scholars such as Mycak or Swyripa, or even in reference to Kostash's view that the lovable is better than the problematic. However, Lysenko's early novel prefigures dynamics that continue through the literature that Padolsky mentions right up into the 1990s and the early years of the new millennium, decades shaped by both the conscious problematization of the politics of identity and Ukraine's 1991 declaration of independence from the Soviet Union. The latter opened up a hitherto-closed Ukraine to the west, when Ukrainians in Canada could conceive of themselves as part of an international Ukrainian diaspora with the ability to travel "back" to Ukraine (a Ukraine that many of the Canadian-born have never seen).[54] If Ukrainian Canadian literature of the late 1990s and early 2000s need not imagine Ukrainian identity as intimately connected to the Canadian prairie—because Ukraine itself could be seen as the locus of identity formation for members of the Ukrainian diaspora—then why do texts from this era still revisit the Canadian prairie? The answer lies in baba.

Read straightforwardly, the many Ukrainian Canadian prairie tales following the publication of *Yellow Boots* may run the risk of situating home in outmoded ways, as a mere fixed point around which a stable identity can cohere meaningfully.[55] But, homes, as George and others contend, are not mere givens—spaces "already marked out in symbolic and material dimensions for the occupant"— but are often fractured, mutable, and multiple.[56] A simplistically stable notion of home fails to grapple with more contemporary ways of understanding subjectivity that foreground instability and mutability rather than stability.[57] Attending to the ways that Ukrainian Canadian authors have created complex and complicated baba figures offers insights that these prairie-focused stories are often doing more than merely replaying a "hackneyed prairie pioneer myth," which can be read as more complicated than critics generally acknowledge even back as early as Lysenko's novel.

A close examination of the later literature reveals a baba not so very different from Lysenko's portrayal. Even in a post-Soviet era, after Ukraine's 1991 independence, we still see Ukrainian Canadian literature creating babas on the prairie, and she remains much more than a celebratory repository of Ukrainian folk culture and identity; rather, her presence in texts often dramatizes the complicated negotiations underlying the split subjectivity of a Canadian-born, English-speaking, minoritized, ethnic subject.

For instance, Marusya Bociurkiw's 2006 novel *The Children of Mary* presents a baba who is much more a feminist figure of agency than a conduit for Ukrainian-ness. This novel offers an account of Sonya's coming of age as she learns how to deal with her abandonment by her father, her sister Kat's death, her mother's cancer, and her own queer sexuality. Sonya traces the story of her sister's death, and ultimately discovers that one summer while she was staying with her baba, the father sexually abused Kat and is ultimately responsible for her death as well. Within this narrative arc, the novel explores memory, womanhood, family, and grief—and the interplay of these very personal things in a larger, public context. Bociurkiw often casts the private sense of Sonya's loss and grief in the public domain, with references to TV shows, pop culture, and news events. In addition, *rusalky,* or Slavic water spirits, figure prominently, representing a commingling of the female in Ukrainian folk culture and the sisterhood of lesbianism.[58] Like *Yellow Boots'* positioning of its witch-like baba in rural Manitoba, *The Children of Mary* also creates a rural Manitoba baba who employs herb craft. Bociurkiw constructs baba's home as an herbalist's dream filled with dried weeds, boiling concoctions, and dark containers with mysterious contents.[59] Yet unlike Lysenko's novel that offers only a limited narrative point of view—Lilli's image of her grandmother—Bociurkiw's lets us into baba's own mind, through which we discover that this baba hates cooking traditional Ukrainian foods and likes working with healing herbs instead.[60] Abandoned by her husband, this baba earns her independence through her healing arts; she says: "in those days people came to see me, for one sickness or another. Word spread, I didn't mind…. In this way I did not become so bitter. I had something to give."[61] Like Granny Yefrosina, whose concoctions save Lilli and represent her power, Baba Maria ("always just Marie, or Mary, or Mrs. M." in the mouths of non-Ukrainians) claims independence and autonomy through her healing.[62]

Where Lilli needs her grandmother's healing help to cure her of a physical sickness, Sonya needs her baba's intervention to help heal her soul. As the immigrant herself, split between the Old Country and Canada, she mixes up her memories and blends places together, the *here* of now and the *there* of memory.[63]

In contrast, when Sonya returns to the prairies after a time in Toronto, she reflects on it as her plane lands: "The prairie looked beautiful from the air, in a way I didn't remember, a picture postcard, ugliness airbrushed away. Canola and wheat fields for miles, as you come in by plane. The land divided into circles and squares, every shade of blue and green. *Home*. I tried out the word on my tongue, like a candy from childhood, one you couldn't get anymore. A place you could be from, a place you thought could save you, a place you made up in your head."[64]

This rumination on the complexities of home—its imaginary status, its glossy superficiality, its impossibility—articulates Sonya's relationship to the Canadian prairie rather than to the Old Country that her grandmother recalls. While her grandmother's psyche vacillates between the two homes inhabiting her memories, Sonya's psyche is torn by the loss of her sister, "what haunts her," such that her baba figures she "should slip some medicine into her tea."[65] Baba, in this book, appears powerful at first, seeking to heal her granddaughter, not merely transmit her cultural knowledge to her. Baba here is also angry. When her daughter considers her herbal healing arts nothing more than magic and superstition, she says: "Many times did I long to strike my own daughter's face."[66] As that daughter grapples with her cancer treatments through the channels of mainstream medicine, baba wishes she would be allowed to intervene with her alternative approaches; she screams and rails at her daughter, but ultimately must accept the limits to her herbal remedies. She cannot save her dead granddaughter, and she cannot prevent her daughter's cancer from spreading.

In an eerie echo of *Yellow Boots*, Kat, Sonya's sister, whose death serves as Sonya's narrative focus, appears as another version of Lysenko's Tamara (or Warwaruk's Marusia). When Kat returns from a summer with her father, Sonya notes that she has become an utterly sexualized teen. She tells us "Kat started dressing kind of slutty."[67] Ultimately Kat leaves home and starts living on the streets; one of the final times Sonya sees her sister alive, Kat lies on a bare mattress on a floor in a commune, her face "turned toward the wall, a man on top of her."[68] Tamara's sensuality develops out of her loneliness as a widow, Marusia's develops out of her unhappy marriage; and Kat's develops in response to her sexual abuse. In each case, the younger, sexualized woman dies a violent death, while the less sexually threatening baba survives just long enough to die a natural death and to be seen as angry or forceful, but ultimately impotent against the forces swirling about her. Granny Yefrosina cannot prevent Lilli from growing up and away, and Baba Maria ("always just Marie, or Mary, or Mrs. M.") cannot heal her daughter's cancer, salve her granddaughter's wounds, or overcome her own anger. In both novels, the protagonists, not their grandmothers, move forward and develop a sense of their own agency, either as a renowned folk singer or a woman learning to put her ghosts to rest.

Grekul's novel provides yet another alternative, a version of an angry but impotent baba. While Lilli and Sonya love their babas, Grekul's protagonist feels a much greater sense of disconnection from hers. Grekul writes her novel as a kind of corrective or complement to the existing genre of pioneering stories set at the turn of the twentieth century, setting it in the late 1980s and early 1990s in both Alberta and Africa. *Kalyna's Song* tells Colleen Lutzak's coming-of-age story, first in the small Alberta town where she finishes high school, and then in Swaziland, where she attends school for a year. Her simple-minded cousin, Kalyna, personifies Ukrainian folk culture, and her traumatized piano teacher, Sister Maria, personifies Ukrainian classical culture. Colleen tries to come to her own definition and understanding of what it means to be Ukrainian in contemporary Canada in reference to these women.[69] When in Africa, Colleen becomes friends with Rosa Richardson, an artist obsessed with eggs and embryos. As I have written elsewhere, if Kalyna represents simplistic Ukrainian folk culture, and Sister Maria represents sophisticated Ukrainian high culture, then Rosa represents all culture as an embryonic *tabula rasa*.[70] Tellingly, by the end of the novel, all these women are dead, as are the kinds of cultural options they symbolize for Colleen. Like Lysenko, who juxtaposes Granny Yefrosina with Tamara and kills them both (in back-to-back chapters), or Bociurkiw, who links baba to Kat through Sonya and kills them both (one at the start and the other at the end of the novel), Grekul creates parallels amongst these three women who influence Colleen and kills them all. Like Lilli and Sonya, who must move forward after the deaths of the witch figures—the non-sexualized babas and the eroticized younger women—Colleen, too, functions as the character in Grekul's novel who bears the burden of continuation after the deaths of Sister Maria, Kalyna, and Rosa. Moreover, Grekul creates in Colleen's baba the antithesis of the "saintly 'baba' " critics see as ubiquitous on the Canadian prairie.

Colleen's baba features in one important scene of the novel: the Christmas just before Colleen leaves for Africa, when her family meets for a traditional Ukrainian-Christmas meal in the town of Vegreville, famous for its giant statue of a *psyanka*, or Ukrainian Easter egg. The Ukrainian symbolism of the scene is as obvious as Grekul can make it—the Ukrainian food, the Ukrainian traditions, the Ukrainian Canadian prairie setting—and in this setting, Baba makes her only significant appearance in this novel. She terrifies the teenaged protagonist and is specifically not the "saintly" baba that critics would lead us to expect: "*Baba's* face is all veins—grey-brown liver spots and veins—and *Gido* looks like a skull. A bony, fleshless skull. I'm afraid to touch them…. Our *Baba* can't cook anymore, and she needs a walker to get around…. Neither of them speaks more than a word or two of English."[71] Colleen's baba is not a robust figure of Ukrainian culture, presiding like a matriarch over all things Ukrainian Canadian, happily awaiting the opportunity to gift her culture to her granddaughter. While Sonya's baba admits to hating cooking the expected Ukrainian Canadian dishes, Colleen's baba has moved to a level of decrepitude where she no longer can cook. This baba appears as a deathly crone, stripped of her ability to perform the cultural acts over which she should be mistress, and grotesque in appearance. She has no natural medicines or witchcraft to bestow, nor stories to pass on. Her inability to communicate with her granddaughter in English underscores her impotence as a traditional, matrilineal figure of cultural transmission. She never teaches her children or grandchildren the folk arts she is expected to; Colleen does not learn Ukrainian folk songs from her grandmother, nor does she learn *pysanky* making from her. Rather, her cultural learning comes from old folk song recordings and books with directions for how to make Ukrainian Easter eggs.[72] When Colleen's plans to leave Alberta for Africa are shared with her grandmother, Baba sees this adventure as a tragedy. This baba is rooted in her prairie context, but that context appears limited and culturally abridged. Upon hearing the news of Colleen's imminent departure, her baba "cries quietly," repeating "*Bozhe, Bozhe,*"—God, God—"as she rubs her eyes with the edge of her apron."[73] The Christmas dinner breaks up, and Colleen departs for Africa, leaving her grandparents behind as near-dead figures of a limited and limiting culture rooted in outmoded traditions, unable to communicate with the younger generation. By the end of the novel, when Colleen realizes that she had to go away in order to change and recognize her Alberta town and her familial context as home, her aged and impotent grandparents are only one part of the complex and complicated dynamic that shapes it, rather than fixed cultural points defining a stable, unmutable ethnic identity for her.[74]

Both Lysenko and Bociurkiw create babas with an affinity with witchcraft, healing, and dissidence who die before the end of each novel, and Grekul creates female characters—Kalyna, Sister Maria, and Rosa—who die and a baba who is impotent. Each of these novels, set in the Canadian prairie and addressing notions of Ukrainian-ness in Canada, offer much more ambivalent portraits of baba as a symbol of Ukrainian-ness and prairie-ness than critics generally tend to acknowledge. Each novel refuses to offer a "revered pioneer grandmother," and offers instead figures who resist, but who also function as mere foils for the protagonists whose journeys of self discovery are shaped, in part, by their relations with their grandmothers. These babas are less the touchstones of culture to which the granddaughters can refer and more unresolved and open-ended figures, ones who are not completely understood by their granddaughters and who seem strangely linked and connected to their more tragic younger counterparts, Tamara and Kat (and Warwaruk's Marusia).

In this disconnect between baba and her Canadian-born granddaughter in these stories set on the prairies, we see Ukrainian-ness as something uncomfortable and unresolved, not neatly confined within a stock baba symbol. Poet Elizabeth Bachinsky writes at the end of her collection *God of Missed Connections*, in which she struggles to articulate her own relationship to her ethno-cultural heritage, "by now, it is impossible to encapsulate all that is Ukrainian. It is an ethnicity that is, by its very nature, fractured, diasporic, transient; there is no one definition of what it is to be Ukrainian."[75] The ambivalent feelings apparent in the construction of babas in many of the prairie-set texts, showing her at once a powerful healer or an angry woman while simultaneously killing her or demonstrating her impotence, hints at some of the instability inherent in attempts to affix Ukrainian-ness to a straightforward homesteading mythology, or its contemporary iteration in the stories set in the contemporary prairie and focusing on the descendants of immigrant pioneers.

Grekul suggests that books set not in the Canadian prairie, but in Ukraine itself offer a more productive complement to the insistence that Ukrainian-ness and prairie-ness must somehow be synonymous.[76] However, another way of understanding these texts that feature a journey "back" to Ukraine notes that often they construct the most powerful moments of connection between the female protagonist and her Ukrainian ethno-cultural heritage in ways that evoke the ambivalent feelings towards baba and "home" on the prairie seen in the other books. Thus these memoirs may not necessarily challenge the prairie myth—they may just be an alternative form of it.

Kostash's *Bloodlines: A Journey into Eastern Europe* and Kulyk Keefer's *Honey and Ashes: A Story of Family*, for instance, construct their narratives of travelling to Ukraine as journeys into a past that evoke intergenerational conflicts and understand a Ukrainian Canadian identity through the lens of nineteenth-century peasantry, which looks very much like some of the Canadian-based stories. Exemplifying the typical journey Ukrainian Canadians make to Ukraine to meet distant relatives and capture something of a lost ancestral connection, both Kostash's and Kulyk Keefer's travel memoirs locate ethnic identity in a rural, ancestral place that looks remarkably like the Canadian prairie. Both texts also situate the grandmother-granddaughter relationship as paramount in both author/narrators' experiences of Ukraine, once again foregrounding baba as in the stories set in the Canadian prairie.

Even though Kostash travels to Ukraine during the 1980s when it is under Soviet control, and many of her observations are thus politically based, she also recognizes that, for Ukrainian Canadians, Ukraine is loaded with meaning as a potential originating source for ethno-cultural identification.[77] She does not find this originating source in the cities of Lvov or Kyiv, which fill her with rage at their "grossest Stalinist bravura."[78] Instead she finds something to connect with in the rural village from which her grandmother emigrated to Canada. Before leaving Canada, she looks at photographs of her extended relatives in Ukraine and seems disappointed to see them dressed in present-day suits or skirts with nylons; she prefers the image of "the matriarch," who is the one member of her family dressed in traditional, peasant clothing, "an embroidered blouse and a thick kerchief and looks wizened and worn out," completing her idealized "image of all Ukrainian women from the village."[79] Like the many critics who see in baba a stock and satisfying image of Ukrainian-ness, she wants to find a "saintly" baba presiding over her family of "real Ukrainians."[80] However, as she seeks this idealized baba figure in Ukraine, she finds something much more complicated, an image which evokes the ambivalent baba figures in the prairie-set stories.

One Sunday, Kostash's Ukrainian relatives take her to her "baba's natal village," despite the fact that in 1980s Ukraine, the region in which the village is located is closed to westerners.[81] In her baba's village, Kostash discovers the poignant feeling of her baba's absence, and through that absence, her own disconnect from Ukraine, the place of her baba's birth. Following a Derridean attention to the spectral in her account of haunting and the in-betweenness occupied by the figure of the ghost, Avery Gordon links photographs to the spectral. She sees in photographs the opportunity to affix an absence, to render the absent person ghostly.[82] Kostash creates this sense of photographs as evidence of absence as she describes her experience of her grandmother's village: "A neighbour, stout, baggy-bosomed and kerchiefed, knee-deep in red and yellow tulips. Click. The church where Baba used to go, still in good shape, white-walled and tin-roofed with a single, squat, hexagonal dome. Click. The very pathway along which she used to drive the sheep out of the village and into the upland meadow. Click."[83] With each "click" of her camera, she captures images that omit her baba. Like the photograph that Gordon analyzes that does not include the missing Sabina Spielrien who was supposed to be present, providing "photographic evidence of her absence," these photographs that Kostash takes provide evidence of her baba's absence.[84] Like the babas on the Canadian prairie who inhabit a rural space, but who ultimately die and who seem unable to provide for their granddaughters a neat and tidy Ukrainian cultural legacy, Kostash's baba here appears as a hint, a ghost, an absence.

If Kostash's journey to Ukraine creates a Ukrainian-ness in ghostly images of a missing baba, then we find this dynamic even more pronounced in Kulyk Keefer's *Honey and Ashes*. Unlike Kostash, who visits the actual village from whence her grandmother departed, Kulyk Keefer does not find the house that her ancestors left behind; rather, she finds her connection to the past through a museum. Like the dead, dying, or impotent babas in the prairie texts, or

Kostash's empty photographs evoking a ghostly absent-present baba, Kulyk Keefer constructs her connection to her own baba through the lens of loss. Museums, like photographs, attempt to fix moments, but are just as illustrative of what is absent as they are of what is present. Like Kostash, who finds echoes of her baba and "clicks" to preserve that absence, Kulyk Keefer finds her grandmother's absence affixed in a peasant museum that recreates a rural, Ukrainian home, much like the homesteads that the prairie pioneers would have inhabited. As she approaches the museum, she remarks with wonder: "Out of time, out of place, I've found my grandmother's house, the very room where my mother was born."[85] In this museum that she allows to become a stand-in for her own ancestral home, she sees "images formed on wavy glass, as tentative as breath. They dissolve into shadows first, then emptiness: the disappearing tricks of ghosts."[86] She takes off her shoes to walk barefoot in the recreated peasant house to feel the "ghostprints" of her ancestry.[87] In many ways, this is the climax of the memoir. This small house, not unlike the pioneer homes constructed in the prairie stories, represents a sense of ethnicity that Kulyk Keefer claims. Once again, a granddaughter's journey of self-discovery develops in relation to her baba, and once again, the baba is dead and gone, impotent in her own right.

While witches can be seen as figures of gendered dissent and both Derrida and Gordon analyze the agency of the ghosts they theorize (such as Hamlet's father rising from the grave and demanding retribution for his murder), these Ukrainian babas who reside in prairie settings or rural Ukrainian ones—that seem very similar to Canadian prairie ones—as witch-like crone figures and ghostly absences have much less agency. Rather, their granddaughters have agency. Lilli's baba dies, but Lilli goes on to become a famous folk performer, making sense of her Ukrainian-ness as part of a larger ethnic socio-economic group; Sonya's baba dies, but Sonya goes on to learn about herbal remedies and healing, not just from her baba's notes, but from a wide variety of sources; Colleen's baba appears as an impotent crone, unable to cook or communicate, but Colleen blends her Ukrainian folk songs with the music she learns in Africa; Kostash's grandmother is an absent figure, glaring as an empty space in a photograph, but Kostash returns to Canada to master the Ukrainian language and develop that lost connection; and Kulyk Keefer's grandmother is nothing more than shadows and ghostprints in a museum, but Kulyk Keefer creates the connection through her imagination and her creative arts. In looking at these texts, therefore, baba is less of a "saintly" figure of cultural specificity presenting a safe image of Ukrainian-ness, but more of an ambiguous figure. She is angry and frustrated at times, impotent and absent at others. This corpus of prairie pioneering stories and their more contemporary prairie-set cousins offer us a more complicated baba embodying Ukrainian-ness in Canada. Her appearance suggests that we turn our attention from her in all her unresolved and possibly irresolvable complications and focus rather on the Nasha Meri and Katies of Ukrainian Canadian English-language literature.

At the end of the introduction to her scholarly survey of English-language Ukrainian Canadian writing, Grekul writes that she hopes readers will take away "the realization that keeping ethnic identity alive requires acts of will, courage, and, above all, imagination," highlighting "the crucial role that literature plays in nurturing—imagining and re-imagining—ethnic identity."[88] The narratives that focus on prairie settings and babas, dramatizing the stories of Canadian-born granddaughters, articulate this creative sense of imagining and re-imagining. They suggest that if she is anything, baba is a catalyst for change, not a repository of Ukrainian culture, *tout court.* The Lillis, Sonyas, Colleens, Myrnas, and Janices who narrativize a struggle to articulate Ukrainian Canadian-ness do so in a way that looks forward as much as it looks backwards.

NOTES

1   Wsevolod Isajiw, "Olga in Wonderland: Ethnicity in Technological Society," *Canadian Ethnic Studies* 9, 1 (1977): 82.

2   Sneja Gunew, *Haunted Nations: The Colonial Dimensions of Multiculturalism* (New York: Routledge, 2004), 97.

3   Robert Klymasz, review of *Echoes from Ukrainian Canada*, ed. Jars Balan, special issue of *PrairieFire* 13,3 (1992), in *Canadian Ethnic Studies* 26, 1 (1994): 163.

4   J. Douglas Porteous, "Home: The Territorial Core," *Geographical Review* 66, 4 (1976): 385.

5   Rosemary Marangoly George, *The Politics of Home: Postcolonial Relocations and Twentieth century Fiction* (Cambridge: Cambridge University Press, 1996), 5.

6   Myrna Kostash, Introduction to *All of Baba's Children* (1977: Edmonton: NeWest Press, 1987), xv–xvi.

7   Sonia Mycak, *Canuke Literature: Critical Essays on Canadian Ukrainian Writing* (Huntington, NY: Nova Science Publications, 2001), 68.

8   Lisa Grekul, *Leaving Shadows: Literature in English by Canada's Ukrainians* (Edmonton: University of Alberta Press, 2005), 116.

9   Mycak, *Canuke Literature*, 51–53, 81; Grekul, *Leaving Shadows*, 116–17.

10   Mycak, *Canuke Literature*, 47; Frances Swyripa, *Wedded to the Cause: Ukrainian-Canadian Women and Ethnic Identity 1891–1991* (Toronto: University of Toronto Press, 1993), 225; Grekul, *Leaving Shadows*, 116.

11   Grekul, *Leaving Shadows*, 117.

12   Mycak, *Canuke Literature*, 50, 93.

13   Myrna Kostash, *All of Baba's Great Grandchildren: Ethnic Identity in the Next Canada* (Saskatoon: Heritage Press, 2000), 30, 32.

14   Margaret Atwood, "Death of a Young Son by Drowning" in *The Journals of Susanna Moodie* (Toronto: Oxford University Press, 1970), 31.

15   For an overview of Ukrainian Canadian contributions to this larger debate, see Bohdan Bociukiw, "The Federal Policy of Multiculturalism and the Ukrainian Canadian Community" in *Ukrainian Canadians, Multiculturalism, and Separatism: An Assessment*, ed. Manoly Lupul (Edmonton: University of Alberta Press, 1978), 98–128.

16   Swyripa, *Wedded to the Cause*, 221.

17   Mycak, *Canuke Literature*, 57.

18   Grekul, *Leaving Shadows*, 118, 202.

19   Mycak, *Canuke Literature*, 85–86, 88.

20   Janice Kulyk Keefer, *Dark Ghost in the Corner: Imagining Ukrainian-Canadian Identity* (Saskatoon: Heritage Press, 2005), 19.

21   Grekul, *Leaving Shadows*, 118.

22   Ibid., 116.

23   Grekul, Introduction to *Leaving Shadows*, xv.

24   Gerald Friesen, "Introduction" in *The West: Regional Ambitions, National Debates, Global Age* (Toronto: Penguin, 1999), xvi.

25   Klymasz, Review, 163.

26   Biddy Martin and Chandra Mohanty, "Feminist Politics: What's Home Got to do with It?" in *Femininity Played Straight: The Significance of Being Lesbian*, ed. Biddy Martin (New York: Routledge 1996), 165.

27   Swyripa, *Wedded to the Cause*, 64.

28   Ibid., 64.

29   Ibid., 240.

30   Frances Swyripa, *Storied Landscapes: Ethno-Religious Identity and the Canadian Prairies* (Winnipeg: University of Manitoba Press, 2010), 174–175.

31   Andrew Suknaski, quoted in "Ethnic Identity: The Question of One's Literary Passport" in *Identifications: Ethnicity and the Writer in Canada*, ed. Jars Balan (Edmonton: CIUS Press, 1982), 75.

32   Swyripa, *Wedded to the Cause*, 64.

33   Illia Kiriak, *Sons of the Soil*, Trans. Unknown (1939–1945 *Syny Zernli*; Winnipeg: Trident Press, 1959); Vera Lysenko, *Yellow Boots* (Edmonton, CIUS and NeWest Press, 1992 [1954]).

34   Lysenko, *Yellow Boots*, ix.

35   Carolyn Redl, "Neither Here Nor There: Canadian Fiction by the Multicultural Generation," *Canadian Ethnic Studies* 28, 1 (1996): 23.

36   Alexandra Kryvoruchka, Introduction to *Yellow Boots* (Edmonton: CIUS and NeWest Press, 1992): xi–xxiii; Tamara Palmer Seiler, "Including the Female Immigrant Story: A Comparative Look at Narrative Strategies," *Canadian Ethnic Studies* 28, 1 (1996): 51–66; Tamara Palmer Seiler, "Multi-Vocality and National Literature: Toward a Post-Colonial and Multicultural Aesthetic," *Journal of Canadian Studies* 31, 3 (1996): 148–65; Beverly Rasporich, "Retelling Vera Lysenko: A Feminist and Ethnic Writer," *Canadian Ethic Studies* 21, 2 (1989): 38–52; and Janice Kulyk Keefer, Review of *Leaving Shadows: Literature in English by Canada's Ukrainians*, by Lisa Grekul, *University of Toronto Quarterly* 76, 1 (2007): 539–40.

37   Grekul, *Leaving Shadows*, 45, 35–46.

38   Palmer Seiler, "Including the Female Immigrant," 56.

39   Marian J. Rubchak, "Ukraine's Ancient Matriarch as a Topos in Constructing a Feminine Identity," *Feminist Review* 92 (2009): 132.

40   Kryvoruchka, Introduction, xxi.

41   Mycak, *Canuke Literature*, 33.

42   Lysenko, *Yellow Boots*, 20.

43   Ibid., 23.

44   Ibid., 29–30.

45   Silvia Bovenschen, Jeannine Blackwell, Johanna Moore, and Beth Weckmueller, "The Contemporary Witch, the Historical Witch and the Witch Myth: The Witch, Subject of the Appropriation of Nature and Object of the Domination of Nature," *New German Critique* 15 (1978): 85.

46   Ibid.

47   Lysenko, *Yellow Boots*, 166.

48   Ibid., 178.

49   Ibid., 187.

50   Ibid., 188, 189.

51   Ibid., 194.

52   Ibid., in *Ethnicity and Culture in Canada: The Research Landscape*, eds. J. W. Berry and J. A. Laponce (Toronto: University of Toronto Press, 1994), 363.

53   Enoch Padolsky, "Canadian Ethnic Minority Literature in English," 364; Mary Kirtz, "Old World Traditions, New World Inventions: Bilingualism, Multiculturalsm, and the Transformation of Ethnicity," *Canadian Ethnic Studies* 28, 1 (1996): 8.

54   Satzewich, *The Ukrainian Diaspora*, 202.

55   Porteous, "Home," 386.

56   Marangoly George, *The Politics of Home*, 21.

57   Marangoly George, *The Politics of Home*, 27–29; Kaplan, "Deterritorialiations," 189; Diana Brydon, "Postcolonialism Now: Autonomy, Cosmopolitanism, and Diaspora," *University of Toronto Quarterly* 73, 2 (2004): 700.

58   Lindy Ledohowski, Review of *The Children of Mary* by Marusya Bociurkiw, *The New Pathway* 77, 30 (2006): 8.

59   Marusya Bociurkiw, *The Children of Mary* (Toronto: Inanna Publications, 2006), 17.

60   Ibid., 41.

61   Ibid. 41–42.

62   Ibid., 41.

63   Ibid., 57.

64   Ibid., 54.

65   Ibid., 57.

66   Ibid., 72.

67   Ibid., 25.

68   Ibid., 30.

69   Lindy Ledohowski, Review of *Kalyna's Song* by Lisa Grekul, *Canadian Ethnic Studies* 39, 3 (2007): 232–34.

70   Ibid., 234.

71   Lisa Grekul, *Kalyna's Song* (Regina: Coteau Press, 2003), 221.

72   Ibid., 365–66.

73   Ibid., 223.

74   Ibid., 383.

75   Elizabeth Bachinsky, *God of Missed Connections* (Gibsons, BC: Nightwood Editions, 2009), 75.

76   Grekul, *Leaving Shadows*, 118.

77   Myrna Kostash, *Bloodlines: Journey into Eastern Europe* (Vancouver: Douglas and McIntyre, 1993), 168.

78   Ibid., 164.

79   Ibid., 163.

80   Ibid., 186.

81   Ibid., 185.

82   Avery Gordon, *Ghostly Matters: Haunting and the Sociological Imagination* (Minneapolis: University of Minnesota Press, 1997), 32–35.

83   Kostash, *Bloodlines*, 185.

84   Gordon, *Ghostly Matters*, 32, 33, 35.

85   Janice Kulyk Keefer, *Honey and Ashes: A Story of Family* (Toronto: HarperCollins, 1998), 255.

86   Ibid., 256.

87   Ibid.

88   Grekul, *Leaving Shadows*, xxiii.

EMBODYING FAMILY VALUES
IMAGINARY BODIES, THE *CANADIAN MEDICAL ASSOCIATION JOURNAL*, AND HETEROSEXUALITY IN WESTERN CANADA

HEATHER STANLEY

The baby boom era holds a special place in the hearts of many Canadians. The years between the end of World War II and the beginning of social and cultural upheaval in the 1960s seem for many a touchstone of normality, family values, and national social cohesion. Compelling as this image is for many Canadians, it has been problematized by several historians seeking to free post-war history from what Stephanie Coontz has termed "the nostalgia trap."[1] These historians have demonstrated that the post-World War II-era focus on normality and middle-class heterosexual nuclear family values was used to disenfranchise certain members of society and that, despite the hegemonic power of "normal," the boundaries of normality had to be constantly (re)defined, enforced, and protected.[2]

One of the many ways that the boundaries of normal were continuously enforced and reinforced was through focusing hegemonic discourses upon the body. Dominant groups such as the medical community examined and sorted citizen's bodies into binary categories, dividing those who were deemed normal and useful to the wider state from those bodies deemed abnormal and deviant, according to the dominant episteme.[3] This concentration on the body helped increase the authority of the medical community, empowered through structures such as the hospital, to gather information about the body and to ultimately set parameters for the disciplining of both normal and aberrant bodies. The medical community was empowered "not only to distribute advice as to a healthy life but also to dictate the standards for the physical and moral relations of the individual and society in which he lives."[4] This search for control of bodies is demonstrated clearly in the *Canadian Medical Association Journal (CMAJ)*, the primary national medical journal of the day. The journal is a remarkable archive of discourse: it represents not only a voice of the medical profession but one intentionally edited and presented to create at least the appearance of a united medical opinion. In a sense the *CMAJ* is not only a reflection of the dominant hegemonic voice of Canadian medicine; it was a dominating and hegemonizing voice from within the medical profession itself.[5] In its pages, the contributors, editors, letter-writers, and advertisers attempted to create a discourse that would police the gendered boundaries of Canadian men and women and to create sexualized hegemony on a national scale.

Yet, this project was never entirely successful, and this incongruity is aptly demonstrated by the oral histories of individual embodied experience. Oral histories, the product of eighteen open-ended interviews with women who lived and married during the baby boom period (1946–1966), demonstrate an ambivalent response to this dominant medical narrative. The women benefitted from their own bodies' "normalcy" as heterosexual women in monogamous marriages, but at the same time problematized the dominant narrative through the persistent individuality of their experiences.[6]

Foucault applied his insights into medical knowledge and power mainly to the Victorian era; however, his notion of how the medical profession as an authoritative structure was tasked to sort citizens' bodies into normal and abnormal, useful and deviant categories is relevant for Canada during the baby boom. As the nation continuously sought stability in the wake of a deep economic depression and two world wars, there was an increasing focus on the heterosexual nuclear family, with its concomitant gender roles, as the bedrock upon which to build a stable state.[7] Medical doctors and psychiatrists were increasingly called upon to provide solutions to issues affecting the family such as juvenile delinquency, divorce, pornography, and sexual education. In giving such advice the medical community usually portrayed the family as both crucially important and incredibly fragile. As one editor of the *CMAJ* remarked in 1959, "it seems to be generally agreed that in Western countries the stability of family life is not what it was in a less enlightened age."[8]

A close examination of the journal demonstrates a startling continuity in its articles, letters, and editorials; a hegemonic voice that both reflected and projected wider societal concerns about Canada's citizen bodies.[9] When viewed as a whole this dominant discourse creates what Moira Gatens identifies in her 1996 work *Imaginary Bodies: Ethics, Power and Corporeality* as "an imaginary politic"—an imagined, non-corporeal body created by discourses and against which individual bodies are judged.[10] Gatens argues that any bodies deviating from the "imaginary body politic" are immediately disenfranchised from full participation in society and their actions deemed ugly or inappropriate. For Gatens this ultimate body politic was a male "Leviathan" corpus created to disenfranchise women; if we expand Gatens' framework, however, the juxtaposition of imaginary ideal bodies to the fleshy bodies of individual citizens becomes an even more useful tool of analysis.[11] Within the dominant discourse of the *CMAJ*, two "Leviathan" bodies were created during the Canadian baby boom: one male and one female. These were imbued with the normalized gender values of the day and created to complement each other to further reinforce discourses of the importance of the heterosexual nuclear family.

Such rigidly defined body politics disenfranchise "problematic bodies" from full and open participation in society. The *CMAJ* body politics, in its embodiment of, and emphasis upon, strict gender roles of male breadwinner and female homemaker and its normalization of heterosexual marriage, disenfranchised homosexuals as well other "deviants" such as unwed mothers.[12] However, these "dominant bodies" also impacted "non-deviant" citizen bodies that they, as an idealization, were supposed to represent and reflect. Yet because these corporeal bodies were assumed to exist within the range of "normal" (because of their relative closeness to the ideal imaginary body), it is much more difficult to see the effects of the imaginary body. Further, because these bodies do derive many societal benefits from this closeness to the imaginary ideal, it is easy to fall into the trap of assuming these "normal" bodies were unproblematic. But the *CMAJ* body politics and the heterosexual couples they were meant to represent were not perfect mirrors which, if held facing each other, would simply reproduce endless copies of the same "perfect" body into infinity. Instead individual Canadian bodies were imperfect copies, at best reflecting some of the features of the *CMAJ* body politics back onto themselves, while distorting others, sometimes beyond recognition.

This essay seeks to explore these distortions by comparing and contrasting one of the dominant Canadian medical body politics, that of the female, to the bodies of individual women who, by engaging in married heterosexual relationships, were assumed to fall within the range of "normal." These individual bodies demonstrate an often uniquely western Canadian perspective, suggesting the importance of place, but problematize dominant, overarching national narratives, using their local bodies to displace such claims to legitimacy. Thus, while the bodies of these eighteen women are not meant to be representative of all women in Canada, and indeed are not meant to even be a representation of western Canadian heterosexual married women, they do demonstrate the ways that individual corporeal or "fleshy" bodies could both reflect and contradict the national medical body politic as presented in the *CMAJ*. They also demonstrate how such reflections and contradictions both further empowered the dominant body politic and, in subtle and often indirect ways, counteracted it.

The primary characteristic of the medical body politic, and the one that allowed the medical profession authority over the female heterosexual body during the baby boom, was its knowability—its permeability—to the outside world. At a time when science and medicine were still invested with a great deal of authority, discourses of the body within the *CMAJ* emphasize a body whose most intimate secrets could be unlocked by a trained medical professional. Not only were doctors deemed able to "know" a patient's body through their ability to interpret clinical data such as symptoms, they also had the instruments and the authority to penetrate the skin of their patients and, thus, to "know" that body from the inside out.

Medical authority came with a sense of assumed responsibility. The medical community was clearly concerned about disseminating its own vision of heterosexual normalcy, via their particular body politic, to the public. Several *CMAJ* articles discussed how medical doctors should conduct themselves in radio and television broadcasts and the importance of medical input and control over sexual education within schools.[13]

While the *CMAJ* body politic was clearly visible, knowable to the doctors and thus able to be penetrated by the external medical world, the individual bodies of the women I interviewed were more defined by their very opacity to their owners, who remained largely ignorant of their bodies' function and biology. This opacity came out most clearly in reoccurring narratives of their loss of virginity, which for many was their first real introduction to their body as a sexual entity. Many women, especially those who married at the beginning of the time period, were confronted with their lack of knowledge on the very eve of their weddings. Margaret Brown recalls, "I remember um when I knew I was getting married...and I remember sitting in the bath and getting out and drying myself and I thought how is it all going to work...? We never look at ourselves... we never looked.... I knew there was something going to happen but I couldn't imagine *how* it would happen."[14] Ruth Bell, after losing her virginity on her wedding night, not having been told that some bleeding was to be expected, actually cut off sexual relations with her husband because she thought she had begun menstruating. She notes, "I can't imagine that there are grade school children that are that innocent [nowadays]. But I was. I was completely a virgin and I had no experience."[15]

On the surface this opacity seems to support the authority of the medical profession over the female body and the profession's right to disseminate information about it to lay people. However, even those women who had access to medical information about their bodies usually relied more on rumour for information about sexuality. Jessica Bateman, who was training to be a nurse when she became engaged to her husband, remembers that, though they learned about STDs and cleanliness in regards to sex, the "old matron" who taught them was a "spinster" and would get very embarrassed when discussing the actual mechanics of intercourse. Jessica's main sources of "information" were her sexually experienced friends, and, she notes that, as she was pretending to know more than she did, it is quite possible that they too were attempting to seem more "worldly" than they actually were. Indeed, she found out later through her own experiences that much of the information she heard was wrong.[16] Bateman's story demonstrates a plurality of non-official sources through which most of the women interviewed gained their information about their bodies, sex, and sexuality. They were not reliant upon medical knowledge in this regard. Indeed, a reoccurring theme amongst women who grew up on farms was that their sexual education was facilitated "behind the barn" through their observations, and subsequent questioning of, the breeding of the farm livestock.[17]

The post-World War II Canadian medical profession gained a new tool to "know" the body in new ways—Freudian-based psychoanalysis. This new tool had a profound impact on the way that the female body was medically perceived. Though Freudian psychoanalysis had been around since the turn of the century, it gained legitimacy in the post-war period as its efficacy in dealing with veterans' postwar stress was determined.[18] This adoption of Freudian concepts allowed the Canadian medical community to make new connections between the mind and body. This further pushed medical body politics, especially its view of the female, to embody ideals of masculinity and femininity within a heterosexual binary.

As the last vestiges of the Victorian image of the sexless woman were swept away and sexuality was seen as normal and even healthy, there was an attempt to contain female sexuality within marriage. The medical community suggested that only abnormal women expressed sexuality outside of marriage or were unwilling or unable to express sexuality within a marriage. Thus, a connection between mind and society was made. If a woman was having abnormal sexual symptoms it meant that she was transgressing societal boundaries and the transgressions had to be addressed as part of the cure. In this sense the contributors to the *CMAJ* were able to embody femininity—to make femininity flesh.

For example, in a 1958 article reporting on a study of women suffering from Premenstrual Tension Syndrome (PTS), doctors J.N. Fortin, E.D. Wittkower and F. Kalz directly linked the symptoms of PTS to their patients' supposed inability to embrace their femininity and adjust to their feminine role. In the study they compared women who did not have PTS (the "control group") to women who experienced symptoms such as "tension, irritability, depression, anxiety...swelling of the abdomen and limbs, itching, thirst, and various tendencies to migraine, asthma and epilepsy."[19] They concluded that PTS was often a response to guilt over sexuality and resentment at being a woman. They noted: "the control group demonstrated a better acceptance of the feminine role and of the inevitable restrictions imposed on a girl; a reaction of pride to the menarche with emphasis on the positive aspects of femininity; a dependant relationship to the mother with fewer hostile features; and a better sexual adjustment."[20] In contrast, those in the experimental group who had PTS were unable to embrace their femininity, resented their mothers, and envied boys' freedom from both social and biological restrictions. Further, the experimental group girls often came from homes where marital discord was common, apparently signalling their mothers' inability to fulfil their own feminine roles (according to the researchers).

Many *CMAJ* contributors viewed pregnancy and motherhood as the culmination of a woman's journey to biological and emotional maturity. Daniel Cappon, in a 1954 article, argued that "pregnancy crowns a female psychosexual evolution.... Though ambivalence may exist, there is triumph of life over death, of motherhood over self-preservation, of motherliness over sexuality, of passivity and submissiveness over aggression and of femininity over masculinity."[21] He continued that the proper motivation for a woman to get pregnant was not only to show love and gratitude to her husband—by providing biological proof of their healthy heterosexual relationship—but also "to prove her womanhood."[22] That is, by having a baby a woman could provide the world with physical proof of her normality, fulfil her gender role, and generally demonstrate the viability of her marriage and her own psychosexual maturity. This privileged normality was only extended to women in heterosexual marriages. Pregnancies that occurred out of wedlock or as a result of adultery were pathologized in direct opposition to "normal" pregnancies. Instead of indicating the strength of a marriage and a woman's psychosexual maturity, these abnormal pregnancies demonstrated that the mother was "an essentially frigid, masculine protesting Western woman... who has exhibited class striving and arrogance, rejection of family and aggressive emancipation,"[23] or that she had marital conflicts and was generally, "unable to accept femininity."[24] These abnormalities would make themselves known by physical symptoms such as extreme nausea during pregnancy, intermittent or absent orgasm during heterosexual relations, a problematic relationship with the father of her child, and resentment of, or disconnection with, her own parents.[25]

Crucially, this embodied femininity did not translate to embodied masculinity in the *CMAJ*'s complementary male body politic. Indeed, if a woman's husband refused, or was unable to fulfill, his male gender role it was usually she, not he, who suffered. His gender transgressions were written on her body. This demonstrates how, for the contributors to the *CMAJ*, the female body politic did not, in a sense, belong to itself. The female body politic was a familial body placed, like a keystone, in the centre of the family body politic both supporting it and reflecting its inadequacies. In a 1952 article on postpartum psychosis, Doctor F.E. McNair presented two cases in which he directly attributed a patient's psychosis to their husband's inability to fulfil his masculine role, thus forcing the woman outside of their normal feminine role. According to McNair, Mrs. J.G.'s psychosis was caused, and later exacerbated, by her husband's inability to be a "man." McNair noted in the case records that, "while pregnant she routed a thug's attack on herself and her husband." Later, "as her illness developed momentum her husband became indecisive, did not assume responsibility and her elder sister took over." In another case study, Mrs. D.G. was the "war bride of a husband whose mother still dominated him."[26] In both cases the patient's husband was unable to fulfil the requirements of his gender role—whether through the application of physical force to protect his wife and unborn child, take control of the household, or even simply to govern the other women in his life. This inability, according to the physician, forced the wife into a more masculine role, causing, or contributing to, her illness.

In her role as keystone of the embodied nuclear family, it was the wife and mother who was supposed to make adjustments to her body and whose role it was to preserve, as much as possible, the gendered and sexual normality within the family. Many decisions that affected individual women's bodies were deemed familial decisions by the *CMAJ* body politic. This can be most clearly seen in cases of birth control. In some ways the *CMAJ* was very progressive in its attitudes towards birth control. Most contributors argued that despite the fact that mechanical or pharmaceutical birth control was illegal, taking birth control actually strengthened a marriage by allowing the couple to maintain physical closeness, free from the fear of maternity or potential pregnancy. Indeed, many contributors to the *CMAJ* argued that without birth control the stress on married couples would cause marital breakdown. In a 1963 editorial, the editor argued, "complete continence in a happily married couple can be reasonably looked upon as an impossibility" and "fear of pregnancy produce[s] much human misery, ill-health, marital tension and unhappiness."[27] However, any limitation of fertility was to be a joint decision and many articles and editorials warned doctors that to prescribe birth control without the husband's consent was potentially to deprive him of his right to progeny within marriage, which raised both moral and even potentially legal complications for the doctor.[28] Further, when *CMAJ* contributors reported on trials of different types of birth control, including the Pill, the feelings of the husband about the wife's reaction to the particular kind of birth control and his comfort level with using it was included and contributed to their overall assessment of the method. For example, in a 1965 trial of the acceptance of oral contraceptives for married women the questionnaire included the line "Husband's opinion of the method."[29] In a 1966 study of intrauterine devices (IUDs) the authors noted that "the husband of one woman suffered a penile hematoma after being 'stabbed' by the tail of the device. The woman's coil was removed because of alleged excessive vaginal bleeding and cramps. We were unable to determine whether she actually had these symptoms or whether her husband had insisted that the coil be removed."[30]

In contrast to birth control, which reaffirmed the familial body, abortion was usually framed as the result of a selfish desire on the part of the woman and thus a decision she made on her own, divorced from family considerations. Though there were articles suggesting that abortion laws be relaxed within the *CMAJ*, during this time they focused on placing more control over the decision whether an abortion was appropriate into the hands of doctors. This measure was to help protect doctors from prosecution and was not a call for women's right to access safe abortion on demand.[31] According to Dr. E. Zarfas in a 1958 article "Psychiatric Indications of Termination of Pregnancy," women who sought out therapeutic abortion were usually engaged in problematic marriages where their own gender inversion was the main cause of the problem. Dr. Zarfas diagnosed several of the patients in his study as being overly masculine, describing one patient, a German immigrant, as an "aggressive, demanding, intolerant woman who hated her husband."[32] In a 1963 letter to the editor C.P. Harrison argued that women who wanted to be rid of a pregnancy were divorced from their inherent femininity and maternity: "surely Nazi Germany lives in memory as an example. Sacrifice the weak to the strong is the cry—a strange travesty of motherlove."[33]

In addition to giving up full control over her own body, the wife and mother, in her role as family keystone, was expected to adjust herself to maintain sexual normality within the family. In 1960 three Montreal doctors published an article entitled "Impact of Sudden Severe Disablement of the Father Upon the Family" wherein they traced several families in which the husband and father had had a debilitating accident or sudden onset of a disabling disease. They argued that the importance of understanding such family dynamics was paramount to treatment, as "when a person marries he and his wife enter marriage with a series of conscious and unconscious needs which they expect to be fulfilled through interaction with each other."[34] These conscious and unconscious needs included the discipline of bodies to the heterosexual model, which supported the male as breadwinner and the female as homemaker and the preservation of masculinity and femininity derived from that binary. The authors ultimately concluded the families that attempted to maintain these gender roles after the husband was incapacitated were the most successful in the long term. For example, in "Family C" the mother, according to the authors, showed "remarkable understanding, skill and tact..." by taking a job only while her husband was too ill to work and quitting it as soon as he was well enough to return to work, noting that "she said 'we have to let him feel that we are dependent on him.' "[35] The authors concluded the article by suggesting: "By and large, one had the impression that families in which the respective roles of father and mother were clearly defined functioned better than those in which some uncertainty in role functioning existed."[36] It should also be noted that in cases where the roles could not be not maintained because of a long-term disability, the wife and mother was criticized if she tried to take on patriarchal authority in addition to her new role as family breadwinner.

It is clear that some sense of responsibility over the maintenance of gender roles did transfer to the individual bodies of the women I interviewed. When asked to identify how their marriages were different or similar to marriages of today's generation and what advice they might have for women getting married, many echoed the sentiment of the wife in "Family C." Alice Hall, when asked what she thought was the secret to a long, happy marriage answered: "well I think you have to let the husband be the boss. Because it makes them feel stronger."[37] Margaret Brown compared her two daughters-in-law noting that, while both were very clever, only one of the women was clever enough to still allow her husband arenas within the marriage to demonstrate his capability. "I mean it's a different world. But I still think ideally boys need to see some sort of a male role model Dad making certain decisions.... You see I have a husband that can fix *anything* and all that...and I've seen [my sons] look with admiration at Dad and I think that's probably good."[38]

There is a key difference, however, between the *CMAJ* body politic and the views of individual women whom I interviewed. In the *CMAJ* a woman who took over a man's normal role was immediately pathologized as abnormal. Her gender role inversion, even if inadvertent, could cause mental and physical anguish for both her and the rest of the family; the most concerning outcome was that a dominant and overbearing mother would actually cause her male children to become homosexuals.[39] However, the interviewees' decisions to *allow* their husbands to "be the boss," or at least feel like he was, was not an attempt to prove their normality; nor did they blame themselves or other women if they failed to live up to that standard. For them it was an eminently practical, even empowered, situation that helped to maintain peace in their marriages. Moreover, all of the women were still able to assert themselves to their husbands in cases where they felt the issue was too important to relinquish control, such as if they believed their husband was drinking too much, in cases concerning their children, and also in cases of infidelity.[40] Thus, this process of allowing their husband to feel like the boss was clearly not a mere imposition of patriarchal will or total maternal sacrifice—it was a negotiation. There was only one case in which a woman chose to sacrifice her own body to preserve that of her husband without his knowledge. Fiona Shortt was told by her family doctor that her husband's blood pressure was dangerously high and that she should go to work to take some of the financial strain off of him. She was also told to keep him from worrying too much. "I saved him.… I was told not to let him worry. If there were any problems with the school I dealt with it. I dealt with my children. I never took problems to him and I just did whatever I could. And then we moved to Vancouver and I went out to work and my son said to me 'please mum don't go out to work'.…[but] better that I be a working wife than a working widow." This strain eventually manifested itself on Fiona's body; she collapsed from nervous exhaustion and suffered a miscarriage.[41]

There is also some evidence of the efficacy of the medical familial body in terms of birth control. All the women interviewed used some form of birth control during their reproductive lives and most used a few different kinds as new innovations such as the Pill became available. Several of the women did make the decision, with their husbands, to take birth control and modified their use of it according to his wishes. In some cases, like that of Mary Johnston, there was a direct transfer of the medical discourse to her through her doctor. Mary, who married an older man, was told to go on birth control to protect her husband's health since he was in his fifties when their last child was born. The doctor was concerned that the stress of having more children would make her husband ill and it was not fair to expect that of him. Up until that point Mary, a Roman Catholic, had been using the rhythm method to limit their fertility.[42] In other cases the use and modification of birth control came from both the doctor and the husband. Joyce Martin's doctors modified her birth control to suit her husband by cutting off the tail of her IUD because it bothered her husband during intercourse. This caused problems later when another doctor tried to remove it.[43] However, in most cases the women I interviewed went to get birth control on their own and did not remember the doctor asking if their husband approved. The women's main concern was preventing unwanted pregnancy; STDs did not concern them, since only "nasty" people had STDs. Perhaps since an unwanted pregnancy would affect their bodies most, especially in cases of premarital sex, it seems to have been a responsibility undertaken primarily by the women.[44]

Only one woman out of the eighteen interviewed admitted to having an abortion. Yet her story is particularly interesting as it directly counteracts the images of female selfishness presented by the *CMAJ* body politic, fitting instead with the idea of the familial female body seen in *CMAJ* birth control discourses. For Margaret Brown, obtaining an illegal abortion was a sacrifice that she made for her family and one that she and her husband went through together as a couple. Margaret explained that her husband, who originally had a career installing television antennas, had to quit because of a back injury. He returned to school to train to be a teacher and Margaret went to work to make ends meet. As she tells it, "I worked for a real estate company.... I was a shorthand typist and bookkeeper and have been for all my working life. And anyway suddenly I found out I was pregnant. And we [her and her husband] cried a lot but I cried and I said 'you know what this'll be the end of the dream. You'll have to stop what you're doing.' "[45] A short time later Margaret found out from a male colleague at work the name of a doctor who would perform illegal abortions. She went to a secret office with her husband and had the procedure and described the aftereffects. "It was worse than having a baby. Oh God! Cause then you lose it. That was when I lost it and oh we did cry. We both cried. I wish I had never done it. But I had no choice! It was either that or [he] I don't know what he would have done for a living. He had no other skills."[46] Margaret went on to explain that both she and her husband would have liked to have had another child had the circumstances been different, and that for her having the abortion was something that she undertook out of love for her husband and concern for the entire family's well-being. Though not ashamed of the decision she said, "I feel regretful though. I'm sorry I had to do it."[47]

Both Fiona Shortt's miscarriage narrative and Margaret Brown's abortion narrative demonstrate imperfect reflections of the *CMAJ* body politic through subtle modifications to the hegemonic script. Though Fiona acquiesced to her determined role, placing her body in the service of maintaining her husband's health, this gender role alignment did not have the successful outcome of a return to health for the whole family. Instead, the strain of such a sacrifice caused Shortt to miscarry and the loss of her child is a clear deviation from the image of the heterosexual family as a stronghold. Further, Brown, though she accepted the narrative of the familial female body, applied that script in a way the medical community deemed inappropriate. Her husband's involvement in the decision to get an abortion and in facilitating that abortion repurposes the familial body discourse, and counteracts the image of the abortive mother as selfish.

Another distortion appears when the maternal *CMAJ* body politic is compared to the individual maternal body. Given the importance of maternity to the "wholeness" of the *CMAJ* female body politic it would seem natural that any issues of infertility, especially when due to the loss of actual physical reproductive ability rather than situational infertility, would be a major event in a woman's life. However, this turned out not to be true. Two of the women interviewed had faced damage to their reproductive organs. Edith Small had an ectopic pregnancy which destroyed one of her fallopian tubes and reduced her ability to conceive. However, though Edith Small describes the event as physically trau-matic, repeatedly recounting the "terrible excruciating pain," when asked about the psychological trauma of losing a fallopian tube and the subsequent reduction in her fertility so early in her marriage she replied, "well I was so glad to be out of this thing I mean it was pretty painful and pretty serious. I don't really go into tizzies about things you know not unless it's really necessary and I realized it was serious and they had told me that it might be difficult to get pregnant then you see cause they said usually it's your best side that goes but I wasn't in the habit of worrying about things ahead of time and look at it we had six pregnancies after that."[48] This attitude was echoed by both Nancy Wilson and Joyce Martin. Nancy had a cyst on her ovary which required that the ovary be removed and which ultimately delayed the conception of her two sons. However, this event was given only a passing mention as she discussed her children more broadly.[49] Joyce Martin, who was treated for infertility of unknown causes, remembers the treatment as more of an inconvenience than a psychological trauma. "It was a pain because I had to use the thermometer. I had to keep a record and I had to collect my urine for twenty-four hours and take it back. We were living in Mile-stone and I was doctoring in Moose Jaw because we had been living in Moose Jaw when I was trying to get pregnant at first I just kept with the same doctor."[50]

Why did the experience of infertility seem to be minor in the face of the cult of motherhood and the medical importance given to maternity for these women? The answer is perhaps because they all went on to have children, and in the case of Edith Small quite a large family. The *CMAJ* body politic was dissected from any past or future, forcing each medical event to be studied in isolation and potentially giving it a false sense of significance. In contrast, the women I interviewed, looking back upon their lives with the benefit of hindsight, saw these events as less significant parts of a larger health and sexuality spectrum. Further, in contrast to the embodied femininity of the *CMAJ* body politic, the women interviewed did not tie their own femininity to its biological signifiers. For both Edith Small and Nancy Wilson the loss of their biological functionality did not reflect itself negatively on their image of themselves as women.

This refusal to tie their femininity to biological signifiers, such as intact re-productive organs, highlights the other way in which the individual body dis-torted the generalized body politic within the *CMAJ*. One of the great ironies of the *CMAJ* body politic is that despite the fact that it was essentially an imagi-nary body and thus had no corporeality, its consistent state of illness forced it to be constantly embodied and aware of its own embodiment. Thus, though the "metabody" created by combining and de-individualizing all the singular cor-poreal bodies within the *CMAJ* had no corporeality, by their very nature each body within the *CMAJ* was ill and looking for relief. So each body was conscious of itself, the body's feelings and reactions, by virtue of that illness. Further, because the *CMAJ* body politic is made up of ill bodies, the sense of embodiment is usually negative and associated with pain or loss of function. In contrast, the women interviewed rarely thought about their own bodies, and remained largely unaware of their embodiment except for key moments of their lives when they experienced a clear bodily change—and this was not always negative. For example, I noted above the prevalence of loss-of-virginity narratives amongst the interviewees—this is likely because both the pain and pleasure of that experience resonated over the years. Pregnancy, especially difficult symptoms such as nausea or the discomfort caused by trying to do house or farm work in a state of advanced pregnancy, was also one embodied experience that was usually clearly remembered and a feature of most interviews. However, the interviews also make it clear that these women, like most people, went about their day-to-day lives not being aware of their bodies at all. Aside from a few flashpoints their bodies merely served to house them as they went about their daily lives, and it is this lack of body consciousness that directly contradicts the medical body politic's image of the consistently ill embodied woman.

Despite these distortions, many of the interviewed women did reflect the *CMAJ* female body politic in one crucial way: they desired to be seen as sexually normal. Though their definitions of normal did not always directly align with that of the *CMAJ* body politic, it is clear there was some transference of the importance of sexual normality, which manifested itself in an aversion to being seen as different. When asked about the frequency of sexual contact between themselves and their husbands, most of the women replied with some variation of "probably average." When pressed to define what a normal amount of sexual intercourse was for a married couple, most were uncomfortable saying a firm number and instead looked to me to give them a suggestion of what was usual.[51] Jean Simpson originally answered that she and her husband had sex about four times a week but when she discovered that was higher than average she was anxious to change her answer. "Maybe I'm closer to two than four I don't know. I was going to say two to three and then I thought four covers the whole thing…. I think that's another myth that one has; this idea that if you're happily married you're sort of having sex all the time, yeah, but nobody tells you what is an average amount."[52] Thus, though the interviewed women did not fully accept the idea of embodied femininity, they did internalize the post-war discourse of the importance of normality which the *CMAJ* body politic certainly enforced.

The final distortion between the *CMAJ* body politic and the individuality of the interviewees' bodies can be seen in the relationship of those bodies to the medical community itself. Within the *CMAJ* the image of doctor is fairly hard to pin down, as actual medical men and women rarely enter the narrative of patient care. Clinical case reports, which made up a majority of the content, were written deliberately with an air of detachment deemed appropriate to scientific enterprise. This detachment and hesitancy to write themselves into the narrative of patient care projects the image of a faceless and monolithic medical community working to bring people to health but not really interacting with them on any personal level. Indeed, even when the focus of an article or an editorial was the doctor him- or herself, the image of detached objectivity was maintained. For example, in a 1966 editorial on doctors' relationships with their own wives the editor noted that, "the doctor, it is postulated, has been giving direction to others all day and suppressing his own emotional feelings, and he feels unable to switch to a two-way and emotionally tinged communications system with his wife.... The doctor is expected by most patients to wear a mantle of omnipotence and may therefore come to feel that way."[53]

However, individual doctors with whom the interviewees engaged counteracted this image of the detached doctor focused only on the patient's body. Brown's story of the doctor who performed her illegal abortion was not the only case of doctors forced by personality or situation to change the patient-doctor script. The most common reason for this deviation was the difficulties associated with rural practice. Verna King's doctor was forced to transport her son, very ill with bronchial pneumonia, in his personal car from their rural farm in Manitoba to Winnipeg during a terrible snowstorm. After hitting a snowbank he was forced to drive the rest of the way holding the driver's side door closed because it was damaged.[54] This highly personalized image of the doctor driving while holding his door shut, as well as the fact that the doctor, who had the only car in the area, used his personal transportation to move a patient counteracts the image of the medical profession as cold and faceless. Similarly, Joyce Martin's interaction with her doctor was mostly over the telephone because her farm was so isolated. They often worked together to find home remedies or to use what medicine she had on hand to treat her family in order to save a costly and time-consuming trip into town to see him: "He knew our lifestyle. My husband had a ringworm in haying season and I phoned him and I said 'listen, I have some salve here that we use on the calves; can I use it on my husband?' He said 'well, read off the ingredients' and he said 'yeah' he said 'it might work.' "[55] Just as the individual bodies of the interviewed women counteracted the truncated and silenced body parts that made up the *CMAJ* body politic, the relationship between individual women and their doctors defied the image of a medical profession focused solely on bringing those ill parts to health. The locality of these narratives further breaks down the false image of national urban hegemony presented by the *CMAJ* in its very structure. Each clinical article published within the journal was identified by city of origin, and the placement of teaching and experimental hospitals meant that urban spaces were overwhelmingly overrepresented. Thus, the prescriptive discourse within the *CMAJ* usually assumed urbanity, including the near proximity of hospitals and specialists, when suggesting avenues of treatment. However, when rural doctors were faced with treating rural patients the urbanized body politic did not always transfer.

Though many Canadians view the time period making up Canada's baby boom as a time of innocence and social cohesion, studies of the body politics responsible for promoting this image of hegemony, as well as the individual bodies they were meant to influence and reflect, demonstrate the fragility of categories of "normal." This is not to say that the women interviewed did not benefit enormously from their even-partial reflection of dominant body politics, though these benefits can be hard to identify. Primarily they were able to live their lives out in the open and, though their heterosexual bodies were often pathologized within the *CMAJ*, to a certain degree they were protected enough by their veneer of normality to move within fairly wide boundaries of actual behaviour. In contrast, bodies within the *CMAJ* identified as deviant, such as homosexual bodies, were subject to much more surveillance and thus much more limited.[56] One of the reasons for this comparative room to manoeuvre is that the medical community's body politic was one of several sources of "normal" jockeying for position during this time period, and the women interviewed could pick and choose variations of normal from their medical community, their religious community and from the realm of popular culture. At the same time, it is clear that many of the elements of the *CMAJ* body politic did transfer onto the fleshy bodies of the interviewees. Most accepted, at least partially, a division of gender roles that privileged the male head of household and worked to maintain an image of his authority. Further, the general desire of most of the women to be seen as sexually normal demonstrates the power of the normal-abnormal binary.

Despite these elements of body politic–corporeal body congruity, distortions from the "perfect" body politic demonstrated by the individual corporeal bodies of the women I interviewed argues for the need to examine the resistances of not only those who were completely disenfranchised by hegemonic body politics but also those who reflected that body, albeit imperfectly. The bodies of the women interviewed did, though usually passively, disrupt medical claims to be the sole centre of knowledge about their bodies as well as attempts by the Canadian medical profession to make their bodies into living embodiments of femininity and familial sacrifice. Even Fiona Shortt and Margaret Brown, who in many ways followed dominant scripts for female interaction with the medical community and society, changed those scripts in ways which significantly disrupted their hegemonic power.

This form of largely passive resistance is not only more difficult to see than the active denunciations of completely disenfranchised groups; its impact is also more subtle and less effective in dismantling the dominant medical body politic—at least in the short term. Indeed, many of the women refused to be identified as feminists or "women's libbers" and identified those labels with extreme action and being "anti-men" or even "crazy."[57] Yet through the subtle distortions they made in the mirror of the body politic, the connections between the baby boom era and the activist feminist era of the 1970s become clear. Often this was in the way that they raised their own sons and daughters, subtly rewriting gender scripts to include housework for their sons, narratives of premarital co-habitation in their children or grandchildren, and new roles for the female body. Ruth Bell consciously discarded narratives of female innocence and outside authority over the female body when she took the time to personally teach her daughter about her own body in a way that she had never been taught.[58] Like water finding small imperfections in a stone wall over time, the minute resistances of the baby boom women would weaken the structure of hegemonic "normality" and ultimately aided in its destruction and reconstruction by subsequent generations.

NOTES

1   Stephanie Coontz, *The Way We Never Were: American Families and the Nostalgia Trap* (New York: Basic Books, 1992).

2   Mary Louise Adams, *The Trouble with Normal: Postwar Youth and the Making of Heterosexuality* (Toronto: University of Toronto Press, 1997); Mona Lee Gleason, *Normalizing the Ideal: Psychology, Schooling and the Family in Postwar Canada* (Toronto: University of Toronto Press, 1999); Valerie J. Korinek, *Roughing it in the Suburbs: Reading Chatelaine Magazine in the Fifties and Sixties* (Toronto: University of Toronto Press, 2000). For works that examine this time period in an American context see, Beth L. Bailey, *Front Porch to Back Seat: Courtship in Twentieth Century America* (Baltimore: Johns Hopkins University Press, 1988); Wini Breines, *Young, White and Miserable: Growing Up Female in the Fifties* (Boston: Beacon Press, 1992); *Not June Cleaver: Women and Gender in Postwar America, 1945–1960*, ed. Joanne Meyerowitz (Philadelphia: Temple University Press, 1994); Elaine Tyler May, *Homeward Bound: American Families in the Cold War Era* (New York: Basic Books, 1988); Jessica Weiss, *To Have and to Hold: Marriage, the Baby Boom and Social Change* (Chicago: University of Chicago Press, 2000).

3   Michel Foucault, *Power/Knowledge: Selected Interviews and Other Writings 1972–1977*, trans. Colin Gordon (New York: Pantheon, 1980) 55–57.

4   Michel Foucault, *The Birth of the Clinic: An Archaeology of Medical Perception*, trans. A.M. Sheridan Smith (New York: Vintage Books, 1975), 34–5.

5   The archival data demonstrates that the *CMAJ* also believed themselves to be the dominant voice of the profession and actively attempted throughout this time period to increase their scope of influence. For example, they gave free copies of the *CMAJ* to returning medical veterans of World War II and medical missionaries (LAC, Canadian

Medical Association fonds, R3676-0-6-E, Microfilm reel M-7487). Their assertions to authority were also supported by the fact that throughout this time period they continuously raised the rates for advertising within the journal. As the managing editor reported in 1953, "Three advances in two and a half years totalling more than 50% have been accepted by our clients remarkably satisfactorily—all of which bears testimony to the position which our journal occupies as the medical medium of choice in Canada." (emphasis in original—Canadian Medical Association fonds, R3676-0-6-E, Microfilm reel M-7491).

6   These oral histories were gathered according to the guidelines provided by, and with the approval of, the University of Saskatchewan's and the Tri-Council's Ethics Boards. The interviews were solicited via a number of invitations through public organizations such as seniors' centres throughout western Canada. These invitations called for women who married between the years 1946 and 1966 who were willing to discuss their sexual histories with me, and only those interested were contacted. These interviews were open-ended and varied in length from half an hour to three hours. All interviewees were given pseudonyms and all identifying details were removed from the transcripts.

7   This national drive to promote and protect the heterosexual nuclear family is not only demonstrated in the secondary literature but also by the number of national commissions and conferences dedicated to the family. One of the largest of such endeavours was the Vanier Institute of the Family endowed by the Governor-General and his wife in 1965 to study and provide assistance to the family unit. The medical community as well as the religious community and the educational community were involved in the Vanier Institute a great deal in both creating and implementing its discourse and programs (LAC, Vanier Institute of the Family fonds, R2782-0-4-E, 1943–1978).

8   "Crises in the Family," *Canadian Medical Association Journal* [hereafter *CMAJ*] 15 September 1959, 494.

9   Of course no source is ever totally monolithic and the *CMAJ* is no exception. There were calls for tolerance to those people who stepped outside the boundaries of normality such as unwed mothers or homosexuals but they were by far in the minority.

10   Moira Gatens, *Imaginary Bodies: Ethics, Power and Corporeality* (New York: Routlege, 1996).

11   Gatens, *Imaginary Bodies*, 10–18.

12   For examples of gay and lesbian resistance to the heteronormativity of the baby boom era, see Brett Beeymn *Creating a Place for Ourselves: Lesbian, Gay, and Bisexual Community Historians* (New York: Routledge, 1997); Jonathan Ned Katz, *The Invention of Heterosexuality* (Chicago: University of Chicago Press, 2007); Heather Murray, *Not in This Family: Gays and the Meaning of Kinship in Postwar North America* (Philadelphia: University of Pennsylvania Press, 2010).

13   "National Health Week," *CMAJ*, January 1950, 87; "In the Doctor's Hands," *CMAJ*, February 1952, 188; Robert R. Robinson, "Public Relations Prescription for M.D.'s," *CMAJ*, December 1953, 649; M. B. Etziony, "Repetitio Ad Nauseam?" *CMAJ*, 15 December 1955, 992; L. W. Holmes, "The Doctor Speaks," *CMAJ*, 1 March 1956, 396; L. W. Holmes, "Medicine on the Air," 1 April 1956, 571; L. W. Holmes, "Doctors on Camera," *CMAJ*, 15 April 1956, 652; "Is This You Doctor? Or Is Your Halo Getting Tight?" *CMAJ*, 15 January 1957, 146; L. W. Holmes,"Preventive PR," *CMAJ*, 1 February 1957, 229; H. D. Baker, "Doctor-Patient Relationship or Doctor-Public Relationship," *CMAJ*, 15 January 1958, 129; Hereford Still, "Medical Broadcasting," *CMAJ*, 1 March 1958, 369; "Medicine and the Mass Media," *CMAJ*, 15 May 1958, 786; "Doctors on Television," *CMAJ*, 1 June 1958, 866; "Teenage Morals," *CMAJ*, 21 October, 1961, 952; Raymond Miller, "The Facts of Life," *CMAJ*, 15 January 1966, 147; G. W. Piper, "Facts of Life," *CMAJ*, 12 February 1966, 352; W. E. Armour, "Sex Education in the Schools: The Doctor's Role," *CMAJ*, 3 December 1966, 1212.

14 Margaret Brown (pseudonym), personal interview, June 27, 2010.

15 Ruth Bell (pseudonym), personal interview, September 21, 2010.

16 Jessica Bateman (pseudonym), personal interview, July 19, 2010.

17 Joyce Martin (pseudonym), personal interview, December 2, 2010.

18 Nathan G. Hale (Jr.) also notes this in *The Rise and Crisis of Psychoanalysis in the United States: Freud and the Americans 1917–1985* (Oxford: Oxford University Press, 1995), 4–5. This was also noted within the *CMAJ*, see: "Let Us Be Practical About the Psychoneuroses," *CMAJ*, August 1949, 102.

19 J.N. Fortin, E.D. Wittkower and F. Kalz, "A Psychosomatic Approach to the Pre-Menstrual Tension Syndrome: A Preliminary Report," *CMAJ*, 15 December, 1958, 978.

20 Ibid., 980.

21 Daniel Cappon, "Some Psychodynamic Aspects of Pregnancy," *CMAJ*, February 1954, 148.

22 Ibid., 149.

23 Ibid., 153.

24 M. Straker, "Psychological Factors During Pregnancy and Childbirth," *CMAJ*, May 1954, 512.

25 For abnormal pregnancy symptoms see, N.W. Philpott and Christina F. Goodwin, "Case of the Unmarried Woman and Her Child," *CMAJ*, September 1946, 294; Cappon, "Some Psychodynamic Aspects of Pregnancy," 147–154; Straker, "Psychological Factors During Pregnancy and Childbirth," 510–513; E. Zarfas, "Psychiatric Indications of the Termination of Pregnancy," *CMAJ*, 15 August 1958, 230–236.

26 F.E. McNair, "Psychosis Occurring Postpartum: Analysis of 34 Cases," *CMAJ*, December 1952, 638–639.

27 "Oral Contraceptives," *CMAJ*, 10 August 1963, 270.

28 In one article doctors were warned that they could be involved in divorce cases and risked being sued by the husband if they did not obtain his consent. G.P.R. Tallin, "The Legal Implications of the Non-Therapeutic Practices of Doctors," *CMAJ*, 4 August 1962, 210.

29 "The Emotional Responses of Married Women Receiving Oral Contraceptives," *CMAJ*, 5 June 1965, 1207.

30 C.A. Douglas Ringrose, "Clinical Experience with Margulies Intrauterine Contraceptive Device," *CMAJ*, 2 July 1966, 15.

31 J.J. Lederman, "The Doctor, Abortion, and the Law: A Medicolegal Dilemma," *CMAJ*, 4 August 1962, 216; Tallin, "The Legal Implications of the Non-Therapeutic Practices of Doctors," 207; Walter Simpson, "The Doctor, Abortion, and the Law," *CMAJ*, 13 October 1962, 821; C.P. Harrison, "The Issue of Legalized Abortion," *CMAJ*, 9 February 1963, 329; S.G. Stern, "The Issue of Legalized Abortion," *CMAJ*, 27 April 1963, 899; "Abortion," *CMAJ*, 28 September 1963, 676.

32 Zarfas, "Psychiatric Indications of the Termination of Pregnancy," 30-236.

33 Harrison, "The Issue of Legalized Abortion" *CMAJ*, 26 January 1963, 329.

34 R. Castro De La Mata, G. Gringras and E.D. Wittkower, "Impact of Sudden, Severe Disablement of the Father Upon the Family," *CMAJ*, 14 May 1960, 1015.

35 Ibid., 1016.

36 Ibid., 1018.

37 Alice Hall (pseudonym), personal interview, June 28, 2010.

38 Margaret Brown (pseudonym), personal interview, June 27, 2010.

39   Marvin Wellman, "Overt Homosexuality with Spontaneous Remission," *CMAJ*, 15 August 1956, 273.

40   Florence Anderson (pseudonym), personal interview, September 20, 2010; Jessica Bateman, (pseudonym), personal interview, July 19, 2010; Ruth Bell (pseudonym), personal interview, September 21, 2010; Karen Rand (pseudonym), personal interview, July 7, 2010; Fiona Shortt (pseudonym), personal interview, July 5, 2010; Diane West (pseudonym), personal interview, July 19, 2010.

41   Fiona Shortt (pseudonym), personal interview, July 5, 2010.

42   Mary Johnston (pseudonym), personal interview, April 19, 2010.

43   Joyce Martin (pseudonym), personal interview, December 2, 2010.

44   Jean Simpson (pseudonym), personal interview, July 5, 2010.

45   Margaret Brown (pseudonym), personal interview, June 27, 2010.

46   Ibid.

47   Ibid.

48   Edith Small (pseudonym) personal interview, September 19, 2010.

49   Nancy Wilson (pseudonym), personal interview, April 19, 2010.

50   Joyce Martin (pseudonym), personal interview, December 2, 2010.

51   Jean Simpson (pseudonym), personal interview, July 5, 2010.

52   Ibid.

53   "The Doctor and His Wife," *CMAJ*, 8 January 1966, 93. There were other examples of doctor's dealing with the expected detached clinical image including a flurry of articles about doctors and public relations as the question of universal healthcare in Canada came to a head. Ian MacNeill, "Is the Profession Misunderstood?" *CMAJ*, January 1952, 79; "In the Doctor's Hands," 188; A.D. Kelly, "Why Bother With Public Relations?" *CMAJ*, May 1952, 493; Robert. R. Robinson, "Public Relations Prescription for MDs" December 1953; L.W. Holmes, "Enter the Patient," *CMAJ*, 1 December 1955; Etziony, "Repetitio Ad Nauseam?," L.W. Holmes, "The Doctor and Community Relations," *CMAJ*, 15 January 1956, 158; L.W. Holmes, "The Doctor and the Press," *CMAJ*, 1 February 1956, 224; Kenneth G. Gray,"Sexual Deviation," *CMAJ*, 15 February 1956; L.W. Holmes, "Medicine on the Air," *CMAJ*, 1 April 1956, 571; L.W. Holmes, "Doctors on Camera," F.B. Bowman, "Public Attitudes Towards Doctors," *CMAJ*, 1 January 1957, 64; "Is This You, Doctor?," 146; L.W. Holmes, "Preventive PR," *CMAJ*, 1 February 1957, 229; Francis T. Hodges, "Medicine's Seven Deadly Sins," *CMAJ*, 15 April 1957, 660; L.W. Holmes,"PR Aid For Doctor's Offices," *CMAJ* 1 October 1957, 707; Harry Baker, "Doctor-Patient Relationship or Doctor-Public Relationship," *CMAJ* 15 January 1958, 128; "Medicine and the Mass Media," *CMAJ* 15 May 1958, 786; "Doctors on Television," *CMAJ* 1 June 1958, 866.

54   Verna King (pseudonym), personal interview, November 25, 2010.

55   Joyce Martin (pseudonym), personal interview, December 2, 2010.

56   See for example, S.R. Laycock, "Homosexuality—A Mental Hygiene Problem," *CMAJ* September 1950, 245; B. Kanee and C.L. Hunt, "Homosexuality as a Source of Venereal Disease," *CMAJ* August 1951, 138; William R. Thomson, "Homosexuality," *CMAJ* 1 November 1955, 760; Marvin Wellman, "Overt Homosexuality with Spontaneous Remission," *CMAJ* 15 August, 1956, 273; William R. Thomson, "Homosexuality," *CMAJ* 1 November 1957, 901; P. G. Thomson, "Sexual Deviation," *CMAJ* 1 March 1959, 381; Ian K. Bond and Harry C. Hutchinson, "Application of Reciprocal Inhibition Therapy to Exhibitionism," *CMAJ* 2 July 1960, 23; John F.H. Stewart, "Living with Homosexuality," *CMAJ* 1 September 1962, 517.

57 Margaret Brown (pseudonym), personal interview, June 27, 2010; Alice Hall (pseudonym), personal interview, June 28, 2010.

58 Ruth Bell (pseudonym), personal interview, September 21, 2010.

MAPPING OUT THE CULTURAL PRESENCE OF FRANCOPHONES IN THE WEST VIA THE RE-VISIONING OF LOUIS RIEL AND GABRIELLE ROY IN NFB FILM ADAPTATIONS

ELSPETH TULLOCH

Through documentaries, animations, live-action dramas, and more recently through clips incorporated into interactive materials on new media platforms, the National Film Board of Canada (NFB) has been mapping out a cinematic version of Canada as it pursues its evolving mandate related to the telling of Canada to Canadians, a nation-building and nation-maintaining goal. One way it has mediated the laying claim to cultural space has been through the selection and reworking of diverse literary texts for cinematic adaptation. The retention, erasure, and changing of source content for film adaptation can reflect adapters' intentions as well as the social and political contexts to which they may be responding, particularly in an institutional setting, as the scholarly work of Brian McFarlane, Robert Stam, and Linda Hutcheon variously suggest. Although live-action drama never became a major form of production at the NFB for budgetary reasons, some filmmakers remained committed to trying their hand at it, in part through adaptations. In this context the pointed selection of material for the relatively small number of live-action adaptations actually made gains of significance. They arguably reflect a greater fascination for the selected subject matter than the actual quantity of such productions would at first suggest.

In the 1970s and 1980s, after decades of neglect, a small surge of interest in exploring the francophone presence in the West through adaptations that were rendered either entirely or partially through live-action film was manifested at the NFB, notably by reworking texts by, about, or addressed to one of two iconic francophone figures: Louis Riel and Gabrielle Roy.[1] This interest in finding ways to represent cinematically French-language writing from the West coincides with the general movement towards regionalization at the NFB, which resulted in numerous documentaries on francophones in the West after an apparent near dearth of any production interest.[2] It also parallels the development of regional and alternative theatre that fostered and mounted productions on local themes, some of which were showcased in NFB films.[3]

Marginalized in the West and marked by a history of periodic contestation both in the West and at the NFB, francophones constitute a group with an evolving set of relations with the dominant political and cultural apparatus. Although francophones from the West have received relatively little attention in NFB adaptations, whether in the form of live-action drama or otherwise, representations of them have been varied. These representations not only reflect the changing dynamic of those relations and disparate anglophone perceptions of francophone cultural contributions, but also reveal the trace of Québécois appropriations of Franco-Manitoban literary heritage. This chapter examines how these films alternatively erase, refashion, perpetuate, contest, or grapple with the claims each iconic figure makes directly or has had made in his or her name to linguistic and cultural, if not national, place. Given that chronologically the first film in this set of adaptations is based on a text by Roy and given that films inspired by Riel carry on after those based on Roy's texts (even though Riel lived and died long before Roy), the adaptations of the Roy texts are examined first, namely: *Un siècle d'hommes/Of Many People* (1970), based in part on Roy's *La petite poule d'eau* (1950),[4] and *Le vieillard et l'enfant* (1985), based on Roy's similarly titled novella published in 1966.[5]

UN SIÈCLE D'HOMMES/OF MANY PEOPLE

Un siècle d'hommes/Of Many People, which boasted English and French versions, was, according to NFB internal documents, a multimedia production consisting of film footage, stills (photos and drawings), slide projections, and music. It was instigated at the request of the Secretary of State and produced for the Government of Canada and the Government of Manitoba in honour of Manitoba's centennial year in 1970 by the NFB's innovative, Montreal-based Studio G, "the multimedia section responsible for sound-film strips for schoolchildren."[6] It thus followed on the heels of Canada's own centennial celebrations, and traces of the evolving federal vision for Canada can be found in the extant production and its files.

Stanley Jackson (1914–1981), a Winnipegger by birth and a long-time NFB director and producer whose work exhibits at times a particular interest in the West, directed the production.[7] Robert Verrall and John Spotton, major creative forces at the NFB, produced it. The production was made during and after the closing of the NFB's first, short-lived attempt at regional production operations in Winnipeg, which were wound down in the 1969–70 fiscal year, and preceded the 1974 opening of the Prairie Studio proper by four years.[8] Premiering on July 1, 1970, it enjoyed an extended run until the end of March 1971, with a projected total of 440 presentations. Shown in smaller communities over the summer of 1970, where it received respectable audiences given the size of the communities, attendance picked up considerably when it was shown in Winnipeg. By the end of the centennial year, the chair of the Manitoba Centennial Corporation declared it "la plus belle réussite de l'année du Centenaire," as reported by the head of Studio G.[9] Considering the technical attention given the production, this success is perhaps unsurprising. The show's publicity material indicates that extensive image research was done, with over 10,000 slides and 8,000 feet of 16mm film considered, and NFB engineers were commissioned to design and build special projection equipment. With a production budget estimated at $60,000, excluding presentation costs, the NFB accorded the means to make a quality production.

Although research to date has uncovered only the fragmentary remains of what was apparently a twenty-five minute show—the most useable material being a print of the French version with approximately eight minutes of film of the original production along with blank spaces where stills would have been inserted or projected and the accompanying soundtrack—it appears, if one accepts the order on the extant print, that the production accorded a paradoxically prominent but muted position to francophone historical presence in the province and that it did so from a particularly Canadianist stance.[10] The production followed the recent passing of the federal Official Languages Act in 1969, enacted on one of the recommendations of the Royal Commission on Bilingualism and Biculturalism, and seems to seek to make the French fact a natural, non-threatening part of not only Manitoba's history but of the nation-building process itself.

The first half of the multimedia production is based on the Roy text, a fact corroborated by the catalogue descriptions of both the French and English versions as well as internal NFB documents.[11] The loose adaptation is rendered partly by film image, partly by the now-missing stills and slides, and most fully by voice-over narration, which is audible although somewhat degraded in the extant French version. Narrating an idealized yet not unrealistic account of the settlement experience of the isolated Tousignant family in what Roy calls Water Hen country in northern Manitoba, Roy's text was selected because of "the tribute [it makes] to the pioneering spirit of the Manitoban," one that NFB officials felt could serve as a representative "story of a province where its early settlers conquered the wilderness to build for later generations."[12] Indeed, the English translation of the source text had become popular among English speakers in the West for these reasons.[13] While acknowledging the conditions of an isolated life, the adaptation tends to highlight the idyllic aspects of the family's pre-mechanized agrarian life, retaining, for instance, references to the Tousignant's beautiful house or "belle maison" and good, sufficient meals. The intent never seems ironic, although the visuals depict the house as small and rustic; rather, the adaptation intimates the pleasures of simple, rural living.

This tendency to lean to a form of idealization, this time in the direct service of nation, continues with the adaptation's portrayal of the education of the Tousignant children. Roy gives extended accounts of their difficulties in acquiring any education, let alone one in French, on their isolated island, recounting their disparate experiences with a series of live-in school teachers sent by the government at the request of their mother, Luzina Tousignant. The adaptation, however, emphasizes the culturally integrative results of their education—its part in the nation-building process. The children's education is shown to be efficiently absorbing them into the Canadian nation-state. In one shot, for example, the camera slowly pulls back from a school map showing the family's location on the Water Hen to reveal the entire nation, while the reminiscing narrator recalls the children's lesson: "Nous sommes des canadiens." While the adaptation does elaborate on some of the teachers' activities, noting humorously, as in the source text, that one of the teachers, Miss O'Rorke, was bothered by the family's sheep, it does not expound much on the latter's active attempts to mould the children into British subjects or her neglect of French-speaking explorers and fur traders, although the film's planning document indicates the adapters foresaw a shot of the raising of the Union Jack sewn under Miss O'Rorke's instructions. Later, the eventual migration of the French-speaking children to the more populated, and we deduce, largely English-speaking, south is naturalized by images of migrating birds. The spectator understands they are contributing to the birth of modern Manitoba, becoming, as the title affirms, "of many people." The complexity of their linguistic future does not seem to have been explored as it had been in the source text.

The rural, non-mechanized settlement experience as expressed through the adaptation of the Roy text in the first part of the production prefaces the province's shift to urbanization and mechanization shown in the review of Manitoba's history in the second half of the production, rendered through a wide assortment of archival film, (missing) stills, and 1970s-style instrumental pop music.

The film images reveal technological progress through, for example, shots of early twentieth-century cars negotiating city streets and threshing machines at work during harvest times. The province is thus shown to have moved beyond the pioneer past of Roy's text, one that while treated with gentle nostalgia is presented as trying, as symbolized by the mailman's cutter tipping over at the beginning of the film while making its arduous way to the Tousignant home through the lonely, snow-drifted lands.

One could cynically argue that the production also inadvertently suggests that, over Manitoba's history, the province moved from ethnic primitivism to superior British ways, since the production's fragmentary remains show the province developing from the less technologically developed French and other non-British immigrant pioneering ways of life into a more advanced, British-dominated society within the British Empire and then the Commonwealth, symbolized in the production's second half by archival footage of the young Queen Elizabeth's visit.[14] However, with no visual evidence from the missing stills, which constitute the bulk of the production, and no such indication in the narration, it is difficult to make any conclusive observations.

Indeed, the more elaborate first draft of the "Centennial Project Handout" reveals that an a-linguistic form of multiculturalism informed the production's publicity material. This is a little different from the form that was soon to unfurl at the national level in which the federal government, under Pierre Trudeau, advanced "a policy of multiculturalism within a bilingual framework."[15] The draft handout describes the contact between the Tousignant family and other ethnic groups as mutually enriching but omits subjects related to language. In a bid to write Manitoba's multi-ethnic heritage into the national narrative, the document states that "Manitoba, a province of many national origins, has benefited from its diverse population, nor is there any doubt that Canada has gained from the unique character of Manitoba and its people."[16] The earlier "Approach to Treatment for Water Hen," however, described one of the production's planned sequences in multilingual terms also, i.e., as containing a "multiplicity of ethnic groups using voice and music. We should hear snatches of Icelandic, German, Ukrainian, Polish.... The sequence ends with very lively Ukrainian dancing."[17] However, Nick Sluzick, the Ukrainian mailman, speaks in English in the extant production material. Although a secondary character in both the source text and the adaptation, he arguably accrues multicultural significance in the latter, while serving as an example of the English-language assimilation of settler populations. During the course of its work, the Bilingualism and Biculturalism Commission had encountered "a certain degree of protest by relatively established 'ethnic groups' such as Ukrainian-Canadians."[18] Greater access to French-language instruction was also accorded in Manitoba during this period, with small steps in 1963 and 1967 and a major one in June 1970.[19] Thus the adaptation's increasing of the narrative importance of this secondary character in conjunction with the muting of the source text's concerns with French-language issues suggest the NFB was using the Roy text to work around the shifting ground of policies and approaches surrounding the fostering of bilingualism and multiculturalism as they were advanced and re-acted to federally and provincially.

Roy, the daughter of a Quebec-born, federal immigration official in Mani-toba, always wrote with interest and sympathy about people of various cultural backgrounds and, in this particular text, repeatedly mentions of Luzina Tou-signant's positive multicultural encounters in her travels south. This character takes deep pleasure in hearing Icelandic, for instance. Studio G's elaboration on the source text's multicultural openness likely contributed to the production's finding such great favour with Maitland Steinkopf, the chair of the Manitoba Centennial Corporation. Billed as Manitoba's first Jewish cabinet minister, he was sympathetic to the multicultural approach to the interpretation of history. Indeed, he literally wore it on his sleeve during Canada's centennial year, going to the point of hamming it up in a multi-ethnic costume in his duties as chair. For example, in the caption of a photo taken in 1967 and held by Library and Ar-chives Canada, he is described in "Indian headdress, Hungarian shirt and vest, German lederhosen, Ukrainian sash, Dutch klompen, and shillelagh."[20]

The spirit of technological progress and multicultural idealism notwith-standing, the production's first and last film images suggest that difficulties en-countered among the early settlers persist into the modern era. The production ends with a reference to Roy's text, having it serve as the overarching narrative tie to the panoramic overview of the province's history, one that ultimately sug-gests that change poses challenges to one's comfortable world. No longer hav-ing to deal with the tipping over of his cutter, as he did at the beginning of the film, Nick Sluzick now drives an early-model car, which he attempts to negoti-ate along a primitive road in the woods. He has decided, as the film's treatment states, "to move further north.[21] As his voice-over explains, in a summarizing of a sentiment he expresses in the source text, "Il commence y avoir trop de monde." ("There are starting to be too many people here.") Placed as it is at the close of the production, the mailman's desire to move northward carries greater weight than it did in its secondary narrative position in the source text. The pro-duction thus ends with emphasis on what is likely unintended irony, with one of the symbols of cultural interaction and negotiation fleeing, albeit with some minor difficulty, the ever-growing, multicultural world of the more southern parts.[22] In spite of itself, the production leaves the spectator wondering about the inherent good of social change.

LE VIEILLARD ET L'ENFANT

The fifty-minute *Le vieillard et l'enfant* (1985) is based on Roy's similarly titled, poetic, semi-autobiographical novella, which was originally published in the collection *La route d'Altamont* in 1966.[23] The film is the only entirely live-action drama adaptation in the NFB corpus based on a strictly literary source text (as opposed to songs, legends, or life-writing) by a francophone from western Canada about francophones from the region.[24] Produced by the NFB's French-language production arm in the West (Production française/Ouest) in 1985, the film was made more than ten years into French production in the West and was shot in Manitoba. The producer, René Piché, was a Franco-Manitoban with a track record of productions about francophones in western Canada. Despite the film's evident connections to Manitoba, the film has a strong Québécois flavour; the director, Claude Grenier, the scriptwriter, Clément Perron, and all the key actors were from Quebec. Notably, the central role of the little girl, Christine, was accorded to the young up-and-coming Quebec actress Lucie Laurier and established Québécois actors were cast in the main supporting roles, with the old man played by Jean Duceppe, the girl's mother played by Patricia Nolin, and the narrator played by Michèle Magny.[25]

This Quebec slant may be attributable, at least in part, to the fact that the film was made in collaboration with the Société Radio-Canada (the French-language CBC), creating an impetus to make a film with broad French-language audience appeal. This aim is suggested in the very French heard in the film. Although standardizing the oral French along Quebec norms may mean the language more closely reflects the French spoken by Roy's fictional family, originally from Quebec, the film silences the very regional voices it is meant to let speak, leaving the impression that there are no competent Franco-Manitoban actors. It also glosses over the origins of the old man, Monsieur Saint-Hilaire, who had emigrated directly from France, something explained in the novella. Although at least once he does use a word more frequent among continental French speakers, the film mutes his French accent and suggests his emigration only obliquely when he explains he arrived in Canada by boat.

While the director, Grenier, was interested in Franco-Manitoban subjects, making several documentaries on them during this period, he also had a prior history of involvement in nationalist-oriented film production on Quebec-centered subjects.[26] This interest is reflected in his casting choices, most notably that of Duceppe, one of the "main artistic proponents for the Yes camp in the first Quebec sovereignty referendum in 1980."[27] Given Duceppe's symbolic status and his popularity in Quebec, and given the adaptation's themes of memory, loss, and change, the film may be read in terms of the concerns of Québécois cinema, which in this period is marked by a response to the sovereigntists' loss of the 1980 referendum (exemplified, for example, in Denys Arcand's documentary *Le confort et l'indifférence*, 1981). This interpretation is arguably as compelling as reading the film as an adaptation of a Franco-Manitoban fictional memoir dealing symbolically with universal themes of memory, "the recuperation of childhood," the desire to explore the world, and the coming to terms with death, themes explored in Gordon Collier's discussion of the film.[28]

The quest to see and experience the great blue *lac Winnipeg*, called the "mirage d'eau libre," can be interpreted in this socio-political context as the eternal desire for the (elusive) francophone nation. The white sails and white gulls against the expansive blue recall the colours of the *fleurdelisé* (the Quebec flag), while the white-tipped waves suggest a period of agitation; the latter concept is reinforced by the lake's steely colour in some shots.[29] The blue and white colour scheme is further complemented by the panoramas of blue sky, at times studded with white clouds during the little girl and old man's visit to the lakeshore. All the main characters can be seen as assuming allegorical roles in the sovereigntist drama: Christine's dead grandmother, whose death Christine must come to terms with, symbolizes the generational death of the dream; the child, Christine, charmed by the idea of seeing the great blue lake, embodies the youthful quest for the site of the dream's eternal regeneration; the old man, who bewitches her with his tales of the eternal lake, acts as the transmitter of that dream; Christine's mother represents the indecisive middle ground, engaged as she is in polishing tarnished, silver heirlooms—the dulled but renewable dreams of the past. Christine pleads for her mother's permission to see the lake, to make her first steps to independence accompanied by the old man, not her mother. "Dis oui," the girl begs, in a line not in the novella, but mimicking the sovereigntists' call in the referendum campaign, while her mother remains, like the undecided voters, pensive and uncertain for a notable period. Returned to the safe fold of her mother's arms at the end of the film after her brief flirt with independence along the lakeshore—the line between stasis and flight—Christine imagines she will eventually meet her grandmother and the old man, whom she will never see in life again, by the waters of the great lake.[30] The dream is not dead.

It is not surprising, then, that the adaptation divests the text of non-franco-phone regional names—gone are terms such as saskatoons and any mention of the neighbouring Saskatchewan—to focus instead on details in the source text that emphasize the francophone presence in the history of the West, details that intimate it could have been a French-speaking land. As in the novella, the word "*coulée*," a regionalism with French origins, finds its way into the film. Most developed is the scene in which Christine play-acts the fur trader and explorer La Vérendrye, in which she and the old man dream that the explorer will take possession of the West "pour le Roi de France" before the English come.[31] In the novella, she had also sometimes imagined herself to be the Chinese launderer or the Italian peddler. These immigrant references are erased in the film, as are her pained imaginings of finding piles of animal bones and corpses, possibly an allusion to the decimation of the buffalo and First Nations peoples or perhaps a fear of the current drought's consequences. Thus over Roy's subtle laying claim to past visions of Franco-cultural space through her nostalgic accounts of people and place—one that acknowledges the hardship and trials of others—Grenier's film superimposes another sentiment. Through symbolic resonance with Que-·bec's post-referendum blues, the film evokes a more recent and pointed sadness over the loss of the French nation in the form of an independent Quebec. The adapters create both a palimpsest and an erasure of cultural-linguistic losses. As the narrator suggestively affirms at the beginning of the film when ostensibly referring to complaints about the weather: "Nous vivions toujours insatisfaits, entre l'avenir et [le] passé, entre l'attente et le regret." (We live forever dissatisfied, between future and past, between expectation and regret.)

That said, the Franco-Manitoban sense of loss and struggle is not without socio-political resonance in the film. Although its narrative is set in 1935, the political situation during the crucial pre-production period could have encouraged the adaptation team to incorporate subtle symbolic traces that would speak to the wider contemporary context. Certainly it encourages the viewer to look for them. Just prior to the adaptation's summer shoot in 1984, Manitoba was embroiled in a language crisis, notably "from May 1983 to the end of February 1984."[32] Fuelled by reactions to the Supreme Court of Canada's decision in the *Forest* case in 1979, which ruled Manitoba's Official Language Act of 1890 "inoperative," it reached a fevered pitch during the meandering of the *Bilodeau* case through the courts. A notable period in the legislative debates was the "long hot summer" of 1983.[33] The Supreme Court of Canada ruled on the latter case in 1985, giving the provincial government three years to translate its major laws and statutes into French.

Given this context, it is possible to read the film as subtly weaving the colours of the Franco-Manitoban flag into its visual narrative—yellow (for wheat), red (for the Red River), and green (for a plant emblemizing francophones, which is evoked on the flag by two back-to-back F shapes illustrating the plant from roots to leaves). The large white background into which the plant reaches can also be detected in the film. With the flag adopted in 1980, not long before the film's production, its colours carried important symbolic weight. Except for yellow, mentioned to describe drought-stressed grass, none of the veritable colours are mentioned in the novella.[34]

Although, as a visual medium, film inevitably adds to a scene described in print and although colour film, in particular, immensely multiplies ·visual signifiers, careful direction can select clusters of images that suggest, under-score, or contain certain colours of symbolic significance. Since colours accrue political meaning in a charged socio-political context, they cannot be dismissed as a signifier in a cultural text. Yellow, evoked at the opening of the film through shots of expansive wheat fields, conveys a sense of cultural rootedness. This sentiment is then visually and aurally reinforced with a shot of a sad, young Christine missing her deceased grandmother, her feelings explained by the voice-over of her adult self. Neither wheat fields nor yellow are mentioned in this opening scene in the novella. White as a wide wash of comforting non-colour is also put to emblematic use early in the film, with the panning of the length of the sheltering, outer white walls of the family home behind which the mother draws white curtains and white blinds to take refuge from an oppressive heat wave. The peeling paint on the walls suggests the pressure that they and, by extension, the family within are under from outside forces. Later this wearing but invisible meteorological event leaves the young Christine, the symbol of the future, prostrate with heat stroke; her mother soothes her burning forehead with a white cloth dipped in cooling, restorative water, the element that becomes the object of Christine's quest in the film. None of this type of use of white is in the novella, and it is the old man who is more affected by the heat.

Red and its derivatives also form motifs in the film, connoting the care for, transmission, or furtherance of Franco-Manitoban heritage or culture. For in-stance, the mother frequently wears some type of red dress, such as when she nurses her heat-stricken daughter or polishes the family silver in the decision-making scene. In Christine's early adventure scenes, she regularly dons red shoes, for instance when she takes risks with her make-believe voyages on stilts or pre-tends to be La Vérendrye. During some of her imagined exploits she also fre-quently wears ruddy overalls or a dress edged with reddish trim. During Christine and the old man's visit to the lake, red stands out as a protective colour on umbrel-las, clothing, or the inside of a kiosk, underscoring the sheltering of self from the blistering sun. The dotting of diverse red coverings along the shore that skirts the great blue expanse of the white-capped waters symbolizes the complementarity of Quebec and Franco-Manitoban aspirations in protecting French heritage as well as the relative bigness of Quebec's occasionally disruptive ambitions.

With the film shot in the summer, it is unsurprising that lush shades of deep green proliferate visually in the form of plants, canopies of tree leaves, shrubs, and varieties of grasses. The more specific suggestion of the cultivation of the francophone socio-cultural presence does find expression in this generalized green context, however. For instance, following a scene in which the old man replenishes Christine with a glass of milk and they exchange tidbits that re-veal their estrangement from certain family members, they go outside to garden together.[35] At their leisurely task, the old man shares with Christine his sense of wonder about the eternal presence of the vast *lac Winnipeg*, an entity she has never seen and which for him eclipses the greatness of the land of the girl's uncles. With only its *coulées* and wells, it lacks sufficient and—by implication nurturing—water in his view. Their exchange culminates with Christine generously watering the flowerbeds thick with tall, green leafy flower stems that boast large red and red-variant blossoms, an action suggesting the sustaining of the local francophone community with the nourishing waters derived from the larger French one.

Green is also used to embody the road to cultural roots, a road the narrative intimates one must not stray from. For example, heavy, tall, green growth edges the same path that leads Christine into the forest where she remembers her deceased grandmother and that then guides the worried old man to the quietly grieving girl. Comforting her in the green enclave, he affirms, "On [ne] contrôle pas toujours la barque [lorsqu'on voyage loin].... L'important...c'est de... retrouver son chemin." (We can't always control the direction of our little boat [when we travel far]. The important thing is to find our path again.) In another scene, Christine's mother nurtures her love and nostalgia for the past; she play dresses with a green gown of her youth while her daughter and the old man enjoy their precious time between past and future by the great blue lake. Made during a time of uncertainty for Franco-Manitobans and Quebec sovereigntists, the adaptation holds out the hope that assuring one's cultural future lies in cherishing those elements that are beautiful and sustaining from one's heritage and caring for them into the present so that one's culture may one day fully blossom on its own.

LOUIS RIEL

Issues related to cultural loss and the French presence in the West are also bound up in the story of Louis Riel. The NFB has paid less attention than one might expect to either him or the Métis resistance of the nineteenth century when compared to that accorded to him by historians and other cultural producers. This is surprising considering the political significance of the resistance movement with which he was associated (and for which he became the leader), his broad appeal to the Métis and francophones and to Westerners, historians and otherwise,[36] and the amount of study to which his story has been subjected by numerous anglophone and francophone scholars, regardless of their regional affiliations.[37] In the over 125 years since his death, he has been the subject of an array of cultural texts, both in English and French, including plays, novels, poetry, children's literature, and a television mini-series.[38] The interest continues unabated in the twenty-first century with, for example, Chester Brown's graphic novel *Louis Riel: A Comic-Strip Biography* (2003) and Pascal Boutroy's independent documentary *Mon Riel à moi* (2008). Indeed, except for the two short adaptations discussed in this chapter—*This Riel Business* (1974) and *Louis Riel: dernier songe* (1983)—and two other projects outside the scope of this chapter, no other NFB production specifically names him in its title, and few others deal with the events of either 1869–70 or 1885.[39] He is a secondary figure in several other productions, as he is, to a certain degree, in the English-language adaptation examined in this chapter.[40]

The idea that the NFB may be eschewing the "great men in history" approach to historiography—an approach reflected in some of its earlier films and series—is undercut by the fact that the NFB continued to make historical portrait films of well-known political figures both around the time of and after the films on Riel. It also continued to make films that either explore the influence of key political figures or survey constellations of figures of political significance. Perhaps the NFB felt others had Riel's story well covered. Whatever the case, the lack of overall film production on Riel by the NFB means that the film adaptations related to him, while minor works, gain importance as far as how they convey the history surrounding him, what he advocated, and the group with whom he particularly identified, "les Métis canadiens-français."[41]

Grappling with a mythologized figure upon whom has been projected a wide range of divergent readings, reflecting at times French-English socio-political tensions, these adaptations serve as barometers for linguistically inflected perceptions—not surprising given that they emanate from an institution structured along linguistic lines. While the scholarship on Riel has gone through various phases depending on the linguistic, regional, and ethnic affiliations of history-tellers—and while he was largely neglected by Québécois scholars from the 1950s to the mid 1980s in spite of Quebec's early sympathy—to this day he still attracts strong partisan commentary among some francophone scholars and remains a central figure in Métis and Western iconography and history.[42] These linguistic-inflected interpretations of Riel are reflected in the two adaptations from literary sources to which I will now turn: *This Riel Business* (1974), based on Rod Langley's comic play *Tales from a Prairie Drifter* (1972), and *Louis Riel: dernier songe* (1983), inspired by correspondence Riel received from loved ones.

THIS RIEL BUSINESS

Directed and produced by Ian McLaren as part of a 1973–74 English-language documentary series on the West (called simply *West*) that was broadcast on the CBC,[43] *This Riel Business* was originally conceived as a documentary showing the mounting of a performance of Langley's play, selected scenes and historical visuals, and reactions of an invited audience of Métis and First Nations people.[44]

However, as the NFB's online catalogue indicates, the NFB categorizes the film as an adaptation of a literary work, and in so far as it makes a coherent selection of episodes from one particular performance of the play at the Regina Globe Theatre in the fall of 1973, it is. In the end the documentary never showed the behind-the-scenes efforts; rather it focused on showing a performance of some scenes inter-cut with on-the-spot and later audience reactions, some from Howard Adams and Gordon Tootoosis, location shots of battle sites, and historical stills. The result is a layered and partial re-recounting of historical events interpreted by the playwright (who sets up the play as a story within a story), reinterpreted by director Kenneth Kramer and his theatre company, reselected by the film director, and finally commented on by audience members. Their commentary takes the form of inter-cut observations and opinions laced with alternative and diverse versions of historical memory and oral histories involving Riel. As a complicated set of mediated adaptations and interpretations of the original events, the filmed version serves as an especially rich example of the appropriation of history of national import.[45]

While some scholars have expressed discomfort with the play's blatant use of caricature and its simplistically negative portrayal of Riel, reviews suggest audiences responded positively to its burlesque treatment of history in which all the main characters, except perhaps Gabriel Dumont, are satirized, some more successfully than others.[46] The playwright, who empathized with the plight of the Métis and First Nations people under Western expansion, acknowledged he saw history "as a series of cartoons."[47] This less sanctimonious approach to history helps explain audience reactions. According to McLaren's proposal, "the play… invariably [brought] the house down." Moreover, Métis audiences responded well. During its initial run "a couple of busloads of Métis" were brought to the play by activist Howard Adams. The audience gave it "a ten-minute standing ovation, and several Métis women were weeping."[48] Since the play came out during a period of Métis and First Nations activism, it provided the NFB with an opportunity to capture some of the spirit of that activism through the safe filter of professionally sanctioned theatre.[49]

Large swaths of the original two-act play are deleted so that it and the audience commentary could fit the half-hour format. Numerous scenes dealing with a range of historical events and peoples involved in the westward expansion of Canada and contributing directly or indirectly to the events of 1885 are simply cut. Excised content includes a Protestant clergyman sermonizing on the righteousness of white settlement, white buffalo hunters hoping to make a quick buck, and political negotiations involving Sitting Bull. It is thus difficult to assert that the depiction of issues involving one particular ethnic, religious, or linguistic group is specifically or uniquely deleted. Nevertheless, it is noteworthy that the explicitly French-speaking fact of the main players in the historical event, already secondary in the play, disappears in the film completely, a trend seen in the anglophone appropriation and depiction of Riel in other cultural texts, as Albert Braz has shown.[50]

The fact that Riel was French-speaking is only indirectly acknowledged in both texts and in the minimalist of ways, while Kramer, who plays Riel in the version of the play recorded in the film, makes no attempt to convey the fact in his speech patterns.[51] The farcical, stereotypical scene depicting the Métis population's growth, resulting from the coupling of "Frenchmen" and "Indian Maidens," is also deleted, removing all overt explanation of mixed ancestry.[52] Two scenes in the play depicting the Métis sending petitions in French written for them by a priest to the Ministry of the Interior are also cut from the film version, excising from the text all indication of the Métis' use of French in such a context. The play's burlesque vision of the Ministry's reaction to the petitions is highly xenophobic and even anachronistic. Statements like "[i]t's the French.... Not only are the beggars totally illiterate they can't even speak white" no doubt did not help matters in the linguistically charged atmosphere following the federal government's passing of the Official Languages Act in 1969.[53] Michèle Lalonde's galvanizing poem "Speak White," recited first at *Poèmes et chants de la résistance* in 1968 and then in a triumphant encore at the famous *La Nuit de la poésie* in 1970 and published in its official form in 1974, cast a long political shadow over the disparaging term. Originally written to help raise funds for the defence of, notably, the incarcerated Front de libération du Québec member Pierre Vallières, author of *Nègres blancs d'Amérique* (1968), the poem decries the linguistic, cultural, and economic subjugation of French Canadians. Its socio-political import did not go unnoticed at the NFB. The French program released one film containing a reading of the poem in 1970 and would go on to release two more, one in 1977 and one in 1980.[54]

To return to the Riel film, the inserted audience reactions do not directly comment on the French factor, either because audience members did not mention the language issue, or, if they did, because those remarks were cut. The commentary that is included reflects an a-linguistic interest in First Nations or Métis interpretations of decisions regarding the respective peoples' part in resistance activity. These challenge ideas advanced in the play and by fellow commentators, creating a dynamic text that acknowledges alternative historical narratives between the play's version of a non-Indigenous view and Indigenous views and among Indigenous peoples themselves.

In steering clear of all allusions to French-English linguistic tensions, the film focuses on a select set of issues related to period discontent among the Métis, and to some degree the First Nations people, including the suffering following the decimation of the buffalo. It also spends time on the military events that culminated in the Battle of Batoche. The filmmaker's intention seems to have been to open a space for First Nations and Métis viewpoints on this history through audience commentary. The suppression of some of the play's French content, however, raises the question of whether the NFB perceived it easier in this period, so soon after the October Crisis and the move to bilingual federal government services, to broach—in English-language films at least—issues related to Indigenous peoples rather than ones related, even historically, to the French language. None of the other films in the *West* series are about francophones in the West, but one is about an up-and-coming chief, Noel Starblanket.

LOUIS RIEL: DERNIER SONGE

Unlike the wide-ranging, multi-character Langley plays, the approximately eight-minute *Louis Riel: dernier songe* (directed by Claude Grenier and produced by René Piché at the NFB's western French-language production arm, Production française/Ouest) offers an intimate and sympathetic portrait of Riel. Released in 1983, two years before the centenary of his execution, it focuses exclusively on him through the enactment of a daydream the filmmaker imagines Riel may have had on the eve of his hanging. In it Riel returns alone to his empty family home in St.Vital, Manitoba. The fact that the film is in French—with about one-third devoted to Riel remembering two letters written to him in French, one from his (now deceased) sister Sara and the second from his former fiancée, Evelina Barnabé[55]—reinforce Riel's French linguistic heritage. French is shown to be part of his daily, private life, connecting him with his loved ones. Indeed, his sister Sara writes to him about his mother thinking of her son. These few lines reinforce the notion of French as mother tongue. Riel's mere use of French in the film while reflecting on the fate of "la nation métisse" and the "les ennemis" who, in his words, have risen against it and him shows the language to be integral to his Métis identity. This identify is further underscored by his wearing of the Métis sash. Visual and verbal signals thus adroitly and succinctly build the concept of the Métis as French-speaking.

Grenier's film more positively depicts Riel's Roman Catholicism than Kramer's production of Langley's play in *This Riel Business*. The latter caricatures Riel as a dictatorial, mad prophet bent on martyrdom; he is shown bearing an enormous processional cross in such a way as to emphasize his messianic tendencies.[56] By contrast, Grenier's film naturalizes Riel's Roman Catholicism, which when coupled with his francophone identity has often been used to other him.[57] Setting the film in Riel's family home allows the filmmaker to integrate emblems of his deep faith naturally into the *mise en scène*. Shots from Riel's vantage point of crosses commonly found in home décor during the period and other cross-suggestive POV shots—notably of the cross-like elements in the home's multi-paned windows and glass cupboard door frames and of cross shadows from those window panes—intimate that Christianity informed Riel's very act of seeing. Gentle pans to an open Bible from which Riel eventually silently reads and over a picture of the Madonna and the Christ child further weave worship into the domestic space, normalizing it. His Roman Catholicism is also alluded to through his remembering a letter from his sister who became a nun. While her vocation is not revealed in the film, it is familiar to those who know Riel's personal history. In addition, his allusions to his period of alleged madness suggest that his mental breakdown during his exile was triggered by his neglect of his health when he was separated from family, rendering this episode more understandable than the relentless focus on his esoteric religious vision for the West highlighted by Langley in *This Riel Business.*[58]

While Grenier focuses on Riel the man, humanizing him by returning him to domestic space and his familial roots, the director reminds the spectator that ultimately Riel remains a mystery. A prologue acknowledges the many conflicting ways historians have labelled him: hero, traitor, prophet, madman. More significantly, the film never shows the face of the actor playing Riel. All shots are either from the back, in shadow, or in profile. The only face-on shots are of photographic reproductions of the historical Riel, reminding us that we only have a projected image of him; we cannot really know him. Thus while the film returns him to his French Catholic roots, it underscores that even they do not reveal him fully to us. As his voice-over asks: "Où se cache la vérité de mon être?" (Where does the truth of my soul hide?) He remains a freedom-seeking enigma, caught between the sounds of the military might from which he attempts to flee in the film and the silence of the spaces he will leave behind—an imagined presence, a spirit of the place.

CONCLUSION

With the production of *Of Many People* marking Canada's centennial year and the production of *Louis Riel: dernier songe* leading into the centenary of Riel's execution, it becomes evident that the NFB perceived film adaptations based on or inspired by texts by or about iconic francophone figures as instrumental in helping shape the national imagination. But the question remains: Whose national imagination? With the production of *Le vieillard et l'enfant* contributing to the recognition of the official regionalization of French-language production in the West, it also becomes evident that the NFB saw the adaptation of such texts as central to the fostering of regional imagination. Again, however, one might ask: Whose region? The answer is partly determined by the linguistic group to which the adaptation team belonged. Indeed, the four examples of NFB adaptations examined here betray differences in the French- and English-language approaches to texts by or about iconic francophone figures and the claims to place made within their texts (or that these figures symbolize through their texts).

Gabrielle Roy's texts are used to look back to assert nationalist-inflected claims of factions of the particular official language group making the adaptation. These claims are contemporaneous to the period in which the adaptation is produced. Made by English-language adapters, the multimedia presentation *Of Many People* draws on Roy's *La petite poule d'eau* to portray what was considered a foundational settlement period, the paradoxically hardy yet romanticized and multicultural period from which the province of Manitoba and, by extension, the nation of Canada are shown to spring. Still the fragments of the extant production betray a sense of uneasiness with the change that population growth and technological development have brought, an equivocal sentiment inspired by the source text. The adaptation is thus an unstable expression of nationalist pedagogy, to use Homi K. Bhabha's term. This is unsurprising, given that the source text, itself, was never intended as such a tool. While not a direct response to the production of *Of Many People/Un siècle d'hommes*, *Le vieillard et l'enfant* can be read as replacing or effacing the multicultural ideology promoted by the multimedia production. In focusing exclusively on the French social and historical context, *Le vieillard et l'enfant* erases the cultural heterogeneity evoked in Roy's novella to centre the adaptation around the symbolic expression of the loss and renewal of the dream for a French nation. As such, it intimates the need to keep cultural memory strong and to foster nurturing links with the larger French nation of Quebec, symbolically evoked in the adaptation's performance and aesthetic interpretation of the source text and subtly articulated by means of the adaptation by the director and scriptwriter of Quebec origin.

Although the selections of a performance of the play *Tales from a Prairie Drifter* recorded in the film *This Riel Business* do convey Riel's claims to nation for the Métis, the play also locates his views within the realms of the messianic and the mad. In caricaturing Riel, the play seeks to debunk his iconic status, as it does with that of various other historical characters, but it also ends up perpetuating a more commonly perpetuated one-dimensional view of Riel. However, the film's insertion of audience commentary and interviews around the recordings of the performance shows Métis and First Nations audience members grappling with the play's representation of the history of Western settlement and Riel's role within it, revealing that there is a counter-reading beyond the caricature. Offering individual interpretations that contest some of the historiographical views of the dominant settler society, this commentary allows *This Riel Business* to offer a more complex engagement with the Riel myth and to give voice to the larger Métis and First Nations communities and their views regarding claims to place. The film reveals the willingness of the English-language adapters to give cinematic space to this view, while they temper the francophone aspects of the history. In contrast, while acknowledging the range of historical interpretations of Riel's character and deeds, *Louis Riel: dernier songe* builds on none of them, deciding instead to recuperate his basic humanity. By situating him within the linguistic, cultural and religious womb—the family home—that nourished his formative years, the film seeks to replace cultural stereotypes with a more sympathetic and enigmatic glimpse of someone we ultimately can never truly know. Here the filmmaker of Quebec origin merely seems intent on giving Riel, as a francophone and a Métis, a place in the local landscape. Perhaps because Riel's fate was historically so contested in Quebec, the adapter makes no attempt to recuperate Riel for the larger Québécois national narrative.

In the end these adaptations can be read in dialogue with their times as well as one another—voicing, even debating, various claims to place and, in some cases nation, of the Franco-Manitoban and Métis peoples. These NFB productions also show how, in some cases, the adapters attempt to harness these claims for either the Canadian or Québécois national narratives. These four relatively short adaptations thus become complex sites where place is alternatively and, at times, simultaneously contested, reworked, and re-appropriated, underscoring the fact that the cultural mapping of place is ultimately an unstable process.

ACKNOWLEDGMENTS

I wish to thank my research assistants Sheila Mawn and Ramla Belajouza as well as Catherine Holmes of the Saskatchewan Archives Board and the personnel of both the University of Saskatchewan Archives and the National Film Board of Canada, notably Richard Cournoyer at the NFB Conservation Laboratory and André D'Ulisse at the NFB Archives. Darren Préfontaine of the Gabriel Dumont Institute also gave me helpful leads.

FILMOGRAPHY

Le vieillard et l'enfant, directed by Claude Grenier (NFB Production, 1985).

Louis Riel: dernier songe, directed by Claude Grenier (NFB Production, 1983).

This Riel Business, directed by Ian McLaren (NFB Production, 1974).

Un siècle d'hommes, directed by Stanley Jackson (NFB Production, 1970).

NOTES

1   An exception to this disinterest in live-action drama involving francophones from the West is the short film *Ti-Jean s'en va dans l'Ouest* directed by Raymond Garceau (NFB Production, 1957). It documents the foray of the folkloric figure Ti-Jean into the West in one of several adaptations of the Ti-Jean legend. For a discussion of NFB live-action drama adaptations of English-language literary sources about the West, see Elspeth Tulloch, "Screening the Outsider In/Out in NFB Adaptations of Western Canadian Literature" in *West of Eden: Essays on Canadian Prairie Literature*, ed. Sue Sorensen (Winnipeg: CMU Press, 2008), 219–242.

2   Apart from an early documentary in French entitled *Les Canadiens français dans l'Ouest* (1955), the NFB online catalogue lists no films about francophones from the West until 1976 under its most obvious category *Francophonie canadienne (à l'exclusion du Québec/Ouest du Canada)*, although a few other films categorized elsewhere are of some relevance, such as *L'Âge du castor* (1951) and *Les voyageurs* (1964), which have English and French versions. Some thirty documentaries are listed under the former category from 1979–2009, the vast majority produced in the 1980s. This calculation excludes films made in co-production, the odd animated film, as well as film compilations that repackage individual films as group sets.

3   One of the films discussed in this study, *This Riel Business*, was partly filmed at a performance by Regina's Globe Theatre, a professional, regional theatre that became known for mounting works by playwrights, from the region and otherwise, whose plays addressed social and political concerns of interest to the audience. See Mary Blackstone, "Globe Theatre," *Encyclopedia of Saskatchewan*, http://esask.uregina.ca/entry/globe_theatre.html, accessed April 10, 2011. In 1979, the NFB showcased a play by the alternative theatre movement: Saskatoon's 25th Street Theatre's production of *Paper Wheat*. It is featured in a film by the same name as well as in *Scenes from Paper Wheat*.

4   Gabrielle Roy, *La petite poule d'eau* (Montreal: Boréal, 2009).

5   Gabrielle Roy, "Le vieillard et l'enfant," *La route d'Altamont* (Montreal: Éditions HMH, 1966), 61–154. The article will not consider *Mirage de la plaine* (1978), an experimental short that borrows a line from Gabrielle Roy, given that the film is not strictly an adaptation.

6   Gary Evans, *In the National Interest: A Chronicle of the National Film Board of Canada from 1949 to 1989* (Toronto: University of Toronto Press, 1991), 304.

7   Joining the NFB in 1942, he immediately began directing documentaries about agricultural production during the Second World War: *Battle of the Harvests* (1942), *Hands for the Harvest*, and *Home to the Land* (both in 1944). A later film he directed with a Western connection is *Cornet at Night* (1963), an adaptation of the Sinclair Ross short story. He also produced *Ukrainian Festival* (1947), set on the prairies.

8   For more on regionalization, see Ronald Dick, "Regionalization of a Federal Cultural Institution: The Experience of the National Film Board of Canada 1965-1979" in *Flashback: People and Institutions in Canadian Film History*, ed. Gene Walz (Montreal: Mediatexte Publications, 1986), 107–133, at 114, 118, 121. For information on the production schedule see NFB Memorandum, *Of Many People* production files, "Water Hen Display," Don Hopkins to Pierre Fontaine, May 25, 1970.

9   See NFB, *Of Many People* production files, letter from Don Hopkins to Paul-Marie Paquin, December 14, 1970. The letter from Don Hopkins, head of the NFB's Multi-media Division, to Paul-Marie Paquin, director of Éditions littéraires, Librairie Beauchemin (Gabrielle Roy's copyright representative) is on the subject of extending the program's run to 440. The request was subsequently approved. The same letter cites the chair (or the "président" in French) of the Manitoba Centennial Corporation (mistakenly called the "commission") commenting on the production's success. More positive feedback from the chair, Maitland Steinkopf, is paraphrased in the following

letter: NFB, *Of Many People* production files, letter from Graham Glockling, Secretary of State, to Don Duprey, National Film Board of Canada, October 21, 1970.

10   The extant English material was less intact than the French. The NFB's conservation unit has so far been unable to recover any of the stills used in the production. Citing the limited copyrights accorded to the production at the time and anticipated extra costs to procure extensions on them, the NFB declined the University of Manitoba's request to donate the prints from the production to the university. See NFB, *Of Many People* production files, Memorandum, "La petite poule d'eau," Lucile Bishop to Don Aylard, Winnipeg, August 10, 1972. It is unconfirmed whether this donation occurred later.

11   The NFB memorandum "Water Hen" stipulates, "In all cases reference to the novel is to say 'based on the novel,' rather than 'adapted from,' " suggesting that the NFB understood it was making a loose adaptation, one little concerned with fidelity. See NFB, *Of Many People* production files, "Water Hen," Don Hopkins to Ron Jones, June 17, 1970.

12   NFB, *Of Many People* production files, "Centennial Project Handout," First Draft, Revised Draft, and Printed Pamphlet, n.d., 1 and 2.

13   Linda Clemente and Bill Clemente, *Gabrielle Roy: Creation and Memory* (Toronto: ECW Press, 1997), 178.

14   It is not clear whether the production even included images of First Nations peoples.

15   Pierre Elliott Trudeau, "Federal Multicultural Policy: House of Commons Debates, October 8, 1971" in *Multiculturalism and Immigration in Canada*, ed. Elspeth Cameron (Toronto: Canadian Scholars' Press, 2004), 401–407, at 402. Although the production's actual content avoids language issues, the production, itself, indirectly expresses support for the notion of bilingualism via its English and French versions.

16   NFB, "Centennial Project Handout," 2.

17   NFB, *Of Many People* production files, "Approach to Treatment for Water Hen," 2.

18   Eva Mackey, *The House of Difference* (London: Routledge, 1999), 64.

19   Raymond M. Hébert, *Manitoba's French-Language Crisis* (Montreal and Kingston: McGill-Queen's University Press, 2004), 17–20.

20   Library and Archives Canada, photo PA-185504. It is hard to overlook the fact that nothing in the costume signals the province's French heritage. Admittedly, though, it was donned for comic effect, so its mix of cultural references was not meant to be taken too seriously. More *à propos* for Roy's case, when the Canadian Permanent Committee on Geographical Names accepted to commemorate Gabrielle Roy by naming an island on the Waterhen River in her honour, it respected the Waterhen Community Council's rejection of the use of the French "île," so the island is officially called "Gabrielle-Roy Island" and not "Île Gabrielle-Roy." See Ismène Toussaint, "Inauguration de l'île Gabrielle-Roy dans la rivière de la Poule-d'Eau (Manitoba)," *Cahiers franco-canadiens de l'Ouest* 2, 1 (1990): 91–95.

21   NFB, "Approach to Treatment for Water Hen," 2.

22   He was, after all, the one who brought Luzina Tousignant, the central figure, south every year to give birth.

23   An English version was released in 1986.

24   Since the NFB had never done a documentary on Roy and since she had just died in 1983, perhaps the film, with its concern with memory and death, was thought to be a fitting tribute, following the NFB's partial involvement with the adaptation of her novel *Bonheur d'occasion* (1983) set in Montreal. It was certainly intended to mark the tenth anniversary of "la Régionalisation Ouest" of the NFB; see Michel Larouche, "*Le vieillard et l'enfant*: le scénario de Gabrielle Roy," *Cahiers franco-canadiens de l'Ouest* 9, 1–2 (1997): 3–17, at 4.

25   Jean Duceppe (1923–1990) was a stage and film actor who remained popular over his nearly fifty-year career. An established stage, film, and television actress, Patricia Nolin began teaching at the Conservatoire d'art dramatique de Montréal in 1987. Graduating from the École nationale de théâtre du Canada in 1968, Michèle Magny went on to enjoy an active stage career and teaching at her alma mater.

26   For example, he directed *Le pays de Menaud, Félix-Antoine Savard* (1970) with the production company Cinéastes associés, founded by three nationalist directors (Denys Arcand, Gilles Groulx, Michel Brault) disaffected by the NFB.

27   Canadian Encyclopedia, "Jean Duceppe" by Stéphane Baillargeon, www.thecanadianencyclopedia.com, accessed April 2, 2011.

28   Gordon Collier, "Childhood in Prairie Film," in *Screening Canadians: Cross-Cultural Perspectives on Canadian Film*, eds. Wolfram R. Keller and Gene Walz (Marburg: Schriften der Universitätsibliothek Marburg, 2008), 99–117, at 103, 101–04. Other critics have also observed these themes.

29   Gabrielle Roy, "Le vieillard et l'enfant," 99. Blue appears rarely in the novella. It is the colour of the old man's eyes and the lake, objects holding wonder for the girl. White is rarely mentioned and is linked both to passion and death. It is used to describe the agitated lake and allude to the girl's excitability. Once it refers to the whites of the old man's eyes, visible when he is sleeping, causing the girl to fear he has died. Given the cultural context, it would be a misreading to interpret the blue and white in terms of the Métis flag, although themes of eternity, the symbol of which is on the flag, imbue both texts and although the girl is eight, and she draws the symbol 8 in the sand, in an ironic comment on eternity.

30   The old man and the girl's relationship involves a make-believe courtship dance and carries subtle sexual connotations, for example, in their positioning when lying on the beach in the film. I thank my graduate student Cristina Artenie for her seminar observations on the sexual suggestiveness of this relationship. Collier, "Childhood in Prairie Film," refers to its "illicit nostalgia," 103.

31   Gabrielle Roy, "Le vieillard et l'enfant." *La route d'Altamont*, 61–154, at 66. The phrase appears in both the novella and the film.

32   Hébert, *Manitoba's French Language Crisis*, xi.

33   Ibid., 32, 104–117.

34   Although it may be the subject of debate whether white is a colour, I am not including it as one in this statement. White is, in fact, mentioned in the novella but does not and cannot carry the same connotations that I read in the film, since the novella predates the adaptation by nearly twenty years.

35   In this scene she also dons his daughter's straw hat, ribboned in symbolic blue. Her gesture visually puns on the verb "chapeauter," suggesting that the larger francophone "nation" can serve to shelter and oversee the smaller Franco-Manitoban society with its emerging sense of self, symbolized by the ruddy-clad Christine.

36   See Douglas Owram, "The Myth of Louis Riel," *Canadian Historical Review* 63, 3 (1982): 315–336, at 336.

37   Apart from the films discussed in this article, Riel is mentioned in the following NFB productions or productions for which the NFB offered assistance: *Les Canadiens français dans l'Ouest* (1955), *La Ceinture d'Elzéar Goulet* (co-production company: Les Productions Tilt, 1987), *Making History: Louis Riel and the North-West Rebellion of 1885* (CD-ROM, 1997), *Chiefs: The Trial of Poundmaker* (production agency: Galafilm, 2002), *Engage-toi! La blogue (Site Web)* (2008), which includes a clip of the blogger's, Andréanne Germain's, pilgrimage to Riel's gravesite. He is a near-mythic figure in the NFB documentary *Riel Country* (1996). A visual reference is made to him in the animated short *Jours de plaine* (1990).

38 See Albert Braz, *The False Traitor: Louis Riel in Canadian Culture* (Toronto: University of Toronto Press, 2003) for an extensive analysis of this cultural production. Also see Jennifer Reid, *Louis Riel and the Creation of Modern Canada: Mythic Discourse and the Postcolonial State* (Winnipeg: University of Manitoba Press, 2012), 32–48.

39 The only other projects that feature him in their titles are *Riel Country* (1996) and the CD-ROM *Making History: Louis Riel and the North-West Rebellion of 1885* (1997). Indeed the CD-ROM and *This Riel Business* (1974), are the only entirely NFB productions listed under the English-language category History-Canada 1867–1919/ Northwest Rebellion in the NFB's online catalogue, although a few other productions (see earlier note) refer in some way to these events. There is no specific sub-category for the "Northwest Rebellion" in the French online catalogue.

40 The NFB has shown, however, some interest in Métis subjects more largely, with over twenty productions (dramas or documentaries) on various aspects of Métis life, apart from the films under consideration here.

41 See his brief outline of the positive characteristics of the "Métis canadiens-français," in Louis Riel, *The Collected Writings of Louis Riel*, vol. 2, ed. Gilles Martel, under the general editorship of George F.G. Stanley (Edmonton: University of Alberta Press, 1985), 297–298.

42 On the subject of Quebec's sympathy for Riel, one need only recall that in 1885 crowds of thousands (one up to 50,000) demonstrated against his hanging. See Jacques Mathieu and Jacques Lacoursière, *Les mémoires québécoises* (Sainte-Foy: Les Presses de l'Université Laval, 1991), 359–60.

43 McLaren, who was born in England, raised in Ottawa, and fluently bilingual, was an experienced director and producer by the time of this production. He had worked in these capacities at the CBC in Montreal, where, among other things, he made documentaries about Quebec separatism before coming to the NFB in 1972, when he produced *Adieu Alouette*, another series about Quebec. After a successful career at the NFB, culminating with his appointment as Director of English Production in 1977, he went on to administrative positions at the Secretary of State, Telefilm Canada, and in the private sector. For information on the broadcast of the West series, see Blaine Allan, "CBC Television Series, 1952–1982/Directory of Television Series." *Queen's Film and Media*, 1996, http://www.film.queensu.ca/CBC/, accessed April 15, 2011. McLaren's film was broadcast March 20, 1974, according to a Globe Theatre press release (March 11, 1974).

44 NFB, *Tales from a Prairie Drifter* production files, Ian McLaren, "Proposal for the Western Series for a Film on Dramatic Expression/Working Title *Tales from a Prairie Drifter* or Just Simply *Tales*," July 11, 1973, 3–4.

45 For more on the cultural phenomenon of appropriating history, see Julie Sanders, *Adaptation and Appropriation* (London: Routledge, 2006), 138–146.

46 Positively qualified as a "myth-breaking play" and "lively agitprop," the play has also been described as a "political cartoon" that champions Dumont and blames Riel for the defeat of the Métis." See Chris Johnson, "Riel in Canadian Drama, 1885–1985" in *Images of Louis Riel in Canadian Culture*, eds. Ramon Hathorn and Patrick Holland (Queenston, Ontario: Edwin Mellen Press, 1992), 175–210, at 197, 199, and 198, respectively. It has been qualified as a darkly cynical burlesque by Margaret Gail Osachoff in "Louis Riel in Canadian Literature: Myth and Reality" in *Canadian Story and History 1885–1985*, eds. Colin Nicholson and Peter Easingwood (Edinburgh: Edinburgh University, Centre of Canadian Studies, 1985), 61–69, at 67, and it has been seen to exhibit "contempt for Riel, a scorn bordering on hatred." See Albert Braz, *The False Traitor: Louis Riel in Canadian Culture* (Toronto: University of Toronto Press, 2003), 171. For an example of a review that testifies to a mainly positive audience response, see Jean Macpherson, "Premiere Pleases Playwright," *Star-Phoenix*, February 2, 1973.

47   Saskatchewan Archives Board, Globe Theatre Production Files, unidentified newspaper, "How the West Was Stolen!" February 2, 1973.

48   NFB, *Tales from a Prairie Drifter* production files, Ian McLaren, "Proposal for the Western Series...*Tales from a Prairie Drifter*," 1 and 3.

49   For background on Métis activism, see John Weinstein, *Quiet Revolution West: The Rebirth of Métis Nationalism* (Calgary: Fifth House, 2007), 33–34.

50   The part of the story dealing with the particular situation of First Nations people is greatly reduced but not completely eliminated. Their suffering as a result of the elimination of the buffalo is documented. Riel states that he wants Big Bear and Poundmaker at his side. The point of view of First Nations people is introduced and maintained through some of the audience commentary. For an example of the effacing of Riel's French identity, see Albert Braz, "Western Canada's Man: Rudy Wiebe and the De-Frenchification of Louis Riel," unpublished paper presented at the colloquium *Imagining History in the Literatures of Canada and Quebec*, Congrès national des sociétés historiques et scientifiques, Quebec City, June 6, 2008. Also see Braz, *The False Traitor*, 178–179.

51   In both texts, Riel affirms he is Métis and will found "a new church...the Catholic and Apostolic Church of the French Canadian Métis." In other scenes, the play reiterates the fact that the Métis speak French.

52   Rod Langley, *Tales from a Prairie Drifter* [copyright 1972] (Toronto: Playwrights Co-op, 1974), I.6.5.

53   See ibid., I.7.7 for the reference to "speak white" in the play.

54   In 1970 it released the film *La nuit de la poésie 27 mars 1970*; in 1977 it released a separate clip of Lalonde reading her poem as part of the series *Extraits de la nuit de la poésie*, and in 1980 Pierre Falardeau and Julien Poulin directed an illustrated version of a reading of the poem by Marie Eykel in a new, six-minute film.

55   His sister's lines are from a letter she wrote to Riel in September 19, 1870. See Sara Riel, Letter No 42, in *To Louis from your sister who loves you Sara Riel*, ed. Mary V. Jordan (Toronto, Griffin House, 1974), 112–113. It is yet unconfirmed whether the quotation from his former financée, Évelina Barnabé, is from an actual letter. They did correspond.

56   While in interviews Langley claims that Riel was insane (see Saskatchewan Archives Board, Globe Theatre Production Files, unidentified newspaper, "How the West Was Stolen!" February 2, 1973) and while McLaren does not shy away from the scenes depicting him as a religious fanatic, including Langley's depiction of Riel as a "cardboard prophet," audience commentary from Howard Adams argues that the federal government was constructing Riel as a "religious demagogue" in a political manoeuvre to discredit him in the eyes of devout Roman Catholics in Quebec and that the play merely reflects this situation.

57   One audience member's comment on the Langley play qualifies the notion of "other" along racial and cultural rather than Christian denominational lines, explaining Riel's religion was "a white man's religion," which led to his lack of support from "the Indian people."

58   Some, such as Gilles Martel, argue Riel was a Millenarian, "one of a long list of Christian mystics," Riel, *The Collected Writings*, xxvi. Others believe he was insane. In the play Riel expounds on his ideas for the Exovidat, "a special council," composed of ten Métis men of God, who will pass laws and run the nation (Act II, Scene 8, 34).

BADLANDS AND BONES
TOWARDS A CONSERVATION AND SOCIAL HISTORY OF DINOSAUR PROVINCIAL PARK, ALBERTA

STERLING EVANS

Dinosaur Provincial Park in southeastern Alberta's Red Deer River Valley represents Canada's largest area of badlands topography and is the country's crown jewel in paleontological research. More dinosaur fossils have been discovered in and around this nearly 7,500-hectare preserved area than any other single place on Earth. It is, as the director of the Royal Tyrrell Museum of Paleontology has called it, "one of the few places on earth that provide a nearly complete picture of dinosaur-dominated ecosystems in the latest Cretaceous." Due to the park being in an area that once was situated on the shores of a great inland sea, its sediments contain "an unbelievably rich fauna and flora."[1] This combination of badlands and bones, then, became a *cause célèbre* for Albertans in the early-twentieth century to advocate for protection of the region—something that became reality in 1955, Alberta's jubilee year as a province, when the province established Dinosaur Provincial Park (DPP). As the largest badlands in Canada, and representing conservation initiatives in the oft-overlooked arid plains of the Prairie provinces, DPP must be understood in its larger context. This chapter offers a corrective approach to the more localized reading of DPP in the extant literature, and promotes a more complete telling of the environmental, social, and political history of Alberta's badlands region. Matters to consider include the importance of geology and paleontology to the park's development, especially as those disciplines tell us a great deal about past ecological change, the perceptions of this landscape held by Aboriginals and newcomers, the history of conservation efforts and policies leading to the area becoming a provincial park, and how tourism developed around the area famous for its badlands and bones.

The first point here, however, is to define badlands. One useful definition suggests that badlands are characterized by "steep, barren land, usually broken by narrow channels and sharp crest ridges that result from rapid erosion, often of unconsolidated sediments," and are "most common in dry areas."[2] Its geomorphology reflects that wind and water, over time, eroded clay-rich soil and softer sedimentary rocks to form ravines, gullies, canyons, outcrops called hoodoos, and other geological forms. The descriptions are certainly accurate for DPP and the area around Drumheller, Alberta, where residents have marketed their badlands topography, especially the many hoodoos and dinosaur fossils, for tourism. Likewise, the provincial government's tourism ministry promotes Alberta's southeastern corner as the "Canadian Badlands."[3]

Alberta's topography reflects the reason why badlands are sometimes referred to in common vernacular as "inverted mountains," dropping off the plains while various isolated hills and mountain ranges rise above them. They are part of a larger system of "islands on the plains" that helps to refute the description that historical geographer Walter Prescott Webb used many years ago when calling the Great Plains arid, treeless, and flat, or more specifically, "characterized by a plane, or level, surface."[4] Residents and scholars of the Great Plains region, however, know that there are so many exceptions to that rule that it should be dismissed outright. Upland rises such as the Wichita Mountains in Oklahoma, the Black Hills in South Dakota, the Bear Paw Mountains in Montana, and other isolated ranges, as well as rolling hill areas such as Saskatchewan's Great Sandhills and Manitoba's Spirit Sands, prairie canyons, and badlands that dot geographical maps of the Great Plains all illustrate that the region as a whole, despite popular misconceptions, is hardly level or flat. Ecologists understand these areas as unique bioregions and study them in terms of island biogeography associated with high degrees of organic endemism (species found there and nowhere else).[5] Granted, there are indeed areas within the region that are completely flat, but the variety of contoured areas within the region should not be neglected.

Although this region in Alberta is unique to Canada, it is not for the greater North American West. From northern Mexico, across the western United States, and into the Prairie provinces there are dozens of so-called badlands units. The map in Figure 1 indicates the locations of these units, and divides them into what I classify as badlands of the Great Plains grasslands, of the Great Basin and Southwest deserts, and volcanic lava flows (not geologically "badlands" by the definition of erosion, but ones that people in the region, over time, have termed badlands). Combined, the total size of the badlands in the greater West is roughly five million hectares or 50,000 square kilometres, nearly equivalent to the size of Nova Scotia.[2] If somehow that chunk of land were merged together in one place, it would be an astonishing wilderness in the middle of western prairies, basins, or deserts and would surely be the topic of countless studies and books. But because the units are scattered throughout this large region and over three countries, their histories have only been told locally and in many cases, inadequately, although there is no scarcity of studies, articles, and books on the areas' geology and paleontology.[6] Figure 1 also shows that badlands are intrinsically a western phenomenon. The vast majority of them occur west of the 100th meridian, also known as the aridity line, more or less where rain is too scarce to water crops adequately. The dryer the area the more prone it becomes to erosion, and the formation of badlands.[7]

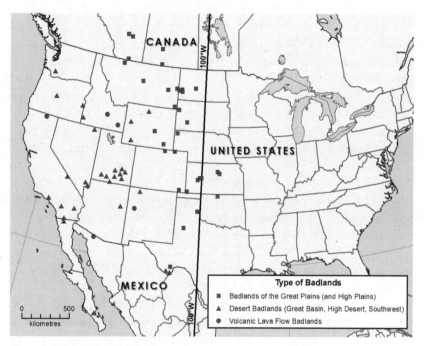

Figure 1 *Badlands locations and typology (Map courtesy of Wenonah Fraser Van Heyst, Dept. of Geography, Brandon University; Brandon, MB)*

The map also shows how DPP is located at the northernmost arc of the grassland badlands zone, illustrating how it should be located historically within this broader regional and transnational context. Like other badlands in the region, DPP is comprised of sandstone, shale, clay, and bentonite, with canyons and gullies formed over eons of erosion. The sediments that remain can be observed in the strata of the buttes and ravine walls; they comprise the bedrock of three different geologic formations in the park, including the middle one named for the park itself. From the ground up they are: the Oldman Formation (76.5 Ma [*Mega annum*, or millions of years ago]); the Dinosaur Park Formation (75.3 Ma); and the Bearpaw Formation (74.8 Ma). Thus, the badlands were formed over a span of 2.8 million years during the late Campanian Stage of the Cretaceous Epoch (145.5 to 65.5 Ma). The sediments in these formations are the remnants of enormous ancient rivers and coastal lowlands that characterized the area those eons ago.[8] An Alberta Recreation, Parks, and Wildlife official explained to a researcher for the National Geographic Society that the sandstone formations are composed of sediment deposited by "slow-moving rivers 70 to 75 million years ago." Then, as time passed, the deposits deepened and the earth cooled; when the glacial ice melted 10,000 years ago, the rushing meltwater "cut swaths into the newly exposed earth, revealing the 75 million-year-old deposits." And the process continues, with the badlands always growing and thus exposing "new" dinosaur bones.[9]

The majority of the park's fossils are found in Dinosaur Park, that middle formation where the number and diversity of discoveries has been nothing short of extraordinary. Phillip J. Currie has written that "the Park is one of the richest sources of Late Cretaceous terrestrial vertebrate fossils and has produced important specimens for more than a century," and paleontologist Dale Russell has argued that DPP's ancient landscape "nourished the apogee of dinosaurian excellence, as reflected in their diversity, activity levels, and behavioral complexity." As the badlands continue to form, the ravines disclose remains of ancient animals "unduplicated elsewhere."[10] Paleontologists have discovered some sixty species of dinosaurs from forty-five genera and seven families including a vast array of the famed *Tyrannosaurus rex* and *Albertosaurus* species—named in honour of the establishment of the province in 1905. The park is especially rich in evidence of *Hadrosaurs* (the ornithischians, or duck-billed dinosaurs such as the *Trachodon* and the *Edmontosaurus*, also named in honour of the province). There is also a large assortment of other reptiles such as ancient crocodilians and turtles, a great variety of freshwater vertebrates (e.g. sharks, rays, paddlefish, bowfins, gars), ancient amphibians, and mammals (e.g. shrews, marsupials, and rodents); however, the evidence of mammals is more from fossilized teeth than from entire skeletons. Thousands of specimens have been removed from DPP for study and exhibition at museums around the world. This activity was especially robust between 1979 and 1991, when paleontologists collected a total of 23,347 fossil specimens including 300 dinosaurs from thirty-five species.[11] As Russell concludes, "the great fossil field stands as a benchmark for assessing dinosaurian evolution, ecology, biogeography, and extinction," all of which is compelling information for the studying of the area's environmental history.[12]

While the ancient environment of this place was semi-tropical, few mega-plant fossils have been discovered in DPP. As paleobotanist Eva Koppelhus writes, plant fossils are not the "resource that made Dinosaur Provincial Park world famous." Fossilized pollen, spore samples, and petrified wood collected in the badlands, however, show that the region was part of a vast coastal plain characterized by mixed forests made up of sycamore, magnolia, bald cypress, sequoia, and other conifers. The evidence has come from carbonized compressions and impressions, petrifications, and amber commonly found in "coaly layers in laminated vegetable units and carbonized logs."[13] There is also fossil evidence of a great variety of ferns and flowering plants, although little research on them has been published. Paleontologists have compared the region of 72 million years ago to something resembling today's cypress swamps of coastal North and South Carolina.[14]

The human prehistory of this area is in some ways more difficult to track than that of the prehistoric megafauna. There is far less evidence to go by, but archaeologists have discovered several sites within DPP that are representative of the Indigenous culture that stretched across the northern Great Plains. Artifacts discovered include a vision quest site, teepee rings, arrow points, scrapers, medicine wheels, rock writing, burial sites, and boulder figures that date human habitation of the region to as early as 8,000 years ago.[15] This part of southeastern Alberta is home to the three tribes of the Niitsitapi (Blackfoot Nation): the Kanai (Blood), the Piikani (Peigan), and the Siksika (Blackfoot). Likewise, the Nakoda (Stoney) and Assiniboine peoples travelled, hunted, and lived in this part of southeastern Alberta.

But what were Aboriginal people's views and perceptions of the badlands? More research is needed on this question, but some authorities have hinted at valid possibilities, and comparing more well-known notions of badlands by other Northern Plains people could be useful here. Philip Currie, for example, has asserted "the badlands of this area inspired the indigenous peoples of North America for thousands of years." He has written that the Piikani peoples knew very well about the bone beds in the badlands and showed fossils to the Jesuit priest Jean-Baptiste L'Heureux in 1871. In what is probably the first historical record of these fossils, L'Heureux wrote an unpublished account of the bones that he said the Piikani referred to as coming from the "grandfather of the buffalo."[16] In similar fashion, Dale Russell hints that the area's First Nations may have considered the badlands as a kind of sacred topography: "Long before the arrival of Europeans, the badlands of Deadlodge Canyon [in DPP] were special to the people of the Blackfoot [Nation]. There, they contemplated relationships between the material and spiritual worlds, as well as to the massive bones of the 'Grandfather of the Buffalo.'" To Indigenous peoples (as well as to immigrant peoples later), he writes, the badlands' "barren landscapes evoke[d] vistas of time without conceivable limits."[17] Russell's analysis meshes with what archaeologist Linea Sundstrom has discovered on how Native peoples often did see Great Plains anomalies such as mountains and canyons as "sacred islands." The "special landscape features" had "specific religious significance for aboriginal Plains dwellers" who would also "maximize their access to usable resources," both uses indicating a special "human-landscape interaction."[18]

South of the forty-ninth parallel, however, there is evidence to indicate that some Indigenous peoples did not always consider badlands areas in the Northern Plains as sacred. The Lakota used the term *mako sika,* meaning "no good land" or "bad soil" for the badlands in what is now eastern Montana and western North and South Dakota. The terrain, replete with all the gullies, canyons, buttes, and outcrops, was certainly not conducive for hunting bison, nor was the land suitable for agriculture for the more sedentary First Nations in the region, such as the Mandan, Hidatsa, and Arikara, who grew corn and beans to trade with the Lakota, Crow, Assiniboine, and other Indigenous groups in the Northern Plains. It was also difficult terrain to cross, and nomadic groups avoided the badlands when possible, although assuredly they used the cottonwood bottoms along the rivers for hunting deer, gathering wood, and occasional encampments, and perhaps used badlands for vision quests.[19] Thus, the impressive badlands areas that are today in the Little Missouri National Grassland, Theodore Roosevelt National Park, and Little Missouri State Park in North Dakota, Badlands National Park and Buffalo Gap National Grassland in South Dakota, and Makoshika State Park in Montana were indeed that—*mako sika.*[20]

The Siouan peoples were not alone in thinking that the badlands of the Northern Plains were "no good lands." As European explorers and settlers moved into the region, the badlands were barriers to transportation, trapping, trade, and agriculture. The first European account we have of reactions to badlands is that of the expedition of Pierre Gaultier de Varennes, Sieur de la Vérendrye, who sought to discover an inland sea that could connect the interior of North America with the Pacific Ocean. In 1738 he and his expedition party stumbled upon the badlands of what is today North Dakota and Montana and, as legend goes, declared them to be *les mauvaises terres*—French for "the bad lands"—they were bad lands to cross ("*Ils sont les mauvaises terres a traverser!*")—and hence perhaps permanently adding that term to the geographic lexicon of such terrains.[21] Further south (and outside the scope of this essay, but worthy of mention here), Spanish explorers were looking for mineral wealth across the far northern frontier of New Spain when they happened onto the vast expanses of volcanic lava flows of what is today western New Mexico. Also viewing them as barriers in their way and as lands unsuitable for mining or agriculture, the Spaniards called the area *el mal pais*—"the bad country." Today it is preserved as El Malpais National Monument under the administration of the U.S. National Park Service. Thus, the monikers of *mako sika*, *les mauvaises terres*, *el mal pais*, and "bad lands" linguistically represent common perceptions of North American badlands by Indigenous and newcomer peoples.

In the Northern Plains, other explorers continued to encounter badlands areas and were struck with their uniqueness. The journals of the Lewis and Clark Expedition (1803–1806) refer to some of the badlands in the Missouri Breaks area of Montana as "the burnt hills" and William Clark wrote that what are today's Terry Badlands were of "various Coloured earth," red and coal black, and "washed into Curious formed mounds and hills and…cut much with reveens." Early Anglo settlers who encountered badlands in the area often complained that the terrain was "hell with the fires put out." In the DPP area of Alberta, there were few such non-Native settlers, but "Happy Jack" Jackson and John Ware were two of the most well-known and colourful characters to attempt ranching in the region. Both were rugged homesteaders engaged in trying to eke a living out of a harsh terrain. According to accounts, Jackson was a "whisky-sopping, gun-toting hermit" who lived in a modest cabin on the "Mexico Ranch" in the Red Deer River badlands. Ware, a six-foot-three-inch 200-pound African-Canadian cowboy and superb horseman, built a short-lived ranch in the badlands but eventually left the area, adding to its reputation as no good for farming or ranching. His L-shaped cabin is preserved in DPP near the visitors' centre and is open for tourists. An old gravel road running from Brooks to the park follows what was known as the John Ware Trail.[22]

South of the border, Theodore Roosevelt found solace and loved ranching and hunting out in the badlands of western North Dakota (known then as Dakota Territory). Although he described them as having a "desolate and grim beauty," a "dreary and forbidding aspect," and a "look of savage desolation," he admired the "fantastic shapes," how in "their coloring they are as bizarre as in form," and that they made for "good cattle country" with "plenty of nourishing grass and excellent shelter from the winter storms."[23] Famed architect Frank Lloyd Wright had an even more perceptive and artistic description than most easterners may have had viewing the badlands; having seen them for the first time in 1935, he proclaimed that the ones in South Dakota that later became Badlands National Park left him with "an indescribable sense of mysterious otherwhere." He wrote that although he had seen much of the United States, he was "totally unprepared for that revolution called the Dakota Bad Lands before sunset…. Ethereal in color and exquisitely chiseled in endless detail, they began to reach to infinity spreading into the sky on every side; an endless supernatural world more spiritual than earth but created out of it." Calling for painters and architects to visit this place with its unique light and lines, he concluded, "Yes, I say the aspects of the Dakota Bad Lands have more spiritual quality to impart to the mind of America than anything else in it made by man's God."[24]

More specifically to the DPP area of Alberta, one of the first written descriptive accounts of the region came from the Palliser Expedition that passed through in 1859. Captain John Palliser, a geographer, led the British North American Exploring Expedition through Rupert's Land from 1857 to 1860 to catalogue geological and botanical information about the region. In June of 1859, en route from the Rockies back to Ottawa, the team entered the Red Deer River Valley and proceeded southeast into the barren areas between the Red Deer and South Saskatchewan rivers. Although there is no specific mention of "badlands" in Palliser's accounts, we have hints of that terrain from the various descriptions. Soon after his arrival in the area, the expedition geologist James Hector discovered a variety of fossils and "salicified" trees in the strata of the riverbanks. There is also a great deal of detail about the dryness of the area, miles of burning sand, the intense heat of the prairie July, and a land rife with rattlesnakes, all of which led Palliser to conclude that the area was not fit for agricultural development. But there was also mention of amazing scenery, long prairie views, and the beautiful sweep of the country—indicative of Palliser's eye for detail and beauty in an otherwise barren terrain.[25]

Other expeditions entered the region for other purposes and made similar discoveries. In 1874, the British North America Boundary Survey (1872–74), whose goal was to mark and map the U.S.-Canadian border from Lake of the Woods in Minnesota/Manitoba to the Rockies, entered the Palliser Triangle region. The survey's geologist and naturalist George Mercer Dawson, son of the famous McGill University paleontologist Sir William Dawson, discovered fossilized dinosaur bones in the Wood Mountain area of southern Saskatchewan and in the Milk River badlands area of Alberta. Paleontologists consider Dawson's accounts and specimens to be the first officially reported dinosaur discoveries in western Canada. Then in 1882 and 1883 the Geological Survey of Canada conducted research and surveying in the same region. Dawson's assistants Richard George McConnell and Thomas Chesmer Weston worked for the Survey and found and recovered more dinosaur fossil specimens from around Scabby Butte, near Lethbridge, and other places in southern Alberta.[26] As the area became known for its coal reserves, geologists studied coal beds, especially in the Horseshoe Canyon Formation. In 1884 geologist Joseph Burr Tyrrell, while examining a particular coal seam, as the story goes, was startled to come face to face with a well-preserved skull of the dinosaur that was first thought to be a *Dryptosaurus*, but renamed *Albertosaurus sarcophagus* in 1905. Meanwhile, Weston returned to the area in 1889 and floated the Red Deer River, observing more and more fossils, especially in the Horseshoe Canyon Formation near Drumheller and at Berry Creek and Deadlodge Canyon that are now a part of or near the boundaries of DPP. He recorded that there were vast quantities of dinosaur bones in these places, opening the floodgates for many paleontologists in the 1890s and ever since.[27]

The Canadian Geological Survey continued sponsoring field research to the DPP area in the late-nineteenth century. Its studies represent the evolution from amateur scholarship and freelance collectors to the professionalization of advanced paleontology, especially with the research of Lawrence Lambe, who led the Survey in 1897 and 1898 and published papers on the importance of the bone beds in the Belly River (now Dinosaur Park) Formation.[28] The bone beds attracted scientists from across Canada and the United States, and later many other parts of the world, who sent fossils from even the earliest excavations to natural history museums and universities in Philadelphia, Montreal, Toronto, Ottawa, New York, London, San Diego, Washington, and many other places. What has become known as the "Great Canadian Dinosaur Rush" took place between 1910 and 1936 when forty different professional paleontological expeditions worked in the badlands of what is today DPP.[29]

One of the most famous paleontologists of the early twentieth century, Barnum Brown, from Kansas, had gained a reputation for his dinosaur bone excavations, especially with his discovery of *Tyrannosaurus rex* specimens in Montana. It was there that he heard of the bone beds in the Red Deer River Valley and visited the area in 1910. He uncovered a huge *Albertosaurus* bone bed at Dry Island Buffalo Jump (today also a provincial park) and sent most of the bones to the American Museum of Natural History in New York. The fact that in what is the DPP area there were more fossils than anywhere else he had seen in his career convinced him in 1911 to stay and work there for the next few years. Brown worked steadily in southeastern Alberta through the 1910s, excavating over 300 crates of fossils in that decade. The American Museum of Natural History displays more dinosaurs from Alberta than any other museum in the world, which speaks to Brown's work in the 1910s.[30]

That Brown sent his finds to New York for research, preparation, and display angered many of his counterparts in Canada, leading the Canadian Geological Survey to take a more active role in paleontological research in Alberta and to compete directly with Brown. To do so, perhaps oddly and coincidentally, the Survey hired another well-known Kansas fossil collector, Charles Hazelius (C.H.) Sternberg who, with his two sons Charles (C.M.) and Levi, came to Alberta in 1912 and started work immediately in the park environs.[31] Even more oddly, one of Brown's best assistants was Sternberg's other son, George, although by the next year he ended his contract with Brown and went to work with his father and brothers. Despite some rivalry, the teams remained cordial and tried to stay out of each other's way. By 1913 they were both working in the DPP area where there were plenty of fossils for everyone. In fact, on the Sternbergs' very first day in the area, C.H. discovered a marvellous skeleton of a *Gorgosaurus* while the others were setting up camp! For the next few years, many of the fossils uncovered by the Sternbergs and the Geological Survey were designated for the Natural History Museum in London, with apparently less concern for them leaving Canada for England because of the Imperial connections. The Sternbergs remained important collectors in Alberta off and on until the early 1960s.

As for Canadian museums, the Royal Ontario Museum in Toronto employed zoologist Benjamin Bensley and others, including Levi Sternberg, to collect dinosaur fossils from Alberta for research and display. Museums in Ottawa, Montreal, and of course later in Alberta, display the paleontological wonders uncovered from DPP. Most importantly, in 1985 the Royal Tyrrell Museum in Drumheller, near DPP, opened to display dinosaur fossils uncovered from the area and to employ a team of paleontologists to continue the excavation and research. The Alberta premier at the time, Peter Lougheed, was instrumental in its development and declared that it was the "absolutely right" idea for the museum to be located in Alberta and so near the discoveries. The Royal Tyrrell Museum has been a huge boon to local and provincial tourism, with 10 million visitors since it opened twenty-five years ago. Former premier Ed Stelmach observed that, "We always think of Alberta as oil and gas and maybe agriculture, but you take 10 million people and that is a huge boost to...tourism."[32] There will be plenty of work for the Tyrrell paleontologists and other scientists from around the world for a long time in DPP. As someone who has devoted twenty-five years of his own work at the Tyrrell, Philip Currie notes that, "Even ignoring the rapid erosion of the badlands, which is constantly exposing new fossils, there are enough resources known in the Park (including bone beds and uncollected skeletons) to maintain the collection of data for another century."[33]

Other paleontologists at the Tyrrell not only recognize the importance of the fossil wealth of DPP, but their perceptions about the badlands reflect an important understanding of place. Museum director Bruce Naylor recalls that, "When I first visited the badlands of Alberta's Red Deer River...over thirty years ago with my father and brothers, I little realized what a place of magic it truly is. There is more romance, more importance there than any thirteen-year-old could ever imagine of a single place on this earth." This "romance" and "magic" are matched by the significant role that science plays there. Naylor continues, "Dinosaur Provincial Park—the three words cannot properly convey what this little part of the Earth's surface has meant for the world of paleontology and for

Alberta's place in the world." The area has "been the playground of a dedicated group of American and Canadian paleontologists…. Dinosaur paleontologists, paleoherpetologists, paleomammalogists, paleobotanists, palynologists, invertebrate paleontologists, and geologists of many stripes have used this ancient laboratory to understand the world of 72 million years ago."[34] His colleague Dale Russell agrees, poetically describing the badlands as "an eroded remnant of a world far removed from us in time…. Ghosts of creatures that until recently remained unnamed emanate from fragments of brown bone littering surfaces of white sand…. The badlands are a tangible, delimited site that represents a geometric midpoint in the evolution of terrestrial life. They link humanity to the great, positive living stream issuing from deep time, and thereby carry a spiritual as well as paleontological value."[35]

Paleontologists played an important role in the effort to preserve the area that became DPP in 1955. Efforts to establish a park began as early as 1912 when Canadians became alarmed at the numerous U.S. paleontological expeditions into the badlands that allegedly were depleting the area of fossil resources. Area resident Dr. W.G. Anderson proposed the park idea in 1915, although finances were scarce during the war and there was little support. In the 1930s amateur fossil collecting intensified in the region, especially as badlands rocks and fossils became popular in urban rock gardens. Investigations of illegal pilfering led to some legislation against depleting valuable paleontological resources, but the crisis also led to renewed efforts for developing a protected park. The Great Depression, World War II, and the discovery of large oil reserves in Alberta in 1947, however, diverted attention and funds away from those efforts, and it was not until the spring of 1955, when the Alberta Parks Board convened a meeting with land owners in the DPP area and with various other interested parties, that the park effort was resurrected. Anderson had stayed involved, and forty years later many of his efforts started to pay off.[36] Representatives at the meeting included officials from the local irrigation district, the Parks Board, the Calgary Zoological Society, and paleontologists with the Canadian Society of Petroleum Geologists.

C.M. Sternberg had been one of the most vocal in encouraging the Alberta government to create a conservation unit in the Red Deer River badlands. Supporters used his 1952 survey of the area to help illustrate its importance to be protected for scientific study. After a few other meetings later that spring, the final hurdles were cleared with landowners, especially as Alberta law then permitted park boundaries to enclose private lands, which at that time accounted for nearly a quarter of the park. With that, the legislative assembly, using Order-in-Council 829/55, created Steveville Dinosaur Provincial Park that was originally 8,994 hectares. A timely boost for the park designation came with that year's Golden Jubilee celebration as provincial leaders hastened the park's creation, among other acts, to honour Alberta's fiftieth anniversary as a province. The government shortened the name to DPP in 1961 (Order-in-Council 1928/61) as the Steveville community had basically disappeared and the park maintained no connection to it.[37] Just a few years later, a development-minded provincial government sought to transfer DPP to federal administration with Parks Canada in return for the federal government transferring the much larger Wood Buffalo National Park, in northern Alberta, to the province. The idea was to make "better" use of timber and oil and gas reserves and potential agricultural lands found in Wood Buffalo (established primarily as a large refuge for the last remaining herds of wood bison and whooping cranes) in exchange for the more "barren" DPP. The swap, however, never materialized.[38]

The planning and operation of DPP are guided by the principles outlined in the province's guidelines entitled "Putting the Pieces Together: An Alberta Provincial Parks System Plan" that was adopted in July of 1977 under the category of "Preservation Parks." The principal goal is "to ensure the preservation of representative and unique features of natural or cultural significance for interpretation, education and appreciation." The ministry developed specific goals and objectives for the park within those guidelines in 1978, stating that DPP characterized this larger goal and "was precipitated by the internationally significant paleontological resources occurring in the area" coupled with "the interesting geomorphological formations known as 'badlands'. " Thus, this combination of badlands and bones "provided the basis for Dinosaur Provincial Park's establishment." The document states that DPP's goal is "to preserve the historical and natural resources contained within its boundaries for the purposes of providing the people of Alberta, now and in the future, with the opportunity to understand and appreciate the role of the park's historical resources in the context of natural (paleontology, geology, geomorphology, ecology) and anthropological (native people) evolution and natural settlement." It also includes a statement of explanation regarding the badlands, suggesting that the park's landscape "is unique and still relatively free of the obvious intrusion of man," making it "mandatory that the landscape be protected from further adverse development."[39]

The make-up of the park is unique in the way it is carved up. The majority of the park (63 percent) is public land owned by the province of Alberta, 19 percent is still in private holdings, and the remainder (18 percent) is owned and controlled by the Eastern Irrigation District. Mineral rights, however, are held by the Crown and are freehold, the majority of which are owned by the Canadian Pacific Oil and Gas Company.[40] The park protects what the United Nations Environment Program has called "an outstanding example of ongoing geological processes and fluvial erosion patterns in a semi-arid steppe environment." Likewise, it protects valuable remnants of riparian cottonwood forests along river bottoms that are highly threatened in semi-arid regions. The landscape is also characterized by sagebrush, open shrubland, and grasslands that provide critical winter range for native ungulates such as pronghorn antelope, mule, and white-tailed deer. Likewise, DPP is home to some 160 species of breeding birds, including endangered raptors like golden eagles, prairie falcons, ferruginous hawks, merlins, perching birds such as loggerhead shrikes, plus Brewer's and grasshopper sparrows as well as the threatened Plains spadefoot toad.[41] In the early 1970s there were discussions about reintroducing bison to DPP, as is the case in the badlands national parks of North and South Dakota, but that plan did not materialize primarily out of deference for paleontological research. According to the provincial minister of lands and forests, DPP was more of an "historic type park" and due to the "nature and ecology of badlands areas," the park was "very delicate and could not stand a great deal of abuse." Reintroducing bison, he warned, could lead to "a large number of problems" and to "the destruction of the things in the park we're trying to preserve."[42]

A number of policies and laws help regulate wildlife protection in DPP. The park is zoned for the natural preserve only, with no other development possible within its boundaries. Equally vital and bringing more international attention and protection to the park was the decision of the United Nations Educational, Scientific, and Cultural Organization (UNESCO) in 1979 to designate DPP as a Natural World Heritage Site, one of fifteen across Canada. It was a big affair for Canada and especially for Alberta to secure the UNESCO designation. The Alberta Ministry of Recreation, Parks, and Wildlife worked hard with the federal minister of Indian and northern affairs, J. Hugh Faulkner, and Albertan legislators to rally support, especially when UNESCO delegates visited the site.[43]

To legislate against illegal bone-picking and collecting, the provincial legislative assembly passed the Alberta Heritage Act of 1973 and the Alberta Historical Act of 1978 that protect all paleontological, prehistoric, and historic resources on both Crown and private lands. The ministry mandated updated resource management and general management plans in 1990 and 2003 respectively to provide for periodic reviews of future uses, development, management, and interpretation and education in the park. The plan strictly controls visitor access to all areas within the park; most of the park is only accessible via small buses, with park rangers giving guided tours of the trails and some of the historic dinosaur-dig sites.[44]

The access limitation regulations were central to protecting DPP's badlands and paleontological resources, but they were contentious with some visitors. Jim Butler, head of Interpretation and Education at DPP in the 1970s, explained that "virtually all of Dinosaur Provincial Park is restricted in access…because of the fragile landscape and value of the fossils." Thus, the bus tours were the only way to control the number of people who went into some of the interior areas of the park, and were the only opportunity available for the elderly, families with small children, and handicapped visitors to "experience the badlands first-hand." But he admitted the vans were hot, especially when temperatures climbed up to 40°C or higher. And in those years, the park had only one older van; the park needed a newer and upgraded model, Butler advised.[45] This upset some tourists who wanted to use their own vehicles. One visitor from Elkwater, Alberta, wrote park officials to say that he had driven an "Econoline [van] full of guests" wanting to go to the restricted area. The park administration did allow occasional waivers if a party that wanted access went through the proper permit procedures; for example, in 1974 park officials allowed a field trip sponsored by the National and Provincial Parks Association of Canada, which was convening its annual meeting in the park that year, into some restricted areas.[46]

Guided tours and an adequate, if somewhat small, visitors' centre, complete with dioramas and fossil samples, represent how park interpretation has always been an important facet of DPP. In fact, Butler cited how the park's activities that his office planned were highly popular with visitors, with 86 percent attending interpretative programs. "The chief recreation activity is interpretation," he wrote in a memo. "Park visitors do not travel to Dinosaur to participate in the usual recreation activities [read: boating, skiing, fishing]. They come to see the badlands and to hear about the dinosaurs."[47] Some of the rangers and employees in the 1970s, graduate students who worked in the parks over the summer, really got into the spirit of interpretation, especially regarding children's programs. They called themselves "The Singing Hadrosaurs" and came up with sing-along songs for the bus tours, campfires, and amphitheatre events. Some of their numbers included "The Dinosaur Park Song," "The Ballad of the Dinosaur Hunters," and the motion song "If You're a Pterodactyl, Flap Your Hands." "The Dinosaur Park Song" included lyrics about the four main park themes: badlands, dinosaurs, fossil hunting, and preservation. Much of this was from the creative mind of DPP interpretive naturalist Jay Kassirer, who worked in the park in the summer of 1977. He claimed that the staff used music to help set the mood, to convey information, and to encourage kids to get involved with what they were learning. He especially liked leading the songs "out in the badlands at sunset" and on bus tours at scenic overlooks and at the end of the tours. He and other staff also developed skits and other ways "to reinforce togetherness."[48]

Many visitors appreciated these efforts, and members of several travel and camping clubs (including the Alberta Roamers Camper Club) wrote in support of the park's programs. Most of the letters were consistent in their high praise of the "helpful" or "outstanding" staff. One guest from St. Albert, Alberta, mentioned in a letter that he and his family especially liked the "Badlands at Night" with all of the singing. Members of a "trailer club" from Calgary wrote to say the kids in their group loved the "dinosaur songs" and went home knowing "a lot more about dinosaurs." A group from the Golden Mile Senior Citizens Centre in Moose Jaw, Saskatchewan wrote directly to Premier Lougheed to say how much they enjoyed their whole visit to DPP.[49] An attendee of a Women in Uniform conference that took place in June of 1977, went to lengths to explain how pleased she, a first time visitor to the park, and others in her group were with DPP and how struck she was by the park's features. She especially appreciated how "great" the restricted areas were that they visited in the park van. She wrote that it was a "terrific idea" to have created a park in such a "unique area" and that it provided "an excellent opportunity to introduce people to a completely different environment, but one which represents a particular combination of sequence of universal processes and ecological structure." Park officials always took the time to answer the letters, expressing appreciation for the visitors' praises and trying to answer complaints. J.E. Potton, an official at DPP, responded to one kind letter saying the praise was "shared by almost all visitors" and that the park's resources "will be protected for the enjoyment of future generations." This was another reason that the park authorities included so many educational programs, as according to Potton, "thousands of school children visited Dinosaur" in the months of May and June.[50]

Similar letters came in from all over North America. One particularly enthusiastic couple from Sarasota, Florida, mentioned how much their family loved DPP and how they thought the national and provincial parks of Canada were "one of the few saving graces of this century." George Mitchell from Edmonton wrote to say that after his visit to park he thought DPP was "one of the most interesting and unique parks in the world." A medical doctor from Virden, Manitoba, visiting with his "seven young daughters" in 1977 commented that he had noticed that a *Brontosaurus* tail bone on display had fractured and healed on its own, and how he would discuss this with other bone specialists he knew.[51] An Edmonton grade six teacher wrote about a field trip to the park she took her students on, as did a leader of a Girl Guides camping trip there, both in spring of 1973, and both praising the experiences their students had enjoyed in the park. One particularly noteworthy letter came from the lieutenant commanding officer of the Royal Canadian Sea Cadet Corps "Resolute" (from Leduc, Alberta) who brought his corps to DPP in May 1974 for its annual "camping expedition." He appreciated how "the uniqueness of Dinosaur Provincial Park provided much educational and recreational benefit to the cadets," and he specifically thanked the park workers for providing "invaluable advice and assistance when mechanical troubles plagued our logistics truck—a bit of a dinosaur itself."[52]

Tourists were not always pleased with their experience, with some visitors complaining about the presentation of the dinosaurs. A disappointed but surprisingly uninformed visitor from Wilkie, Saskatchewan, was the harshest, writing directly to the minister of the Alberta Department of Natural Resources about his park experience in 1973:

> The sign announced that dinosaur skeletons from this park had been sent to museums all over the world! However, for the park, not one complete skeleton had been kept for display. In three display cases I saw fossil teeth, toes, claws, vertebrae, even parts of two skulls. Out in the field under three buildings [pavilions] I saw the skeletons of two duck-billed dinosaurs, neither one complete, and a like skeleton of a young ceratopsian, half complete. This was all! In Delta, Colorado, a Mrs. Jones, who is only an amateur, has more fossilized bones on the floor of her garage than your park has in all its display cases, and yet this is called a dinosaur park! The wealth of Alberta comes from oil. The beds for oil were laid down in the age of dinosaurs. Is this the best tribute your government pays to that vanished age?

He attached an article from the *Brooks Bulletin* (11 July 1973) that mentioned, to his great alarm (as indicated with a series of exclamation marks he wrote in the margin) that some 120 dinosaur skeletons from the area had been sent to museums all over the world, but caustically exclaimed, "not one complete one for the park!! What kind of management is this?"[53] An official at the ministry responded a few days later providing some of the important historical background to address this complaint. "I would suggest to you that most of these specimens were removed prior to the time that the province had any control over this land," he began, informing the visitor that public lands administration in the Prairies was held by the federal government until the 1930s. Moreover, much of the park used to be private property outside the control of any governmental regulation until the passage of the Alberta Heritage Act in 1973—the very year of his complaint. The letter went on to explain that park development had also been slow due "to a lack of funds and also the possibility that the area might be taken over by the Federal Government for National Park purposes."[54]

Many letters arrived at DPP headquarters criticizing long waits, made worse with antsy children, for the buses to take them to the limited access parts of the park. Others faulted the facilities and access roads. This was particularly true of representatives of area chambers of commerce and those in the tourism industry. M.A. Valli editorialized in his local paper that the road from Brooks to the park "is a dusty much-travelled road and is no inducement for the tourist to take" and he recommended that the province pave the John Ware Trail to the park.[55] But the question that park officials struggled with was whether better roads would bring in *too* many tourists, especially as more and more people started coming in the late 1970s with the park's "proximity to the Trans-Canada Highway," as a representative of the club Travel Alberta noted. Likewise, the park's campground in the 1970s could only accommodate fifty units, and park personnel did not want to have it expanded to fit any more. An internal letter from one official to another stated that "random camping" when the campground was full was starting to show its wear: "As a result of uncontrolled camping…ecological damage to the campground area has become very apparent."[56] Overcrowding led to other disadvantages, as a representative of the Big Country Tourist Association from Hanna, Alberta, observed in the late summer of 1978. He complained of what he called "deplorable conditions" at DPP, fielding complaints from his association membership of an "overabundance of litter," "dirty cook stoves," and insufficient water, advising that "maintenance should get on this." A park official countered, "I cannot agree that conditions are deplorable," but did offer that despite "ever increasing visitor use" the park was still "comparatively underdeveloped," making it difficult for the maintenance personnel to keep up with needs.[57] Finally, a particularly unorthodox complaint surfaced in 1977 when a visitor told a park ranger that during an interpretive presentation slide show all of a sudden a picture of a nude female park employee was shown to the audience. There was no mention as to why this took place, and no written complaints ever came in about the incident, but in an internal letter, a park official recommended "better oversight" to avoid a repeat offence.[58]

In order to evaluate management strategies in the park's twenty-some years of existence and to compare strategies and results in other paleontologically rich badlands preserves in the greater West, DPP officials originated the idea to host a Creative Planning Workshop "Think Tank" for October 1978. They invited officials from the Western Region of Parks Canada, Badlands National Monument (now National Park) in South Dakota, Dinosaur National Monument in Colorado, environmental education consultants, members of the Calgary Board of Education, paleontologists, geologists, a variety of officials from other provincial parks in Alberta, and natural historians from museums for a three-day workshop. Some of the goals of the sessions were to discuss growing pains, land acquisition problems, a "should we or shouldn't we" discussion of camping and alternatives, and the growing concern with oil and natural gas exploration and development in the region. The meetings generated not only good discussion of these issues, but also an exchange of ideas and research materials "regarding the future development of the park."[59]

The "Think Tank" workshop was a place to offer some conclusions on DPP's development and how to locate it within a transnational history of North American badlands. Commonalities surfaced at the meeting in terms of management, relationship to, and problems associated with area tourism (especially as community leaders in Drumheller, blessed with the Royal Tyrrell Museum and its own badlands and hoodoos, started to market the town as the "Dinosaur Capital of the World"), how other areas performed their balancing act between paleontological research and badlands conservation, and the struggles with more recent efforts to develop oil and natural gas in the area.

As essential as the comparative analysis is, DPP remains, in many ways, a unique place. It is unsurpassed as the world's leader in dinosaur fossil recovery. Its findings fostered the development of one of the world's best paleontological research centres and museums, and the only such facility located *in* a remote badlands environment. The park is Canada's largest badlands and continues to evolve practically before our eyes. "The badland areas are eroding at the rate of approximately one-half inch per year," posited Alberta Director of Parks T.A. Drinkwater, "thus creating the possibility of uncovering new specimens at any time." That is why he advised that "restricted areas will still be necessary to protect this very important heritage resource for Albertans and indeed Canadians."[60]

Discussion of these themes offers an environmental history approach to the larger trans-border Northern Plains, especially as a corrective to the lacuna in the historiography of badlands and their preservation. An important part of that larger story is how various parts of human society have perceived badlands, something this essay reflects. Perceptions are important to consider, as they have dictated understandings and policy formulation in the region. Can they continue to do so? What role will the geology and paleontology of places like DPP have in our understanding of environmental change? As Dale Russell has pondered, "how does a world separated from the present by 80 million years inform us of the world in which we live today?"[61] And thus the question answers itself. Science will continue to place high value on a place like the badlands of Dinosaur Provincial Park as a limitless laboratory to explore past ecological history. And in the process of conserving such a space, its educational and recreational opportunities, not to mention its stunning geographical beauty, are equally limitless.

NOTES

1   Bruce G. Naylor, "Preface," in *Dinosaur Provincial Park: A Spectacular Ancient Ecosystem Revealed*, eds. Philip J. Currie and Eva B. Koppelhus (Bloomington: Indiana University Press, 2005), xxi.

2   Chris Park, *A Dictionary of Environment and Conservation* (Oxford: Oxford University Press, 2007), 39.

3   See, for example, www.tpr.alberta.ca, www.traveldrumheller.com, and www. comeexplorecanada.com for maps indicating these regions and tourism designations.

4   Walter Prescott Web, *The Great Plains* (Lincoln: University of Nebraska Press, 1981), 7.

5   For a good example of scholarly work on this notion of island biogeography in the Great Plains, see Marcel Kornfeld and Alan J. Osborn, *Islands on the Plains: Ecological, Social, and Ritual Use of Landscapes* (Salt Lake City: University of Utah Press, 2003).

6   A rare exception is Chuck Haney, *Badlands of the High Plains* (Helena, MT: Farcountry Press, 2001).

7   This essay is part of a larger manuscript to be entitled *Badlands: A Landscape History of Canyons, Breaks, and Badlands of the North American Great Plains.*

8   David A. Eberth, "The Geology," in *Dinosaur Provincial Park*, eds. Currie and Koppelhus, 54–55. For more on creation of badlands, see Robin Digby and Linda Ecklund Digby, *The Drumheller Badlands* (East Coulee, AB: Groundwork Natural Science Education, 1991), 3–5.

9   Provincial Archives of Alberta (hereafter PAA) GR1988.0155, Box 3, Vol. 7, David McIntyre to Jennifer West, 7 December 1978.

10   Philip J. Currie, "History of Research," *Dinosaur Provincial Park*, 3; Dale A. Russell, "Foreword," *Dinosaur Provincial Park*, xviii.

11   United Nations Environment Program (UNEP), World Conservation Monitoring Centre, fact sheet on Dinosaur Provincial Park, Alberta, Canada, 2, 3, http://www. unepwcmc.org/sites/wh/pdf/Dinosaur%20Park%20Canada.pdf(2007) (accessed 1 August 2011). For details of the history of these excavations, see Currie, "History of Research," 3–33. For more general information, see Renie Gross, *Dinosaur Country: Unearthing the Badlands' Prehistoric Past* (Saskatoon: Western Producer Books, 1985), or his updated version, *Dinosaur Country: Unearthing the Alberta Badlands* (Warlow, AB: Badlands Books, 1998).

12   Russell, "Foreword," xviii.

13   Eva B. Koppelhus, "Paleobotany," *Dinosaur Provincial Park*, 13.

14   Russell, "Foreword," xvii–xviii.

15   PAA, GR1988.0155, Box 3, vol. 5, p. 2 "The Dinosaur Provincial Park, Alberta," unpublished memo, Alberta Ministry of Recreation, Parks and Wildlife, 1975; UNEP fact sheet, 2.

16   Currie, "History of Research," 3, 8.

17   Russell, "Foreword," xvii. I borrow the term "sacred topography" here from Sabine MacCormack, *Religion in the Andes: Vision and Imagination in Early Colonial Peru* (Princeton: Princeton University Press, 1991), 433.

18   Linea Sundstrom, "Sacred Islands: An Exploration of Religion and Landscape in the Northern Great Plains," in Kornfeld and Osborn, *Islands on the Plains*, 258.

19   This theory matches what others have written about Indigenous use of prairie canyons and badlands. See William E. Banks, "Catchment Basins as Islands in West-Central Oklahoma: Farra Canyon," in Kornfeld and Osborn, *Islands on the Plains*, 67–88. Banks explains that archeological evidence suggests strongly that early Indigenous people in

the area used Farra Canyon "primarily for hunting and related processing activities and short-term occupations."

20 Another angle to pursue here is the idea of badlands as refuges, as secure hiding places for First Nations people against enemy pursuits. Did Hunkpapa leader Sitting Bull take refuge in the badlands of southern Saskatchewan (possibly the Big Muddy area or parts of what is today Grasslands National Park—they did not go so far west as DPP), and if so, what perceptions and memories can we trace about their understandings of badlands?

21 Digby and Digby, *The Drumheller Badlands*, 3. On the Vérendrye expedition, *see* Hubert G. Smith, *The Explorations of the La Vérendryes in the Northern Plains, 1738-43* (Lincoln: University of Nebraska Press, 1980); Grace Flandreau, *The Vérendrye Overland Quest of the Pacific* (Seattle: Shorey Bookstore, 1971); and Lawrence J. Burpee, *Pathfinders of the Great Plains: A Chronicle of La Vérendrye and His Sons* (Toronto: Brook, 1915).

22 "The Dinosaur Provincial Park, Alberta," 1–2; M.A. Valli, "Buck the Shepard," editorial in *Brooks Bulletin*, 30 Aug. 1972, 14.

23 Theodore Roosevelt, "Ranching in the Bad Lands," in *Hunting Trips of a Ranchman: Sketches of Sport on the Northern Cattle Plains* and *The Wilderness Hunter: An Account of the Big Game of the United States and Its Chase with Horse, Hound, and Rifle* (New York: Modern Library, 1885, repr. 2004), 17–18.

24 Frank Lloyd Wright to Robert D. Lusk, reprinted as "Bad Lands" in *South Dakota History* 3, 3 (Summer 1973): 271.

25 Irene Spry, *The Palliser Expedition: An Account of John Palliser's British North America Expedition, 1857–1860* (Toronto: MacMillan of Canada, 1963), 218, 222–223.

26 C.M. Sternberg, "Early Discoveries of Dinosaurs," *Natural History Papers, National Museum of Canada* 21 (26 Sept. 1963): 2–3; Currie, "History of Research," 8–9.

27 Details of these and other expeditions can be found in Currie, "History of Research," 8–10.

28 Russell, "Foreword," xvii.

29 For more on the Rush, see chapter 8 "The Canadian Dinosaur Bone Rush" of Lowell Dingus and Mark A. Norell, *Barnum Brown: The Man Who Discovered Tyrannosaurus Rex* (Berkeley: University of California Press, 2010).

30 Dingus and Norell, *Barnum Brown*, 128–129, and Appendix 3, 312–313; Currie, "History of Research," 10–11.

31 For Sternberg's pre-Canada fossil hunting history, see Charles H. Sternberg, *Life of a Fossil Hunter* (New York: H. Holt and Co., 1909).

32 Reported in the *Drumheller Mail*, 25 Sept. 2010, 1.

33 Currie, "History of Research," 31.

34 Naylor, "Preface," xxi.

35 Russell, "Foreword," xvii, xviii, xix.

36 His son, Jack Anderson of Medicine Hat, sought to have a plaque commemorating his father's work in creating of the park erected at DPP in the 1970s. See PAA, GR1988.155, Box 3, vol. 6, Jack Anderson to V.A. Wood (Chairman, Alberta Lands Forum), 29 May 1974, Wood to Anderson, 31 May 1974, and T.A. Drinkwater to Anderson, 13 June 1974.

37 "The Dinosaur Provincial Park, Alberta," 1; Currie, "History of Research," 12. 15; PAA, GR 1988.0155, Box 3, vol. 7, p. 2. "Park Goal and Objectives for Dinosaur Provincial Park—July 1978," Ministry of Recreation, Parks, and Wildlife, For more on the park's connection to the 50-year anniversary of the province, see Frances Swyripa, "1955, Celebrating Together, Celebrating Apart: Albertans and Their Golden Jubilee," in

Alberta Formed, Alberta Transformed vol. 2, eds. Michael Payne, Donald Wetherell, and Catherine Cavanaugh (Edmonton: University of Alberta Press, 2006), 591.

38   Max Foran, "1967, Embracing the Future…at Arm's Length," in *Alberta Formed, Alberta Transformed*, 635.

39   "Park Goal and Objectives," 1, 3–4.

40   PAA GR1988.0155, Box 3, vol. 5, T.A. Drinkwater (Director of Parks, Province of Alberta) to Dr. Allan A. Warrack (Minister of Parks and Lands), 6 June 1973.

41   UNEP fact sheet, 1-2.

42   PAA GR1988.0155, Box 3, vol. 5, Minister Allan Warrack to Gene M. Johnson (Iddesleigh, AB), 3 October 1972.

43   PAA, Details of the negotiations are in Faulker to J. Allen Adair (Alberta Ministry of Recreation, Parks, and Wildlife), 25 October 1978; and Adair to Faulkner, 29 November 1978.

44   Ibid, 3.

45   PAA, GR1988.0155, Box 3, vol. 7, Jim Butler, "Touring Bus for Dinosaur Provincial Park" memo to Burn Evans, Executive Assistant DPP, 8 June 1976.

46   PAA, GR1988.0155, Box 3, vol. 6, Office of Park Administration to Robert C. Scace (Calgary), 8 May 1974.

47   Butler, "Touring Bus for Dinosaur Provincial Park."

48   PAA, GR1988.0155, Box 3, vol. 7, memo, Jay Kassirer, "The Humming Hadrosaurs: Musical Interpretation at Dinosaur Provincial Park."

49   PAA, GR1988.0155, Box 3, vol. 6, Alberta Roamers Camper Club to Dinosaur Provincial Park, 31 July 1977; Bryan Nordstrom (St. Albert) to Dinosaur Provincial Park, 25 August 1977; Mr. and Mrs. Carrell (Calgary) to DPP, 7 Aug. 1977; and Golden Mile Senior Citizens Centre to Peter Lougheed, 13 June 1977.

50   Susan Bramm to Potton, 8 July 1977, and Potton to Bramm, 27 July 1977; Potton to Colin Brun (Calgary), 21 July 1977, ibid.

51   George Mitchell (Edmonton) to J.E. Potton (DPP), 6 Aug. 1977; Lt. Col. and Mrs. E.W. Kennedy (Sarasota, FL) to J.E. Potton, 20 Aug. 1977; D.E. Yates (Virden, MB) to Minister of Parks and Recreation, 15 Nov. 1977, Ibid.

52   Sonia Lee (Sherwood Elementary School) to Department of Lands and Forests (Edmonton), Apr. 1973; Mrs. Buckner (Girl Guides) to Department of Lands and Forest, 23 Mar. 1973; J.E. Smith (Sea Cadets) to Director Alberta Provincial Parks, 7 May 1974, Ibid.

53   PAA, GR 1988.0155, Box 3, vol. 5, Walter Bieber (Wilkie, SK) to The Minister, Department of Natural Resources (Edmonton, AB), 29 Sept. 1973.

54   Drinkwater to Bieber, 9 Oct. 1973, ibid.

55   Valli, "Buck the Shepard," 14.

56   PAA, GR1988.0155, Box 3, vol. 7, D.W. Smithson (Travel Alberta) to Gerald Beach (Big Country Tourist Association), 31 Aug. 1978; T.C. Hall (Regional Manager) to G.J. Strudwick (Chief of Operations), 12 Sept. 1978.

57   Beach to Travel Alberta Office (Edmonton), 25 Aug. 1978; Strudwick to Beach, 19 Sept. 1978, ibid.

58   Hall to Strudwick, 8 July 1977, ibid.

59   Dinosaur Provincial Park Creative Planning Workshop "Think Tank," memo, ibid.

60   PAA, GR1988.0155, Box 3, vol. 5, Drinkwater to Warrack.

61   Russell, "Foreword," xviii.

PRAIRIE TOWNS
PROCESS AND FORM

BEVERLY A. SANDALACK

Much contemporary discourse in environmental design has been concerned with trying to understand the values and processes that have contributed to the modern environment, with part of the debate concerned with the loss of distinctive regional and local identity and the construction of that identity.[1] Where local and regional identity were once produced almost incidentally and resulted in distinct and unique landscapes, towns, and cities, the visual character of places is now more frequently produced, or protected, intentionally.

At the beginning of the twentieth century, Darcy Thompson argued that the form of an object or organism is a "diagram of the forces" that have acted upon it. Although he was, at the time, referring to biological forms, the concept also applies to the form of a landscape, city, or neighbourhood.[2] The growth of a cultural landscape, region, or city can be understood as the product of the forces acting upon it, and this form can be "read" and the processes explained.

Cultural landscapes refer to geographic areas modified by human activity or given special meaning by a group of people resulting in an area that is distinctive or definable in the form it presents or the values it reflects. They are illustrative of the evolution of human society and settlement over time, under the influence of the physical constraints and/or opportunities presented by their natural environment, and of successive social, economic, and cultural forces, both external and internal. Cultural landscapes are important sources, as well as receptacles, of individual and communal identity, and are often profound centres of human existence to which people have deep emotional and psychological ties.[3] The values cultures place on the land are reflected in changing patterns of land ownership and land development, and consequently in the spatial, visual, and experiential qualities of the built environment. The evolution of a cultural landscape cannot simply be dealt with as a chronology of events; it also reflects the evolution of ideas and ideologies. This paper considers the evolution of Canadian prairie towns, from the settlement era to the present day, not as a strictly historical process but via several forces or form determinants through which ideas of place and identity will be discussed.

The Prairies, as a cultural landscape, have been affected by layer upon layer of human intention and action. Over the past few decades, the determinants that shaped prairie settlement at the turn of the twentieth century, such as the need for regularly spaced grain handling and service centres, have changed. Many towns have failed, but in the towns that persist the practicality, expediency, and distinctiveness of the early morphologies have given way to town planning practices and urban forms that raise concerns about sense of place and urban quality.[4]

LAND

In his address to the Canadian Society of Landscape Architects in 1997, author and commentator Rex Murphy argued that Canadian identity is rooted in its various landscapes, and that our love for these landscapes is what unites us as a nation. He also suggested that we have yet to live up to our landscapes. This may be particularly true of the Prairies, which in some ways is a more challenging region than many.

The Prairies are a region of ethereal and ephemeral beauty, but also the kind of landscape that usually evokes strong feelings, either positive or negative, in people. It can attract and compel, but can also intimidate and repel. The detractors often speak of the Prairies as boring, flat, and tedious; others, however, are attracted to the beauty of the "austere land of violent mood."[5] The relationship between the Earth and sky is important, and the sense of space contributes to its character. The Prairies are both a place and a state of mind.[6] This is powerfully expressed by writer Wallace Stegner, in his autobiography *Wolf Willow*:

> The geologist who surveyed southern Saskatchewan in the 1870s called it one of the most desolate and forbidding regions on earth. Yet... I look for desolation and can find none.

> It is a long way from characterless; "overpowering" would be a better word. The drama of this landscape is in the sky, pouring with light and always moving. The earth is passive. And yet the beauty I am struck by, both as present fact and as revived memory, is a fusion: this sky would not be so spectacular without this earth to change and glow and darken under it. And whatever the sky may do, however the earth is shaken or

darkened, the Euclidean perfection abides. The very scale, the huge-
ness of simple forms, emphasises stability...

Desolate? Forbidding? There was never a country that in its good moments was more beautiful. Even in drought or dust storm or blizzard
it is the reverse of monotonous, once you have submitted to it with all
the senses.[7]

European settlement in the Canadian prairie region is historically recent, and
it took place over a compressed period of time. Following scientific expeditions
to the West during the mid-1800s, the new nation-state of Canada purchased
Rupert's Land from the Hudson's Bay Company for the sum of 1.5 million dollars plus some land claims in 1869. The Canadian government envisioned the
West for white agricultural settlement, despite its centuries-long history as an
Aboriginal-European fur trade society and the longstanding presence of Indigenous peoples on the land. In the late 1800s and early 1900s, the Government of
Canada embarked on a massive promotional campaign to attract non-Aborigi-
nal farmers to the West. Simultaneously, through the treaty and reserve system,
Indigenous inhabitants were dispossessed of their traditional territories, and
Métis resistance movements were suppressed, resulting in the dispersal of Métis
homelands. The conversion of the prairie into farmland occupied by white settlers proceeded relatively quickly, with agricultural development following the
spread of railway branch lines and the accompanying waves of homesteaders.
The boldness of this vision, and the extent of the subsequent ecological transformation of the land, are staggering in their scope. The alteration of the original
prairie ecosystem to today's agricultural landscape is a significant man-made
environmental change that is profound and permanent.

LANDSCAPE

The Prairies are vast and largely uniform, and only occasionally do features of
strong relief occur. The topography falls away to the east from the boreal aspen
forest and the rolling foothills, and three more-or-less distinct sub-regions make
up the prairie region. These coincide generally with differences in elevation, soil
type, moisture regime, and the native vegetation that existed before European
settlement, and result in distinctions in the agricultural practices that proved
successful and the density of population that remains.

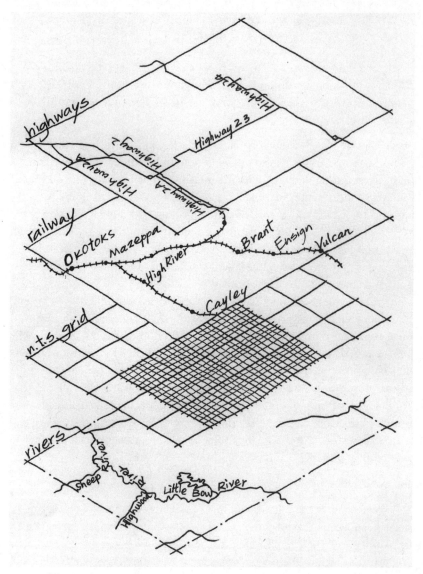

Figure 1 *The original topography and hydrography of the Prairies have been overlain by several patterns. (Drawing by the author)*

In the last decades of the nineteenth century, the land was surveyed and subdivided according to the one-mile grid of the National Topographic System, and a grid road network connected the dispersed farmsteads. The regular grid survey was a convenient and effective way of subdividing and selling land. It influenced the size of farms, as land was settled, bought, and sold according to sections and quarter-sections, and has had a lasting effect on the location of roads and the distribution of the population. It is clearly discernible from the air, and the rhythm of the grid roads is sensed while driving any significant distance.

Figure 2 *The cumulative effect of landscape, survey, and roads have produced the distinctive and much-marked prairie landscape. (Google Earth)*

SETTLEMENT PATTERN

The conversion of the Prairies into occupied farmland proceeded quickly during the late 1800s and early 1900s, with agricultural development following the spread of railway branch lines and the accompanying waves of homesteaders who were attracted by the Government of Canada's massive promotional campaign.

Farmsteads were located close to the roads, and timber-frame houses and barns constructed, often through cooperative efforts. Although the Prairies were largely treeless, it was easier to transport wood than other building materials; entire houses could be ordered from mail-order catalogues, and frame construction required only carpentry skills. Clusters of simple and utilitarian wood sheds built over the first century of settlement are now mostly replaced with equally functional aluminum silos. The original and the newer objects on the agricultural landscape have an aesthetic and a geometrical simplicity that could provide a vocabulary for a regional architecture, but so far has yet to be tapped in any significant way.

Homesteads of one quarter-section (160 acres) were granted and until the end of World War I, homesteaders could purchase an adjacent quarter-section at a nominal price. The early process of land subdivision and homesteading produced the dispersed pattern of settlement, which is a distinguishing characteristic of the prairies. Over time, technological changes replaced horsepower with tractors, and combines did the work of harvest labour gangs so farmers could work more land. Pesticides and fertilizers have continued to improve yields and productivity, but the new machinery and chemicals require larger and larger contiguous fields in order to be used economically and efficiently.

Figure 3 *Farmsteads were established on quarter-sections or larger parcels of land, setting up a spatial order and a social distance, and requiring each farmstead to deal individually with the extremes of climate, through, for example, establishment of trees as shelter belts. (Photo by the author)*

Quarter-section or half-section farms invariably proved to be inadequate, and larger farms, and consequently fewer farm families, are now more common.

As the Prairies were opened up, a rail system was required in order to help bring in the settlers and to move the agricultural produce. A well-developed transportation network was necessary to assert Canadian sovereignty over the adjacent United States who had interest in the lands, and also over Indigenous and Aboriginal territories, and to promote the economic base of the region.[8] The Canadian

Pacific Railway (CPR) negotiated a contract with the Canadian government that provided a land grant of 25 million acres, along with cash, the cost of surveys, and other concessions, which assisted it economically and gave the railway a powerful position in western development that it retains in many ways to this day. The railway was also conceived for its political mission of uniting the country, and its presence, although now much diminished, still has nationalistic symbolic meanings.[9]

Contrary to traditional locational theory whereby gradual and random incremental growth transformed a crossroads hamlet into a town or city, western railway-town establishment and development occurred according to railway company directives.[10] Railway routes were determined taking into consideration such factors as grade, terrain, hydrography, and agricultural potential of the area, and they inscribed a second pattern upon the survey grid. Along the prospective route, land was reserved, the right-of-way purchased, and then from the reserved blocks, townsite location would be considered. Sidings were located at six- to ten-mile intervals, a convenient distance for hauling grain with a horse and wagon, and some of these sidings would become townsites.

The ones that were destined to become towns became distribution points for agricultural implements, feed, coal, lumber, and general merchandise. Larger centres developed at divisional points approximately 110 to 130 miles apart, which was the distance a locomotive of the day could travel without refuelling. These points were where engines and train crews were changed, and they required additional services, such as hotels and banks, and were more actively developed by the CPR. The resulting dispersed nature of the towns (and of the homesteads) established a social distance and a sense of isolation, but also a system of co-operation and mutual care, where the towns functioned for the farmers and ranchers as important social, as well as service, centres.

Transportation technology change has probably had a greater impact than any other force on settlement patterns: the period of establishment and exploitation depended upon the establishment of the railway network, which began in the 1870s and was complete by the early 1930s. The purpose of towns during this period was utilitarian. Construction of a network of highways and improvements of the prairie road network began in the 1930s, a period that saw either the consolidation and expansion, or the collapse, of prairie towns; those that remained usually became established communities. Highway and air travel eventually began to dominate passenger and freight activity. Until the 1950s road networks were generally locally oriented, and the highways were more closely linked to the United States than to neighbouring provinces. In 1950, construction began on the Trans-Canada Highway to provide an east-west route linking the entire country; Highway 1 was opened in 1962. Over time, the inter-city highways were paved and widened, and the grid network of country roads was improved. The Trans-Canada Highway is an element of great importance to the Prairies. It links the cities, and is the first in the easily perceived hierarchy of roads. Rail passenger service was discontinued beginning in the 1970s, and grain handling and transport entered a process of rationalization that introduced new patterns and forms that create another layer on the land.

The concept of distance has a profound meaning on the Prairies—major centres are between 200 and 300 miles apart, and high-speed driving is required to comprehend the spatial order. Travel from the main divided highway to a secondary highway to a gravel or dirt road takes one from a high-speed ribbon of whizzing cars and trucks to a place where space and time are measured in quarter sections and grid roads. Unless one makes the effort to get off the Trans-Canada and onto one of the smaller tributaries, the highway remains as its own place—an asphalt conduit giving few hints of the subtle richness of the landscape that it slices through, or of the population centres that might be located there.

RAILWAYS AND THE GRAIN ELEVATOR SYSTEM

To transport grain to distant markets, more than a railway was needed. Grain elevators combined with and depended upon the railway system, enabling vast amounts of wheat and other grains to be marketed in a relatively cheap and efficient manner. Farmers hauled their crops to the railway siding, where they would be stored in an elevator until loaded on a train, to be transported to a terminal grain elevator at a larger centre.

Grain elevators were painted with the elevator company colours and logo, and usually the town name in large letters near the top. Towns were therefore recognizable from a distance, and the grain elevators were the most prominent buildings in every town, symbols of relative wealth and prestige. Ronald Rees described how the elevators suited the prairies: "The prairie landscape is a landscape of extreme dimensions, described by Frank Lloyd Wright as 'a great simplicity', and it calls for extreme, yet simple, forms. Two seem particularly suited: the low, spreading structure, submitting to the prairie; and the vertical, opposing its dominating horizontality. Only the grain elevator really belongs— its height, firm lines, and strong colours harmonising with the bland prairie and parkland and taking full advantage of the abundant sunlight. It is a self-assured form, confident of its function."[11]

Figure 4 *A long row of elevators in communities such as Vulcan (top, photo by the author, 1993) once signified their regional importance (Vulcan was the largest among the regularly spaced string of places on the line between Calgary and Lethbridge: Mazeppa, Blackie, Eltham, Brant, Ensign, Vulcan, Kirkaldy, Champion, Carmangay, Peacock, Barons, Nobleford, Whitney). Only one elevator remains within the town of Vulcan today (middle, photo by the author, 2008). The new order is represented by concrete structures no longer situated within the towns (bottom, photo by the author, 2005).*

Where the system of towns was originally formed and responded to specific and directed forces, they are now part of the larger and more coarsely grained international community. Over the past few decades, the determinants that shaped prairie settlement at the turn of the century, such as the need for regularly spaced grain handling and service centres, have changed. Transportation methods have shifted from rail to automobile and freight truck, and the network of railways is in decline.

Concurrently, competition and the mechanization of agricultural practices have favoured large corporate agribusiness over the family farm, and the prairie economy has undergone a major structural transformation. Improvement in roads and truck transportation, and a shift to custom hauling of grain which utilizes larger semi-trailer trucks and covers longer distances, means that the short-distance elevators are no longer required. New high-throughput elevators (HTE's or "cement plants") are spaced fifty to 100 miles apart, with catchment areas of a radius of fifty to seventy-five miles and a much larger capacity. Overlap is common, as agri-businesses compete. These massive structures can be more efficiently operated outside of town where huge trucks can access them more easily, therefore this process is now disengaged from, and independent of, the settlements.

As more and more of the high-throughput elevators are constructed, a new order is emerging. Although massive in scale, they still exhibit the same functional efficiency and integrity typical of agricultural buildings. Many of them employ distinctive company colours, and the structures are visible from a great distance. Perhaps this new form will come to represent a new spatial order, and visually express it in the same way as the system of wooden elevators did for the first century. Nearly 6,000 country grain elevators were standing in the 1920s and 1930s; since then their numbers have steadily decreased, as the need for close spacing of elevators became obsolete. In the late-twentieth century, this shift accelerated; from 1982 to 1992 the number of country grain elevators in the Canadian prairies fell from 2,934 to 1,498; and in Alberta, where there were over 500 elevators standing in the early 1990s, there are now fewer than 100.[12] Most of the wooden elevators that still remain are either privately operated, or are vacant. The loss of this highly visible and meaningful symbol of the prairies has spurred efforts to save elevators and to find other uses for them; however, their decline in numbers continues.

The impact of this transformation is important to local and regional contexts. The presence of grain elevators gave the Prairies visual identity and legibility, and provided one of the only ways of orienting oneself on the landscape that otherwise does not have many visual landmarks. On the flat Prairies, grain elevators were the first structures to be seen from a distance, signalling clearly the town's function as an agricultural service centre, emphasizing its location on the rail lines, and signifying refuge and the presence of other people in the otherwise empty land. The potentially disorienting vastness of the Prairies was made human and tolerable by those visual landmarks. Towns which were otherwise largely invisible on the flat plains were identified by the number and colour of the elevators; without the elevators, the towns disappear into the horizon. The elevators gave structure and order to the towns, which now have few differentiating forms; most towns are now clusters of houses and commercial buildings, and there are few visual clues as to the reason for their presence or location. As a result, the social and economic life of the towns has suffered, since farmers no longer have to travel to the towns to ship grain, and at the same time socialize, buy goods, and frequent cafes.

TOWNSCAPE

Sir Sanford Fleming, at one time the chief engineer and surveyor for the CPR, gave directives regarding stations, town plots, roads and crossings. In his *Report on Surveys on the Canadian Pacific Railway*, produced in 1877, Fleming proposed a model plan for town layout, with the station at the centre and the streets radiating out from it.[13] Although it was never realized, and although the CPR did not appear to have a clear policy on townsite layout, subsequent town plans located the station at the centre, with the commercial district huddled around it and the settlement developing outward from there. Plans that could be easily expanded were the norm. The rectangular grid formed the base for general townsite layouts; other plan arrangements were viewed as difficult to use due to their increased complexity of survey.[14]

The major elements used to generate railway town form were the presence of a siding, the railway station, and the main street. The main street was characterized by its larger dimensions, sixty-six feet (the length of a surveyor's chain) or often ninety-nine feet wide, with narrow commercial lots of twenty-five feet in width as compared to residential lots of fifty feet. Towns conformed to a simple structure. There were two linear functional axes—an industrial axis along the railway tracks, and a commercial axis along Main Street, either parallel or perpendicular to each other, depending on town plat. The town centre grew around that intersection in a grid pattern of blocks. Residential streets typically had sixty-six-foot allowances, and included sidewalks and treed boulevards.

Characteristic features were grain elevators along the railway line, the railway station (across the tracks from the elevators), Main Street perpendicular or parallel to the rail line, and a grid network of streets. The attractiveness of the railway stations as social centres increased when railway agents began to plant gardens, a practice that began voluntarily but eventually became company policy. Station gardens were considered valuable in convincing arriving settlers of the fertility of the land, and often gardens were planted in a way to appeal to their cultural values and make them feel more at home.[15]

Figure 5 *The town of Olds, Alberta ca. 1920, typical of prairie railway towns, is legible as a grain handling centre, as a component of the railway system, and as a dense and leafy settlement on the otherwise sparsely inhabited prairies.[16] (Glenbow Archives)*

Early town form was expressive of an "inside-out" development, a form that also reflected how the town was experienced. Goods and people typically arrived at the railway station, and worked their way outward through successive layers of public function. The railway station was not only the first thing that people saw, it was the social and cultural heart of the town, and was imbued with many layers of meaning and association. From the railway station and grain elevators, one could easily locate services such as hotels, banks, and stores. The street patterns were legible, and the size and organization of the buildings were harmonized. The main street and adjacent commercial streets constituted the heart of the town, and were more than just streets, services, and spaces: they were places, and they were a measure of a town's success and prosperity.

In the late decades of the 1900s, and paralleling the changes in grain-handling technology, passenger travel on the Prairies shifted from rail to automobile, and freight transport from train to truck, and the railways experienced a general decline. The transition has generally not been graceful; as railway stations became obsolete, distinctive buildings were either demolished or replaced by utilitarian concrete sheds, the gardens are long gone, and the public and social function of the stations and gardens have not been replaced. The land adjacent to the railway stations is often used for parking lots, or is left vacant, creating what Trancik calls "lost space."[17] The CPR owns most of the land adjacent to the railways, which in most towns means that a large strip of land through the centre of the

Figure 6 *The railway station in Virden, Manitoba has been vacant for many years (top); the original station in Olds, Alberta (a similar structure to Virden's) was replaced by a concrete block shed in the mid-1960s (bottom) after the railway garden adjacent to that station was bulldozed and a strip mall (poignantly named "Garden Park Plaza") and parking lot were built in its place. (Photos by the author, 1991)*

town is in the control of one very powerful absentee land owner. These vacant sites that are left in the middle of the town are destructive to the town's character and erode its functional cohesiveness.

MAIN STREET

Prairie towns, while certainly not identical, had a recognizable vernacular, particularly of Main Street, that was expressive of the traditional materials and ways of building. Timber frame construction, building right up to the property line, doorways that were set back, large storefront windows, and false fronts to present the largest facade for advertising were all features of Main Street. These characteristics are all expressive of the environmental conditions, of the light, and of the culture—the way of doing and being that is easily recognized as being of the Prairies.[18] The architecture of Main Street typically consisted of one- or two-storey buildings with false fronts that concealed the pitched roof behind them, presenting an impression of size and solidity. Most were wood, although significant buildings such as banks were constructed later of sandstone or brick.

Traditionally, there were a limited number of building materials and techniques, and there were consistent ways of doing things, so that the streets hung together as cohesive townscapes. However, there was enough variety from town to town, in terms of local variations in building materials and local businesses, for each town to have a distinct identity; as other materials became available and as traditional construction techniques evolved or new ones were imported, various eras became identifiable through the historic record of built form. Although there was change, it was gradual and related to what came before; and as the streets and public spaces provided an underlying unifying structure, there was continuity.

Many historic downtown commercial centres began losing business in the last decades of the twentieth century to highway strip malls or to out-of-town shopping centres, which are better positioned to capture the transient automobile traffic. This resulted in local economic loss, in a decline in social vitality in the town centres, and in corporate homogeneity replacing local individuality and character. The issue received significant professional and public attention.

As early as the mid-twentieth century, the decline of the prairie town economy and image was being recognized. The cultural heritage of the small town, embodied in the historic business districts, and its economic vitality, traditionally localized on Main Street, was threatened by the strip malls that were springing up along the highway entries. Coupled with this was the visual deterioration of the historic commercial and residential areas, as original buildings were demolished or renovated beyond recognition, or mutilated and obscured by signage and additional layers of "modernizing" features.

Figure 7 *The Main Street in Olds, Alberta is recognizably of a prairie town: the false-fronted buildings facing right up to the property line, the local businesses, and the angle parking are typical and characteristic. Although there was variation in materials and design, the buildings formed one cohesive whole (top, photo c. 1950 by D. Becker). The main element of the highway strip mall ca. 1970 in Olds (middle, photo by the author) is the large parking lot in front. The latest variation is the more recent construction of big-box stores, in this case a Walmart on the edge of the town of Pincher Creek, Alberta (bottom, photo by the author).*

Attempts to address the economic decline of Main Street businesses began in the 1970s, most notably and successfully by the federal and provincial Main Street Programs, which focused revitalization around heritage resources. In the initial Main Street Canada projects, seven communities with important heritage

Figure 8 *The Main Street Canada pilot project in Fort Macleod, Alberta attempted to combine image enhancement through period restoration with marketing strategies. The aim of that project, started in 1982, was to restore the image of the commercial buildings in the downtown historic area to an approximation of the 1920s, while improving their usability for business. The program also had economic benefits, and Fort Macleod's restored Main Street continues to be one of the town's primary tourist destinations. (Photo by the author, 2002)*

resources were selected. From 1981 to 1985, Heritage Canada Foundation coordinators worked with the business communities of these towns to become more effective in competing with the strip malls, not by "promoting the prettification of Main Street" but by "encouraging communities to restore the life that was already there, by working with the people who were already there."[19] By 1990, over seventy communities throughout Canada had become involved in the second phase of the program. The goal of the program, "to combine preservation techniques with economic and social revitalization of a community's commercial centre through a gradual process of incremental change," involved organization and management, marketing the downtown and individual businesses, as well as urban design and economic and commercial development strategies.[20]

Figure 9 *Especially notable in High River are some individual properties that reflect many of the qualities and characteristics of Main Street (which are now also considered to be some of the qualities of good urbanism) including a small set-back, permeable facade (entry off the street and large windows), mix of uses (including commercial at grade and residential above), and compatible materials—and all of this within a contemporary architectural envelope. (Photo by the author, 2006)*

In 1994, Heritage Canada Foundation withdrew from Main Street Canada, and main street improvement programs have since then been maintained at the provincial level. The Alberta Main Street Program was created in 1987, and has more recently adopted the document "Standards and Guidelines for the Conservation of Historic Places in Canada" as its guide. It works with the Municipal Heritage Partnership Program to help municipalities manage their historic places.[21] As of 2009, the program had undertaken work in twenty-three communities.[22] Main Street Saskatchewan[23] is a new project through which four communities (Wolseley, Indian Head, Maple Creek, and Prince Albert) were selected in 2011 to pilot a demonstration program, and the Hometown Manitoba program[24] was introduced in 2004 to provide funding in two categories: Meeting Places and Main Streets; since then it has provided funding through a competitive process.

In addition, initiatives by property owners and developers have attempted in various ways to reflect historic ideas, with varying results and implications. Positive examples can be found in High River, Alberta, which has managed to maintain a viable downtown commercial area through a combination of economic initiatives, streetscape improvements, Main Street Programs, and design guidelines, despite competition from newer commercial areas along the highway entries.

In some cases, the enthusiasm for revitalization led to the creation of forms that have little to do with the actual history or context of the town. For example, the town of Battleford, Saskatchewan had Victorian and Edwardian beginnings, but has been "updated" to a Wild West theme, with false-fronted cedar-sided buildings complete with hitching posts.

Vulcan, Alberta, an agricultural town established in the early 1900s, was once renowned for its row of nine grain elevators, distinguishing it as a major regional grain handling centre. As the elevators were demolished ca. 1970 and its commercial main street declined, the town struggled to maintain its attractiveness as a place to live, and its identity. After Main Street improvements in the early 1980s did little to stimulate its economy, Vulcan embarked on a series of programs, all linked to the TV show and movie series *Star Trek*. Since approximately 1990, Vulcan has attempted to distinguish itself through its name, which it shares with the fictional planet Vulcan—birthplace of the show's Dr. Spock—and the town's website now identifies it as the "official *Star Trek* capital of Canada." The tourist information booth is in the form of a spaceship, and people visit for the opportunity to photograph themselves alongside plywood models of the *Star Trek* crew or to buy a set of plastic Vulcan ears. Tourists are attracted to what has become the yearly "Spock Days" festival, and year-round to the attraction of the tourist centre and town murals that depict scenes from *Star Trek*.

An even more perplexing example is Langdon, Alberta; it is important to briefly review the history of its evolution in order to comment on current developments. Langdon was established in 1883 on a branch line of the CPR. It grew to a population of 800 by the early 1900s, and to 2,000 by the early 1920s. Main Street was located perpendicular to the rail line, and a couple of blocks of commercial buildings were developed to the north. However, due to a number of issues including high water table and poor drainage, and construction of a duplicate rail line ten kilometres to the southeast, it lost its prominence, and declined to 100 residents by 1950.

Figure 10 *In Langdon, construction of a building is intended to appear as a false-front commercial building and replicate the Main Street type (top). A boardwalk on top of a concrete sidewalk, a brick veneer facade, the separated buildings (to conform to the current fire code), the parking lot in front, and the "1908" sign are all peculiar elements (bottom, both photos by the author). This development has injected vitality into the hamlet and provides some commercial and professional services, but one wonders what the residents make of this new "history."*

Langdon lost its Village status in 1975 and was designated a hamlet. It was not until construction of a new sanitary sewer line in 1983 and improvement of the local highways that the town was again seen as being a desirable place to live. With the expansion of Calgary's suburban edge, Langdon became viable as a bedroom community, and started a new period of growth in the 1990s and 2000s.[25]

A mixed-use development nearing construction completion as of 2011, is designed as a reconstruction of Langdon's Main Street in 1908, albeit in a different location several blocks north of the original town centre and 100 years after the fact. Also different is the building type; where the original Main Street conformed to the Main Street typology of individual but linked false-fronted mixed-use buildings, the new development is essentially a strip mall on the main highway entry and with a parking lot in front. It is private property, and not a public street.

Although the Main Street and similar programs can bring some economic benefits to a town, period restoration can also result in preservation of the past, but prevention of the future.[26] The spatial structure and visual symbol of the prairie town embodied during its early development became a cultural icon, even though prairie towns evolved significantly after this period. Main Street conservation programs became fixated on the early-twentieth-century era as the epitome of prairie town development, and one to which the town should return. However, in reality, towns continued to evolve beyond that original typology.

THE HIGHWAY STRIP

Concurrent with the decline of the railway was an increase in importance of highway travel and transport and the development of the highway commercial strip. Real estate opportunities often became a driving force in town development, where the most important quality of an environment is its "highest and best use." These values and ways of thinking contributed to the shift of the commercial activity from the historic downtown core to the highway strips in order to take advantage of lower land costs, direct access to highway traffic flow, and to enable more parking to be provided. Coupled with this were changes in shopping patterns; regional shopping centres and superstores have been located in a number of towns, where they are able to attract the more mobile rural customers within a regional catchment area. These large developments further erode the commercial viability of local downtowns, and their morphology seems more suited to city suburbs than to small towns.

As the highway gained importance and the railway concurrently declined, the experience of the town is now "outside-in." The "entry" point is the highway strip—a series of fast-food restaurants, service centres, automobile dealers, and big box stores that are positioned to capitalize on the new traffic patterns.

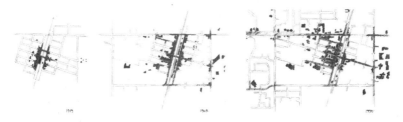

Figure 11 *Impressionistic drawings of Olds, Alberta illustrate how the central commercial heart of the town (darkest tone) has now become dispersed. Drawings by the author.*

Although usually criticized, highway strip developments are the logical developments of the evolution of transportation and technology, and their deliberate urban design as a travel corridor to communicate regional and local identity and as a gateway into the town is, so far, a missed opportunity.

Many people are still attracted to small towns,[27] presumably for their distinctive environment and culture; however, the new pattern of development threatens to homogenize and transplant city suburbia to the country, destroying the very features that make smaller places desirable. In strip malls and big-box developments, there is no contact with the street as a social environment; rather, the street becomes a separator, as parking must be visible to attract customers. The parking lot, rather than the street, becomes the most likely opportunity for informal social encounters, a situation more like that of suburbia than the small town.

ROAD LAYOUT AND NEIGHBOURHOOD STRUCTURE

Although the original railway grid plan can be criticized for its own autocratic system and for its unresponsiveness to local variations of topography, it defined the form of the prairie town and is a historical expression of the development of the west, as well as a convenient and effective method of subdividing and selling land. It is also an urban form that is legible and permeable, particularly in terms of the degree to which an environment offers a choice of ways through it, and from place to place. If attention is paid to issues of scale and variety, the grid often contributes to a high-quality urban structure and way of life.

The original continuous grid resulted in a connected and cohesive town fabric. Towns which have experienced development since the 1950s are now composed of a gridded core surrounded by newer neighbourhoods of cul-de-sacs, crescents and collector roads. The result is a jarring discontinuity—in street layout, building density, building setback, and even sidewalk dimension and species of street tree—as the new developments have been imposed with little regard for their compatibility with the existing fabric. The shift in road layout and streetscape appears as fractures in the town form. Varying street alignments

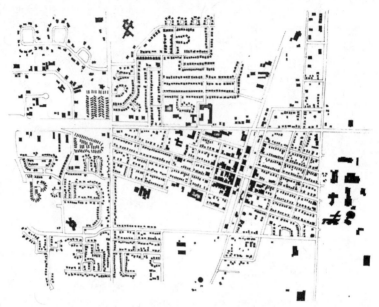

Figure 12 *Town development in the case of Olds, Alberta up to the middle 1960s conformed to the subdivision pattern aligned with the railway grid. The government road allowances contained the town; the railway station, grain elevators and Main Street formed a cohesive town centre. By the 1990s, the town consisted of the original railway grid, but now with several developments of varying densities and configurations surrounding it. As the town expanded beyond the highway grid, new subdivision patterns followed generic engineering models for suburbs, rather than grafting on to the established streets. Streets do not line up, and town neighbourhoods are cut off from each other. Drawing by the author.*

and changes in building density have resulted in parts of the town becoming segregated from each other. It is difficult to find any rationale for unnecessarily interrupting block pattern and streets, other than the tendency to attempt to spatially distinguish one neighbourhood from the other for marketing purposes. A more coherent vision of town form, including ideas of road alignment and articulation, should be expressed in the Municipal Plan so that new areas can be grafted onto the old rather than existing in isolation.

In the course of this evolution, changes also occurred at the scale of the street. Where the town had been comprised of narrower streets with treed boulevards and small setbacks, the newer developments consisted of wider streets, wider sidewalks, no treed boulevards, and houses set further back from the sidewalks. Traditional back lanes are usually omitted, and large garages, rather than front porches, dominate the street facades. These newer street types are more suited to vehicles than pedestrians; later evolutions do away with sidewalks and street trees, negatively impacting the social and public function of the street.

Figure 13 *Three streetscapes—all with sixty-six-foot rights-of-way—representing three phases of residential development in Olds, Alberta. In the historic grid (top), there is a clear definition between public and private space, the sidewalk is an important public component, and trees are a structural element. In subsequent development (middle), regular street tree plantings have been eliminated, the human scale has declined, and the sidewalk is a much less comfortable place for walking. In the newest developments (bottom), the street is most important as a device for moving and storing cars; the definition of private and public has become ambiguous, and trees are rarely included. (Photos by A. Nicolai, 1994, used with permission)*

The earlier grid, with the smaller setbacks and treed boulevards, helped to create a feeling of being inside a continuous town. The newer subdivisions, with the emphasis on the individual lot and the lack of unifying elements such as street trees, transfer the feeling of "insideness" to the house. The end product is a suburb—a low-density, self-contained neighbourhood—rather than a continuous town.

WHERE TO NEXT?

Although it was often previously thought that small towns would be destined for extinction as they lost their traditional economic base, such predictions seem to have been based on general statistics and short-term trends, and overlooked both regional considerations as well as the ability of towns to alter the nature of their service roles and/or attract new economic activities in order to survive. They also may not have foreseen the infrastructure improvements that made highway commuting much less inconvenient. The function of the prairie town has changed, but it remains an integral and vital part of the Canadian West.

There are two somewhat conflicting scenarios taking place in the rural prairies. One is the population redistribution caused by agricultural and transportation technology changes which have favoured larger centres.[28] The other is an apparent preference many people have for small-town or country living, contributing to a counter-urbanizing process identified by Bollman and Biggs and continuing today.[29] This is most pronounced in Alberta, and in towns that are within easy commuting distance of larger cities. Alberta's population growth was 10.8 percent between 2006 and 2011 (compared with Canada's growth of 5.9 percent during that same interval, Manitoba's of 5.2 percent, and Saskatchewan's of 6.7 percent (up from the 2001–2006 decline of 1.1%). Some of the towns within one hour's commute of Calgary had the following population growth rates between 2006 and 2011: Black Diamond 19.2 percent, Carstairs 27.5 percent, Didsbury 14.1 percent, High River 20.6 percent, Langdon 43 percent, Olds 13.5 percent, Okotoks 42.9 percent.[30]

But what will these towns become next? If sense of place and authentic identity are important ideas, then this question should be considered carefully. As Michael Hough observed, "the question of regional character has become a question of choice and, therefore, of design rather than of necessity."[31]

Canadian prairie towns are distinct, and are the product of particular geographic and historic processes. Many emerged over a short period of time in the late nineteenth and early twentieth centuries in response to specific needs and as a manifestation of an anticipated future white settler society. The patterns and structures that were first laid upon the land responded to issues of function and expediency. Just finding an easy way of subdividing and selling land, transporting people and goods, and keeping out the elements resulted in simple utilitarian landscapes and structures. But now, with technological innovation and access to global markets, almost anything is possible, including many versions of historical and pseudo-historical themes. But their ability to continue to contribute to a sense of place may not be appropriate or desirable, assuming that we as a society continue to value the distinct and the authentic.

Place image was once a direct outcome of the forces acting to produce it; the line between process and form was direct, and "reading" a landscape was an activity that could provide true insights. Many recent developments are more obscure, and in some cases completely indecipherable. It is more difficult for a resident or visitor to a place to be able to understand where the buildings and spaces came from, and why they take the form that they do.

While historic conservation programs have been effective in preserving physical pieces of the past, they have tended to be site- and period-specific (rather than treating history as a dynamic process which affects the entire town); they also do not provide sufficient guidance for new development within a modern context, but tend to propose one- or two-dimensional solutions to multi-dimensioned issues.

Change and transformation are part of landscape and settlement evolution. When they build on and reinforce qualities and patterns that are considered to be distinctive and supportive of high-quality physical environments and a high-quality way of life, then change is positive. When transformation results in a loss of identity and a decline in quality, however, those changes need to be questioned. What do we do as technology changes, and when railway stations, or grain elevators, or mills, or mines become obsolete? What do we do with our landmarks when they are no longer viable and have become part of history? It is important to find ways to reconcile local and regional identity with modern aspirations, and if the questions are properly framed, then perhaps elements such as highway commercial developments, town entries, abandoned railway lands, and obsolete agricultural structures could be approached as opportunities for celebration of place and acknowledgment of contemporary conditions.

The ingredients for cohesive and place-specific town form are often found in the historical record. Many elements of the early towns, such as the Main Street typology, the permeable and coherent grid block pattern, walkable residential streets, and the development of a town centre are what urbanists have now been advocating for several decades, following the unsuccessful post–World War II era characterized by excessive land use zoning, urban clearance, and rationalization of services. There are also important landscape approaches and elements suited to the Prairies that first arose in response to the need to make it home— and then to cope with droughts, winds, and the peculiarities of the prairie environment—including the simple elements of trees, shelter belts, and many practical ways of coping with a finite water source. These urban and landscape elements are great sources for planning and design.

Reviving or maintaining a sense of place does not lie in the preservation of towns as museums or the creation of themed environments. It is important not to romanticize or to give way to a nostalgia for what is often a largely imagined past. But it is also true that when historic urban forms are recreated, they are not without social and political meaning, even though they may be removed from their original context. The inherited meanings of these forms, therefore, may be used to provide a legitimizing vocabulary for newly created buildings and public spaces. This can likely only be done successfully if it is approached honestly—by understanding the fundamental elements of the Main Street typology that contributed in a positive way to town form and town life, and learning to reflect those in new construction rather than simply replicating the facade image. If this could be done successfully, then new buildings could be signed as the actual date of construction, and not, as in the case of Langdon, as 1908. Thus, in the accumulated history of the town, expressed in its public spaces, buildings, landscapes, and institutional forms, a typology could be developed that would go beyond the simple relationship between form and function, to express a continuing tradition of morphology and of community life.

NOTES

1   See for example Michael Hough, *Out of Place* (New Haven and London: Yale University Press, 1990); Edward Relph, *The Modern Urban Landscape* (Baltimore: Johns Hopkins, 1987).

2   Darcy Thompson, *On Growth and Form* (Cambridge: Cambridge University Press, 1917, repr., 1961).

3   Edward Relph, *Place and Placelessness* (London: Pion, 1976)

4   Ronald Rees, *New and Naked Land: Making the Prairies Home* (Saskatoon: Western Producer Books, 1988); Gerald Friesen, *The Canadian Prairies: A History* (Toronto: University of Toronto Press, 1984).

5   Ronald Rees, "The Prairie: A Canadian Artist's View," *Landscape* 21, 2 (1977): 31.

6   *A Region of the Mind*, ed. Richard Allen (Regina: Canadian Plains Research Center, 1973); Rees, *New and Naked Land*; Neil Evernden, "Beauty and Nothingness: Prairie as Failed Resource" in *Landscape* 27, 3 (1983); Sharon Butala, *The Perfection of the Morning: An Apprenticeship in Nature* (Toronto: HarperCollins Publishers, 1994).

7   Wallace E. Stegner, *Wolf Willow* (Toronto, Penguin Books, 1962), 6–8.

8   R.F. Legget, *Railways of Canada* (Vancouver: Douglas and MacIntyre, 1973).

9   See Legget, *Railways of Canada;* and J. Edward Martin, *Railway Stations of Western Canada* (White Rock, BC: Studio E, 1980) for further reading on Canadian railways; and Edwinna von Baeyer, *Rhetoric and Roses: A History of Canadian Gardening, 1900–1930* (Markham: Fitzhenry and Whiteside, 1984) for a chapter on railway gardens.

10 John Reps, *Cities of the Way West: A History of the Frontier of Urban Planning.* (Princeton: Princeton University Press, 1979), 10.

11 Rees, "The Prairie," 32.

12 A. Paavo, "Never say forever," *Briarpatch* (June 19, 1993): 13.

13 Legget, *Railways of Canada.*

14 A. Holtz, "Small Town Alberta—A Geographical Study of the Development of Urban Form" (MA Thesis, University of Alberta, 1987), 66.

15 Von Bayer, *Rhetoric and Roses,* 14–33.

16 Glenbow Archives, PA-3689-632.

17 Roger Trancik, *Finding Lost Space* (New York: Van Nostrand Reinhold, 1986).

18 See Donald G. Wetherell and Irene R.A. Kmet, *Town Life: Main Street and the Evolution of Small Town Alberta, 1880-1947* (Edmonton: University of Alberta Press, 1995); and Beverly A. Sandalack, "The (sub)Urbanisation of Prairie Towns," *Prairie Forum* 27, 2 (2002): 239–248 for further discussion of town form.

19 Deryk Holdsworth, ed., *Reviving Main Street* (Toronto: University of Toronto Press, 1985), ix.

20 John J. Stewart, "A Strategy for Main Street," *Canadian Heritage* 40 (May-June 1983): 5. The program is described in considerable detail in Holdsworth, *Reviving Main Street.* See Andrei Nicolai and Beverly A. Sandalack, "Hometown: Urban Design Issues in the Canadian Prairie Town" in *Issues in Canadian Urban Design,* ed. C. Charette (Winnipeg: Institute of Urban Studies, 1995), 149–182; and Beverly A. Sandalack, "Continuity of History and Form: the Canadian Prairie Town" (PhD Diss., Oxford Brookes University, UK, 1998) for a discussion of these programs and some of their effects.

21 http://www.albertamainstreet.org/ Accessed July 2011.

22 Heritage Canada Foundation for Saskatchewan Tourism, Parks, Culture and Sport, *Main Street Programs Past and Present,* March 2009 (http://www.tpcs.gov.sk.ca/MSProgramHCF).

23 http://www.tpcs.gov.sk.ca/MainStreet, accessed July 2011.

24 http://www.gov.mb.ca/agriculture/ri/community/ria01s04.html.

25 Langdon community website http://www.goodlucktown.ca/, accessed December 2011.

26 B. Goodey, "The Healthy, Happy History Show: the Evolving Image of the Urban Heritage" in *NSCAD Papers: Beyond Form,* eds. Beverly A. Sandalack and Nick Webb (Halifax: Nova Scotia College of Art and Design, 1997).

27 An overview of population and dwelling counts by Statistics Canada comparing 2006 and 2011 indicates that many towns are experiencing population growth above the national mean.

28 Jack Stabler, *Restructuring Rural Saskatchewan: Challenge of the 1990s* (Regina: Canadian Plains Research Center, 1992).

29 *Rural and Small Town Canada,* ed. Ray D. Bollman (Toronto: Thompson Educational Publishing, 1992).

30 Government of Canada (2011) Census Canada.

31 Hough, *Out of Place,* 2.

DEFINING
PRAIRIE POLITICS
CAMPAIGNS, CODES,
AND CULTURES

JARED J. WESLEY

INTRODUCTION

Considering their many geographic, economic, demographic, and institutional commonalities, the three prairie provinces ought to feature very similar political environments. Indeed, this is the assumption underlying the tendency among many academics to group the three provinces into a common region for comparative analysis.[1] In this, "the probability that combining data for the prairie provinces may be about as meaningful as combining data for Ontario and Quebec and calling it Central Canada hasn't occurred to everyone yet."[2] Closer examination of their provincial party systems reveals that prairie Canadians live in three distinct political terrains.

Since Confederation only twice, for a total of nine years, has the same party formed government in all three provinces.[3] Moreover, each province's party system has its own unique "tilt." Clear relationships exist between the dominance of conservatism and right-wing parties like Social Credit and the Progressive Conservatives in Alberta, and socialism and the success of the left-wing CCF-NDP in Saskatchewan. The balance between the forces of left and right in Manitoba help to set it apart from its prairie neighbours in this respect. Aside from the major parties involved, the dynamics of competition between them varies drastically from province to province. Recent contests in Manitoba have involved "three enduring and competitive parties and the periodic experience of minority government,"[4] whereas Saskatchewan elections have been closer to a "two-plus" party model, and Alberta campaigns a "one-party, non-competitive" type.[5] In sum, despite sharing a relatively similar topography, industrial base, and set of political institutions, Canada's three prairie provinces maintain distinct patterns of party competition.

This chapter suggests that by downplaying the role of ideas and agency, structural theories offer only partial solutions to this "paradox" on the Canadian prairies. In ignoring the rhetorical boundaries dominant parties place on their party systems through their campaign messages, the academic community has neglected the extent to which parties themselves help shape the climates in which they compete. As discussed below, successful parties and their leaders have crafted unique dominant discourses—or "political codes"—that have helped promote freedom in Alberta, security in Saskatchewan, and moderation in Manitoba as each province's fundamental value. In doing so, these parties have helped create an atmosphere in which they succeed, both ideologically and electorally.

THE PRAIRIE PARADOX

The political diversity found on the Canadian plains is puzzling. Manitoba, Saskatchewan, and Alberta are each separated by essentially artificial boundaries, their borders based on arbitrary longitudinal lines rather than topographic or ethnic divisions.[6] All three are associated with a common iconic landscape: vast stretches of prairie, bounded only by mountains to the west and the Canadian Shield to the east. Tied so closely to the land, their populations have been historically small and rural compared to their neighbours in British Columbia and Ontario. In natural resources and primary industry, the three prairie provinces share a common economic base, dependent as it is on the unpredictable climates of the international market and the weather, and (according to some) vulnerable as it is to the economic engine of central Canada.[7] Furthermore, like all provinces, Manitoba, Saskatchewan, and Alberta operate under the same Westminster style of parliamentary government and plurality-based electoral systems. Thus, at first glance, one might expect the prairie provinces to share a common political climate. They do not, and the contrasts are starkest in terms of the region's three provincial party systems.

Most accounts characterize Alberta's various governments as "right-wing," reinforcing the province's image as the bastion of Canadian conservatism. Only four parties have governed Alberta—a fact that divides the province's history into distinct eras. Over sixteen years, the Liberal Party formed the province's first four majority governments. Their successor, the United Farmers of Alberta (UFA), also enjoyed massive majorities throughout its fourteen years in power. Also true to form, the Farmers were unceremoniously removed from power by a new political party, William Aberhart's Social Credit. The Socreds would win nine successive elections between 1935 and 1967, earning Aberhart (1935–1943) and his protégé,

Ernest Manning (1943–1968) majority governments for over three decades. This dynasty came to an end under Social Credit premier Harry Strom (1963–1971), whose loss of power in 1971 marked the most recent change of party government. Since that time, five Progressive Conservative (PC) premiers—Peter Lougheed (1971–1985), Don Getty (1985–1992), Ralph Klein (1992–2006), Ed Stelmach (2006–2011), and Alison Redford (2011 to the present)—have presided over a Canadian-record twelve consecutive majority governments.[8] In sum, not once over the province's first century have Alberta voters elected a minority government, with victorious parties winning an average of nearly half of the popular vote and enjoying an average seat advantage of five to one over the opposition. What is more, no governing party has ever returned to power once ousted. In this, Alberta features the very definition of dynastic party competition.[9]

This conservative, dynastic pattern contrasts sharply with Saskatchewan where, since World War II, the province's "natural governing party" has been avowedly social democratic.[10] As Marchildon describes, "in the typical stereotypes of these contrasting identities, Saskatchewanians are depicted as collectivist-inclined social democrats who emphasize security and egalitarian social development while Albertans are portrayed as entrepreneurial 'small c' conservatives who are dedicated to the individualistic pursuit of liberty and prosperity."[11] In Saskatchewan, the New Democratic Party (NDP) and its progenitor, the Cooperative Commonwealth Federation (CCF), have formed governments following twelve of the last eighteen elections.

In this vein, there are two prominent features of Saskatchewan party politics. First, the system is cyclical in nature, featuring regular, if relatively infrequent, alternation of parties in government. Second, the party system is highly competitive and polarized, in partisan if not ideological terms.[12] Since World War II, the main combatants have been the left-leaning CCF-NDP and a succession of three rightwing challengers—the Liberals, Conservatives, and Saskatchewan Party. Hence, the Saskatchewan party system has featured four distinct eras, each roughly separated by pivotal elections in the province's history:

The Liberal-Conservative Era (1905 to 1934);
The Liberal-CCF Era (1934 to 1978);
The NDP-PC Era (1978 to 1999); and
The NDP-Sask Party Era (1999 to present).

Four parties have governed Saskatchewan since its entry to Confederation in 1905.[13] As a single organization, the Liberal Party has won the most elections, forming a total of ten majority governments over the province's first seven decades. The Conservatives have led a total of three governments, including the Depression-era Anderson Coalition and Grant Devine's two consecutive majorities in the 1980s. As heirs to the province's right-wing tradition, the Saskatchewan (Sask) Party formed its first governments in 2007 and 2011. With the notable exception of the pre-war Liberals, none of these three parties has enjoyed sustained success. Since World War II, each has formed government only once, for a maximum of two terms (the Liberals, 1964 to 1971; the Conservatives, 1982 to 1991; and the Saskatchewan Party, 2007 to present). In this, episodes of right-wing party rule have served as interludes in the recent history of Saskatchewan politics.

Combined, the CCF and its successor, the NDP, have won the remaining twelve Saskatchewan elections. Indeed, since running in its first campaign in 1938, the Saskatchewan CCF-NDP has won two of every three elections it has contested. Only one other Canadian party (the Ontario Conservatives), has enjoyed a better winning percentage over the same period. In terms of its consistency, the CCF-NDP is the only Saskatchewan party (and one of only a handful in Canadian history) to have governed in every decade since World War II.[14] Over this period, every one of its leaders—from Douglas to Calvert—has served as premier; the party is the only one in post-war Saskatchewan to have won three consecutive elections, performing the feat on three separate occasions (1944 to 1960; 1971 to 1978; and 1991 to 2003). Moreover, of all political parties in Canada, only five have averaged a higher proportion of the popular vote in the post-war period, none east of the Ottawa River.[15] The depth of its dominance may not compare with right-wing dynasties in Alberta; nonetheless, considering its longevity, the Saskatchewan CCF-NDP ranks as one of Canada's most successful "natural governing parties."[16]

Its ideological identity is what distinguishes the Saskatchewan CCF-NDP most, however. Since inspiring Lipset's *Agrarian Socialism* over fifty years ago, the party remains the most successful social democratic organization in North America. Many accounts—including the myriad based on Lipset's observations—attribute the CCF-NDP's success to its innate connection to Saskatchewan's collectivist political culture; that is, the party has been portrayed as a beneficiary of a socialist-inclined electorate.[17]

Further east, party competition in Manitoba has been more evenly balanced between the left and right. A self-proclaimed "non-partisan" government ruled the province from 1922 to 1958. Under the amorphous "Liberal-Progressive" banner, a succession of coalition administrations was held together loosely under a platform of laissez-faire politics before giving way to a series of moderate partisan governments beginning in the late 1950s.[18] Since that time, Manitoba has alternated between Progressive Conservative and New Democratic governments, with each serving twenty-six and twenty-seven years in power, respectively. Thus, the Manitoba party system has evolved through three key eras: a traditional period

(1883 to 1922); a semi-partisan period (1922 to 1958); and a cyclical period (1958 to the present).

Following a decade of non-partisan administration, provincial party politics emerged in earnest in Manitoba in the mid-1880s.[19] For the next four decades, election campaigns featured heated competition between Liberals, headed by Premiers Thomas Greenway and T.C. Norris, and Conservatives, whose most prominent leaders included Hugh John Macdonald and Rodmond Roblin. As in Alberta, the Progressive era ushered in a new form of party politics in Manitoba. Having pushed the Liberals into a minority position in 1920, the United Farmers of Manitoba (UFM) toppled the government—and the party system—two years later. Under various labels, the Farmers governed Manitoba, uninterrupted, for the next thirty-six years. After fusing with the provincial Grits in 1932, the party settled on the title "Liberal-Progressive"—a moniker that suited the diverse nature of its constituent elements, but is somewhat misleading with regard to the party's ideology. Under Premiers John Bracken, Stuart Garson, and Douglas Campbell, the Liberal-Progressives were as committed as any other Canadian party to the laissez-faire doctrine of classic liberalism. The Liberal-Progressives also preached a distinctive brand of "business-like" politics that was rhetorically "non-partisan" but "semi-partisan" in practice. Based on these principles, Bracken assembled a series of coalition governments throughout the 1930s and 1940s, making his party the only one in Canada to remain in power through both the Great Depression and World War II.

The Liberal-Progressives were ousted by a second "Progressive" party in 1958—Duff Roblin's Progressive Conservatives—whose brand of red and blue toryism marked the beginning of Manitoba's modern province-building era. Roblin's definition of "progress" differed distinctly from the laissez-faire approach of the Liberals, however, who had now begun serving five decades as Manitoba's marginalized third party.[20] The Tories' promotion of the "active state" provided a rhetorical and institutional foundation for the rise of Edward Schreyer's New Democrats in 1969. Indeed, the rightward drift of the Conservatives under leaders Walter Weir and Sidney Spivak left much of the middle ground to Schreyer's message of moderate social democracy. This mode of moderate politics shifted dramatically, if briefly, under Conservative premier Sterling Lyon, whose new right ideology polarized the party system from 1977 through the mid-1980s.[21] Lyon's zealous approach to partisanship earned him a single term in office, however, making him the only premier in Manitoba history to win one (and only one) election without retiring. Since that time, Manitoba politics has settled into its conventional mould, with the New Democrats (under social democrat Howard Pawley and third-way democrats Gary Doer and Greg Selinger) and Conservatives (under Tory-turned-new-right-conservative Gary Filmon) trading places in government. Since 1969, neither party has garnered the support of more than half, nor much less than a quarter, of Manitoba voters.[22] Selinger's victory in 2011—the NDP's historic fourth consecutive majority—leaves some questioning whether the New Democrats have emerged as the province's new "natural governing party." This said, consistently strong performances by the Progressive Conservatives and the survival of the Liberal Party have helped keep the two-and-a-half-party system intact.[23]

In sum, Alberta's pattern of party competition has been *right-wing dynastic*, involving long-term, one-party dominance by conservative parties, interrupted by relatively sudden changes in government. Since 1944, Saskatchewan's pattern has featured a *left-wing natural governing party*, whose control of the legislature has been less dominant and more frequently overturned. The pattern of party politics in Manitoba has been the most *balanced and competitive*, both in terms of the electoral strength of its major parties, and in terms of their centre-leaning ideologies. The question remains: how could three such distinct party systems develop within a single region?

"CODE POLITICS" ON THE PRAIRIES

The paradox can be explained, in part, by combining a series of four prominent theories. To solve the origins of the dilemma, I have relied in my previous work, *Code Politics*,[24] upon Wiseman's seminal research to suggest that each provincial political culture was formed in the early-twentieth century by a unique combination of settlement patterns (fragment theory), economic activity (staples theory), and pivotal episodes (formative events theory). Alberta's conservative political culture was attributable to an early influx of right-leaning, populist American settlers whose livelihoods in the agricultural and petroleum industries tended to reinforce a capitalist ethos in the province. In this regard, the striking of oil at Leduc in 1947 served as a formative event. By contrast, Saskatchewan's social democratic political culture was imported by a group of Fabian-inspired immigrants from Britain whose approach to the young province's agricultural industry was decidedly collectivist. The onset of the Great Depression, and the political class's response, helped reinforce the dominance of communitarianism in Saskatchewan. Manitoba's more moderate political culture—which strays neither left nor right, but remains fixed in the "progressive centre"—was the result of the approach of early, ideologically eclectic ("Tory-touched liberal") immigrants from Ontario. Unlike its western neighbours, whose economies were tied to the highs and lows of global commodity markets, Manitoba's economy was given to neither boom nor bust, thus sheltering its political culture from the extremes of political ideology. Rare, transformative events, like the Winnipeg General Strike, served as punctuations in an otherwise calm political atmosphere, helping to reinforce the exceptional nature of pitched conflict in the province.

Supplementing Wiseman's findings, I argue that the persistence of these cultural differences could be attributed to the powerful, enduring campaign narratives crafted by each province's dominant politicians. Examining the rhetoric found in hundreds of speeches, platforms, pamphlets, and other campaign materials, I have found that prairie politics have been defined by three distinct "political codes"— unique, elite-level projections of each province's over-arching values. In Alberta, campaigns have revolved around the concept of "freedom," with dominant parties emphasizing the importance of preserving the province's individualism, populism and autonomy. "According to this code, the Alberta government—and, by extension, the party in power—serves as the defender of provincial interests against external, oppressive forces, be they the federal government, a socialist menace, or any other Big Shot foe of the Alberta community."[25] In nearby Saskatchewan, the code has been defined by the notion of "security," combining an emphasis upon dirigisme, collectivism, and polarization to reinforce the importance of the state "as a pioneer in Confederation, a provider of social services, and a director of the provincial economy."[26] Meanwhile, Manitoba's political discourse has been defined by "moderation," with leading politicians stressing the values of progressive centrism, pragmatism, and trans-partisanship throughout their campaigns, reinforcing the state's role as a "broker in federal-provincial relations, moderator of internal social issues, and participant in the provincial economy."[27] In short, "by transmitting distinct, age-old value systems through a series of unique campaign narratives, and by perpetuating these codes over time, dominant party leaders have helped sustain the three different political cultures that now characterize the Canadian prairies."[28]

Left unaddressed in *Code Politics*, however, was the fact that, once established, these dominant forms of discourse actually affect the structure of party politics in each province. In other words, these political codes were not merely *symptoms* of the long-term dominance by certain political parties; they were also *sources* of those very patterns of party competition.

It seems straightforward to draw the causal arrow in the former direction, from patterns to narratives. From this perspective, the fact that the Alberta code is grounded in the right-wing concept of "freedom" is due, quite simply, to the longevity of conservative parties in office. The same is true in Saskatchewan and Manitoba, respectively, where left-leaning and centre-straddling parties have prevailed at the polls and in establishing their own ideologies as paramount. Yet, the causal arrow could just as easily point in the opposite direction. Left-wing parties could enjoy natural governing status in Saskatchewan, and moderate parties could thrive in Manitoba, because separate codes of elite discourse help ensure their success. As narrative constructs, these codes could structure the way parties compete, and establish a system of advantages and disadvantages for certain organizations. Hence, rather than *resulting* from party competition, these dominant narratives could actually *shape* the party systems we see on the Canadian prairies today.

Like most questions of structure versus agency, this dichotomy is largely artificial. As the following discussion reveals, the causal arrow runs in both directions: patterns of party competition and dominant narratives reinforce one another. While the stability of the former contributes to the durability of the latter, at the same time, the persistence of a code makes the continued success of dominant parties more likely. Party dominance begets ideological prominence, and vice versa —a point Duverger made decades ago: "a party is dominant when it is identified with an epoch; when its doctrines, ideas, methods, its style, so to speak, coincide with those of the epoch.... Domination is a question of influence rather than of strength: it is also linked with belief. A dominant party is that which public opinion *believes* to be dominant."[29]

In Alberta's case, the parallels between the dominance of Social Credit and the Progressive Conservatives appear obvious. Both have been described as populist, right-wing, province-first parties whose appeal stems from the intimate connection between their shared ideology and the province's conservative political culture.[30] Indeed, my analysis confirmed that these dominant parties have drawn on a common campaign theme—a "socially shared political understanding"— in each of the past twenty Alberta elections.[31] From Aberhart's Social Credit to Redford's Conservatives, representatives of both dynasties have emphasized the importance of keeping Alberta strong and free. This notion of "freedom" constitutes the code—the persistent, core narrative—of Alberta politics, favouring right-wing parties like Social Credit and the Progressive Conservatives, and marginalizing opposition parties like the CCF-NDP and Liberals.

In Saskatchewan, many claim the CCF-NDP has tapped the vein of the province's political culture, be it rural populism, progressivism, pragmatism, the cooperative spirit, or simply a desire for good government. While not disputing their accuracy, *Code Politics* reversed the causal arrow in these interpretations. An examination of their campaign rhetoric reveals that the CCF-NDP not only draws upon, but actively promotes, three key facets of political life in Saskatchewan: collectivism, dirigisme, and polarization. Under the broader concept of "security," these three elements constitute Saskatchewan's political code—a tradition of elite-level rhetoric that extends back to the Liberal Party's dominance in the pre-war era. By emphasizing the concept of "security," the province's natural governing parties have cultivated a unique field of political competition in Saskatchewan, one that sets the province apart from both Alberta and Manitoba and has helped guard against the success of right-wing and overly-centrist parties.

Despite its easternmost position, Manitoba represents the Prairies' political middle ground. Ideologically, its politics span the spectrum between right-tilting Alberta and left-leaning Saskatchewan, and its most successful elites have conscientiously avoided either pole. Indeed, throughout most of its history, centrist parties have dominated Manitoba politics. At the height of their influence, each of its three post-Depression governing parties—the Liberal-Progressives, Progressive Conservatives, and New Democrats—have epitomized this search for moderation. This began with "Brackenism," the middle-of-the-road ideology promoted by Manitoba's longest-serving premier, John Bracken. Thus, whereas Aberhart staked out the right and Douglas the left, Bracken defined the "progressive centre" as the fertile "middle ground" of Manitoba politics. His successors, Stuart Garson and Douglas Campbell, reinforced this vision before ceding power to Duff Roblin's Progressive Conservatives in the late-1950s. Yet, as transformative as it was, Roblin's arrival did not represent a comprehensive reinvention of the provincial code. Just as Lougheed and Romanow adapted their parties' ideologies to fit within the broad boundaries of their respective provincial discourses, shifting their codes in the process, so, too, did Roblin reshape Progressive Conservatism in Manitoba. When his successors pulled the Conservatives back to the right, joining the Liberal-Progressives on that side of the spectrum, room was left for a second adaptation of the progressive centre: Ed Schreyer's moderate version of New (Social) Democracy. Ever since Schreyer's rise to power in 1969, Manitoba politics has featured a two-party-plus system, with the Progressive Conservatives and New Democrats alternating in power to the exclusion of the Liberal Party. Theirs is a recipe for political success and failure that dates back to the Bracken era: when any major party strays too far from the principles of progressive centrism, pragmatism, and flexible partisanship, its opponents sit poised to assume the mantle of government.[32]

Drawing on these lessons, this chapter advances a neo-institutional solution to the Prairie paradox, in which dominant narratives both reflect and constrain party behaviour. On the latter point, codes help determine the *tilt* of party competition by defining the acceptable role(s) for the provincial government, and the *competitiveness* by identifying key "enemies" of the state. Opposition parties often find it difficult to overcome these constraints, as their own visions typically conflict with, or are marginalized by, the prevailing discourse. As a result, unique patterns of competition develop in each polity, bestowing certain parties with advantages, and penalizing others, depending on the content of the dominant narrative.

CODES AS INSTITUTIONS

Codes shape politics in much the same way as do constitutions, laws, and other more conventional institutions. In addition to rules, norms, and customs, codes provide symbols, cognitive scripts, and moral templates that shape, consciously or subconsciously, the conduct of political actors, namely parties and their leaders.[33] Through these constraints, "(1) players are identified, (2) prospective outcomes are determined, (3) alternative modes of deliberations are permitted, and (4) the specific manner in which revealed preferences, over allowable alternatives, by eligible participants, occurs."[34]

By creating an array of incentives and disincentives, codes forge a sense that "there is no alternative" but to abide by the established rules of political competition. By defining the scope of debate, this type of "T.I.N.A." politics restricts the ability of opposition parties to express opinions that conflict with, or lie outside, the dominant discourse.[35] In this way, codes constrain all parties in a system, whether in terms of their behaviour or their performance. As Berman notes, "Many scholars have found that ideas can influence political behaviour even if political actors have not internalized or do not believe in them. In such cases, ideational variables work indirectly; they influence the translation of interests into outcomes by shaping the incentive structures associated with different courses of action. Even if actors do not believe in particular norms, they might abide by them if non-compliance carries a high cost."[36]

In the case of codes, these "high costs" are often felt at the polls. Parties that do not speak "in code" are often marginalized during political debates, labelled as extremists and outsiders, or, as discussed below, branded as enemies of the polity, itself. These labels often define a party's legitimacy, both among elites in the party system and among voters in the electorate.

It is important to note that, while constraining their behaviour, codes are nonetheless constructed by dominant elites themselves. In this sense, party politics on the Prairies "is not simply a matter of negotiating coalitions of interests within given constraints of rights, rules, preferences, and resources. Politics extend to shaping those constraints, to constructing accounts of politics, history, and self that are not only bases for instrumental action but also central concerns of life."[37] The question becomes, then: precisely which rules, norms, or expectations do codes establish, and how do these constraints help to determine patterns of party competition?

DETERMINING TILT AND COMPETITIVENESS

This study suggests codes impose two sets of constraints on political parties and their leaders: they (1) establish the "proper" functions of government, while (2) defining which types of opposition are "acceptable" within a given party system.

First, as elsewhere, elites in each prairie province have fought over the proper role of government in a variety of different spheres.[38] The dominant discourses that have evolved from these debates have established three specific roles for the provincial state: one in terms of representing the community's position in Confederation; a second with regard to domestic and social needs; and a third vis-à-vis the provincial economy (see Table 1).

STATE'S ROLE IN:	*Alberta*	*Saskatchewan*	*Manitoba*
Confederation	guardian	pioneer	delegate
Society	ombudsman	provider	moderator
Economy	liberator	director	participant

Table 1: Codes and the Role of Prairie States

In Alberta, for instance, the dominant narrative portrays the state as a guardian against outside influence, specifically from the federal government and other central Canadian elites. In terms of social affairs, the code describes the state's role as more of an ombudsman—reactively and prudently responding to citizens' concerns as they arise. Lastly, in their campaign rhetoric, dominant elites in Alberta have defined the state as an economic liberator, preserving the "freedom" of individuals and businesses to compete in open markets. In Saskatchewan, the state has been defined as a pioneer among Canadian governments—an innovator in developing government programs and approaches. On the domestic front, Saskatchewan elites have touted the state as a provider of key social services, and a director of the provincial economy. In all of these ways, dominant elites have promoted the importance of state-sponsored "security" in Saskatchewan. By contrast, Manitoba's dominant elites have portrayed their state as a delegate in federal-provincial relations, a moderator of internal social forces, and an active, but not overpowering, participant in the economy. Reflected in their campaign messages, Manitoba premiers have been among the country's most conciliatory and diplomatic at the first ministers' table, providing both a buffer and a bridge between the interests of east and west and the haves and have-nots.[39] The state has been viewed as having a similar role within Manitoba society, moderating between the varied social, economic, ethnic, geographic, and other interests in the province. Befitting the province's code of "moderation," elites have also depicted a middling position for the state vis-à-vis the economy, neither as interventionist as its neighbour in Saskatchewan, nor as laissez-faire as its Alberta counterpart.[40]

Flowing from these definitions, the various tilts of party politics we see on the Prairies today are attributable, in large part, to the different ways in which dominant provincial elites in each province have conceptualized and confined conflict. By defining "the normal" or "the acceptable" limits of political debate, these codes have "organized out" certain opposition parties by virtue of their identities or ideologies. In addition to conditioning the behaviour of established elites, as discussed below, codes affect political aspirants' attitudes about government, politics, and partisanship. This deters certain types of individuals (e.g., socialists in Alberta, neo-liberals in Saskatchewan, or utopians in Manitoba) from seeking public office, particularly under opposition party banners. This, in turn, only serves to reinforce the existing patterns of party competition by granting dominant parties a greater proportion of the political talent in a given community.

Beyond the definition of the "proper," however, a second key component of code politics—and the mechanism behind its impact on the competitiveness of each party system—lies in the identification of a polity's greatest "enemy." In some ways, codes lie at the heart of what some observers label "the politics of fear": they identify the objects in need of protection and single out oppressors to give the public a "clear target for their unrest."[41] During periods of uncertainty, the identification of "enemies" is especially powerful—so much so that leaders may be tempted to manufacture crises in order to derive the positive benefits of being the community's saviour.[42] This strategy amounts to the cultivation of a "wartime psychology" in which the party is portrayed as society's defender.[43]

In their broadest terms, the "villains" in Alberta have been those forces that impinged on the province's liberty and autonomy.[44] Throughout the last seven decades, the various threads of the province's populist, individualist, alienated political culture have been tied together by an underlying theme: "If we pull together we can defeat the 'enemies' and return Alberta to prosperity and its natural state of grace."[45] These foes have ranged from the federal government and eastern Canadian capitalists to atheists and socialists; from individual prime ministers and federal parties to abstract concepts like Keynesianism, "big government," and "the debt." By invoking these themes, Alberta's dominant party leaders have proven masterful at *externalizing opposition*.[46] Aberhart's marriage of evangelism and Social Credit turned any criticism of his government into an attack on God Himself.[47] Manning's portrayal of Socred ideology as the natural antithesis of Soviet-style communism made any opposition seem un-liberal, un-democratic, and un-Canadian. Years later, Peter Lougheed's promotion of a "quasi-colonial mentality" to link provincial Liberals and New Democrats to their unpopular federal cousins made "enemies" of Alberta's Official Opposition.[48] And Ralph Klein's parochial appeals to the province's frontier roots made resistance to his party's ideology "unseemly, anti-Albertan, and, to some extent, traitorous."[49] On most occasions, in fact, Alberta premiers have refused to name or engage the provincial opposition altogether; when they have been forced to do so—as Richard Reid, Harry Strom, and Don Getty have discovered—their fortunes wane.[50]

As Elton and Goddard described, "In such a milieu, the mass electorate, it would appear, becomes depoliticized, allowing natural intergroup conflicts to be smothered under a screen of consensus of support for the elites in their battle against external threats."[51] This presents opposition parties, like the Liberals and New Democrats, with the unenviable choice between being anti-Albertan and tacitly supporting the dominant party. In these ways, the ability of Social Credit and the Progressive Conservatives to externalize opposition, embodied in the provincial code, adds to existing explanations of one-party-dominance in Alberta.

One province to the east, "enemies" of the Saskatchewan state have been defined quite differently. There, the natural governing CCF-NDP has identified the province's primary threat as a domestic, right-wing challenge to Saskatchewan's collectivist traditions. By highlighting the polarized, partisan nature of provincial politics throughout their campaigns, leaders from Douglas to Calvert have portrayed their party as the dirigiste defenders of the Saskatchewan welfare state, resource sector, and crown corporations. Douglas and Lloyd touted their achievements in medicare and public automobile insurance, for instance, warning voters that the Liberal Party may reverse these gains. Years later, Allan Blakeney emerged as the champion of the government's role as a resource entrepreneur, cautioning voters not to "sell out" their "birthright" by electing a Conservative government. And Roy Romanow and Lorne Calvert persuaded voters, for a time at least, to move "Forward, Not Backward" by electing the New Democrats to protect core social programs and services against the free-enterprise designs of the Saskatchewan Party.

In this way, the Saskatchewan CCF-NDP have not only helped to sustain their own dominance over provincial politics by presenting themselves as the protectors of Saskatchewan's social democratic traditions. They have also left room—in some ways, even cultivated the space—for a minority right-wing force. Periodically, conservative leaders of various political stripes have exploited this opportunity and risen to power—Ross Thatcher's Liberals, Grant Devine's Conservatives, and Brad Wall's Sask Party have each risen from Opposition to government. Yet their longevity in office has been limited by the prevailing code established by the natural governing party. Thus, just as in Alberta, code politics may help us to better understand the competitiveness of party politics in Saskatchewan, where a left-wing party dominates, but right-wing parties play a prominent, if periodic, role.

While dominant parties have helped shape their environments by *externalizing* opposition in Alberta, and *internalizing* conflict in Saskatchewan, elites in Manitoba have established a more balanced pattern of party competition by *minimizing* such partisan and ideological tensions. Indeed, dominant party leaders in Manitoba have identified extremism—in all its forms, from partisanship to dogmatism—as their province's greatest enemy. John Bracken viewed non-partisanship and "business-like" administration as the best means of securing "good government" for Manitoba. His definition of politics marginalized both Social Credit and the Cooperative Commonwealth Federation—both of whom rose to power elsewhere on the Prairies, and both of whom joined Bracken's coalition governments in the 1930s and 1940s. Building on similar premises, Duff Roblin constructed his brand of Progressive Conservatism as a middle-of-the-road alternative to the more "extreme" versions of laissez-faire liberalism and state-first socialism being advocated by the Liberals and CCF in the 1950s and 1960s. Upon his departure, Roblin's cultivation of "progressive centre" provided fertile ground for the more moderate version of social democracy developed by Ed Schreyer and the New Democrats, while continuing to marginalize more doctrinaire conservatives on the right. Following a brief period of polarization—during which neither Sterling Lyon's new-right Conservatives, nor Howard Pawley's old-left New Democrats could retain power for more than a single, full term—the party system once again settled under the code of moderation. After the rightward drift of Gary Filmon's PCs, the moderate, third-way approach of Gary Doer and Greg Selinger has kept the New Democrats in power for over a decade. Hence, just as in Alberta and Saskatchewan, the nature of the dominant political discourse has played a role in determining the shape of party politics in Canada's original prairie province. There, moderation has bred balance, with the most successful parties trading places in the "progressive centre" and taking turns in office.

CONSTRAINTS ON OPPONENTS

Minor opposition parties have struggled to gain traction in each of these provinces, thanks in large part to the constraints placed upon them by each of these codes. In Alberta, for example, the CCF-NDP has enjoyed little success compared to its eastern prairie cousins. Beyond the many economic, cultural, and institutional barriers typically cited, the present analysis suggests that the electoral weakness of social democratic parties in Alberta is attributable, in part, to their inability (or unwillingness) to frame their ideology to fit the province's freedom-based political narrative. In this, "the ideology of the NDP appears to be somewhat antithetical to the political culture of Alberta, with its greater emphasis on individualism."[52]

Notwithstanding subtle changes in their adaptation of social democracy—most notably in the 1980s—the New Democrats have remained the most ideologically consistent party in Alberta (indeed, the entire prairie region). Perhaps this is as much a symptom of the party's distance from power as a source of its (limited) success. As Dyck suggests, since the onset of the Tory dynasty "the NDP, with its limited audience in the province, strives to represent an ideological alternative—greater public ownership and control of power and other utilities, selective nationalization of resource industries, a pro-union stance on labour legislation, more concern with unemployment, and defense of social programs."[53] These same principles may be traced back to the party's origins in the Cooperative

Commonwealth Federation. From their first campaign in 1940 to their most recent in 2008, the CCF-NDP strategy has been to identify all other major parties as "Tory Twins" (or "Triplets"), portraying themselves as the only real alternative to the conservative Socreds, Conservatives, and Liberals. Hence, while overshadowed by a variety of conservative party ideologies, social democracy has remained a constant—if, at times, marginalized—element of the Alberta political party spectrum.

The Alberta Liberal Party's challenges stem from two additional sources. First and foremost, the party has suffered from its association with the federal Liberal brand. This link has been by name alone throughout much of the post-war period, and persists despite vehement protests by the provincial wing and a formal severance of institutional ties in 1977. Throughout the post-war period, Alberta Liberals continue to hold open discussions about changing their party's name to avoid this brand association, but no such plans have come to fruition. Heated battles between Liberals in Ottawa and Social Credit and Progressive Conservative governments in Edmonton have only served to bolster the popularity of the latter as the defender of provincial autonomy.[54] Second, the Alberta Liberal Party has experienced a long-lasting ideological identity crisis since losing power in the early twentieth century. At certain times, the party has straddled the political centre, incorporating elements of both left-wing "security" and right-wing "freedom" in its platforms; in the process, the Liberals have failed to establish themselves as an authentic champion of either side of the spectrum. At other times, the party has lurched from left to right, leader to leader. The resulting form of political schizophrenia has prevented the Liberals from establishing themselves as a consistent, recognizable alternative to government. In short, if the New Democratic Party has suffered from ideological inertia, the Alberta Liberals have faced the opposite affliction. Neither condition has aided in the opposition in their attempts to unseat Social Credit or the Progressive Conservatives.

In Saskatchewan, right-wing opposition parties have struggled to displace the CCF-NDP as the province's natural governing party. Some of their leaders have spoken in code, at least early on in their careers. All three post-war right-wing premiers entered office by campaigning on toned-down platforms and commitments to uphold the principles and institutions of Saskatchewan "security." Ross Thatcher was fond of mentioning his own early roots in the CCF movement, for instance, while Grant Devine labelled himself as the true heir to Tommy Douglas's legacy during the 1986 campaign. And Brad Wall's breakthrough with the Sask Party in 2007 may be attributed to his commitments to keep several of the province's key crown corporations in public hands. In the two earlier instances, both the Liberals and Conservatives drifted gradually back to their right-wing roots, however. In Devine's case, second-term attempts to rewrite the Saskatchewan code in the image of "Alberta freedom" failed to come to fruition. To this point, none of the CCF-NDP's opponents have managed to crack, let alone supplant, the code of security that has helped keep the party in power more often than not in the post-war period.

Challengers to the dominant parties have faced unique obstacles in Manitoba as well. During the Bracken era, opposition leaders of every label were forced to choose between allying themselves with a very popular premier or sitting alone on the opposition benches. The former option would grant the leader a position at the Cabinet table while in coalition, whereas the latter would earn him the label of an outsider in the non-partisan environment of Manitoba politics. Recognizing the futility of the latter approach, all major party leaders—from Social Credit on the right to the CCF on the left—joined Bracken's coalition at one point or another. Following the premier's departure during World War II, both the CCF and the Progressive Conservatives withdrew from the coalition. It would take a decade before either party could formulate an alternative, moderate vision for Manitoba's future. But once Duff Roblin's vision of the "progressive centre" took hold, it was the Liberal Party that found itself on the wrong side of the provincial code. For decades to come, the Grits were victimized as representatives of an outdated version of their polity's creed—as a backward party in a forward-facing world. (Borrowing from this script, a decade later in Alberta, Peter Lougheed would portray Harry Strom's Socreds in a similar light.) Despite a minor resurgence in the 1980s, when the party managed to position itself in the "progressive centre" during a brief period of polarization, the Liberals remain outside the province's mainstream to this day. Instead, the New Democrats and Conservatives now trade turns in office; when one strays too far from the "progressive centre," the other has proven poised to assume its position in government.[55]

Thus, codes in each of the three Prairie provinces have established unique sets of incentives and disincentives related to party competition. Parties run a significant risk, and incur high electoral costs, by defining the Alberta state's role as anything but a guardian, ombudsman, or liberator; criticizing the Saskatchewan state's position as a pioneer, provider, or director; or ignoring the Manitoba state's function as a delegate, moderator, and participant. Parties that become defined as, or associated with, "enemies of the state" face even greater challenges. Meanwhile, as crafters and champions of their state's role in Confederation, society, and the economy, dominant parties enjoy a significant competitive advantage over their opponents. This ideological edge is just as critical to their continued success as any other formal institutional safeguards they may establish while in office (including electoral systems and other legal barriers).

As a result, minor parties are forced into one of two strategies: to serve as principled actors, committed to their own ideological tenets; or to submit to the dominant discourse and speak "in code." The former route, chosen by the CCF-NDP in Alberta and periodically by all parties in Saskatchewan and Manitoba, has left these organizations on the margins of power. The latter path, chosen at various times by right-wing leaders in Saskatchewan, has secured their parties control of government, if only temporarily. Neither strategy has proven effective in displacing the dominant parties, however. As a result, the right-leaning Socreds and Conservatives in Alberta, left-leaning CCFers and New Democrats in Saskatchewan, and centrist Liberal-Progressives, PCs, and NDPers in Manitoba remain their provinces' only natural governing parties.

CODES AND HEGEMONY

In this way, code politics raises the spectre of hegemony—that, once entrenched in a party system, a set of ideas will determine winners and losers in an almost mechanical and enduring fashion. Continued rule by the Progressive Conservatives, or some other right-wing party, seems inevitable in Alberta. We can predict with confidence that the New Democrats will return to power more often than not in Saskatchewan. And Manitoba will continue to be governed by moderate parties of the left and right for the foreseeable future. These worries intensify when the culture, code, and creed become virtually synonymous with a political party. As one editorialist put it, "Ideologies that control the culture also control the politics."[56]

It is true: patterns of party competition are subject to the same processes of "lock-in" as the codes that help produce them. A code institutionalizes processes of "positive feedback" and "increasing returns" that advantage certain types of political actors depending on their ideology.[57] In turn, the resulting patterns of competition establish their own sets of expectations about the strong and weak players in a given party system. These norms define the level of credibility, respectability, viability, and overall prospects for the various parties (such that the NDP is viewed as a major player in the eastern Prairie provinces, for instance, but not in Alberta). By filtering the world around them, these expectations shape the behaviour of a wide range of political actors—from the media and academics to potential party sponsors and activists to voters and political elites. Journalists and observers talk about "safe seats" and "secure majorities," serving to reinforce those same patterns in the minds of their audience. Donors tend to fund the strongest parties and activists too, focusing their resources on influencing those parties closest to power. Some voters may be drawn toward winners, or to vote strategically for the party most likely to stop their least-favoured alternative. And the norms embedded in a party system can affect the decision of would-be candidates to run under a party's banner, or to even contest an election at all. In these and other ways, existing patterns of party competition generate their own path-dependent momentum by establishing expectations based on the existing hierarchy of power in the system.[58]

In other words, codes limit the choices available to all political actors during elections. Granted, each party system analyzed in this study contained a wide *variety* of choices on the ballot. In some cases at certain times, these ranged from orthodox communism on the left to traditional liberalism on the right or, later, new-left social democracy to new-right neo-conservatism. Yet, in order to establish true "choice" on the ballot, these options must not only be *available*—political actors in the system must view them as *viable* alternatives to government.

According to most theories, the basic premise of democracy is the provision of elections that offer voters a variety of competing visions for the future.[59] This "choice" is rooted in a variety of options on the ballot and, equally importantly, the ability to choose among feasibly electable alternatives. That is, for citizens to make meaningful democratic decisions, the options presented to them during elections must be both distinguishable and viable.[60] In developed countries like Canada, the quality of electoral choice is determined primarily by "its politicians, its political parties, and its patterns of party competition"[61] If these "patterns" dictate that only one type of political party is likely to form government, while others have few prospects of success, the quality of democratic "choice" is compromised.

Gloomy or accurate as it appears, this is an overly deterministic view of political life. Just as codes can be cracked and altered, so too can patterns of party competition. The process is not an easy one, given that both codes and patterns of party competition are deeply entrenched in the political system. Yet, as with any institution, there are ways to erode, convert, layer, or even replace existing constraints. Codes can be rewritten under certain circumstances—that is, when political actors are able to create or exploit an opportunity during a period of intense uncertainty to establish a new way of conceptualizing the state's role in society, the economy, or in Confederation.

Exogenous events may introduce anomalies or uncertainty into the political system—for instance, creating an opportunity for new political ideas (and the actors carrying them) to rise to prominence. Such events—including wars or depressions—are few and far between; moreover, as witnessed on the Canadian prairies, they do not *always* produce dramatic changes to the political status quo. While they may create the prerequisite *demand* for change, political entrepreneurs must *supply* a popular and acceptable vehicle if major transformations are to take place.

More often, to rise above the expectations established for them by the present pattern of party competition, leaders must first learn to "play by the rules" of the game *before* they can convert them to their own advantage. As Pal argues, to succeed in party politics "requires leadership, a capacity to sense instinctively the patterns of accepted discourse and the creative, even artistic ways in which they may be modified to suit different interests and agendas."[62] To break their dominant predecessors' grip on power, for instance, Duff Roblin and Peter Lougheed first adopted, then adapted, their respective political codes. Roblin accepted the Liberal-Progressives' creed of "moderation," progressive centrism, flexible partisanship, and pragmatism, just as Lougheed drew upon the Socreds' principles of "freedom," individualism, populism, and autonomy. Their strategy, however, was to point out the disjunctions between these ideals and the perceived realities of the world around them. Roblin and Lougheed, like Schreyer after them, were able to alter their provinces' patterns of party competition by pointing out these "ironies" and converting the existing code to new ends.

From this perspective, party competition is rarely a matter of opposing sides presenting conflicting codes or paradigms. Rather, it is more often a contest between conflicting *interpretations* of those ideals. The most successful opposition parties seek to highlight not the "anomalies" left unsolved by the dominant narrative, but rather the disjunction between the realities of political life and the promise contained in the existing code. These ideals constitute the community's "creed"—a relatively unsystematic conglomeration of symbols, values, and beliefs that serve as the guiding principles of a society and its political actors. In this sense, ideas can guide political development in that the non-realization of a society's creed may empower an opposition group to challenge the governing party by restating (and often reinterpreting) the basis of that original creed. In this context, Huntington argues, party competition seldom "takes the form of idea versus idea...but rather of idea versus fact. The conflict is between...groups who believe in the same political principles: those who find it in their interest to change existing institutions immediately so as to make them comply with those principles, and those who accept the validity of the principles but who perceive existing institutions as being in accord with the principles insofar as this is feasible."[63]

None of this is to suggest that parties must conform, ideologically, to the norms of their respective provinces if they expect to gain office. A party does not have to be arch-conservative to be successful in Alberta; nor orthodox socialist to attain power in Saskatchewan. (Peter Lougheed and Roy Romanow have dispelled these notions.) For one, the norms of each community are seldom so rigid. As the history of Prairie politics reveals, there is much room for interpretation within the bounds of these guiding codes and creeds. Rather, in order to gain and retain power for a significant period of time, party leaders must at least speak (if not act) "in code." To dominate politics in Alberta requires speaking with a freedom-based accent. There, dominant party leaders may emphasize "freedoms from," if they are from the right, or "freedoms to" if they are from the left. By the same token, long-term success in Saskatchewan entails talking security. Once again, there is room for interpretation of the provincial code; however, those on the left may emphasize "freedom through security" while those on the right may offer "security through freedom." And consistent victory in Manitoba means promoting moderation from either side of the spectrum.

Once in power, these parties may work toward shifting the norms of party competition in their favour. If the experiences of Ross Thatcher and Grant Devine in Saskatchewan or Sterling Lyon and Gary Filmon in Manitoba offer any guidance, such an undertaking is a long-term process.

CONCLUSION

As Wiseman puts it, whatever broad similarities there may be among Manitoba, Saskatchewan, and Alberta, "treating them as a single region is akin to trying to tie…watermelons together with a single piece of string."[64] In particular, the partisan diversity in the region poses a dilemma: considering they were divided rather arbitrarily just over a century ago, why have Manitoba, Saskatchewan, and Alberta developed into three worlds "thriving in the bosom of a single region?"[65] This chapter suggests that by downplaying the role of ideas and agency, structural theories offer only partial solutions to this Prairie paradox. Formative event, fragment, and staple theories neglect the extent to which parties themselves help shape the climates in which they compete.

As revealed, campaigns in each of the three Prairie provinces are characterized by a unique modes discourse that helps to define their politics and structure their party systems. The Alberta code centres on the concept of "freedom," such that successful parties in that province have emphasized themes like individualism, populism, and autonomy. This dominant discourse differs from those found in Saskatchewan and Manitoba, where the most successful parties have stressed "security" and "moderation," respectively. By crafting these unique "codes," major party leaders have set the bounds of acceptable debate in their respective provinces, and constrained their opponents by labelling them as outsiders or enemies of the provincial community. In this way, dominant parties have helped perpetuate their own success, shaping the distinct patterns of party competition in the process. Such an emphasis on ideas and agency is missing in conventional accounts of party politics; adding it brings us one step closer to solving the "paradox" on the Canadian Prairies, and to understanding the ideational foundations of party systems beyond the region.

NOTES

1   André Blais, Elisabeth Gidengil, Richard Nadeau, and Neil Nevitte, *Anatomy of a Liberal Victory: Making Sense of the 2000 Canadian Election* (Peterborough: Broadview Press, 2002); Harold D. Clarke, "The Ideological Self-Perceptions of Provincial Legislators," *Canadian Journal of Political Science* 11 (1978): 617–633; Michael Lusztig, Patrick James, and Jeremy Moon, "Falling from Grace: Nonestablished Brokerage Parties and the Weight of Predominance in Canadian Provinces and Australian States," *Publius* 27, 1 (1997): 59–81; David E. Smith, "The Prairie Provinces" in *The Provincial Political Systems: Comparative Essays*, eds. D.J. Bellamy, J. Pammett and D.C. Rowat, (Toronto: Methuen, 1976).

2   David E. Smith, *The Regional Decline of a National Party: Liberals on the Prairies* (Toronto: University of Toronto Press, 1981), xvi.

3   The Liberals governed all three provinces from 1915 to 1921, and the Conservatives did so from 1988 to 1991.

4   R.K. Carty and David Stewart, "Parties and Party Systems" in *Provinces: Canadian Provincial Politics*," ed. C. Dunn (Peterborough: Broadview, 1996).

5   Peter McCormick, "Provincial Party Systems, 1945–1986," in *Canadian Parties in Transition: Discourse, Organization and Representation*, eds. A.-G. Gagnon and A.B. Tanguay (Scarborough: Nelson, 1989).

6   D.K. Elton, *One Prairie Province? Conference Proceedings and Selected Papers* (Lethbridge: *Lethbridge Herald*, 1970).

7   Smith, "The Prairie Provinces," in *The Provincial Political Systems*, 47–50.

8   In Ontario, the Progressive Conservatives won an unprecedented twelve consecutive elections from 1943 to 1981. They failed to achieve majority status on three occasions, however (1943, 1975, and 1977).

9   Edward Bell, Harold Jansen, and Lisa Young, "Sustaining a Dynasty in Alberta: The 2004 Provincial Election," *Canadian Political Science Review* 1, 2 (2007): 27–49.

10 Jocelyne Praud and Sarah McQuarrie, "The Saskatchewan CCF-NDP from the *Regina Manifesto* to the Romanow Years," in *Saskatchewan Politics: Into the Twenty-First Century*, ed. H. Leeson (Regina: Canadian Plains Research Center, 2001); Ken Rasmussen, "Saskatchewan: From Entrepreneurial to Embedded State," in *The Provincial State in Canada: Politics in the Provinces and Territories*, eds. Keith Brownsey and Michael Howlett (Peterborough: Broadview, 2001).

11 Gregory P. Marchildon, "Why the Heavy Hand of History?" in *The Heavy Hand of History: Interpreting Saskatchewan's Past*, ed. G.P. Marchildon (Regina: Canadian Plains Research Center, 2005), 4.

12 John Wilson, "The Canadian Political Cultures: Towards a Redefinition of the Nature of the Canadian Political System," *Canadian Journal of Political Science* 7, 3 (1974): 438–483; Jane Jenson, "Party Systems," in *The Provincial Political Systems;* David Stewart and R. Kenneth Carty, "Many Political Worlds? Provincial Parties and Party Systems," in *Provinces: Canadian Provincial Politics*, 2nd ed., ed. C. Dunn (Peterborough: Broadview, 2006); Peter McCormick, "Provincial Party Systems, 1945–1993," in *Canadian Parties in Transition*, 2nd ed., eds. A.B. Tanguay and A.-G. Gagnon (Toronto: Nelson, 1996); Christopher Dunn and David Laycock, "Saskatchewan: Innovation and Competition in the Agricultural Heartland," in *The Provincial State: Politics in Canada's Provinces and Territories*, ed. K. Brownsey and M. Howlett (Mississauga: Copp Clark Pitman, 1992).

13 In this count, I consider the CCF-NDP to constitute a single party.

14 The federal Liberals, Saskatchewan CCF-NDP, Ontario Conservatives, and the New Brunswick and PEI Liberals are the only Canadian parties to have governed in every

decade since World War II. (The Quebec Liberals governed up to the end of World War II, and have served in government in every decade since.)

15   The Saskatchewan CCF-NDP has earned an average of 44.8 percent of the popular vote in elections since World War II. Only the PEI Liberals (49.8) and Conservatives (47.4), and the Liberals in Newfoundland (49.4), New Brunswick (48.9), and Quebec (46.3) have performed better over the same period.

16   Praud and McQuarrie, "The Saskatchewan CCF-NDP," 143; Rasmussen, "Saskatchewan," 258; Nelson Wiseman, "Social Democracy in a Neo-Conservative Age: The Politics of Manitoba and Saskatchewan," in *Canada: The State of the Federation 2001: Canadian Political Culture(s) in Transition*, eds. H. Telford and H. Lazar (Kingston: Institute of Intergovernmental Relations, 2002), 218.

17   Numerous studies dispute the extent to which the Saskatchewan electorate is, in fact, "socialist." See for example Don Baron and Paul Jackson, *Battleground: The Socialist Assault on Grant Devine's Canadian Dream* (Toronto: Bedford House Publishing, 1991); Rand Dyck, *Provincial Politics in Canada* (Scarborough: Prentice-Hall, 1996); Evelyn Eager, *Saskatchewan Government: Politics and Pragmatism* (Saskatoon: Western Producer Prairie Books, 1980); Michael D. Ornstein, "Regionalism and Canadian Political Ideology," in *Regionalism in Canada*, ed. R.J. Brym (Toronto: Irwin, 1986).

18   Jared J. Wesley, "The Collective Centre: Social Democracy and Red Tory Politics in Manitoba," paper read at Annual Meeting of the Canadian Political Science Association, York University, Toronto, 2006.

19   Dyck, *Provincial Politics in Canada*, 397; W.L. Morton, *Manitoba: A History* (Toronto: University of Toronto Press, 1967), 221.

20   The Liberal-Progressives dropped the term "Progressive" from their party name in 1960. The Liberals enjoyed a brief resurgence in the 1980s, under leader Sharon Carstairs. The party formed the official opposition from 1988 to 1990—the first time it had done so since 1969.

21   David K. Stewart and Jared J. Wesley, "Sterling Lyon," in *Manitoba Premiers of the 19th and 20th Centuries*, eds. B. Ferguson and R. Wardhaugh (Regina: Canadian Plains Research Center Press, 2010).

22   Since 1969, the New Democrats have garnered between 23.6 percent (1988) and 49.4 percent (2003) of the popular vote. The Conservatives have won between 35.7 percent (1969) and 43.8 percent (1977).

23   Chris Adams, "Manitoba's Political Party Systems: An Historical Overview," paper read at Annual Meeting of the Canadian Political Science Association, Toronto, 3 June 2006; Dyck, *Provincial Politics in Canada*, 419; Donald Swainson, "Manitoba's election: patterns confirmed," *The Canadian Forum* (September 1973): 4–7; Nelson Wiseman, *Social Democracy in Manitoba: A History of the CCF-NDP* (Winnipeg: University of Manitoba Press, 1983), 147.

24   Jared Wesley, *Code Politics: Campaigns and Cultures on the Canadian Prairies* (Vancouver: UBC Press, 2011).

25   Ibid., 236.

26   Ibid.

27   Ibid.

28   Ibid., 237.

29   Maurice Duverger, *Political Parties: Their Organization and Activity in the Modern State* (New York: John Wiley & Sons, Inc, 1967), 308.

30   Some analysts disagree with this interpretation. For instance, Archer and Hunziker argue that while "there is a popular assumption that the province's long history of one-party dominance is the product of a set of homogeneous political attitudes and beliefs...

[in fact] Alberta is characterized by significant attitudinal diversity"; "Leadership Selection in Alberta: The 1985 Progressive Conservative Leadership Convention," in *Leaders and Parties in Canadian Politics: Experiences of the Provinces*, eds. L. Erickson, D.E. Blake and R.K. Carty (Toronto: Harcourt Brace Jovanovich Canada, 1992), 81. See also Doreen Barrie, *The Other Alberta: Decoding a Political Enigma* (Regina: Canadian Plains Research Center, 2006).

31   Nelson Wiseman, *In Search of Canadian Political Culture* (Vancouver: UBC Press, 2007), 240.

32   Jared J. Wesley, "Staking the Progressive Centre: An Ideational Analysis of Manitoba Party Politics," *Journal of Canadian Studies* 45, 1 (2011): 143–177.

33   *Structuring Politics: Historical Institutionalism in Comparative Analysis*, eds. Sven Steinmo, Kathleen Thelen, and Frank Lonstreth (Cambridge: Cambridge University Press, 1992).

34   Kenneth A. Shepsle, "Studying Institutions: Some Lessons from the Rational Choice Approach," *Journal of Theoretical Politics* 1, 2 (1989): 135.

35   British prime minister Margaret Thatcher coined the term "TINA" in her defence of market supremacy, alluding to the pre-eminence of neo-liberalism in the 1980s.

36   Sheri Berman, "Ideas, Norms, and Culture in Political Analysis: Review Article," *Comparative Politics* 33, 2 (2001): 242.

37   James G. March, and Johan P. Olsen, "Institutional Perspectives on Political Institutions," *Governance* 9, 3 (1996): 257.

38   *The Provincial State in Canada*, 14–15.

39   Gerald Friesen, *The West: Regional Ambitions, National Debates, Global Age* (Toronto: Penguin Group / McGill Institute, 1999), 9; Morton, *Manitoba*, 420-421; Dyck, *Provincial Politics*, 381; Paul G. Thomas, "Manitoba: Stuck in the Middle," in *Canada: The State of the Federation 1989*, eds. R.L. Watts and D.M. Brown (Kingston: Institute of Intergovernmental Relations, 1989); Paul Thomas, "Leading from the Middle: Manitoba's Role in the Intergovernmental Arena," *Canadian Political Science Review* 2, 3 (2008): 29–51.

40   There are obvious disjunctions between what has been *portrayed* by these elites in their campaign rhetoric, and the actual *performance* of these states. At various times, Saskatchewan governments have reduced their state's role as a pioneer, provider, and director. Likewise, Manitoba elites have, from time to time, abandoned their code of "moderation" by choosing sides at the federal-provincial table, in debates over private versus public development, or in domestic social disputes. And, in Alberta, the code of "freedom" is difficult to reconcile with the development of the province's expansive welfare state and programs of corporate assistance. See Dyck, *Provincial Politics*, 514; Mark Pickup, Anthony Sayers, Rainer Knopff, and Keith Archer, "Social Capital and Civic Community in Alberta," *Canadian Journal of Political Science* 37, 3 (2004): 617–645; *Government and Politics in Alberta*, eds. Allan Tupper and Roger Gibbins (Edmonton: University of Alberta Press, 1992), xv; Kenneth H. Norrie, "Some Comments on Prairie Economic Alienation" in *Society and Politics in Alberta: Research Papers*, ed. C. Caldarola (Toronto: Methuen, 1979); Mark Lisac, *Alberta Politics Uncovered: Taking Back our Province* (Edmonton: NeWest Press, 2004), 2–3.

41   Edward Bell, *Social Classes and Social Credit in Alberta* (Montreal and Kingston: McGill-Queen's University Press, 1993), 153.

42   Christine de Clercy, "Leadership and Uncertainty in Fiscal Restructuring: Ralph Klein and Roy Romanow," *Canadian Journal of Political Science* 38, 1 (2005); Trevor Harrison and Gordon Laxer, "Introduction" in *The Trojan Horse: Alberta and the Future of Canada*, eds. T. Harrison and G. Laxer (Montreal: Black Rose, 1995), 7–8; Jean Blondel,

Political Leadership: Towards a General Analysis (Beverly Hills: Sage Publications, 1987), 93–7.

43   Keith Archer and Roger Gibbins, "What do Albertans Think? The Klein Agenda on the Public Opinion Landscape" in *A Government Reinvented: A Study of Alberta's Deficit Elimination Program*, eds. C. Bruce, R. Kneebone and K. McKenzie (Toronto: Oxford University Press, 1997), 466.

44   Wiseman, *In Search of Canadian Political Culture*, 248, 250.

45   *The Trojan Horse*, 5–7.

46   Michael R. Georgeson, "A One-Party Dominant Party System: The Case of Alberta," (Calgary: University of Calgary Press, 1974).

47   Edward Bell, *Social Classes and Social Credit in Alberta* (Montreal and Kingston: McGill-Queen's University Press, 1993), 153–154; Carlo Caldarola, "The Social Credit in Alberta," in *Society and Politics in Alberta: Research Papers*, ed. C. Caldarola (Toronto: Methuen, 1979), 40.

48   David K. Elton and Arthur M. Goddard, "The Conservative Takeover, 1971," in *Society and Politics in Alberta: Research Papers*, ed. C. Caldarola (Toronto: Methuen, 1979), 68.

49   Linda Trimble, "Comments on Chapter 13" in *A Government Reinvented*, 488.

50   Allan Tupper, "Alberta Politics: The Collapse of Consensus," in *Party Politics in Canada*, 6th ed., ed. H.G. Thorburn. (Scarborough: Prentice-Hall Canada, 1991), 459.

51   Elton and Goddard, "The Conservative Takeover," 68. Blondel discusses how dominant leaders often "close their borders" to competing ideas, "branding foreigners as potential enemies" to the domestic consensus (*Political Leadership: Towards a General Analysis*, 32). In Alberta, for example, "Governments in the province have been successful in deflecting attention towards the deficiencies of the federal government and away from any shortcomings of the provincial government. In these contemporary intergovernmental battles, the population invariably lines up behind the Premier like Albertans did generations ago…. [A] unique Alberta identity has been forged in part by driving a wedge between Albertans and the national government and, by extension, the national community." Barrie, *The Other Alberta*, xiii.

52   David Stewart and Keith Archer, *Quasi-Democracy? Parties and Leadership Selection in Alberta* (Vancouver: UBC Press, 2000), 172.

53   Dyck, *Provincial Politics*, 518.

54   James Fischer, "Liberals in Alberta: Studying the Lessons of History" (MA thesis, University of Alberta, Edmonton, 1986).

55   Wesley, "Staking the Progressive Centre," 143–177.

56   Susan Martinuk, "Harper spinning his wheels in pursuit of elusive majority: Ideologies that control the culture also control the politics," *Calgary Herald*, January 18, 2008, A20.

57   W. Brian Arthur, *Increasing Returns and Path Dependence in the Economy* (Ann Arbor: University of Michigan Press, 1994); Douglass C. North, *Institutions, Institutional Change, and Economic Performance* (New York: Cambridge University Press, 1990).

58   Such "expectations" are key to understanding the dynamics of party competition. See Kenneth Janda, Robert Harmel, Christine Edens, and Patricia Goff, "Changes in Party Identity: Evidence from Party Manifestos," *Party Politics* 1, 2 (1995); Graham White, "One-Party Dominance and Third Parties: The Pinard Theory Reconsidered," *Canadian Journal of Political Science* 6, 3 (1973): 400–01; David J. Elkins, "The Perceived Structure of the Canadian Party Systems," *Canadian Journal of Political Science* 7 (1974). As Stern suggests, "interparty competition is usually taken as one of the basic factors defining the state of behaviour in party systems. However, it is the actors' perceptions of interparty competition which in fact underlies their actions in the system." Mark Stern, "Measuring Interparty Competition: A Proposal and a Test of a Method," *Journal*

of Politics 34, 3 (1972): 890. As Pinard argued, "a system of one-party dominance is a party system in which the traditional opposition party (or occasionally, parties) cannot be considered a serious challenge, a viable alternative to the dominant government party.... In the end it is the people's perception of this condition that counts." Maurice Pinard, "Third Parties in Canada Revisited: A Rejoinder and Elaboration of the Theory of One-Party Dominance," *Canadian Journal of Political Science* 6, 3 (1973): 440.

59   E.E. Schattschneider, *The Semisovereign People* (New York: Holt, Rinehart and Winston, 1960), 140–141; Joseph A. Schumpeter, *Capitalism, Socialism and Democracy* (New York: Harper and Row, 1942).

60   J.A.A. Lovink, "Is Canadian Politics too Competitive?" Canadian Journal of Political Science 6, 3 (1973): 342; T.J. Pempel, Introduction, in *Uncommon Democracies*, ed. T.J. Pempel (Ithaca, NY: Cornell University Press, 1990), 9–10; Donald V. Smiley, *The Canadian Political Nationality* (Toronto: Methuen, 1969), 68.

61   Wesley, "The Collective Centre." R. Kenneth Carty, William P. Cross, and Lisa Young, *Rebuilding Canadian Party Politics* (Vancouver: UBC Press, 2000), 14.

62   Pal, "The Political Executive," 5.

63   Samuel P. Huntington, *American Politics: The Promise of Disharmony* (Cambridge: Belknap Press, 1981), 32.

64   Nelson Wiseman, "The West as a Political Region" in *Riel to Reform: A History of Protest in Western Canada*, ed. G. Melnyk (Saskatoon: Fifth House Publishers, 1992), 280.

65   Smith, "The Prairie Provinces," 46.

INDEX